The Golden Road to Modernity

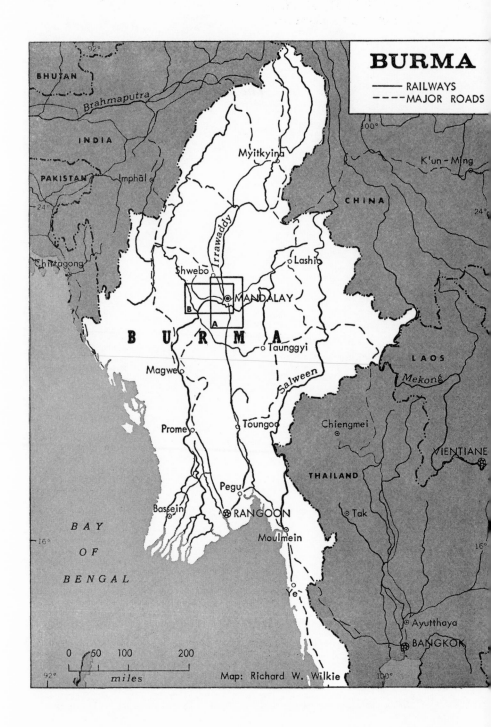

BURMA
— RAILWAYS
--- MAJOR ROADS

Map: Richard W. Wilkie

THE GOLDEN
ROAD TO
MODERNITY

Village Life in Contemporary Burma

BY MANNING NASH   University of Chicago

John Wiley & Sons, Inc., New York · London · Sydney

Library of Congress Catalog Card Number: 65-21437
Printed in the United States of America

Preface

I am indebted to the National Science Foundation for a grant which financed the field work for this study. To the Graduate School of Business of the University of Chicago, I am grateful for the time to do the field work and for the excellent secretarial services, under Hal Fibish, in the making of this book. In Burma, I received help from the Fulbright Foundation, from the Asia Foundation, and from the Ford Foundation. Without the aid of the many district officers and township officers in Upper Burma, the research task would have been impossible. The many friends I made in Burma made my stay there not only anthropologically profitable but a joyous adventure as well. And to my hosts in Nondwin and Yadaw I proffer in this public way my gratitude for their kindness, their friendship, and their wry humor and tolerance as I stumbled and bumbled my way into their lives and societies.

Some of my colleagues have given generously of their time and knowledge, either in conversation or in the painstaking reading of this book. I want especially to thank Dr. F. K. Lehmann of the University of Illinois for his aid with transliteration, Professor M. E. Spiro of the University of Chicago, who not only shared in some sense the joy of Burma when we met in the field but also gave many helpful corrections, Dr. E. M. Mendelson of the School of Oriental and African Studies, London, John K. Musgrave of Yale University for clearing up many points of Burmese usage and spelling, and Dr. Hla Myint of Oxford. Professor Clifford Geertz of the University of Chicago proffered many useful suggestions after a careful reading of the manuscript.

Professor Milton Singer of the University of Chicago encouraged and aided me throughout the study and underwrote a summer which I devoted to writing this manuscript. The Committee for the Comparative Study of New Nations at the University of Chicago generously gave me funds to survey the villages of Upper Burma, and seminars with members of the Committee have contributed materially to the content of this book.

Barbara Cropper served valiantly as my research assistant while I was writing this book, and she devised the ingenious kinship charts. Maps of the villages were drawn by Mrs. Della Friedlander of the Department of Geophysical Sciences, University of Chicago, and by Mr. R. Wilke of the Geography Department at the University of Washington.

Finally, Dr. June Nash's professional skills enter into this study in many ways. My son Eric and my daughter Laura, who went to Burma with me, gave me the love and human warmth to complete this task. It is to their bubbling sense of life, of joy, and of love that I dedicate this book.

MANNING NASH

May 1, 1965

Contents

1. VILLAGE LIFE IN CONTEMPORARY BURMA   1

2. THE SETTING OF A MIXED CROP COMMUNITY   9

Technology and Economy, 15
  Technology, 15
  Economy, 17
    Classification of Land and Crops, 18
Land Distribution: The Best Index to Wealth, 28
  Household Budgets, 33

3. SOCIAL AND POLITICAL ORGANIZATION   44

Social Organization: The Household, 45
Political Organization, 73
  The Village Government, 73
    Village Administrators, 74
  Ties between the Village and the National Government, 93
The Gap between Social and Political Organization, 101

4. BUDDHISM, THE MEANING AND ORGANIZATION OF
   RELIGIOUS LIFE   104

The Meaning of Religious Life, 105
  Kan and Kutho, 105
    Buddhist Giving, 115
The Organization of Religious Life, 140
  Funeral Ceremonies, 151
Effects of Buddhism, 156

5. NATS, SPIRITS, PREDICTIVE, DIVINATORY, AND
   CURING SYSTEMS   166

The Nats, 167
Spirits, 175
  Witchcraft, 177
Predictive and Divinatory Systems, 182
  Astrology, 183
  Alchemy, 190
Curing Systems, 192
  Traditional Medicine, 192
  The HA, 201
Summary, 203

6. YADAW, AN IRRIGATED RICE GROWING COMMUNITY   207

Technology and Economy, 214
  Technology, 214
  Economy, 223
    Rice Growing, 224
    Categories of Wealth, 231

7. SOCIAL AND POLITICAL ORGANIZATION   246

Social Organization: The Household, 246
  Marriage and the Family, 247
  Burmese Interpersonal Behavior, 267
Political Organization, 274
  Village Government, 274
    Outside Effects on Village Government, 281

8. BUDDHIST BELIEF AND RITUAL AND PREDICTIVE
   AND DIVINATORY SYSTEMS   291

Village Buddhist Belief, 291
Interplay between Belief and Practice, 295

9. CONCLUSIONS   312

BIBLIOGRAPHY   325

INDEX   327

The Golden Road to Modernity

1

Village Life in Contemporary Burma

The new nations of Asia and Africa are in the foreground of current history. The emergence of a host of new nations since the end of World War II is one of the most dramatic and portentous phenomenon of this era. Breaking loose from colonial domination the new nations of Asia and Africa are discovering ways and means of transforming traditional societies into modern ones. The process of social and cultural transformation they undertake has few analogs in past history. Modernization on this scale, and with this speed, has rarely been conceived, and more rarely carried out. The kinds of societies and cultures that the African and Asian nations have to work with pose new enigmas and raise grave doubts as to the methods of social transformation and the possibilities of the coexistence of various kinds of institutions within the same social system.

In contributing to policy and theory, the study of Burma offers some special advantages. As a newly independent nation Burma does not suffer from many of the handicaps besetting other Asian and African lands. It is not plagued by overpopulation; it does not suffer from acute land shortage; it is not handicapped by abject and grinding poverty. Burma has the physical and material basis for making the transition to a modern nation. Its future is not caught in those dismal "vicious circles" that seem to make economic and social development a virtual impossibility. If Burma does not succeed in developing a modern economic, political, and social structure, it will be a failure of human effort, a matter of social and cultural variables, a case of organizational and ideological inadequacy. As such a potential of success Burma is particularly inviting to the student of social process. Here can be seen, more clearly than elsewhere, just what the role of a particular social and cultural heritage is in the process of modernization; here can be gauged the play of human agency and choice; here

1

can be charted the emergence and operation of new structures. Burma's particular complex of social institutions is all the more appealing to the investigator because it bears on some of the most mooted questions in social science: what is the role of an otherworldly religion in economic development; how are culturally distinct minorities made into a political whole; how is a polity formed where only an administrative apparatus existed; how are Western institutions and techniques adapted to an agrarian, traditional village and Buddhist society; and what are the effects of a complex division of labor on a relatively homogeneous and unstratified society? These are some of the problems the study of Burma is able to explicate. This book is an anthropological study, and anthropologists naturally gravitate to the lowly hut, to the village, to seek information from the people who make up the bulk of the society. In a complex society like Burma the village is only a segment. But it has been the most neglected segment. Recently economists, political scientists, sociologists, and historians have given us some understanding of Burmese national society. Pye, Silverstein, Furnivall, Badgley, Tinker, and many Burmans like U Nu, Maung Maung, and others have provided data on the national structure of the people and the organizations that make the national decisions and speak for Burma. There is some understanding of the planners and the policy makers, of the plans and the policies attempting to transform Burma into a modern nation. But there is scant information on what effect the plans and policies have. There is little data on what has been and is happening in the villages of Burma where more than 85 per cent of the Burmans live. And it is the response of the villagers, the human and social material from which a modern nation must be built, that in large measure will determine the course of social and cultural change.

This book focuses on the villages of Upper Burma. It centers on the description and analysis of two villages around Mandalay. Its theme is to state the sources of susceptibility and resistance to social change in a newly developing nation, to point out the range of opportunities that appear to the ordinary villager in a modernizing society. Although the description and analysis is mainly confined to the two villages in which I have lived and worked, it is intended to stand for the villages of Upper Burma, to be a model of the "dry zone," the heartland of traditional Burmese society and culture.

The villages presented here were chosen after a survey of some thirty-odd villages in the districts of Sagaing, Mandalay, and Kyaukse. Each village approximates the demographic, economic, and, in gross features, the social modalities of a district. Nondwin is typical of the Sagaing district, of the dry zone mixed cropping of Upper Burma. Yadaw, in the Mandalay district, is an average irrigation rice village of the upper Irrawaddy. By concentrating on the two chief ecological and economic types of communities, it is possible to make a comparison of how differing structures within the same cultural and historical setting respond to change, while, at the same time, examining the range of diversity within Upper Burma.

The published ethnography of modern Upper Burma is meagre, so I find it necessary to give a rather full description of village society and culture. A comparison of the two villages, with some other by-the-way comparisons with other villages, will point up the chief features of social life and underline the dynamics of change.

National and regional society comes into the study in the form of agency, acting upon or attempting to act upon the local societies. For this is the way Burmese national society is organized. Villages and local communities do not initiate, seldom invent or foster innovation. They are exhorted, ordered, or coerced by the national political and economic agencies. In a sense this is what is meant by traditional society in a new nation: a series of agrarian villages in a setting of relatively unchanging technique, limited economic opportunity, and long standing conventional understanding. In this context there grows up that attachment to authority, the respect for the pastness of things, the dependence upon routine, and the exaggerated respect for precedent that are usually entailed in calling a society "traditional." The modernizing element is a small segment of Western educated persons living in the urban centers. Their images of the nation to be, the methods for making it, create the national and regional organizations which impinge upon the villages. This is a multiple society. Segments have different scale and organization. Goals and means are divergent. It is hinged together by a single political network and a national economy, and it is operated by brokers, politicians, go-betweens who mediate between the local societies and the national.

The study, by an anthropologist, of social change in a newly developing nation is, in my view, best done through "microanalysis," that is, the careful observation and description of variation within a social structure amenable to first hand, personal observation. What this microanalysis means as a working methodology, and its relationships to the broader framework will, I hope, become clear as the argument of this book is worked out.

The history of modern Burma begins with the opening of the Suez

Canal. The world demand for rice transformed a virtually subsistence farming society into a huge commercial concern. Furnivall (1957) describes these changes in economy and society. The rich lands of the delta were quickly brought under cultivation. Burmans from Upper Burma migrated to take up holdings in this newly drained swamp; Indians, the Chettiar moneylenders in particular, came to supply the capital for these cultivators, and the British and Europeans built the railroads, the shipping lines, and the financial structure of international trade. Chinese merchants came to set up shops, and Rangoon was transformed from a sleepy fishing town into a bustling, cosmopolitan, commercial center.

In the early days of the rice trade, prosperity was the keynote. The Burman cultivator did better than he had done in Upper Burma; the Chettiar profited; the Europeans grew rich; and the Chinese were beyond poverty. But as time passed the Burman began to feel his place at the bottom of the economic heap. Heavier and heavier indebtedness, the passage of land into the hands of the now disliked "Chetties," and a declining range of welfare and social services weighed on cultivators. Added to that was what Furnivall has called the "decay of organic society," and the rise of violence, crime, and disorder in the delta. Still the Burman did not go hungry; his scanty clothing needs were met; his bamboo and thatch hut were erected; and there was even something left over for religious donations and *pwes*. But Lower Burma was a society held together by only two sets of bonds: the division of labor based on ethnic lines and the coercive apparatus of law, police, and army in the hands of the Europeans. There was little sense of identity as a people, no allegiances beyond the local community, and little consciousness of the world beyond.

Lower Burma specialized in the export of rice whereas Upper Burma, the dry zone, specialized in a mixed cropping system, partly for export, such as sesamum oil, and partly for internal consumption. The irrigated rice grown in Kyaukse, Mandalay, and Sagaing since the times of the Burmese kings did not much enter into world trade. Upper Burma had less of an influx of foreigners than did the delta, and Mandalay, its chief city, never became the kind of hub that Rangoon did. Still, the British apparatus of administration, law and order, rise of tenancy, indebtedness, and increases in violence and crime did come to the upper Irrawaddy.

Although many items of culture, new crops, and new social rules were introduced during this period, Burma, especially Upper Burma, retained its distinctive cast and character. The distinctive dress of the *longyi* was retained by both men and women, the Burmese style of eating *hin* (curry), their way of building houses, the Buddhist religion, and other central aspects of the culture and society stayed virtually intact. What came in was adapted to fit the Burmese context, just as, centuries earlier, religious ideas and political models from India and technology from China had been indigenized to the Burman mold.

The sweep of the British and the movement of conquered Burma into world markets did not greatly modify the life and structure of the Burmese village. Burmese society was, it is true, decapitated. The glory of its king and court, its system of circle headmen and feudatory retainers was swept out and replaced by the British system of administration. Memories and tales of the grandeur of the golden land still linger in Mandalay, and persons who lived under the peacock throne can still be found; the ruined palace walls still reflect the orange sunlight on the moat, but every working vestige of the royal system is gone. But the British administrator and his Indian and hill tribe clerks and soldiers neither sought to penetrate, nor did they penetrate deeply into the life of the Upper Burmese village. They were substitutes for the kingly superstructure, and from the point of view of the villager the official of the Empire replaced the official of the court. There was, however, this major difference: The British rule of a rule of law was rationalized, regular, impersonal. It was administered by a career civil service and it rested on the "book." The villager was less subject to the caprice of authority, sudden demand, and extraordinary levy. And he was excluded from the military service and virtually excluded from all but the very lowest rungs of the administrative machinery. The government of Burma was now alien to the people. They had no deep loyalty, no sentimental attachments for it. It served to keep the peace, to regularize the mode of litigation, and to ensure a modest standard of living.

One feature of the sixty-odd years of British rule in Upper Burma, remarkable in retrospect, is the small impact the modern world made there. No revolution of agricultural technique, no influx of machines, no burst of industry, no greatly widened mental horizons came in the wake of the British. The Burmese villager was as isolated as ever, in daily life, from the modern world. With a history and tradition of Burmese ascendancy over their near neighbors behind them, their attitude of easy complacency, of satisfaction, of trying to perpetuate, not to develop, a way of life continued.

The arrangement of apparently docile villagers living a relatively contented life under the apparatus of British colonial administration received its first shocks in the riots of the 1930's and in the mounting tide of nationalism in the capital city. The precarious nature of the plural society, held together only by economic and military bonds, was fully revealed with the outbreak of World War II. The Burmese welcomed the Japanese invaders, and few Burmans regretted the passing of the British. The conflict of the modern world was beyond the grasp of the Burman, but what he could envision was a return to independence for the Land of Gold, the old glories that would again make the Irrawaddy blaze with gaiety and color.

When the Japanese moved into Burma they began early to antagonize and alienate the villagers. Not only did their demands for labor and for food, heavy because of the rapidly deteriorating Burmese level of living, make the Burmans who welcomed them come to hate them, but also the personal behavior and code of the Japanese army conflicted in many ways with the Burmese mode of social life and with the gentle Buddhism of the villager. The slapping of Burmans in the face and head, the most sacred part of the body, was a constant source of irritation (Nu, 1954). The misunderstandings in conversation were a further source of friction. Burmese have no way of saying hello or goodbye, and they rarely say "How are you?" unless you look ill. The common street greeting is more likely to be "Have you eaten yet?" or "Where are you going?" or "Where do you come from?" These questions put to Japanese soldiers were interpreted as demands for military information, and they responded by slapping and abusing a villager who only wanted to make the conventional greeting.

As the tide of the war turned against the Japanese, the now disillusioned and antagonized Burman turned also. The allied armies were aided in their return and Burmans helped in the expulsion of the Japanese. But now the seed of independence had been firmly planted, and an independence movement was well underway. The movement had roots in the armed bands in the countryside and in the nascent political organizations, almost all of which were left and Marxist at least in talk, and they now spread throughout Burma. Burmese villagers as well as city and town folk strongly favored the demand for independence. A hero emerged from the war years, Aung San, called the *Bogyoke*, the Generalissimo. Aung San succeeded in outfacing the representatives of the British Army, foreign office, and Burmese government in exile (Tinker, 1961). He won independence for the Burmese, and, amid great rejoicing, on a date set by astrologers, the Land of Gold again became a sovereign nation.

But its troubles, rather than ending, had just begun. A decade of civil war wracked the countryside. The government was at times in control of little more than the city of Rangoon itself. A host of private armies, robber bands, and paramilitary organizations ravaged the towns and villages of Burma. All, or nearly all, of the villages had spells of government by white or red flag communists, or by Karens, or by the People's Volunteer Organization. Bit by bit (Tinker, 1961) the coalition government of the AFPFL (Anti-Fascist People's Freedom League) won back the countryside from the rebel bands and reduced dacoity to manageable proportions. Relative peace was restored in Burma proper. In Karen country in the delta, there were still strong outposts of the KNDO (Karen National Defense Organization), who as late as March 1961 successfully blew up the Rangoon to Mandalay Dagon Express. In the Shan States the roads and villages belong to the national government only during daylight hours, while the KMT (Chinese Nationalists) continue to have a quasi-government in the Wa States and on the Sino-Burman border.

With civil order fairly well restored, the government and people could settle down to their huge task of rebuilding the war-devastated land in the image of the "Welfare State," which they had proclaimed as their goal. But politics was not so gentle. The wartime coalition fell apart. The AFPFL was split into a "clean" and a "stable" faction, under the leadership of U Nu and Kyaw Nyein respectively. The factions have become divided into separate political parties: U Nu's, the *Pyidaungzu* (Union) and Kyaw Nyein's, the *Pataza* (AFPFL). And in addition the NUF (National United Front) and the outlawed or underground communist party continue to operate. Above all this stands the single, enduring symbol of national unity, U Nu. U Nu, who turned the reins of government over to a military caretaker regime under Bogyoke Ne Win (see his report of the 18 months of military rule in *Is Trust Vindicated?* (1960)), was handily re-elected in a relatively free, open, and democratic election as Prime Minister.

The tasks facing the government are huge and pressing. A brief statement of them is that, "The task of the new government was to weld the component people into a united nation; to reintegrate social life from the village upwards in an organic national society; to instill into Burmans the discipline of social and economic life in the modern world; and to equip Burma with the political and economic institutions of a modern state" (Furnivall, 1958: 130).

This all too brief sketch of the Burmese background in modern times is offered to place the villages of Upper Burma in perspective. The people in them have lived through strenuous times, in seething up-

heaval, in political turmoil, in war, in occupation, and in daily uncertainty. This recent history could not fail to have marked effects on
the way villagers handle and interpret their immediate world. They
have learned, above all, to regard government and authority with
suspicion and mistrust. From the days of the kings, when the government was one of the five traditional enemies, to the political huckster-
ing of the elections, they have had experiences that have reinforced
this time-tested attitude. They have developed remarkable modes of
dissimulation, so that it is impossible to tell beforehand whether the
villager will be with or against one in a given situation. And they
know the bitter truth that, in last resort, it is force, violence, and
coercive power that counts in political life. They are still prone to
resort to arms when other channels fail; a whole generation schooled
in war and civil war takes a long time to retrain and reorient. They
tend in their relations with authority and political power to be self-
seeking, to ask "What's in it for me?" and to drive bargains for short-
run gains. They have learned that one cannot depend upon the promises
of politicians, and that remote gains turn out to be insubstantial.

This background is given as a setting for the villages of Upper
Burma, for to casual inspection and on superficial acquaintance these
villages appear to belie their recent history. So much of the technology, the economy, the social life, and the religious code appears
unchanged from nearly 80 years ago when Scott (1882) wrote his magnificent study of the Burmans. This is one of the paradoxes of contemporary village life. The villagers have the material equipment of
a mode of life developed centuries ago and a mental outlook more
closely geared to that than to the modern world, but, at the same time,
they are acting members of a working Asian democracy, and they are
participants in the political and economic processes of transformation.
The traditional and the modern are side by side in an odd and unstable mixture. Village life is not dormant, but is an uneasy mixture
of conservatism and radicalism, as is the life of the nation as a whole.

To explicate these contentions about village life in a new nation,
to show the dynamics of change and resistance to change, and to bring
to human dimension the meaning of the transition from traditional
to modern society, I turn to the analysis of Burmese village life.

2

The Setting of a Mixed Crop Community

The road heads out of Mandalay, south and west across the muddy and sluggish Irrawaddy, over the steel span of the Ava bridge. It winds by the pagodas, glinting gold on Sagaing hill, through the dusty streets of Sagaing and passes villages on either side. Buses, trucks, bicycles, oxcarts, cars, and motorcycles all flow down the metaled strip. Following the road past the junction at Ondaw and swinging down the left fork toward Monywa, one arrives at the village of Nondwin. Nondwin lies about 40 road miles to the south and west of Mandalay. The country surrounding it is typical of this part of the Sagaing district. It is brown and sere. In the dry season the dust swirls at every movement of the foot. The sun looks down from nearly cloudless skies. Relentless shimmers of heat rise from the ground. The broad, open vistas are broken now and again by a cluster of green trees and thatch roofs. This is the site of a village.

Nondwin, lying just off the road, has nothing special to distinguish it (see Map of Nondwin Area). Unless there was a deliberate reason for going there, a traveler would pass it, thinking that it was just like the hundreds of other villages that dot the plain of Upper Burma. Its physical appearance is like any other farming village. A bramble fence surrounds the houses. Gates at the south and north ends allow men and cattle to pass in and out of the village. A single street, muddy in the rainy season, dusty in the dry, runs the length of the village roughly from north to south. From it branch smaller paths and footpaths petering out at the bramble fence (see Map of Nondwin Village). The houses are apparently flung out at random. The village has no plan; it is not a grid, a hub, or any design, but rather the accretion of households at convenient sites over time. There is no village center, no place in the web of paths toward which the village orients. A few two-story houses look more imposing than the single-story bamboo and thatch

9

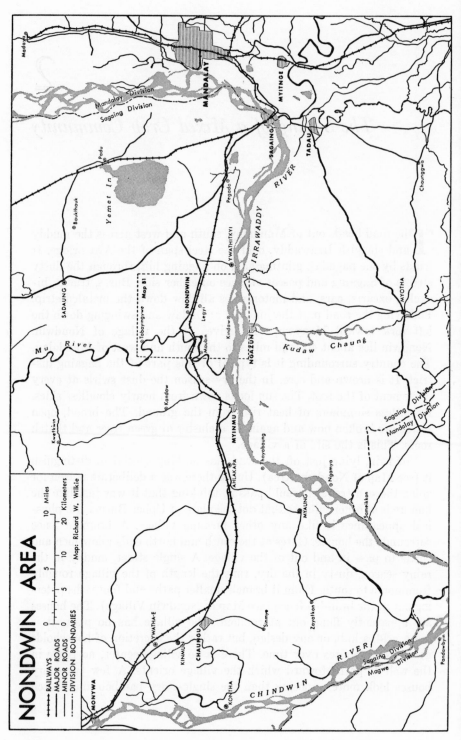

NONDWIN AREA

- +++ RAILWAYS
- —— MAJOR ROADS
- —— MINOR ROADS
- —·—·— DIVISION BOUNDARIES

Map: Richard W. Wilkie

0   5   10 Miles

0   5   10   20 Kilometers

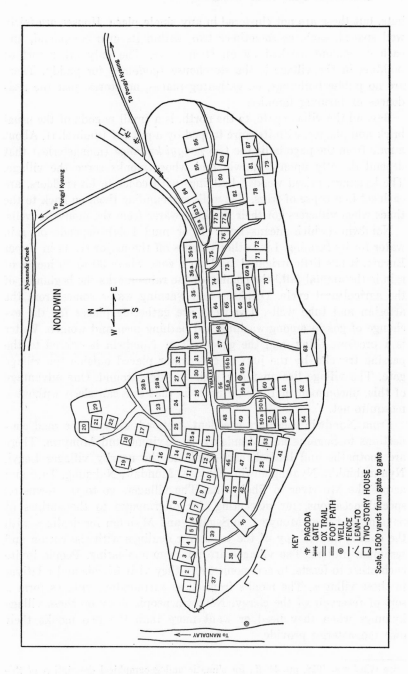

huts, but these are not clustered in any single place. Houses are fairly well spaced, each, or sometimes two, within its own compound, and each compound marked by an open fence. The only other sort of building in the village is the storehouse (*godown*) for paddy. There are no public buildings, no gathering places, no stores, just the residences of farming families.

Beyond the village gate, to the north, is a small pagoda of the usual brick and plaster, with its spire topped by a gilt *hti* (umbrella). About a mile from the pagoda lie the two *pongyi kyaungs* (monasteries) that depend directly upon Nondwin and whose monks serve the village. The kyaungs, raised wooden buildings with concrete lower floors, are each set in a copse of trees. The wells surrounding them go back to the times when villagers got their drinking water from the monastic wells.

Nondwin (which means mud pit or mud hole) depends on rain water for its farming. Like other villages off the major rivers in Upper Burma, it has little irrigated land. In a zone where 30 to 40 inches of rain is the annual fall,[1] the coming of the rains marks the beginning of the agricultural cycle. Drinking and washing water comes from the artesian and tube wells. The wells are gathering places for the exchange of gossip among washing and bathing men and women. Water is a precious thing, and the good will of Nondwin is offered to the passing traveler by the jugs of cool water placed outside the village gate. The village lies on fairly high and dry ground. One advantage of this, uncommon in Upper Burma, is that one can sleep without a mosquito net.

From Nondwin there are excellent, metaled, all weather road connections to Sagaing and Mandalay, to Myinmu and Monywa. There are footpaths and bullock cart roads to the nearby villages Legyi, Nyaungbinhla, Nyaungbinwin, Kinywa, Mondaw, Nakaung, Tatu and across the Mu river to Thabyetha. The villagers go to the towns on special occasions, for marketing, for pilgrimages to the shrines at Sagaing and near Monywa, to Sagaing and Myinmu for dealings with the courts, and to any of the towns for dealings with the cotton and sesamum millers. The villages are intercommunicating. People invite each other to feasts, to ceremonies, and they visit friends and relatives in these villages. The monks from these surrounding villages form a sort of reservoir of the clergy. Nondwin people draw on these village kyaungs when they need or want more than the two monks their own monasteries provide.

---

[1] See Ginsburg, 1958, pp. 440 ff., for climatic and geographical description of this region.

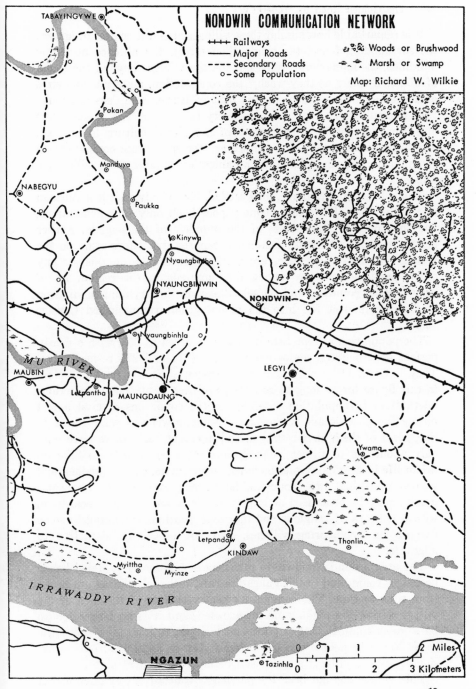

NONDWIN COMMUNICATION NETWORK

++++ Railways
—— Major Roads
– – – Secondary Roads
o – Some Population

🌿🌿 Woods or Brushwood
🌿🌿 Marsh or Swamp

Map: Richard W. Wilkie

TABAYINGYWE

Pakan

Manduya

NABEGYU

Paukka

Kinywa

Nyaungbinbha

NYAUNGBINWIN

NONDWIN

Nyaungbinhla

MU RIVER

MAUBIN

Letpantha

MAUNGDAUNG

LEGYI

Ywama

Letpandaw

KINDAW

Thonlin

Myittha

Myinze

IRRAWADDY RIVER

NGAZUN

Tazinhla

0   1   2 Miles
0   1   2   3 Kilometers

13

It is remarkable how similar these villages are—the scatter of houses, the surrounding fence, the single chief street, the absence of public buildings, the monasteries lying outside the village "beyond the sound of women's voices as they wash," the construction, materials and sizes of houses and compounds. In this part of Burma one does not move from one culturally distinct local society to another. The movement is one from one localized expression of a regional culture to another. The elements of society and culture are the same from community to community, and the planes of organization similar from village to village.

Nondwin is an old village, long settled. Everybody in it is a Burman and a Buddhist. Historical memory goes back only four generations, and then only for the names of the founders of the pagoda. Earlier census reports and British settlement reports give information on the region, but these, of course, are statistically scanty on this, or any other, particular village among the hundreds in the region. As of August 1960, Nondwin and the 86 villages in the Myinmu subdivision of Sagaing district fell into the modal group (unpublished Census, 1960).

The population of Nondwin in 1959 was given as 553, with a nearly perfect split between males and females (276 and 277 respectively). They lived in 116 houses. The village population has remained close to this figure for as long as records have been kept. The only serious fluctuations in population were due to the conditions of civil unrest during the past decade when many residents went to safer towns to live. Most of them have returned, and in recent years there have been only about ten or fifteen out-migrants, who left chiefly to take up urban life in Mandalay and Sagaing. In-migrants, except for men and women marrying into Nondwin, have been even fewer. The community may be visualized as largely stable in size, mainly local born, with a network of religious and marriage relations extending to some five or six neighboring villages, and not especially attractive to migrants.

The area around Nondwin is currently one of security. Rebel bands no longer roam, and dacoit gangs are rare, although alarms are heard from time to time. The compulsory sentry service of the men of the village during the night is no longer used, and it is no longer felt to be a great comfort that a police post is just a few miles down the road. Nondwin people can move freely day or night, and only occasionally does a villager arm himself before going out at night.

This village has not been the particular concern of any government agency, and nothing in its history singles it out from the run of villages around it. The Agricultural Rural Development Corporation had, during my stay, made some visits and attempts to foster the growing of onions, but special government services are not located in or tendered to Nondwin. In this area of Sagaing the land redistribution program has not been carried out, and the ownership and tenancy patterns follow the natural lines of the economic structure of the community rather than governmental plan.

Nondwin is the ordinary village of dry zone Burma, and it is this very ordinariness that makes it a desirable object of study.

TECHNOLOGY AND ECONOMY

Technology

The technological equipment that Burman villagers use is derived from the neolithic Southeast Asia, with some additions and minor overlays from more modern times. In Nondwin an agricultural system based on the plow, the bullock, and metal tipped wood and bamboo implements forms the technological core of the society. An enumeration of the items, the wooden plow with metal share yoked to a pair of bullocks, the wooden toothed harrow, the sickle, the metal bladed hoe, the *dah* (long knife), ropes and twines of various grasses, the forked stick, indicates the long standing complex of the region. Bamboo and wooden items are ubiquitous, and iron and metal nearly so. To see where bamboo and wood, iron and metal are employed is to see all the devices used in Nondwin.

Besides the agricultural implements, some simple machines are found. A rice pounder (*maung*) made of a metal tipped pole beating into a clay or stone lined hole, the apparatus of cotton making and weaving which includes a spindle, whorl, and loom, a metal bladed fodder chopper run by a pedal press, a nutcracker-like betel chopper, a leather bellows, and the pulley and lever or windlass for raising water, are the machines in daily use.

The modern world's technology is represented in the village by the sewing machine, the loudspeaker amplifier system run on batteries, the few shotguns, and one truck. One man has a gasoline motor which he has hooked up to a cotton seed separator, but this is the only nonhuman, nonanimal energy used in the community.

This technology shows all the familiar features of a rather advanced, settled peasantry. The bullock is the largest capital item and the most important piece of equipment, but it still partakes of the essential feature of peasant technology: it is household owned, and household operated. The technology is based on the household unit of production and consumption, and requires neither a capital nor a labor force beyond that scale. Each household tends to duplicate every other in its technological equipment, and each producing unit aims at technological and economic self-sufficiency. Of the 116 households, 88 in Nondwin had at least a pair of bullocks, so that they had the minimal equipment for farming. A good pair of bullocks cost about 650 kyats (the kyat is roughly equivalent to U.S. 21 cents). This is the only item which is beyond the means of the poor, for if a man can afford bullocks, he can afford a plow, harrow, sickle, and dah. If he cannot afford the oxen, he does not need the plow and harrow. Every man owns at least one dah, just as he does the longyi he wears. Not all of the owners of bullock pairs have carts. There are only 70 carts in Nondwin, leaving 18 pairs with nothing to pull. Carts are not essential to farming, and the bullock owners without them are men with small holdings who hire themselves and their teams out to larger holders. The larger landholders have carts which are supplied to the hired hands.

If the technology is adjusted to the economic unit of the household in its capital and labor scale, it can be expected that items added to the basic list will be those that meet these peasant requirements. From the modern world have come the sewing machine, the amplifier, the gun, the gasoline motor, and the truck. All of these are owned within a single household; all of them use only the capital and labor of a single household. No item of technology requiring social invention in the realm of organization has been adopted. New knowledges and new skills needed to run the few modern devices are also limited by the organization of the villages. They are the knowledges and skills that can be transmitted either within the household or by the apprentice method of teaching.

This description of the technological aspect of Nondwin appears to bear out the much debated "dual economy" of the Asian peasantry as conceptualized by Boeke (1953). The equipment of a village like Nondwin does show great persistence over time and a rate of addition and invention that virtually justifies the adjective "static." This agricultural equipment is the same as it was in the times of the Burmese kings. No one in Nondwin recalls a time when it was different, and none can say from experience when a change has taken place in their technology. The cities of Burma, even Mandalay, have a technological complex including "imperial" colonial machines—the cotton and cloth weavers and spinner, the electric dynamos, the forges, and the artisan tools. Mandalay even has the automobile repair shop, the lathes of metal work, and some small factories and mills. This technology exists apart from the village. Villagers do not participate in it, and they have no knowledge of how it works. For the most part the modern world of machines has bypassed the farming communities. Is this because Asian peasantry have a "dual economy," a different structure of mentality and aspiration as Boeke (1953) conceives? Or are there other, simpler reasons and causes that in their cumulative effect result in this technological dualism?

The latter explanation is acceptable when the facts of economic life in Nondwin are considered. The key to technological stagnation is found in the economic structure of the village community. Technological innovation does not come about because the economic motivation for it is small or absent and because the play elements of Burmese village life lie in the religious and dramatic sphere. The economic setting of agriculture explains the technological status quo.

Economy

Nondwin grows the crop mixture common to the Myinmu region. A *mayin* paddy, seven varieties of beans, sesamum, cotton, maize, sorghum, a few bananas, some small gardens of mangos, and onions are planted. The acreage of the three *kwins* (fields) the people of Nondwin farm are kwin 1, 406 acres, kwin 2, 281, and kwin 3, 385 acres. Of this land, only 50 acres, in 1959–1960, were in fallow, while 215 were double cropped. The land is intensively used, and the crop pattern shows a good knowledge of farming possibilities and a close adjustment of land use to its most economic return, given the technology at hand. The close fit of the crop and the land is testified to by the small amount of crop failure. In kwin 1, the best land, only six acres of those planted failed to mature; in kwin 2, 46 acres failed to yield enough to pay tax assessment on, and this was largely due to the withering of 23 acres of *hma peh* (black peas) [2] and 16 acres of other peas because of an insufficiency of rain. In kwin 3, only 20 acres failed to yield.

---

[2] See Sawyer and Nyun, 1927, for plants of Burma.

Classification of Land and Crops. The land, of course, is not uniform either in its goodness or in its ability to bear different sorts of crop cover. The villagers classify the land into three broad categories. The tax collector has a complicated system of assessment, depending upon the crop grown.[3] First class land is river alluvium land, blackish in color. It stays under water for at least a month during the flood tide. Second class land gets rainwater only, but it is low-lying and is under water intermittently. It is a brownish color. Third class land is higher-lying, sandy, and watered only by the rain; sometimes it is stony. The classification of the land is reflected in market price: class I brings around 1,000 kyats an acre, class II, 500–600, and class III, only 200–300. Most of Nondwin's land is class III, with some class II, and less than a score of class I lands. The different classes of land support varying crops. Class I can take any of the crops grown, but it alone can support onions and fruits without irrigation. Class II can take graham, maize, cotton, and sesamum, but its best use is for the more expensive white and red bean cover. Class III is best suited to cotton, sesamum, and maize. Sometimes a bean crop of *kalapè* (literally Indian Bean or foreign bean, but it is the dal or chickpea), or the broad bean *pehgyi* or *pezingon* (the small green bean) may be tried on class III land. Cotton, sesamum, dal, maize, and broadbeans are the chief agricultural products of Nondwin. The others play a much smaller part in the agricultural life, onions are restricted to a single owner, and fruits are grown by three families.

Although all the crops, except paddy, depend upon rainwater, there is some latitude in the timing of agricultural work, and where double cropping is practiced, the phasing of agricultural effort is of some importance. The different crops require varying amounts of human effort, of capital input, and give different yields and monetary returns. The economics of farming in Nondwin must be viewed not only from the geographical-technological perspective, but also from the angle of a village farmer who balances the inputs and outputs as he decides what and when to plant. According to my field census, extending from September to January 1960, 88 households, the economic units of production and consumption, were engaged in active economic life. Of these seven were nonfarming, and five were agricultural laborers without land of their own. This leaves 76 families engaged in agriculture. During this period they worked:

---

[3] See the Village Manual for the official system.

TABLE I

Crops Worked	No. of Acres	No. of Cultivators
Cotton	481	61
Sesamum	239	51
Beans	254	54
Maize	56	29
Paddy	28	12
Peanuts	8	3
Onions	3	1

Information is lacking, or unreliable, on eight cultivators who held 97 acres among them. From the above table it is clear that most Nondwin farmers plant more than one crop. There are seven farmers whose holdings are so small and the land so uniform that they are dependent upon a single crop. Mixed cropping is the rule.

Cotton, the most extensive crop, is grown as a money crop and exported to the nearby mills. Cotton is begun soon after the first rains, sometime in the month of *Kason* (roughly May–June). The earth is broken to a depth of four to five inches, and the wooden toothed harrow is then drawn over the soil. The earth is left in clumps until the rains come, usually in June. The moist earth is then plowed and harrowed again. Using two teams of bullocks drawing the metal tipped plow and the wooden toothed harrow, it takes four mornings to prepare an acre of cotton land. The seed is sown broadcast, sometime in June or July. This is a morning's work for a single man. In about 20 days the plants are nearly 5 inches tall, and the field is weeded. It takes a man five work days to clear an acre. In another 20 days the plants are about 12 inches high, ready for the second cleaning. The man days for cleaning are the same, five to an acre. Cotton begins to ripen in October, blooming irregularly so that the harvest is spaced over two or three months. Picking cotton requires two man days per acre.

Cotton yields vary widely from farmer to farmer and from year to year. The yearly difference is dependent upon the amount and incidence of rain. Individual differences depend upon the quality of land and the quality of the farmer, a topic to be treated later. The 1960 cotton harvest in Nondwin was about 25 per cent below the 1959 yield. In 1960 yields per acre ranged from 63 *viss* to 150 viss (a viss is 3.6 pounds). In constructing averages, I took a sample of 10 cultivators who farmed 120 acres of cotton. (Within the sample the figures are based on a 25 per cent sample of the cultivated cotton land and a 17 per cent sample of the cotton cultivators.)

Seed input in cotton varies from 60 to 80 pounds per acre, the better land getting the heavier seeding. Manuring is about a cartload of 30 baskets (weighing about 20 pounds each) per acre. Cotton prices, of course, vary from year to year, and throughout the selling season from October to February. Just at the beginning of the harvest, cotton sold for Ky 1.25 per viss, rose to Ky 1.30 at the end of October, Ky 1.35 the first week in November, and up to Ky 1.60 at the end of November, its high point. The return per acre is difficult to calculate and is within rather wide limits. Since most of the village cotton was in fact sold at Ky 1.30 per viss, this price is used to gauge the monetary returns. Only ten or so families have the withholding power to wait until the price rises before they unload their cotton. Most farmers must sell the cotton just as soon as it is harvested, and in the three village stores, selling food and sundries, cotton is taken in payment. The price is Ky 1.25 per viss, just under what cotton brings at the mills. The Ky 1.25 per viss price is what a cotton broker gives if he comes to pick up the cotton.

The upper and lower return for an acre of cotton at the selling price of Ky 1.30 per viss works out like this:

TABLE II   Return per Acre of Cotton *

Cost, Ky			Yield per Acre		
			Upper	Average	Lower
Plowing	12	Gross yield, viss	150	100	63
Planting	1	Selling price, Ky	13	1.3	1.3
First cleaning	5	Gross yield, Ky	195	130	82
Second cleaning	5	Cost	−77.50	−77.50	−77.50
Picking	2				
Manuring	25	Net Yield, Ky	118.50	54.50	4.50
Seed	27.50				
Total Cost	77.50				

* Based on 10 cultivators (N = 61, 17%) and 120 acres (N = 481, 25%).

However, the return is higher to the farmer, since for most cultivators the only cash outlay is for seed, labor is provided by themselves or their family or with neighbors on an exchange basis, and the manure comes from their own cattle.

Sesamum is alternated with cotton on a yearly basis. It is also a cash crop, grown for the money return. It uses not only the same sort of land as does cotton (chiefly class III land, although some bits of class II are sometimes under bean crops), but its cycle of planting and harvesting is nearly the same. Sesamum is planted during September and October. To prepare an acre for sesamum is a job of four mornings. One morning is required to broadcast the seed, and, when it matures in about 75 days, it takes three man days to harvest. No cleaning is required for the growing fields. Sesamum is seeded at about 20 to 26 pounds to the acre, just under half a basket. The fields are manured in the same way as the cotton fields. Yields run from one basket of 14 viss to six baskets, with an average of four baskets an acre. The price for sesamum ranged between 21 and 25 kyats per basket at the mill. The lower price was just at the beginning of the harvest. Most of the sesamum is sold at Ky 25 per basket, for, unlike cotton, the demand seems to be continually over the supply of sesamum in the region, so that the 25 kyat price holds for long periods. Table III shows the calculation for sesamum return.

TABLE III   Return per Acre of Sesamum *

Cost, Ky			Yield		
			Upper	Average	Lower
Plowing	12	Gross yield, baskets	6	4	1
Planting	1	Selling price, Ky	25	25	25
Harvest	3				
Manuring	25	Gross yield, Ky	150	100	25
Seed	13	Cost	−54	−54	−54
Total Cost	54	Net Yield, Ky	96	46	Loss

* Based on 10 cultivators ($N = 51, 20\%$) and 60 acres ($N = 239, 25\%$).

When the farmer says that cotton and sesamum are interchangeable, he is noting the near identity of their money incomes, the sameness of the labor input, the coincidence in suitable land, and their place in the agricultural year.

Besides cotton and sesamum, the common crops are pulses, beans, and maize. The chief pulse grown is kalapè (Indian bean, or dal). Beans of several varieties are also grown, white, red, broad, and black beans being the most common. Beans and pulses are restricted to the better lands (class II), although occasionally they are scattered in among growing cotton, sesamum, or maize fields. As I gathered data on beans and dal, I saw the similarity between them and I lumped them together in my census. Beans and dal were grown on 254 acres by 54 cultivators in 1960. The planting of pulses and beans stretches from the end of the first heavy rains in August to the beginning of the cold season in November. But work is bunched in the months of September–October. Whether it be the white or red beans planted in July–August, or the dal planted in October–November, four mornings' work is required in plowing and harrowing, per acre. Broadcast seeding takes a morning. White and red beans require the fields to be weeded after 20 days and this task is spaced over five mornings. Dal fields are not weeded. Harvesting beans is more laborious than the other field crops and requires five man days per acre (for the white and red beans five actual days, for the dal 10 mornings, since dal comes in March and April, and no one can, or does, work in the afternoon heat at the height of the hot season). Bean yields, like other crops in Nondwin, show a range of yield, from two to thirty baskets per acre. From my sample of 10 cultivators, growing various kinds of beans on 64 acres, 15 baskets was the average yield. Beans vary in price from 12 to 15 kyats the basket. As nearly as I can determine, most beans were sold at an average of 13 kyats the basket. Dal was fairly steady in price, and most dal sold at 10 kyats the basket. Table IV shows how the money return on beans works out:

TABLE IV   Return per Acre of White and Red Beans *

Cost, Ky			Yield		
			Upper	Average	Lower
Seed	10	Gross yield, baskets	30	15	2
Plowing	12	Selling price, Ky	13	13	13
Planting	1				
Cleaning	5	Gross yield, Ky	390	195	26
Harvesting	5	Cost	−58	−58	−58
Manuring	25				
	—	Net Yield, Ky	332	137	Loss
Total Cost	58				

* Based on 10 cultivators (19%) and 64 acres (25%).

Money return on dal, from five cultivators on 35 acres of gram, works out, at the average yield and the average selling price, as shown in Table V.

TABLE V   Return per Acre of Gram *

Cost, Ky		Yield	
Seed	8	Gross yield, baskets	20
Plowing	12	Selling price, Ky	10
Planting	1		
Harvesting	5	Gross yield, Ky	200
Manuring	25	Cost	−51
Total Cost	51	Net Yield, Ky	149

* Based on average yield of 5 cultivators and 35 acres.

Beans and the pulses form an economic and technological category as do cotton and sesamum. It is obvious why the Nondwin farmer uses the better land for beans and pulses, why cotton and sesamum are restricted to the sandy lands, and why the market price of the land suitable for beans and pulses is so much greater than that of cotton and sesamum.

The other field crops, maize, under which I included both the *pyaungbu* (human edible maize) and *pyaungkiung* (a sort of grain sorghum used as cattle fodder), and paddy rice form a small part of the economy. The maize yields a return of about 30 kyats an acre and only 56 acres are devoted to it. Paddy on 28 acres among 12 cultivators is very small scale, and discussion will be reserved to a comparison of the irrigated rice economy with that of Nondwin.

There are, however, two crops which form the "enterprise" segment of Nondwin farming. Peanuts and onions, although long known in Upper Burma (since 1892 when they were introduced in the Mandalay region), are experimental crops in Nondwin. By experimental crops I mean crops that within the last few years have been, or are being, tried by Nondwin farmers. They are the crops outside of the normal agricultural activities of village farmers, and normally they are not calculated in the reckoning of what to grow in a year. Not only are they the more recent crops, but their growing requires some different sorts of behavior from the farmer. First is the heavy investment in seed, second the increased work in the field, third the strangeness of some of the technique, and last the greater risk of failure to yield. The above applies much more forcibly to onions than peanuts, and onions may, in Nondwin, be considered the entrepreneurial crop. Compensation for the added troubles of growing onions is a much greater monetary return per acre. Only one man in Nondwin is essaying onion fields. A close view of his operations is instructive in revealing the variables involved in the introduction of a new crop, even in a rational, monetized peasant farming economy.

Onion seed is expensive. Seeding costs between 50 and 60 kyats per acre. Only a cultivator with capital can begin to plant onions, and the one man in the village who has undertaken it is the richest man in the community. He has enough land in the stable field crops so that if the onions do not come in he does not feel a pinch. The onions are pure investment crops. Two or three other families are able to bear the investment in the same way as the innovator, whom we shall here call U Sein Ko. But U Sein Ko has a more entrepreneurial outlook than they, and they say they will wait and see. If he does well, they will consider the growing of onions next crop year. It is clear that the conduction effects of onions are limited in Nondwin. Without credit facilities for new crops, only three or four farmers can essay the raising of onions. The first variable in the introduction of onions is wealth and withholding power.

Onions are a risk crop in Nondwin. The rain makes chances at least even that there will be no yield. An irrigation reserve must be at hand if the crop is to mature. The flooded paddy fields will not do, for they are too long under water. U Sein Ko has guarded against the vagaries of the rain by planting his three acres of onions near a well. His workers have rigged up a bucket system for raising water and his fields are given sufficient moisture. In addition, in the event that the well water is too slow in coming, he has investigated the hiring of a water pump from Sagaing. This element of planning, of rehearsing contingency, is not a common element in the operations of Nondwin farmers. U Sein Ko gets it because he in fact is only nominally a farmer. He is a businessman and spends most of his time in the cotton brokerage trade. He runs the village's largest store, and he is a moneylender. His relation to agriculture is businesslike, not the peasant attachment to growing things. A remark he made one day as we watched his growing onion fields illustrates this. We sat for about half an hour and watched his hired workers watering the tidy beds of onion seed. I turned and asked him, after a rather prolonged silence, what he was thinking. "Dreaming," he replied. "When I look at those fields I see kyats growing."

This second variable, the ability to plan and organize against uncertainty, is part of an entrepreneurial code. U Sein Ko is, when measured against the run of Nondwin farmers, an executive. And growing onions needs executive skills.

The techniques of onion growing are alien to the work routine of the field crops, and the skill and knowledge required are not in the cultural repertory of the Nondwin farmer. To get onions started in Nondwin, U Sein Ko had to import workers from a community that grew them. In his travels, buying and selling cotton, he had heard of the good, in local terms, "fabulous" returns to be gotten from onion growing. He kept this in mind while he hunted about for a man who would move to Nondwin and undertake the growing of onions. He found a family who would come, live in a thatch shack during the growing season and take on the growing of three acres of onions on a half-share basis. The man came to Nondwin to farm because U Sein Ko has a local reputation for fair dealing, trustworthiness, and openhandedness. In this case, reputation and character, as well as wealth and planning ability, are factors in the enterprise of onion growing.

Onion farming requires tight, compulsive, continual cultivation. It looks odd in the casual field cropping situation of Upper Burma. It requires a steady devotion of hard effort, a neatness and attention to minute detail that other farming does not and cuts into leisure and scheduled activity more closely than other crops. Its appeal is therefore limited. Many farmers would not bother with the care, the work, the effort, and attention of this compulsive agriculture, even if they had the land and capital to undertake it. Certainly, U Sein Ko himself would not engage in onion farming. It would interfere with his other business, tear him away from his experiments with alchemy, and cut unbearably into his easy day of chatting and visiting. Nondwin onion growing still depends upon hired labor, not only because knowledge and skill are lacking, but because a farmer has to be disciplined to onion growing. So a landowner's reputation is important, for a half-share onion farmer must trust the man who lays out the money. Wide social contacts are equally necessary, for the entrepreneur must be able to find the man who will uproot and come to Nondwin.

Onions are an abstract economic opportunity. The return from an acre of onions can run from 3,000 to 4,000 kyats. But the opportunity is limited by available capital and credit, technical knowledge, executive ability, contact and communication, the compulsive nature of onion cropping, and the subsistence outlook of most farmers. In this context, onions can only be grown by a rather affluent man with organizational ability who has an entrepreneurial outlook on agriculture.

In contrasting subsistence to entrepreneurial codes in the management of economic activity in Nondwin farming, I do not imply a difference in rationality of matching means and ends. The foregoing description of the use of land for the best return effectively eliminates that sort of interpretation. What I mean to single out is a difference in the aim of agricultural production and the attitudes engendered by it. Everybody is involved in the money and market economy of farming. The crops grown are exchanged for money and this buys the necessities of life. Like other Burman communities Nondwin is not self-sufficient and must trade to live. But the majority of farmers have an orientation to self-sufficiency. The subsistence outlook in farming is predominant, not the entrepreneurial view. The subsistence outlook is based on the canon of freedom from want: Plant what you need, try to be self-sufficient, get your rice and oil in hand, and you have no need to worry; restrict your wants to your means, gauge your resources to meet your wants, shrug off what you cannot have. This is what the subsistence-minded farmer says. It is a kind of outlook that shrinks ends to meet means at hand. Given greater means, ends expand. But the pull of ends to devise, seek, or nurture new means is virtually absent. It is a way of being free of want, but not closed to new wants or new means, and it is very undynamic. This is the structure of motivation accompanying the "dual" economy. The entrepreneur also aims at being free of want, but his way is to avoid want through abundance. Take a risk, get rich, be respected, find a new way to make more money, expand in the hope of reward: This the entrepreneurial code stresses. And this is the attitude that forms the dynamic, market-oriented society. These two attitudes coexist in a society like Nondwin, but it is special experience, and rare experience, that forms the entrepreneurial outlook.

The special experience apparently consists of managing a large enough bundle of resources in a variety of market situations. The traders, the brokers, the storekeepers—the mere five or six of them —are those with the entrepreneurial outlook. Involvement in a market, the use of money, the fluctuation of return are apparently not enough to break the prevailing subsistence code of most farmers. A critical point of scale in resources more than 25 acres and a variety of market entanglements, especially moneylending and commodity speculation, appear to be the catalysts that transform the "get along" farmer to the "get going" farmer.

Peanuts are a crop, grown by three people in Nondwin, that almost spans the gap between subsistence and entrepreneurial farmers. The investment in seed is high, 45 to 50 kyats per acre, and thus requires capital and withholding power nearly equal to that of onions. But the technical skills are not very divergent from ordinary farming, and the planning and organization are no more extensive than in cotton or sesamum farming. The risk is not great, and the return is good. Peanuts can be converted into oil for home use in cooking so that they accord well with both the end of sufficiency and of increased return. Successful peanut growing is much greater in possible spread

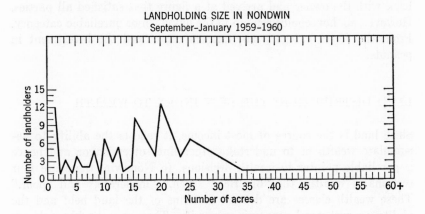

LANDHOLDING SIZE IN NONDWIN
September–January 1959–1960

TABLE VI   Landholding Size
by 5 Acre Interval Yields

Acres	Households
0– 4	17
5– 9	13
10–14	18
15–19	12
20–24	13
25–29	5
30–34	1
35–39	1
40–44	0
45–49	0
50–54	1
55–59	0
60+	1

$N = 82$

than is onion growing. At least 34 of the 82 landholders have the means to take on some peanut growing. Crops with characteristics similar to peanuts represent a real opportunity to many in Nondwin, but they do not have the transforming effect of crops such as onions.

The contention that 32 landholders have the means to be peanut growers is based on the distribution of land in Nondwin. Table VI gives my field census of self-reported landholdings. The reports were checked with three elders in the village. When they concurred with the reported holding, I accepted it; when they did not, I checked back with the owner and arrived at a figure that satisfied all parties. However, six households remain in the unknown or unreliable category. From the 15–19 category on, farmers can afford the investment in peanuts.

LAND DISTRIBUTION: THE BEST INDEX TO WEALTH

Since land is the source of most income, it reflects the ability to accumulate wealth or to undertake other lines of endeavor and hence is a reliable pointer to wealth divisions. In Nondwin, there are four sections of wealth: the "big rich," "rich," "moderate," and "poor." These wealth classes are defined in terms of the land held and the ability to withstand economic adversity. They say the big rich are those who need not worry about the future; they can spend as they like. They have landholdings above 50 acres. The rich are those who can spend, are out of debt, and need to hire some labor to work their lands. They have more than 20 acres of decent land. The moderate are those who earn a livelihood, who with good management need not want. They must be careful how they spend. They have between 10 and 20 acres of land. The poor are those who have less than 10 acres of land, who often must look about for the next day and seek other employment, and who are in continual danger of debt and want. The native categories fairly define the meanings of wealth and land, but since the big rich are so few, I telescoped the wealth division into thirds, rather than quarters, merging the big rich and the rich into the single category of rich.

First I made a division on the basis of land alone, then I checked my categories of wealth with three different sets of informants, one from each wealth class. I need not have been so scrupulous, for with the exception of four persons, who, on the basis of landlessness, I had placed in the poor category, I and the informants from the three wealth divisions were in full agreement. The four households without land, that were moved to different categories, had other major sources of income. Three were moved to the moderate third—an artisan, a pig breeder, and a cattle breeder; one moved to the rich third—a herder of oxen. The wealth categories of Nondwin then are:

Number of Households

Rich	33
Moderate	33
Poor	26

This division breaks the community into fairly even thirds. The wealth division is the basis for an agricultural division of labor. The poor supply the bulk of the labor force. They regularly hire out to do tasks in the fields, such as plowing, weeding, harvesting, and seeding. The moderates tend to be self-sufficient in labor supply—they neither hire out nor hire labor. The rich do the hiring, and, of course, they do not hire out. Of the 12 landless families, seven are completely dependent upon wages for their livelihood (the others have other occupations).

The wealthy are not clustered in any particular part of the village (Map of Nondwin Village), or, except for the prevalence of two-story houses, is a rich man immediately visible. Wealth is expressed in differential consumption and hardly anywhere else in the social structure. Wealth does not necessarily entail power, prestige, or authority. It, of course, is a factor in the pursuit of those ends, but the honored and the powerful need much more than market position or wealth to gain status. Returning to the economic consequences of wealth, the ability to innovate, or the willingness to try new things is the most striking.

From the agricultural description it emerges that only the rich, those with capital and withholding power, can take advantage of the new crops like onions, and only the moderates could even consider peanuts as a crop. The rich, however, do not turn to agricultural expansion. The land market is severely limited, and land transactions are rare. Land is hardly ever sold outright, and for a nine-month period only five acres came into the market. Occasionally land is pledged against a loan. This contract allows the lender to have use of the land for a minimum of three years, after which time the borrower can repay the loan, without interest, and reclaim the land. On land pledges, the title never formally passes to the lender, and generations later, if the connection can be proved and the money raised, a descendant of the borrower may reclaim the land. Besides the scarcity of land in the market, the rich are inhibited from land acquisition by the spectre of the land reform, already carried out in some districts in Upper Burma. But more important is the limit on land that can be well-supervised by a single household economic unit. Land over the 50 acre mark tends to be let out on a half-share basis to a tenant farmer. This effectively passes the management out of the owner's hands, but it keeps the quality of the land up in a way that an unsupervised labor force could not. Half-share lands in cotton and sesamum are not very profitable to the owner; they verge on charity to keep a fellow villager alive. Beans on half-share do not bring startling returns either. Tying up capital in land is safe enough, but higher returns are to be found in moneylending, which the big rich families engage in, in the exciting speculation of the cotton market, and in brokerage in general. So the rich turn to commerce rather than to agricultural modernization. The game of the storing and selling of cotton is very appealing to the love of gambling in the Burmese villager, and the return is worth the effort. A speculative business mentality is built up in the cotton business, and there are families who have been impoverished by wrong guesses and enriched by right.

The three richest families in the community also run its stores. These are small—the largest, U Sein Ko's, has about 100 kyats' intake daily. It is the women of the rich households who take care of the stores and the daughters or hired girls who carry the wares about the village on the woven trays. Men, rich or well-to-do, tend to be released from the productive process. It is not a disgrace to be inactive, to have the leisure to welcome guests, to chat, and to drink tea, but a positive good, and this is one of the rewards for wealth. To fill his time, the rich man is engaged in cotton brokerage, and this requires much visiting about to get current cotton prices, much chatting and talking about the possible shifts in price. If he still has time on his hands and is old enough, he may turn to religion for it is a sort of *summum bonum* in old age to be able to devote full attention to the mediation and devotion that leads to favorable rebirths. Alchemy is another possible outlet. This requires money; it is related to the religious life; it brings one into a social circle of fellow practitioners for the exchange of information; and it has the speculative joy of the possibility of the grand coup of wealth and power unlimited in this life.

The influences of commercial attraction in economic return, the land situation, the emphasis on leisure, the bent toward spectacular return, the joy and sociability of speculation, all underwrite the observable fact that the richer farmer is not strongly drawn toward agricultural innovation or modernization. His growing detachment from the business of farming also prevents his participant grasp of the many simple ways in which farming could be bettered. The rich are a source of agricultural change if the crop promises great return and if somebody else who can be hired has the technical skills needed.

It is fairly obvious that the moderate farmer, the household head who with good rain and decent yields can meet his customary standard of living, is not an innovator. His domestic economy is tightly balanced, and he cannot take even the enticing speculative risks. This is the element that has brought and held a kind of stasis, or slow change, to agricultural life. The moderates have worked out the close fit between land, crops, and labor; they have adjusted to a level of living to fit the returns, and they are content to move within these limits. They are without debt, free of economic bondage, their own masters, and hard working practical farmers. Such men only shift their modes of production when an outside agency—human or natural catastrophe—forces them to do so.

The poor must seek to make ends meet. They eke out a living on a day-to-day basis. They are, or some of them are, receptive to new modes of employment. From the ranks of the poor come the artisans, the men with special occupations, and those ready to adopt bits of new technology. One has even taken on a forbidden occupation of pig breeder. The poor also provide the migrants, from village to village, and from village to town and city.

One of the landless families has its household just at the entrance to Nondwin. This is a family of teakettle makers. It is the only such establishment in Nondwin. Scrap aluminum and other metals are purchased at Ky 2.50 the viss in the Mandalay bazaar (much of the scrap metal comes from wrecked World War II military equipment, chiefly planes). The business is a family operation, with a four-person work crew. The two nephews melt the metal in an open hearth and pour it into molds. The polishing and finishing are done by the husband and wife. On a flywheel, powered by a bicycle chain and pedal, the pots, moistened with mustard oil, are buffed. A bit of heavy sandpaper and more buffing gives the shiny market-ready finish. The family turns out ten finished pots every three days. Each pot sells for five kyats. They make a reasonable living, by Nondwin standards, much better than the six or seven kyats a day they could earn if all

of them were agricultural laborers. The family is not native to Nondwin. They come from Sabyagin, a village in the Monywa district. In
Sabyagin, everyone is a metal worker; competition was too keen. They
picked Nondwin because the kettle maker's aunt (father's sister) is
a Nondwin resident, and she could assure them of a place to settle.
The occupation and its skills remain in the single household. No one
wants to learn, and they do not offer to teach. It is an addition to
Nondwin with almost no effect on any other household.

There is, in another poor household, Nondwin's only machine run
cotton separator. The machine is powered by a one cylinder motorcycle engine which is hooked up by a fan belt to the ordinary, usually foot pedal run, seed separator. Four years ago the owner bought
this machine, repaired it, and started his cotton seed separating business. Where did the idea come from? He was poor and always on the
lookout for ways to supplement his income. In Shanda village, near
Ondaw, about 17 miles from Nondwin, he saw the same sort of machine in operation. He asked about it; every time he was in the vicinity he asked more questions. He found, by way of his brother who
drives an ox cart in Mandalay, a motor for sale; he bought it and
set it up. Now he charges one kyat per viss of cotton processed through
the separator. In the cotton plucking season he will clear five or six
kyats a day. He also hires one or two girls from the nearby village
of Legyi to spin separated cotton into thread, and he sells this thread
for longyi making. His business is not confined to Nondwin, but draws
on other villages. When he brought the machine to Nondwin, it caused
no stir. People did not come to gawk, nobody asked questions, and
nobody else has considered setting up his own separator. Perhaps he
covers the whole demand for this service in the locality.

The course of the adoption of this machine throws some light on
the process of village accretion of items. This man, when questioned,
had never thought of, or considered some rather obvious further uses
of, gasoline motors. Machines like the rice pounder, the fodder chopper, or the sesamum grinder could be easily hooked to gasoline motors.
But he had seen no working models of these machines, and he did not
know how they worked. His drive is not invention or innovation; it
is the poverty-induced need to adapt something that is elsewhere working.

The pig breeding household is also composed of migrants to Nondwin. They have no land, and so turned to pig raising. Their neighbors
think that it is a bad occupation, for Buddhism says that to raise
animals for slaughter is a way of accumulating great amounts of de-

merit. But the pig breeders say they must live. They do not slaughter the animals themselves, and they hope to wipe out the stain of raising them by doing enough good works. But pig breeding will not spread, profitable as it is for a landless family. The religious feeling is too strong against it, and the economic pressures are less than the starvation pressure needed to move people to undertake it.

From these instances, and the case of the tailor, the rope and twine makers, the cigar rollers, and the food sellers, and others which could be added, it is clear that the poor are a source of economic change in Nondwin. But the sort of change they bring tends to be self-isolating and noncumulative. It has small conduction and spread effects, and it hardly, other than through addition, modifies the social structure. Although there is a steady stream of changing economic activity in the wake of the poor seeking means to livelihood, without some external major changes in the opportunities presented to a community like Nondwin, the stream will never become a torrent.

Household Budgets

The categories rich, poor, and moderate have been explored as they bear on economic change and the division of labor. But just what does it mean to be rich or poor in Nondwin? The way to see the life style differences is through the consumption and expenditure patterns of representatives of the different categories. Household budgets exemplify the different levels of living, and they also give clues to the structure of values in Nondwin. For with increased income people move to implement more wants, and the range of things consumed at different income levels indicates, empirically, just how much of a unitary structure the wants of a community are. The budgets presented here are for a month's consumption, somewhat seasonally adjusted for the different products on the market at different times. Adding the food consumption budgets together with the clothing and personal effects budgets and estimating the cost of a house will give a level of living, will translate the bare figures of per capita income that national agencies accumulate into the bundle of goods and services that people actually obtain.

To bring the food expenditure into the total annual expenditure requires some calculation of the way other items are consumed. Religious donations average about 100 kyats a month in this family, except for the months of *Wa*, when such affairs as *hsungywe, athuba,*

TABLE VII Average Monthly Expenditure Pattern of a Rich Household

Item	Amount	Price, Ky/Amt	Total
Cooking	8 viss	4.00	32.00
Firewood	2 bundles	6.00	12.00
Salt	1 v	0.50	0.50
Sugar	1 v	2.00	2.00
Tea	1 v	8.00	8.00
Rice	1 bag *	12–16.00	14.00
Beans	1 basket	10–14.00	12.00
Eggs, duck	40 eggs	0.20	8.00
Eggs, hen	8 eggs	0.25	2.00
Milk	5 v	0.75	3.75
Fish (various)	5 v	3.50	17.50
Dried fish	1 v	8.00	8.00
Tobacco	1,000 cigars	20.00	20.00
Betel, nut		5.00 ky/v ⎫	
Betel, leaf		4.00 ky/v ⎬	8.00
Betel, lime, spice	unknown		
Chili, dry	1 v	4.00	4.00
Ngapi (preserved fish)	2 v	2.50	5.00
Mutton	25 ticals †	6.00 ky/v	1.50
Beef (special occasion food)	1 v	2.00	2.00
Pork (rarely eaten)	1 v	3.50	3.50
Chicken (about 6 times/yr.)		4.00	2.00
Peanuts	1 bask	8.00	8.00
Bananas	5 bunches	0.50	2.50
Cabbage (Dec.–May)	10 heads	0.20	0.67
Carrots (Dec.–Mar.)	3 v	0.50	0.50
Buthi (Nov.–Apr.)	10 gourds	0.20	1.00
Onions	5 v	3.50	17.50
Kayanthi	5 v	0.50	2.50
Tomatoes	5 v	2.00	10.00
Ngabyayei (fish water)	3 v	2.50	7.50
Ginger	25 tics	2.00	0.50
Saffron	50 tics	1.00	0.50
Kayekaya	5 v	1.50	7.50
Mango pickles	3 v	1.00	3.00
Mangosteen (Oct.–Dec.)			1.00
Maize (Oct.–Dec.)	250 ears	1.25 ky/100	0.75
Tamarind	2 v	0.60	1.20

* 1 bag = 3 baskets.
† 100 ticals = 1 v.

TABLE VII (*Continued*)

Item	Amount	Price, Ky/Amt	Total
Subokywe (rainy season)	(picked in forest)		0.50
Bread (or roll)	3 loaves	0.50	1.50
Cake	3 cakes	2.00	6.00
Kyethingathi	2 v	0.50	3.75
Pehmyin	30 v	0.50	3.75
Tea leaf (pickled, to eat)			10.00
Peinu (Oct.)	3 v	0.30	0.10
Potatoes	3 v	0.60	1.80
Pezingon (Dec.–Jan.)	10 v	0.30	0.50
Zadawbe	.5 bask	8.00	4.00
Coffee	1 oz	1.10	1.10
Matches	2 pkg	0.60	1.20
Kerosene	1 tin	8.00	8.00
Fruits (coconuts, papaya, oranges, limes, apples)			3.00
Jaggery	5 v	1.00	5.00
Soap			1.50
Thanakhka (face powder)			2.50
Coconut oil (used on hair)			3.00
Powder, lipstick			1.00
Flowers (for Buddha altar)			5.00
Medical supplies (and treatments)			18.00
Travel			25.00
Total Average Monthly Expenses, Ky			334.82
Annual Food Expenditure, Ky			4,017.84

mingala lethtat, kahtein,[4] etc., are not performed. Then the whole *ahlu* ceremony structure is suspended, and only the feeding of monks, nuns, beggars, and visitors is carried on. But this comes out of the household budget exemplified above. The ahlu (charity or alms) costs are about 900 kyats for the year. Household items that are replaced every year are few. Mats, to sit on and sleep on, wear out at the rate of one per month, and the cost ranges between 3.50 and 1.25 kyats per mat, depending on the kind. An annual cost for mats averages 56

---

[4] To be described in the chapter on Buddhism.

kyats. Kitchen items—pots, pans, spoons, knives, and plates—cost about 15 kyats per year. Furniture is considered virtually permanent. The bed posts, the chairs, the small tables, and woven things that make up the scant furnishings of a Burmese village home can only be roughly depreciated on an annual basis, and, since they tend to be a once for all outlay, I shall not here include them. Other items in the household having an annual cost are blankets, pillows, and mosquito nets. Blankets have a life expectancy of five years, and the annual cost in this household is 6 kyats. Pillows cost about 3 kyats the year, and mosquito nets 15 kyats the year. A rich household's yearly expenditure is then:

TABLE VIII Yearly Expenditure
for a Rich Household

Item	Cost, Ky
Food	4,017.84
Religious donations	900.00
Kitchen items	15.00
Mats	56.00
Blankets, pillows, etc.	24.00
Total Expenditure	5,012.84

This household is made up of five adults, two children, aged 13 and 6, and a baby of under two years.

The clothing and personal effects of a man and a woman in Nondwin are contrasted rich against poor in Tables IX and X. The moderate man will have the same quantities and the same items as the rich man or woman, except for display items. In the range of cost for the different items of apparel, the rich man tends to be at the upper end, the poor at the cheaper end of the scale. The moderate sometimes buys the better grades, sometimes the poorer ones. There is not, in my sample, any consistency. In the comparisons of rich, poor, and moderate, as to clothing and to household expenditure, I have used but single matched families. They are very much like other families in their respective category. I have checked budgets, off and on, in more than 10 per cent of the families of Nondwin, and the ones I present are representative. For those in the following tables, I have gathered daily expenditures for a four-month period, spaced over two of the three seasons of the Burmese year. Other households, against

TABLE IX Men's Clothing Expenditure

Burmese	English	Cost, Ky	Duration	Quantity Poor	Rich
Eingyi	Shirt	11–14	3 yr	2	5
Taikpon eingyi	Jacket	30–50	6 yr	1	2–3
Sutkye	Tee shirt	2.50	3 mo	2	6
Aukhanbaumbi	Shorts	1.50–2.50	3 mo	2	4
Longyi	Wrap skirt	6–20	2 yr	3	10
Bankok longyi	Silk wrap skirt	45–100	6 yr	1	2
Gaungbaung	Hat (wrapped)	15	3–4 yr	only one here	
Tabe	Towel turban	1–5	3–4 yr	2	4
Hnyatphanat	Leather slipper	2.50–13	1 yr	1	3
Honphanat	Wooden slipper	1.25	6 mo	1	1
Chethi	Shirt chain	10–200	—	1	2
Letkainpawa	Handkerchief	1–3		only old men and dandies	
Thou mwei okhtok	Hat	15	7 yr	0	1
Lo eik	Shan carrying bag	7–20	1 yr	1	1
Kamaut	Straw hat	1–1.50	1 yr	1	1
Hti	Umbrella	10–13	2 yr	0	1
Paw okhtok	Topee	5–10	2 yr	0	1

TABLE X Women's Clothing Expenditure

Burmese	English	Cost, Ky	Duration	Quantity Poor	Rich
Eingyi	Blouse	3	6 mo	3	10–15
Nylon eingyi	Blouse	20–30	2 yr	1	2–4
Kot eingyi	Jacket	35–50	5 yr	1	1–3
Htamein	Wrap skirt	5–12	1 yr	2	5
Bankok longyi	Silk wrap skirt	30–50	5 yr	1	2
Chwegan	Bodice slip	2.50–10	3 mo	3	5
Dahpanat	Heeled slipper	8–10	3 yr	0	1
Honhpanat	Wooden slipper	1.60	6 mo	1	1
Hnyathpanat	Slipper	3–9	1 yr	1	3
Nagat	Earring (married women only)	30–100	—	1	1
Nasweh	Earring, dangling (unmarried women)	25–50	—	1	1
Shwegyo	Gold chain	100–500	—	0	1
Letzwe	Necklace	300–1,000	—	0	1
Letkauk	Bracelet	200 plus	—	0	1
Letsuk	Ring	30–500	—	0	1
Shwechgyin	Ankle chain	500–1,000	—	0	1

which I judge their typicality, were visited less regularly but at least once a week during the four-month period. The food expenses are recorded, then, from daily observations, while the clothing expenses are self-reported.

Women may also have an umbrella, straw hat, and sweat towel turbans. The cost and duration of these items is the same as a man's. For the gold chains on shirt fronts, ankle, and wrist, there appears none for the poor. Some of the poor women do invest in cheap, imitations, ranging from 10 to 20 kyats each. But many do not wear any if they do not have gold ones to wear. For the ceremonial occasions when these are worn they will rent or borrow the jewels. All women have a set of eingyi buttons, from the glass and plastic varieties costing 10 or so kyats to the gold ones listed above for rich women. Among the personal effects of a rich man are a straight edge razor, a combination tweezer (for plucking beard hair) and ear spoon (for taking wax from the ear), a comb, a fountain pen, a flashlight, a cigarette lighter, and a leather purse. The richest may also have in their houses a clock (there are only four in Nondwin), some silvered serving goblets (only two houses have these), elaborate lacquer betel boxes, serving trays, and cigar trays. The poorer families tend to have a few of these things, although the cigarette lighter (cost from two kyats up), the ear spoon and tweezer, comb, and straight razor are nearly ubiquitous. Only the richest man in Nondwin has a shotgun, and another rich man has a rifle. Framed pictures (of either religious figures or scenes, the national hero Aung San, or family events) are found in almost every household; only the very poorest tack or nail unframed pictures to the walls or beams.

From the above tables the cost of clothing and effects can be computed for the rich family on an annual basis. By taking the higher prices for all items and prorating them on a year basis, a rich man's clothing costs just over 200 kyats a year. And a rich woman's apparel costs just over 190 kyats a year, not counting the gold jewelry that is only worn on show occasions and represents family investment as much as it does wearing apparel. For this family, the annual clothing costs for five adults (three male, two female) and two children, scaled at half adult costs, is about 1,280 kyats a year. This estimate is fairly accurate, but I know now that I have erred in missing some of the food items (garlic, bought food from sweet sellers, etc., which may run about 30 kyats the year).

TABLE XI   Annual Expenditure for
a Rich Family

Item	Cost, Ky
Food	4,017.84
Clothing	1,280.00
Religious	900.00
Household	95.00
Total Expenditure	6,292.84

Table XII is compiled as a comparison of a moderate and poor family's monthly food consumption. The poor family supplements food intake by eating often with richer neighbors. The poor family is one adult and one child less than the rich and the moderate families described above. The poor tend to have smaller families than the rich, and this family, while violating the principle of strictly matched pairs, is representative of the families in the lower third of the income structure of Nondwin.

The food budgets in Nondwin reveal that the rich man spends more than twice as much on food as does the moderate, and that the moderate spends about twice as much as the poor. The wider range of edibles in the rich diet and diminished intake of the poor is certainly one of the reasons for the greater survival of children in the richer families. The level of living, even in a relatively prosperous village like Nondwin, can go down to one kyat a day per person. That is the bare minimum on which energy to work can be maintained.

Annual expenditure of the rich, poor, and moderate is compared in the following table:

TABLE XIII   Comparison of Annual Expenditures by
Wealth Classification

Item	Rich, Ky	Moderate, Ky	Poor, Ky
Food	4,017.84	1,670.76	708.60
Clothing	1,280.00	750.00	175.00
Religious	900.00	120.00	20.00
Household	95.00	40.00	20.00
Total	6,292.84	2,580.76	923.60

TABLE XII   Monthly Expenditure Pattern of Moderate and Poor Family

Item	Price	Moderate Amount	Moderate Total, Ky	Poor Amount	Poor Total, Ky
Cooking oil	4.00 ky/v	3.50 v	14.00	1.00 v	4.00
Firewood	3.00 ky/cart load	1.00 cart	3.00	.50 cart	1.50
Salt	.50 ky/v	2.00 v	1.00	25 tics	.15
Sugar	2.00 ky/v	50 tics	1.00	—	—
Tea	5.00 ky/v	50 tics	2.50	.10 v	.50
Rice	11.00 ky/bask	3.00 bask	33.00	2.00 bask	22.00
Beans	11.00 ky/bask	.25 bask	3.00	3.00 cans	2.00
Eggs, chicken	.25 ky/ea	—	—	—	—
Eggs, duck	.25 ky/ea	8 eggs	2.00	4 eggs	1.00
Milk	.75 ky/v	1.50 v	1.25	—	—
Fish	4.00 ky/v	2.00 v	8.00	50 tics	2.00
Dried fish	10.00 ky/v	.25 v	2.50	25 v	2.50
Tobacco	5.00 ky/100	100 cigars	5.00	75 cig	4.00
Betel	4.00 ky/v	.30 v	1.20	—	—
Chili, dry	4.00 ky/v	.50 v	2.00	.25 v	1.00
Napi	3.50 ky/v	1.00 v	3.50	.50 v	1.75
Mutton				—	—
Beef	2.00 ky/v	1.50 v	3.00	—	—
Chicken	4.00 ky/v	—	—	—	—
Pork	4.00 ky/v	1.00 v	4.00	.50 v	2.00
Peanuts	8.00 ky/bask	—	—	—	—
Bananas	.50 ky/bunch	—	—	—	—
Cabbage (Dec.-May)	.20 ky/v	1 head	.10	.5 head	.05
Carrots (Dec.-Mar.)	.50 ky/v	1.00 v	.20	.5 v	.10
Buthi (Nov.-Apr.)	.20 ky/gourd	3 gourds	.30	1 gourd	.10
Onions	2.00 ky/v	.50 v	1.00	.25 v	.50
Brinjal	.50 ky/v	—	—	—	—
Tomato	2.00 ky/v	3.00 v	6.00	1.00 v	2.00
Cucumber				—	—
Ngabyabye	2.50 ky/v	2.00 v	5.00	1.00 v	2.50
Ginger	2.00 ky/v	—	—	—	—

Item	Price	Amount	Cost	Amount	Cost
Saffron	1.50 ky/v	.30 v	.50	—	—
Kayekaya	1.50 ky/v	.25 v	.50	—	—
Mango pickles	1.00 ky/v	—	—	—	—
Mangosteen		—	—	—	—
Maize (Oct.–Dec.)	1.25 ky/100 ears	500 ears	1.60	100 ears	.30
Tamarind	.60 ky/v	1 v	.60	1.00 v	.20
Supoyewah	.15 ky/bu	3 bu	.50	—	—
Bread		—	—	—	—
Cake	2.00 ky/cake	1 cake	2.00	—	—
Chainkathi	1.00 ky/v	.10 v	.10	10.00 v	1.25
Pemyit (Nov.–Jan.)	.50 ky/v	20.00 v	2.50	—	—
Potato	.60 ky/v	1.00 v	.60	—	—
Pehzinzau (Dec.–Jan.)	.30 ky/v	1.50 v	.08	—	—
Zadawvwe		—	—	—	—
Coffee	1.10 ky/oz	1.00 pkg	.60	.50 pkg	.30
Candles	.60 ky/pkg	5.00 boxes	.25	4.00 boxes	.20
Matches	.05 ky/box	2.00 bot	.60	.50 bot	.15
Kerosene	.30 ky/bot	1.00 ky/mo	1.00	—	—
Fruits	(various)	1.00 v	1.00	—	—
Jaggery	1.00 ky/v	2.00 cakes	.20	.10 v	.10
Soap	.10 ky/cake	—	2.00	2.00 cakes	.20
Thanakhka		—	2.00	—	—
Coconut oil		—	—	—	1.00
Powder, lipstick		—	2.00	—	1.00
Flowers		—	3.00	—	—
Medical expense		—	15.00	—	—
Travel		—		—	5.00
Total Average Monthly Expenses			139.23		59.05
Annual Food Expenditure			1,670.76		708.60

These differences in the level of living are not as apparent to the eye as the figures would lead one to assume. Poverty in the Burmese village is not of high visibility. There is enough rice, beans, oil, and fish (for these turn out to be the staples of everyone's diet, irrespective of wealth level) even in the poor families. Clothing is uniform in daily life. It is only on festive, religious, or "dress up" occasions that the better off outshine the poor, and, then, not always, for if a poor person can borrow the jewelry he can seem like a rich man. House types are not necessarily tied to wealth. The richest, of course, tend to have the wooden, two-story houses, but beyond that, a man's wealth is not discernible in his house style or in his household furnishing.

In the setting of the village, poverty is not grinding, and being poor is not a disgrace. There exists little envy of the poor for the rich, and there is almost no antagonism or social inequality between them. The absence of social inequality between the wealthy and the moderate and the poor is due to the fact that economic differences between families are not built into the social structure in terms of status or power positions. This (and the social structure will be described in a separate chapter), plus the organization of the economy along household economic units, the absence of a wage labor force, and the small use of capital in the productive process, makes men seldom dependent on each other for economic activity. The familial economic network allows little opportunity for fixed economic relations of employer-employee, capitalist-worker, or patron-client, or any sort of economic relationship that could lay the basis for an expression of inequality. Wealth is not a primary thing that a Nondwin villager strives for. This is not to say that everyone is not united in saying that wealth is a good thing. It frees people from want; it enables them to contribute more to religion, to build up merit in this life for the next, to entertain well; and it bestows on them the highly regarded leisure. But the building up of the land or business underlying wealth is a tricky business and depends on many things beyond the competence and control of the average villager. It depends upon peace and order in the countryside. It depends upon rain and the absence of insect pests. And finally it depends upon the *kan* (the accumulated nucleus of past lives, an idea that will be fully treated in the chapter on religion), the destiny, or luck, or fate that one has.

In a situation like this, with its congruent belief system, failure or success in the economic sphere does not say very much about a person. Villagers do not judge a man on his economic attainments which

are, of course, part of the evaluation of a person, but never the index
or pointer for social placement. Wealth is fluid enough so that it does
not cling to family lines. The rich and the poor are interrelated. Everyone has seen the rise of a poor family and the fall of a rich one. The
poor have none of the cowering, cringing qualities or shame that poverty bestows when economic criteria form the index of social placement, and conversely the rich have none of the pride, arrogance, or
habits of command.

Both the rich and the poor agree that "management" is an important aspect of reaching economic sufficiency. There are stories of bad
managers and good managers. The family from whom the budget of
the poor category is taken is given as an example of poor management. The head of the family tried to get into the cotton brokerage
business. He bought cotton, stored it, and hoped for a price rise. He
guessed wrong and had to borrow money. Next season he tried again,
but he did not pay proper attention to the shifting prices and made
mistakes again. His debts rose; he had to pawn his land; and his living standard consequently dropped from the moderate to the poor
level. Some farmers are also called bad managers. They do not plow
their fields enough; they skimp on manure; and they are generally
lazy. Their yields are less than the more industrious farmers. They
are the farmers who will never build up a hoard or be able to afford
a large social event without getting into debt.

I do not have enough cases to make any generalization about wealth
mobility, but it seems clear that wealth differences are a built-in part
of the Nondwin society. And while wealth is a good, it is not the
greatest good, and poverty is but a minor evil.

Social and Political Organization

The basic social unit of Nondwin is the family. Families are organized into household units, and it is the household, where all the coresidents are in familial relationships, that has a group existence. The family and household occupy a single compound. Each compound is fenced off from its neighbors, and the social separateness of households corresponds to the spatial distinctness. In the Map of Nondwin village there is shown the 94 fenced compounds that make up Nondwin. Some of these compounds contain more than a single conjugal family, but not all of the compounds having more than a single family unit form a single household. The family and households of Nondwin divide into three types: (A) The conjugal family of father, mother, unmarried children (sometimes with secondary relatives as satellite residents); (B) the extended conjugal family, in which a son or daughter has formed a conjugal family and is coresident with the father and mother and jurally subordinate to the father-mother family; and (C) the joint conjugal family, in which relatives such as siblings or cousins or in-laws live in the same compound, with coordinate jural status between or among the families.

The three types do not obscure the underlying dynamic of family and household formation: the drive for each married pair to set up its own compound as the jural superior. The reasons other forms of families are found are obvious enough: they are part of the domestic cycle of independent establishment of a compound, and sometimes the economic or emotional factors are such that conjugal families get rooted into a single extended or joint familial household until the death of some of the members destroys the association.

In the field census of Nondwin the following compound composition was encountered.

Type A	53
Type B	32
Type C	5
	—
	90
Unknown	2
Single persons	2
	—
Total	94

Of the 32 extended conjugal families, 23 were through a female link, making for matri-local residence on the husband's part, and only 9 through a male link, making for patri-local residence for a woman. In type C, four were female-linked, and one male-tied.

SOCIAL ORGANIZATION: THE HOUSEHOLD

The defining social criteria of a family or familial household are:

1. Commensuality: All of the members of the household dine together. Food is cooked on a single hearth. This is the single most telling feature of a group of conjugal families in the same compound. The number of cooking and dining places corresponds nearly exactly to the number of familial and household entities within a compound.

2. Economic Communality: Something is owned in common by the adult members, or else they have a presumptive claim for future ownership of property which they now enjoy use or usufruct of. The most common element is the agricultural land. It is cultivable land which binds single families into larger joint or extended ones. Economic communality extends into common domestic economy, where there is no accounting for shares of cost or return in the consumption and production of the household. Cooperative labor is also performed.

3. Coresidence: Members of the same family occupy a single, spatially delimited compound. Often they reside in a single house, but this is not requisite.

4. Unitary Command: There is a recognized set of dominant adults who have the command and veto powers for familial decision. The breakdown of unitary command occasions the fission of compound families into single conjugal ones.

5. Role Substitutability: All the women of the household (according to age, of course) must be interchangeable for crucial aspects of domestic roles. Women must feed, nurse, train each other's children as they would their own. They must cook for the common pot. Men (age dependent, again) must share the economic tasks, share tools, and work cooperatively. They also look after children other than their own.

6. *Household Altar:* There is a major altar to the Buddha in the compound. It is individuals, not a family unit, who offer respect and devotion to the Buddha. But having an individual altar means that conjugal families are not joined into a single social group.

7. *Kinship:* The members of a familial household who share the above six features are in fact linked by descent and affinal bonds, and any one coresident who is not a kinsman does not have the full six features.

8. *Recognition:* This psychological characteristic means that the persons who share the above seven features do feel themselves a familial unit, with their closest and deepest bonds in that primary group. It also means that other familial groups do in fact recognize an entity sharing the above seven features as a single familial and household unit.

However, for certain official purposes, and for the apportioning of certain tasks (such as rebuilding the fence surrounding the village, or standing turn at sentry duty), a head of household is the standard form of social recognition. On this basis the village, by its own count, sorts out into 88 heads of households. In the villager's arrival at the figure of 88 heads of households, he is not consistent in the application of criteria, but roughly follows the seven features I have given. For allocation of tasks, the very old are exempted, and the poor widow is not required to participate. These considerations bring my census of 94 familial units into coordination with the village official count of 88 familial household heads liable for communal labor.

The eight characteristics of the familial organization of Nondwin are labels for complex social processes. An explication of the labels in terms of the events that underlie them is a description of the forces shaping the composition of families, the roles and duties in the family, and the domestic cycle. It also lays the basis for the understanding of the nature and function of the bilateral kinship system of the community.

Commensuality restricts eating and cooking to a single place. The cooking area of a family in Nondwin may be in a cookhouse, a lean-to, or just in the open on some raised bricks. Commonly a lean-to, or a cookhouse, is combined with an outdoor cooking hearth. The cooking place is not arbitrary, but must be in one of the non-*mingala* (grace, or providential, or auspicious, any one will do now as a one word translation until this idea is more fully treated in the section on belief and religion) directions, that is, West or South. Cooking odors, especially of oil, onions, and fish are offensive to the Burman and felt by him to be injurious to health, and the cooking place is set off, if possible, from the main living and eating quarters. Cooking takes place outdoors as often as indoors. Meals are prepared by all the women of a household, with tasks apportioned in regard to age. Very young girls do not have the jobs of seasoning or of tasting the cooking pots. They are the peelers of the beans, or the onions, or the tomatoes. Or they blow on the fire through a bamboo tube to keep its flame level at the right height. Burmese cooking and cuisine is a rather simple affair, consisting of a rather limited number of basic dishes, garnished with added elements to make the daily diet into a festal one. Rice is the staple, and some sort of hin, a curry, goes along with it to make a meal. Hin does not, as a rule, contain Indian-style spice with turmeric powder. The curry flavor is gotten from a kind of liquid made from dried fish and other spices, or a dash of flavoring bottled in Japan. The techniques of cooking are boiling, frying, toasting, and roasting, but these are not elaborated culinary skills. It is basically a business of applying heat to raw material.

The point is that cooking does not bear the stamp of an individual, and a commensual family unit does not care which of the family hands stirred the pot. The cooking and eating are a group effort. Dining takes place outdoors, or, if the sun is very strong, if it is raining, or in the cold season, under a lean-to, an open-sided and roofed extension to the household. Indoor eating is rare. Sometimes on special occasions when rugs or mats are spread on the floor, visitors or guests are invited to a meal inside the house. But the family usually eats in a more open arrangement. The members of the family eat from several large serving dishes, each member heaping what he wants on his plate. Knives and forks are absent, for the Burman eats with the fingers of his right hand. Serving spoons are used to dish out the food and the *hingyo*, a soup of various ingredients which often accompanies meals. Serving order is males first, in order of seniority, females next, also in seniority order. The custom of each member offering the best piece to the heads of the family (male and female) is not observed in Nondwin, but is part of the recent ethnographic past.

This common cooking and eating arrangement for a family is regarded as defining who is a member. Relatives (*hswemyo*) may come in from other compounds and either help with the preparation of the meal or dine with the family. But unless they have an expected and regular job in the providing and cooking of food, and are regular eaters at this single dining spot, they are not members of the family. This, at first glance, is often confusing. Anybody visiting a Burmese home is invited at least to drink, and if it is meal time he is invited to eat. Meals are not served at fixed periods. There is a morning meal and an afternoon meal with much tea drinking and casual eating between the two. The hours for eating vary from household to household, but the morning meal comes sometime between 7 and 10 A.M. and the afternoon meal any time between 5 and 7 P.M. A stranger, a visitor, or a relative, not of the family, is someone who is asked, *"Htamin sa pibila?"* ("Have you eaten yet?") The odd hours of meal-taking make this a justifiable question to anybody not of the household, and Burmese etiquette requires that it be asked. The giving of a meal to a person moves him into a quasi-familial position. And interdining is expressive of the closest kinds of social ties. If families separate, the measure of the animosity, or lack of it, underlying the separation is the frequency of meal taking between the component units and the ease with which they offer and take meals from one another. Easy commensuality indicates a degree of social adjustment, of intimate intercourse, of understood social duties, of role definition, that is best exemplified in a primary, family group.

The familial unit rests on joint, common ownership or control of some kind of real property. Minimally, it must be the compound and house in which it lives. There are, it is true, four or five household units that live on land not their own. One is a case of a poor widow who lives in the compound of the richest man in town. She is a second cousin of his wife. This is an act of charity to a woman who is a distant relative. The fact that she lives alone is tied to her poverty; she has no real assets and cannot hold her sons and daughters with her, for there is no material basis for them to live. The other cases of nonownership of the dwelling compound represent two different forces. One, a parent or other relative allows a young married couple to live on a piece of land, but the parent or relative remains the nominal owner. No rent is charged, and the young couple stays so long as relations are amicable. They may later buy the land, or it can be given to them, or they can be displaced by other tenants closer to the owner. This is the first part of a cycle, and it is also tied to poverty. It only happens to poor, young couples, who for some reason or other do not form an extended conjugal family household, by far the more common recourse at the beginning of the domestic cycle. The other cause for living on land one does not own is that of in-migration. All the in-migrants have relatives in Nondwin, and these relatives allow them to set up in a part of their compound. They, too, may later buy this or another site. The in-migrants do not have land in the area of the community and are the artisan or special occupation holders.

More important, especially as the basis for the extended or joint conjugal family, is the possession of agricultural land. It is the owner-ship of agricultural land that provides the material base for a familial unit. The joint and the extended families are those having the land base to support more than a single family and to utilize the labor of more than a single family. This follows the observation that the richer families tend to be the extended families; the poorer families tend to be simple conjugal ones. It is only the very rich who can hold on to their sons and have the sons' families live in the same compound and under the authority of the father and mother. The small number, nine, of extended conjugal families through a male line indicates that this is a rare event, as rare as the big rich in Nondwin. On the death of the head of the extended family, the land is divided up, and the sons depart with their own families. No family with less than 10 acres and, more usually, with less than 20 can even remotely hope to keep a son in an extended family. On less than this acreage, he might as well be a field laborer.

On the basis of agricultural land, owned by the head of the house-hold, but with presumptive inheritance rights equally distributed among all the members, both male and female, a common agricultural and domestic economy operates. Cooperative field labor exists among the men and women of the household, and domestic tasks are shared among the women. One of the chief enjoyments of being rich is to be able to surround yourself with relatives, to hold together and to mold an extended family. Fathers of rich boys try to arrange their sons' marriages so that the sons will get women who will come to live in the extended family, and for their daughters they will accept only sons-in-law who will come under their jural authority. This drive to build the extended family sometimes leads to relationships of conflict. The rich prefer to, and do, marry the rich if they possibly can. But this sometimes leads to battles for the allegiance of the newly married pair. Where are they to reside? An economic calculation of best in a utilitarian way would shock a Nondwin villager, although he would admit the reasoning as a logical and necessary part of the argument of residence site.

An example of the kind of conflict generated is this story from the house of the richest man in Nondwin. His daughter married a boy from another village. It was an arranged marriage. The parents of the couple had come to terms and had settled gifts on the couple. The boy moved from his village into Nondwin, and he moved into the house of his father-in-law. The daughter carried on much as before, except she now slept in a separate part of the house with her husband (and later her children). The son-in-law needed to be integrated to his part of the economic communality characterizing a family. Since the head of the family did not work in the fields, the son-in-law was not expected to do so either. He became part of the cotton brokerage business. He went on missions for his father-in-law and helped in the buying and selling. But he also started to do a bit of business on his own. The father-in-law could not, and did not, object to this directly. Instead he began to give tasks which would interfere with the son-in-law's pursuit of his own ends. The son-in-law, one day, wanted to go on his own business; the father-in-law told him to stay home. There was a tense moment as he stood with his bicycle, deciding what to do. The father-in-law said, "If you live under my roof, you follow my orders. I do not like to be contradicted. I have a bad temper. I could kill a man when I am angry." The son-in-law blanched and said, "I am not trying to make you angry. But I promised my father to go home and help there." "If you go now, do not return," said the household head. The boy went. The man's daughter later went to the boy's village and said her father spoke in anger, and her husband returned. But the relationship is highly unstable. The couple now takes turns residing both matri-locally and patri-locally and will eventually become neo-local.

The above incident is meant to illustrate the dynamics of extended family formation through a male link. It shows that the economic communality involves the dependency of a junior male on a senior male. When this is the case the cooperation flows smoothly, and both the domestic and agricultural economy function without friction. But where there are alternatives, or lack of real economic dependence, the extended family through a male link disintegrates. The extended family, given the roles of married males as heads of households, always has this tendency to fission. But a large enough fund of real assets offsets the tendency, and the son-in-law will accept the part of junior male in an extended family easily enough.

Extending the family through the female link is the most usual mechanism. Property is again required to keep the family of the son-in-law and daughter, but not nearly the amount needed to keep a son at home. This difference rests on the definition of the female role, the closeness of the tie between mother and daughter, and a preference for matri-local residence as a consequence. The mother-daughter role is the "keystone" role of Burmese familial life. The notion of keystone is a simple architectural analogy. It refers to a social relationship which supports others. Without it, the whole edifice collapses. The keystone relationship is empirically located by the consequent dissolution of other relationships when it is ruptured. In the village family the mother-daughter bond may be considered the keystone relationship. Marriage does little to attenuate it, and it serves as the chief linkage between households.

Why the mother-daughter bond is a keystone relationship is fairly plain. The role of mother is a stable, house-oriented role. Mothers and daughters spend much time in close proximity, and the daughter is under constant guidance and surveillance. The girl learns how to be a woman chiefly from her mother and other females in the household. She is taught cooking, cleaning, child care, manners, and religion chiefly through her mother. Wives and mothers tend to run the domestic economy, keep the family assets, and to be less of disciplinary figures than fathers. Fathers may spend time in the monastery; they may get caught up in alchemical experiments; they may travel around; they may visit about. The mother is the stable, sure, continuing figure in the household. Moreover, the mother is the clear model for behavior. Daughters grow up to do what their mothers do, in the way their mothers do, and to have the sentiments their mothers have. There is no training for or vision of a break between mother and daughter. Even if the girl marries and moves away, her mother is the chief confidante. A daughter grows up not only hoping to do and be like her mother; she often has the expectation that she will remain in the same place to become this. If a married girl continues to live at home, she has no readjustment problems. She is a member of a group where her role is definite, and she is fully socialized into the nuances of the group. Moving out as daughter-in-law is a very difficult thing to do. In the terminology of village kinship, this is recognized. The word for sister-in-law is *yauma*, "the stirrer-up." And a sister-in-law makes, if not trouble, at least readjustment if she moves in with her husband's family and attempts to form with them an extended conjugal family.

The mother-daughter bond is never thought of as one that can be fractured. Unlike the father-son relationship, in which there is the element of replacement along the age axis or the element of separation when a young man comes into full maturity and an older man passes out of the control and command phase of his life, the mother-daughter role is without the threat of replacement or separation. This makes the group of female siblings a tighter one than the group of male siblings. The ties between women tend toward greater degrees of coordination than the ties between men. The age factor is strong in both sibling sets, but it is stronger among males.

The concept of *pon*, power and glory, enters into these domestic relations. Pon, in the sense of a glory, a religious essence, is limited mostly to men. Women may have a bit (on this informants are unclear), but, if they do, it is so little that it does not really count. Pon is part of the male principle and is derived from the Buddhist understanding that men, and men alone, can reach the final state of the "blowing out" of desire, *Neikban*, as the Burmese call *Nibbana*. Pon places men in a higher spiritual state than women. In daily life, the role of the woman is remarkably coordinate with that of man. Women with opinions voice them. They take the largest part in family councils. They are free to pursue many occupations, and they get equal shares of property. They may as easily as a man initiate divorce and separation. However, the notion of pon gives the flavor to interaction between male and female, husband and wife especially, in which the male is a sort of precious receptacle for an essence which both the man and woman are duty bound to guard, preserve, and extend. So, men are in public deferred to; they are treated with respect; they are served first by women; and they are considered as a slightly higher form of human life than is a woman.

Wives must protect and try to augment the pon of their husbands. Female things and certain feminine acts may diminish or endanger male pon, as this commonly told story indicates.

There were two countries divided by a river. On one side lived a girl, Shin Mwalon, and on the other, a boy, Min Nanda. They fell in love. Now in the river three crocodiles lived: Ngamoyeik, the superior one, and Malato, and Meli. All were man-eaters. Ngamoyeik was the servant of Min Nanda. Min Nanda was able to call the crocodile to him by his magic stick (*kyeinsetkya*). With this stick he would beat on the water and Ngamoyeik would appear and carry him across the river to see his beloved. Of course Malato and Meli wanted to eat the young prince, but they were unable to overcome him. Now Meli and Malato have the power to transform themselves into human form.

So they changed into the form of girl friends of Shin Mwalon, and they urged her to let her beloved use his right arm as a pillow for her head. They said this request, if granted, would show his love for her. If he refused, he really did not cherish her. She agreed to put him to the test. At first Min Nanda refused. She repeated her requests and threatened to leave him if he did not prove his love. At last he gave in. As a result he lost his male power, his pon. The man-eating crocodiles saw this and returned to their reptilian shape. Min Nanda got on his crocodile, Ngamoyeik, and started across the river to his own country, and the crocodiles chased him. They caught up to Ngamoyeik and bit him. Min Nanda took out his knife, but it fell into the water. The crocodile Ngamoyeik said, "To protect yourself come off my back and get into my mouth where you will be safe." He did this. The crocodile swam and he got tired and forgot about the prince and swallowed him. Min Nanda's father began to worry about his son, so he took up the magic stick and beat the water and the crocodile appeared. He asked about his son, and Ngamoyeik vomited him up, still alive. Min Nanda, who had lost his pon, fell dead. His beloved, across the river, was told what had happened. She knew it was because she had made him sleep in the wrong position, and in grief she died on the spot. The bodies of the dead girl and the dead prince were burned on their respective sides of the river, and the smoke from their separate pyres met in the middle of the river and rose up into space together.

The male quality of pon is lodged on the right side of the male body, and a woman sleeping on the right side of her husband lowers his pon. It is never done. She also must sleep with her head lower than his to protect his pon. Female items, especially the longyi, must never be passed over the head of a male. The diminishing of pon is a serious business. There are some remedies for arresting its decline, but none for restoring it to the former level. In Nondwin, the remedy is to shampoo with *kinbun thayaw* (a tamarind-like fruit and a vine creeper) if a woman's acts or things have threatened a man's pon.

The respect and care given to husbands and males in general by women in general is summed up in the pithy saying that, "Having a husband in the house is like having a *nat* around." The nats are powerful spirits, and a husband requires the deference and devotion due to a powerful spirit, and mere women without pon should give it.

In familial relations, then, men are ritually and spiritually apart from women; they are economically destined to be self-supporting; and they are socially expected to head households and to attain jural separateness and autonomy. For women expectations are gentler, more continuous, and less demanding. Women's roles flow one into another as they age; men must change jural status. Because of this distinction, the sentimental and solidary bonds between women, especially mother-daughter, can serve as lifetime links, as ties between households, as ever cooperating dyads.

The Burmese family also rests on role substitutability in many recurrent and significant aspects. Women of the same age must be interchangeable for almost all aspects of domestic duties. Child rearing serves as a good illustration of substitutability.

When a woman is pregnant and about ready to give birth, her husband, aided by other males in the household, will clear a special room for her (the *eikkhan*). The husband prepares a cradle. He and other relatives, both from within and without the household group, gather firewood, boil water, and stand vigil outside the specially prepared delivery room. He calls the *hsayama* (midwife) from the nearby village of Nyaungbintha, if he uses the government provided service, as most do in Nondwin, or he may use a *letthae*, an ordinary midwife. Female nonrelatives and all males are excluded from entering the delivery room. The pregnant woman from a reclining position delivers the baby. If there is trouble, the midwife presses on the abdomen to help delivery. With the baby delivered, the cord is cut with either a bamboo or metal knife. About five inches of cord is left on the baby, tied up, and left to dry and fall off in its own time. The cord must be buried under the edge of the house roof, at right angles to it. Failure to plant it at a right angle will make the child a great wailer and crier. The baby is washed and wrapped loosely and put into its cradle. The mother and baby are secluded for seven days. During this time, some other female kinswoman (usually the woman's Fa Mo, Fa Sis, Mo) must take over the mother's normal duties and keep her household running. Her husband will not, if it is the busy part of the agricultural season, take off from his work, and he must be fed. Other children must be cared for. So kinswomen come and cook, wash, take care of children. If there are other women in the household, kinswomen beyond the compound just visit and go their ways. Only a mother or a sister can be depended upon to come and live in during this period of forced inactivity for the new mother. The baby and mother stay in the house another ten days. Before that period strong sunlight is thought to be injurious to the child and possibly to the mother. So there is a 17-day period at least when someone must take over the job of the woman of the house. It all goes much more smoothly if the woman, or women, taking over is a member of the household. She already knows the likes, dislikes, and habits of the other members. Failing this, a sister or mother is most likely to be and do what the new mother was and did in her household.

Further ceremonies for the child are: the *pakhjtin,* or first placing in the cradle, the *kinbun tattè,* naming ceremony. They require that the guests, relatives, and friends be fed at least rice cakes and tea. And the cooking and serving at these occasions, as on many more occasions, require the time and effort of more than a single woman. Women from other households, sisters, and mother may come to help, but it is much better if there are many women in a single household, for then the responsibility and work can be easily shifted about, no one feels much extra strain, and the whole thing more nearly matches the Burmese idea of a gay crowd at a meal, easily and leisurely prepared.

Children, in the early years in a Burmese family, are given wide developmental latitude. Their abilities, skills, and knowledges are allowed to unfold naturally, as a by-product of growth. Teaching, fostering, cajoling, or even remonstrating children under five is virtually absent. The small child is a bundle of caprice and whim, a crying, demanding, helpless being. It is the task of adults, or older children, to see that caprice is gratified, whim is met, demand satisfied, crying placated, and helplessness overcome. This is impossible for a lone woman to do, or even a married pair to do. It requires that many adults and older children be in contact with the young child. A Burmese child grows up in a circle of relatives and gets much attention and care from many besides his parents. Both men and women are supposed to take care of children.

Small children are never left alone. There is little fear that a child will harm itself; it is allowed to play with whatever it picks up, so long as an adult is about. Children are held in frequent body contact when they are under three years old. There is no strapped-to-the-back tradition that the conjugal family structure demands in Mexico and Guatemala. The presence and willingness of relatives to play with and take care of children obviates this. Children are carried in a hip-astride position during the younger years, by older siblings, by females of the household, by males of the household, by neighbors, by grand-parents. Small children are usually kept within the compound and rocked in the wicker cradles by whoever is at hand.

They are very much indulged. They are fed whenever they appear hungry, and during meal times they can run about or make demands or be generally disorderly without being reprimanded. They must have something in the mouth continually. Children are forever chewing in a Burmese village: a nut, a fruit, a seed, a piece of jaggery, something. The universal pacifier of the breast is continually in use. Not only the mother, but all women of the household give suck to the child, whether or not they have milk at the moment. Neighbors and relatives also breast feed if the mother is away. A crying Burmese child is not told to be quiet, and it is not ignored. All take turns trying to placate it, until finally somebody finds what it wants, and it is silent. Children are not punished for interference with the functioning of the household or because they interfere with adult activities.

In this sort of child rearing, every woman must, according to her age, play the role of mother to all of the children. The women of a household vis à vis the children of a household, all must be mothers. To a Burmese child's cry of *meme*, the closest woman responds, not necessarily the biological or jural mother. The men of the household must stand as either brother or father to the children of the household, for they share large parts of the child care process. There must be, then, from the standpoint of the family, an interchangeability of persons in the familial roles. If a family is not well-integrated, this cannot be done, and a strain is set up. The substitutability extends to men in the economic realm, and all of the males must be conversant with the total economic operations of the household; they must be ready to do their stint without orders, without special rewards.

This role substitutability rests on the feature of unitary command within the household. The senior father-mother pair are at the top of the familial organization. The authority functions are gentle, hardly visible, and rarely expressed. But they are part of the family organization. The unitary command means that in situations where there is opposition of wills, failure of consensus, or need for swift action, it is the decision of the senior married pair that binds the familial unit to a line of action. Role substitutability stops at this limit of the dominant senior pair of the household. The authority of household heads is most commonly seen in situations of dispute. The villagers are not a disputatious lot. Neither in the home nor in the local courts are the Burmans fond of squabbling. The authority of the dominant pair, when recognized by all the others and when operating according to custom, obviates most disputes and forestalls the need for argument.

An instance of familial dispute will make clear just what the authority of the dominant pair is, how it works, and what happens when it is no longer recognized. The father-mother pair have planned a wedding for their son. Not this year but in two or three years, they think he should marry the headman's daughter. The son, however, has other plans. Night after night, he absents himself from home and visits the daughter of the tailor. He is received at her house and they sit outside and talk. His father occasionally asks other members of the family where the boy is. Nobody says, even though some know, as I knew, that Shwe Man (a nickname) is visiting his girl friend. The family all know that the mother-father pair prefer the headman's daughter and that Shwe Man prefers the tailor's. No one takes it upon himself to inform the dominant pair of his knowledge. It is a matter that lies between the father and the son, a question of authority, and no other member has that role substitute as his part to play.

The son makes his plans to run off and marry. He knows that his father will be irrevocably opposed to his marriage to the tailor's daughter. This knowledge means that there is no way he can get parental consent. The only course open to him, if he insists on his own preference, is to run off and present his father with a *fait accompli*. Before leaving the village with the girl, the son contacts his grandfather and tells him that he plans to run off and marry. His grandfather gives his assurances that he will support Shwe Man against his father's anger. The son also goes to see his maternal uncle, living in another village. There he makes arrangements to move in with the uncle if the grandfather does not persuade his father to countenance the marriage and take him and his wife back into the household. He runs off. His father is angered. The boy returns in two days to his household; the girl to hers. The father and the son hardly exchange a word. They are both waiting for the grandfather to come. The grandfather comes and tells his son, the father of the runaway boy, to overlook Shwe Man's failure to get permission. He reminds his son of his wild ways in youth. He tells him that love and trust in a married pair is needed, and that there was really no way to block his son, if he wanted to keep him a son. The grandfather stays around the house for two days, and finally the father of the boy goes to the parents of the girl, now his daughter-in-law, and tells them that he will accept her into the household. They agree because they never had any objections. The girl comes with nothing but a change of clothes. She and Shwe Man get a room to themselves, and they are a recognized married pair. All that remains to be done is to see the *pongyi*, astrologer, and set an appropriate day for the marriage feast itself. This comes about three months after the actual wedding.

This précis of the operation of authority in the family illustrates the main features of authority in particular and in general in a village like Nondwin. Authority rests chiefly and almost exclusively on consensus. There are few sanctions, beyond the rupturing of the social relationships involved, that can be brought to bear on someone who refuses to recognize the authority. Because authority is consensual, a member who wants to go against it has three choices open to him: to contract out (that is, leave the set of social ties which the authority covers); to form a coalition against the power holder, and thus force him to acknowledge a shift in the range of authority; or to directly challenge the authority and thus possibly provoke violence. Most courses of action involve elements of all three. Thus the runaway boy was willing to contract out and live with his uncle, if the need arose. He formed a coalition with his grandfather to persuade his father, and finally he was willing to risk the anger and explosion of his father.

The only way the family can hold together, especially if it is made up of more than one conjugal pair, is for the consensual authority to be fully recognized. If the coalition results in a new person getting authority, the family will break up. If a direct challenge to authority is issued, the family splits. Contracting out is also a way of breaking up family units. In the absence of real sanctions by any authoritative figure in the village (I do not here speak of the township officer, the divisional officers, and the deputy commissioner who have the police, the court, the army, and certain fiscal sanctions to levy against villagers), the ability to command, the quality of *awza*, literally the authority to give an order and to have it carried out, is chance and vague. A family head has awza with his family just so long, and when it is successfully disputed it is gone. For more than familial units, nobody in the village may have awza, including the headman.

What emerges from this analysis is that sheer power, pon, the ability to get someone to do what you want him to do, is virtually absent from either the family or the village. Some men may get pon, and then have awza, that is, their commands will be obeyed (but this phenomenon will be discussed under the political organization of the community). The large spheres of personal autonomy, the careful etiquette of not provoking anyone, the superficial agreement on all issues that pervades both family and village life is tied to the characteristic of unitary command, and that command rests upon consensual authority without a penalty structure. Families stay as units so long as members find it suitable for them. Then they accept the unitary authority structure, the awza of the senior married pair. When there is a dispute which causes the unitary structure to be challenged, or redefined, the social unit fissions into new components. Even a husband and wife, if they have a dispute which is not composed so that the husband's pon and nominal awza are left intact, will separate. This is the dominant reason for divorce.

In this characterization of the village family in Nondwin, one sees a family structure resting on kinship and social recognition, living on its own territory, having real assets, demanding role substitutability, economic cooperation, and working only under a unitary system of authority. It is a family system where the impress of the dominant pairs is light on other members, and where large areas of reservation to each individual are allowed and, in fact, structurally necessary. The strongest, perduring bond is that of mother-daughter, and if a keystone of the structure is sought this relationship is it. It may turn out, on further analysis of other Southeast Asian societies, that the mother-daughter relationship provides the stable element in their familial organizations as it does here.

Families have crosscutting ties with each other. The network linking individuals and families is the kinship system. The nature of kinship in Nondwin must be described and analyzed before the meaning and import of these crosscutting ties can be apprehended. The kinship system of Nondwin is cognatic. From an individual's point of view kinsmen are of equal status on both the mother's and the father's side. A person is not affiliated with any kin-structured group beyond the familial as defined earlier, but he has a host of named and recognized kinsmen. The depth of kinship is not great. Three generations is the norm of recall, although some informants can stretch to five and six generations. Kinship is wide in collateral relation. Cousins to the fourth degree can often be named. A particularly good informant can name nearly two hundred relatives, both in and out of the village. The average recall is less, but somewhere between 50 and 100 kinsmen can usually be named or identified.

The kinship recall by the genealogical method is deceptive. No one in Nondwin has, in fact, relations with 50 to 100 kinsmen. The kinship system is not only bilateral; it is of the optional variety. By optional, I mean that kinship relations, beyond the familial, need to be cultivated. A person has the option of building a structure of reciprocity between himself and a kinsman or the alternative of ignoring the relationship. If the genealogical relationship is not cultivated between kinsmen, it is no different than a relationship between neighbors, covillagers, and casual friends. Without special cultivation, a man will expect and receive no more from a kinsman than he would from a neighbor or fellow villager. Beyond the family, kinship does not necessarily entail mutual rights and duties, but it does confer the

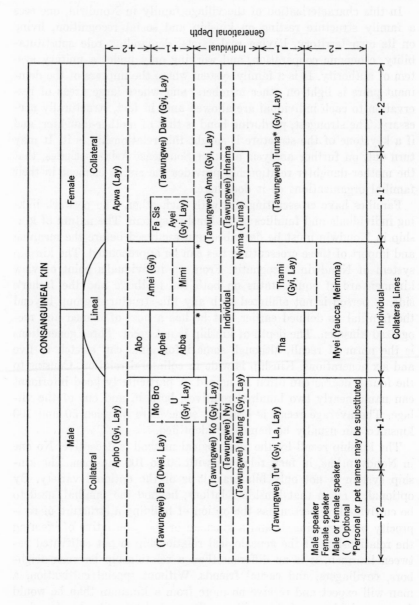

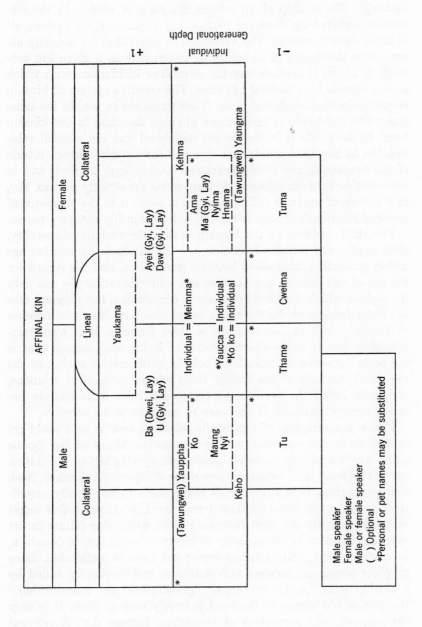

opportunity to develop a role relationship of mutuality, of intimate exchange. The kinship idiom reflects this state of affairs. In the referential terminology there are four or five variants of the system, all of them equally correct. The variations in referential terminology often reflect the degree of formality or informality in a given kin network, or to put it another way the warmth or indifference with which a man regards his potential kin roles. The vocative system of kinship is extremely simplified, and many fewer terms are in use. In the same generation the name is much more often in use than is the kinship term. In daily life it is the named individual and one's social relationship to him that counts, not so much the kinship status. Outside of the household, one rarely hears the kinship term applied, and in conversation between villagers, kinship terms are equally as rare. For, in a system of optional cultivation of kin roles, it is the character of personal relationships that is crucial, not the kinship category per se.

The chief features of the kinship system, beyond its bilaterality, short depth, and collateral relation, are the emphasis on relative age within generation, distinction between generations, and the regard for the sex of the persons linked. Age, sex, and generation are not only the axes on which the kinship system is constructed, but they are also the wider framework for the whole social structure. No social relation in Nondwin fails to take account of these features. It is worth emphasizing that it is the characteristics of living, real, people that is the basis for social relationships, not the categorical meaning of the role itself. Outside of the family there are no categorical relations, and, even inside the family, the categorical roles must operate between narrow trammels if they are to continue to be effective.

This is a description of the dyadic relations, insofar as I could get content from and consensus among informants. Many of the dyadic pairs, which a society could elaborate with specific rights and duties, are left "blank" in the Burmese repertory of expected behaviors. Such content as there is in these dyads never needs to be socially actualized, or evident in behavior, but it does betoken attitudes that ought to, and frequently do, exist between related pairs. The failure to act toward a kinsman in the capacity of kinsman would not, in Nondwin, be a social fault, and probably would not even be noticeable. Since all older people are treated with deference and frequently called by a kinship term "uncle" or "aunt," "grandfather" or "grandmother," the specific kin nature of the bond is hardly ever at issue. It is only the age, sex, and generation of interacting persons that is relevant for most social interaction. The dyads are as follows (excluding the household, whose duties were described in the enumeration of the characteristics of the familial unit):

Fa Bro—Nephew, Mo Bro—Niece. This is an advice and counsel relationship. The uncle stresses that the nephew should be content with what he has. Like other relatives the uncle comes to nephew's naming ceremony, cradle ceremony, induction into novitiate (for boy), or ear boring (for girl), and is present at any funeral, where he will spend parts of seven days. An uncle may also admonish small, younger nephews on the streets if they are misbehaving. When both uncle and nephew (or niece) are adults, the relationship tends to be more of equality and less advice giving. Uncles sometimes take care of children if the parents ask. The kin term is used in vocative form if ages are disparate. Name, or even *ako* (elder brother) term, may be used.

Cousin—Cousin. This dyad is influenced by sex and age factors but is a modified version of the sibling bond. Cousins form play groups if children and if they live near each other. When married, if in separate households, cousins are frequent visitors. They attend all group gatherings, the *shinbyu*, the *nadwin*, the death watch, and they are often invited to monk feeding. Male cousins use names in address if they are about the same age. They use ako (elder brother) or *nyi* (younger brother) and the other sibling terms appropriate to age and sex (see Consanguineal Kin). A referential term of *wungwè* literally means from another womb. It can be prefixed with *ta*, for one, and prefixes up to seven are used. Cousins are often found in work groups together. Female cousins frequently form labor hire groups for transplanting, while male cousins are frequently in vigorous labor teams.

Grandparent—Grandchild. This role is one of deep attachment, and the grandparent plays a large role in bringing up the child, minding it while the parents work, telling it tales, and giving religious instruction. Not only are grandparents indulgent of their grandchildren, in that now familiar pattern of solidarity of alternating generations, but they are often active allies with the grandchild against his parents. Since grandparents usually have much free time, grandchildren spend considerable time with them and the interaction is free, easy, and familiar.

In-law—In-law. Father-in-law and mother-in-law are to be regarded like father and mother and are often called by those kin terms in address. Brother-in-law and sister-in-law are to be regarded as brother and sister, and they, too, often get the sibling term in address.

However, the sister-in-law term translates as "stirrer-up" of the pot of trouble, and patri-local residence often means tensions for the new couple. Son-in-law and daughter-in-law are to be treated like son and daughter, and they are often addressed as son and daughter.

The behavioral repertory of kinsmen in Burmese villages like Nondwin can be collapsed into a few broad categories with few obligations and duties, because the Burmese think and act that way in their kinship behavior. However, it would be erroneous if an impression of kinship as unimportant has been conveyed. Kinship is a significant feature of social organization, and many activity groupings are based on it. But the system of obligation does not, beyond the familial household, lay down or specify a fixed cluster of relations or sets of kin behaviors. Kin and neighbor pervade daily interaction, but one hardly ever finds the same range of kinsmen assembled as one moves from activity to activity or from kindred to kindred. From the observations I have made on the composition of groups for the major tasks of daily life, economic, religious, political, recreational, and for the main sorts of events, birth, death, devotions, ceremonies, visits, group labor, housebuilding, farming, celebrations, and interdining, not even a statistical pattern of predominance emerges. The personal and particular circumstances of each person determine what part of his kindred he will use, and for what ends kinsmen will invoke their particular bond.

In a village like Nondwin, long settled, largely endogamous, with but minor migration outward, most people are related to each other in some manner or another. If they are in a common enterprise, or visiting, or gathered together, they may be kinsmen, but the kin dimension may not be the one that has made them a group or has been the basis for the association. Hence, kinship links are only background for the unfolding of daily behavior and serve as a sketch, not a map, of social relations.

The kinship terminology reflects and is molded by the character of Burmese interpersonal relations. A full, formal set of kin terms may be made for four generations and as far out as fourth or fifth cousin. But no Nondwin villager has at his disposal all of the terms, nor are all of the terms used in any of the genealogies collected. The kinship system laid out below is an artifact of the anthropologist's making. A dictionary and a system of grammar constructed by a linguist is analogous. A linguist may collect the lexical content of a language and syntactical modes of arranging that content, and he may give the elements governing conversation, but he does not say anything about the kinds of extended discourse which in fact take place. So the stipulation of status symbols (kin terms), associated behaviors, and the rights and obligations these entail say little about the concrete social regularities among either kinsmen or nonkinsmen. No social relationship is exhausted in content by its kinship or category stipulation. Other equally important factors enter into even a genealogical relationship.

Just as the families of Nondwin, their form and operation, can be explained by a series of principles or components of organization, so the range of kin relations may be explained by isolating the aspects of interpersonal relationships, which, in various combinations, give rise to the observable regularities in social interaction. This mode of description and analysis is neither a regression to crude empiricism, nor a violation of the analytic principles of viewing society as made up of subsystems. Rather, it tries to formulate those norms, those situational determinants, and those aspects of persons which in fact give rise to role definitions and to definitions of the interaction between persons in those roles. From this viewpoint, the kinship system is one area where the system's pervasive principles configure in a particular arrangement.

Seniority enters into all relationships and is terminologically recognized in most of them. The equation is simple: the greater the age disparity, the greater the respect and deference involved. Age, in its kinship dimension, is expressed along two axes: generation and relative birth order. The suffixes *kyi* (larger or greater) and *le* (smaller or lesser) are fixed to a kin term to express relative birth order in every generation. Kin terms are generationally exclusive. Terms in a person's own generation form one set, those in the first ascending and first descending generations another, and those in the second ascending and second descending generations a third and final set. All kin terms, therefore, take into account a fundamental aspect of the social structure: relative seniority as it is manifest in generation and birth order.

Sex is an equally pervasive fundamental of genealogical categories. Kin terms consider male and female in two ways, by the suffix *ma* (for female) or by different root designations (like *u* for male relative of father or mother and *daw* for female relative of the same category). Any kin term, then, carries this minimum information about those involved: generation, seniority, and sex. The idea of sex implicates a much lesser amount of deference than age. Male is deferred to by female, given parity in age and generation.

Linearity is expressed in most kin terms. The parents, grandparents, children form a distinct set of terms in contrast to uncles, aunts, cousins (of whatever degree), nephews and nieces. Except for the coresident household, linearity may or may not be behaviorally expressed. On the same generation level, among lineal relatives, names are common, or terms expressing only age and/or sex are used. Brothers not living or working together may be much farther apart than cousins who have worked together around some continuing social task. If this is the case, the cousin term may have affixed to it the appropriate sibling suffix, and a literal translation is cousin-brother or cousin-sister.

The collateral interest is much more terminologically variable. Relatives in the first ascending generation may or may not be distinguished terminologically by designating whether it is a female or male link that binds them. Father's sisters and father's brothers are usually distinguished by kin terms. At the same time they are collectively called u and daw when the context refers to all uncles and aunts. Cousins are called by a single term. Their nearness to a person is marked by prefixing a number, one, two, etc. The root for cousin is literally "womb," so cousins are marked as one, two or more wombs away from one's own mother. The terminological concern with placing cousins relative to female connection, the infrequent distinctions between male and female collaterals, and the preeminence of the mother-daughter bond, have caused some speculations as to possible matri-lineal antecedents to the contemporary cognatic system (J. Furnivall, 1911:17 ff.). Since the history of the Burmese family is unknown, and there is no direct evidence that kinship organization was ever other than bilaterally organized, the matri-lineal speculation will not bear scrutiny. But even such a wild hypothesis calls attention to the functional, contemporary significance of the mother-daughter bond and the continued close interaction between genealogically related women. The facts of household composition, of female cooperation, of socialization, and pervasive sex distinctions throughout the system, as they are now operative, are sufficient to account for the collateral bifurcation, whatever the real historical antecedents of it may have been.

The five principles named above are the systemic rules for forming the Burmese repertory of kin terms. But this formal description of how kin categories may be constructed is only a part description of the kinds of relations among the villagers of Nondwin. Whether or not kin terms are used depends upon three further principles: territoriality, task participation, and property stewardship. Kinsmen who are coresident will tend to exhibit the full kin relation; as distance increases, kinship tends to decrease. This is not a simple, mechanical interdependence between spatial and sentimental distances. Territorial closeness is a reflection of sentimental ties. Those kinsmen who get along with each other or do things in common, who do not have outstanding property or personal quarrels, will live together or fairly near each other. The fact of territorial closeness, the idea of vicinity, calls into account the relations between the families of procreation and the families of orientation. The nearness of residence depends on harmony among siblings and parents in the business of growing up and getting married, and on the expectation of land through inheritance. The tie with the family in which one was a child is almost never severed for women, but men are sometimes torn between the families in which they were born and the families they found. The territorial proximity of kin is therefore highly correlated with how well daughters-in-law get along with a man's family of orientation. This is the classic conflict in the Burmese kinship structure. A man has divided loyalties to his own family of procreation and the family in which he is father. For women, the conflict does not arise, since they rarely get or accept demands that will conflict with close attachment to their mother. Men, on the other hand, always take some risks of upsetting their family of procreation by too close attention to the family in which they grew up. A woman with relative impunity may give of her household's goods to her relatives. A man must take account of his wife's willingness to part with their substance if he wishes to help an aged parent or poor relative. I have recorded several cases of divorce turning on this pivot: the wife objects to the use of household resources for the upkeep of her husband's relatives. There were no instances of family breakup because a woman similarly aided her relatives. So even consanguineal ties are conditioned by the interactions among in-laws. And proximity in part depends upon the relations of daughters-in-law to parents-in-law. Wealth of course plays its part in this. If family fortunes are nearly equivalent (within the same broad "third" of the wealth classes sketched in Chapter 2), there is likely to be harmony and, hence, proximity. Conversely if the gap is extremely great (say, between big rich and poor), territorial arrangements will follow the vector of wealth; the poor will be associated closely with the rich as a junior family. It is when the family of the man and the family of the woman are in adjacent wealth classes, when the pulls are not overwhelming in one direction or another, that conflict tends to arise, and the man, not the woman, must decide how much the conjugal bond means in terms of his consanguineal obligations.

Kinsmen who have adjusted their behavior in terms of the norms of familial interaction will do many things in common. The men will frequently carry out agricultural work together; if they hire labor, they will hire kinsmen, and they will cooperate in the cooking, serving, and planning of festal meals. The following counts of the frequency and kind of kin interactions in the main activities of daily interaction, taken over a three-month period from a family in each wealth class, give some indication of how and to what extent kinship forms the basis for social cooperation.

The range of relatives and the occasions for sustained interaction underline the options involved in the Burmese system of kinship. They

TABLE XIV   Number of Occasions of Informal Interaction

Relationship to Person Who Is:	Visited	Sick *	Work Leader	Religious Sponsor	Parturient or Dead	Total
Grandfather †					1	1
Grandmother †						0
Father ‡	2	4		3	1	10
Mother ‡		2		1	1	4
Brother	4	2	4	3	1	14
Sister	2	3	3	2	2	12
Son	1	1	4	2	2	10
Daughter ‡		2		1	2	5
Grandchild	2		2	1	1	6
Uncle	1		1	1		3
Aunt	2	3		1	1	7
Nephew	4	3	4	2	1	14
Niece	5			3	1	9
Cousin	7	1	10	2	1	21
Father-in-law	1	2	1	2		6
Mother-in-law		2		2		5
Spouse			2	1	1	4
Brother-in-law	3	1	1	2	1	8
Sister-in-law	2			2	1	5
Son-in-law			1		1	2
Daughter-in-law	1	1	1	1	1	5
Distant relative	1	2	2	1	2	8

* Child tends to be the one who is sick.
† Grandparents dead.
‡ Mother and father tend to be coresident with daughter in respect to visiting.

make it numerically clear that cognatic kinship functions as a grid of possibilities, and what possibility is employed or ignored by a given person rests on factors extrinsic to the kinship system itself. Cognatic kinship does not, of course, mean that Nondwin villagers are engaged in casting up balance sheets of self-interest and advantage before they make actual or operational a kinship bond. It merely means that the stipulations of a given kin role will or will not become the basis for a social relationship depending on the way the kin dimension intersects with the principles of vicinity, task cooperation, and property stewardship. And, of course, the idiosyncratic play of personal attraction and repulsion has its share in deciding the operational fate of kinship nexus.

Property stewardship involves the overlapping claims of kinsmen in tangible, real property. Tangible property in Nondwin is chiefly land and cattle, house, gardens, plows, and jewelry. Land and cattle and, sometimes, house and house site are the items of real property that may determine the strength or weakness of kin ties. Overlapping claims in real property are always graded claims. A son and daughter, a brother or sister, have putative rights in the land and cattle owned by parents and siblings. The rule of inheritance, almost always followed, of equal shares among offspring, or among a sibling group, is recognition of this overlap in claims to property. If the land and cattle held are large enough (at the top of the moderate range, at least), fathers can exercise longer and greater control over sons, and brothers will work more as a group. The determination of residence at marriage is strongly influenced by the size of the estate involved, and only the very rich manage to hold together multi-generational households. And only the very rich ever bother to check the wealth of potential affines. The possession of graded rights (control by the property holder, inheritance by the offspring, usufruct for the part-time work by brothers, first employment of cousins for labor, gleaning rights by anyone who can establish kin links) ties some contemporaries into tighter kin nets than their fellow Burmese who do not have estates. But property stewardship, by its nature, is tied to the life span of real persons, and, hence, enduring trans-generational bonds cannot be founded on it. Inheritance does in fact sever the bonds built up, and there is no mechanism, once property is divided, to insure or compel the continuity of particular or categorical kin relationships.

The description of the kinship system and the principles through which it is both structured and made operational may be too formal to convey the actual character of social relations in a village like

Nondwin. With an endogamy rate of 93 per cent [5] it is clear that Nondwin's 553 people form a kin community. Almost everyone who is born in Nondwin marries there, lives his entire life and dies there, leaving his offspring there. The crisscross of affinal ties (which incidentally make alliance between families on the same principles that actualize consanguineal kin ties) and the presence of nearly all of one's kinsmen in the confines of the same village combine to make kinship a field of social possibilities. Kin bonds are invoked rarely, for they are but a component of daily life where virtually everybody is some sort of kinsman. As I collected genealogies, checked births and marriages, I sometimes forced, through questioning, the recognition of kin labeling of relatives that had in fact no social meaning. When I uncovered cases of cross-cousin marriage (three, in fact), brother-sister exchanges (three), two cases of parallel-cousin marriage, and three of classificatory cross-cousin marriage, the kin dimensions of these marriages came as surprises to many. The marriages were clearly the result of chance in a kin community, rather than a consequence of the operation of a preferential rule of marriage, or even the vestige of such a rule. In getting the referential kin terms and their associated behaviors, it is clear from the chart that names occur as frequently as do kin terms in any of the social relations that count. When people think of each other, or behave toward one another, they tend to take the situation as existential. I mean by this that they notice or think about just those features that are immediately visible and relevant to the interaction at hand. People react to others in terms of the set of principles I have earlier outlined, but they frequently do not use the kin possibility in making a summation of them. Two other dimensions of interaction, relative power and relative virtue, I leave for discussion under the rubric of religion. All interpersonal behavior, kin or not, is seniority and sex structured. It is obligatory to use a term of kin address, outside of the household compound and often within as well, that puts speakers in the proper relation along these ubiquitous dimensions of social relations. Between men, three terms are used. U is used for anyone a generation ahead of the speaker, anyone of power, anyone of great learning, anyone of great piety, anyone to whom one wants to show respect. *Ko* is used between equals in the dimensions listed above. Ko is reduplicated if the relationship is intimate, so ko ko is a term of fondness. Maung is used to a junior, in all the senses above. The reciprocals to these terms

---

[5] Computed from a field census of the origin of all spouses in 1960–61.

depend on the sentimental closeness of the persons involved. Using *tu*, instead of maung, as a reciprocal does not necessarily mean an actual nephew, but only that the persons feel like uncle and nephew, and the ko ko is used, at times, when the persons feel almost like brothers. Almost all of the older men of the village are called U by the boys and girls under sixteen. In calling out to them, in addressing them, the children will use the U term usually in its uncle connotation, for the elder will usually call out, "What do you want, Maung," followed by the name. With usages of all of these terms, the name follows the relative seniority designation. Of course, nobody with sensitivity calls himself U or even signs any document with U prefixing his name. It is strictly a relational term. Even when the prime minister U Nu issues public statements which appear over his name in the local press, in official papers, he signs them Maung Nu. (Maung and U are also parts of Burmese names, adding to the contexts in which they are used, and the suffixes kyi and le also do double duty in proper names.)

For women the terms of relative seniority are daw and ma, with the very senior generation of women being called *ahpwa*, the grandmother term. Daw and ma also do duty as proper names. The use of daw is like the usage associated with its male counterpart u.

So, in Nondwin, almost everybody, all of the time, is addressed by terms of relative seniority, and the same terms appear as kin terms and proper names. This kin and quasi-kin usage is restricted to the Burmese, whether they are of Nondwin or not. Europeans (and Americans) are called *Bo* (a military term meaning Captain), suffixed by kyi if a fully grown, head of family, or *boma* or *bomagyi* for a female. Chinese are called *tayok*, or *pouk phow* (this latter means literally of common ancestry with speaker, but the kin content is not necessary), and the proper suffixes are added here also. Indians are called *kala* meaning, literally, "foreigner," but in fact connoting "despised foreigner." Other sorts of people are called by their ethnic designation: Shan, Kayin (for Karen), Kachin or Singpo for the relatively infrequently seen Kachin soldier. This digression into ethnic classification clarifies an important aspect of village interpersonal relations and the beliefs that give rise to these relations. Villagers in Nondwin take the world to be made of various discrete kinds of people, with a major axis between Burmans and everybody else. Only the Chinese, who are physically near the people in the plains of Upper Burma and who are religiously tolerant and would as soon be a Buddhist as anything else, almost join the axis by becoming putative "relatives." Within the sector of humanity limited by *Bama bohta bada* (Burmese Buddhist), a villager can work out primordial ties. All Burmans place each other in relational terms by the mode of address. Age and sex take on more and more importance as they have territorial dimensions, task cooperation, property, and face-to-face sentimental attachments as increments. One can move then from stranger, to ethnic cousin, to Burman, to known man, to friend, to brother along the same terminological route, without ever encountering a real consanguineal link.

The relative placement of Burmans to each other by modes of address is built into the language itself. Burmese does not have a system of pronouns like I, you, we, they. Only he and she (*thu* and *thuma*) are functional pronouns in the sense of saying, "that other male or female." To refer to oneself in speech is also a relational act. One must know to whom one is speaking in terms of age, sex, power, virtue, wealth, and learning. The form of "I" to be used depends upon these relational factors, as does that of "we," "you," or "they." The literal translation of personal pronouns is quaint and exotic (like *kyundaw*, your male servant, or *kyunma*, your female servant for "I," or *kyok*, "I," abrupt, insulting, superior to inferior, or *nga*, "I," your clear noble superior, and a host of special terms for use to monks which I shall treat in Chapter 4), but the literal meanings of slave, servant, master, etc., are not functional; they are only the referential components of relative seniority.

The pronoun usage in language follows the category of usages in kinship or personal modes of address. And all of these efforts to mark the visible, socially relevant aspects of persons result in a kaleidoscope of dyadic relations; in some, a person is at one pole, in others, another. The relationships are by nature flexible and shifting. The components that make them up change over time, and throughout a person's lifetime his set of dyadic bonds takes many forms even with the same people involved. What this means in a village like Nondwin is that the relevant aspects of social interaction are publicly accessible, easily ascertained, and subject to shift. The less close a relationship is, the more likely one is "to think the best" of another, to take at face value the presented claims to seniority. So any older villager, about whom one has little information, or little dealings, will be given the best terminological usage the relationship can bear; anyone known a bit more intimately, or dealt with frequently, will get a usage that puts the relationship into the best light one can cast; an intimate will get his name prefixed with the most generous interpretation one can give him. So three kinds of usages are here apparent: the distant ones in which consensus, over the village, is likely, the somewhat fluent interactions, on which some disparity is manifest, and intimate bond, on which there is agreement probably only between the intimates. It is through this existential, personal, and essentially dyadic set of relationships that people interact. And because of this set, its inherent flexibility, room for choice, and its tendency to fluctuate over time, individuals tend to interact in nearly self-created relationships, with definitions of relationships tied to their own personal and situational view.

Such definitions of relationships have been called loosely structured, and, I suppose, this accusation is based on the optionality in kinship, the absence of corporate groups, and the existential basis of norm application. But of course there is a structure in terms of basic, culture-wide principles that, in various combinations, form the groupings, the relationships, and the definitions of roles and persons in a village like Nondwin. The village has structure even in the unsophisticated sense of the word (concrete groups with some temporal durability). The structure needs to be understood not as a visible shape with temporal continuity, but as a series of conventional understandings which shape all the groups, roles, and *personae* in village society.

POLITICAL ORGANIZATION

The Village Government

Nondwin is not only a community of people and families who have adjusted their behaviors over time; it is a political and administrative entity. The political organization of the community is shaped, in part, by the political constitution of the Union of Burma. In the national structure of administrative and political units, the village tract is the lowest level of organization. A village tract may have jurisdiction over, and be composed of, more than one local community. Nondwin is a village tract, and this particular tract corresponds to the settlement bounded by the bramble fence which encloses Nondwin. From the national point of view Nondwin is a political entity because it elects a single headman, is counted in the census as a territorial unit, is assessed taxes on the basis of territorial extent, and has collective responsibility for internal security. Moreover, government services are extended to Nondwin on the basis of the community status as a political and administrative entity. The Ministries of Education, Agriculture, and Defense, tax collectors, road builders, and political parties treat it as a unit, the courts and judges recognize its legal status, and, of course, for the descending line of civil servants, it is the last unit of administrative responsibility.

In a centralized nation, local political identity depends in great measure on the agreement of supra-local bureaucracies to relate in a manner which will define the status of the local society. So, from the Prime Minister to the village headman, there is an unbroken line of political and administrative authority, and the village is the smallest political cell in the structure of the Union of Burma.

From inside the village, its political and administrative unity is expressed in two main ways. All of the households have responsibilities to keep up a section of the village palisade. This task is apportioned among 88 families, and these units form the political community of the village. All those who keep up their section of fence are members of the community and, hence, if of proper age, are entitled to vote for the village headman. Voting for the village headman is the local expression of membership in the political community. The 95 per cent turnout in election for village headman is not an indication of a hotly contested campaign (the headman was in fact unopposed), but a validation of membership in the political community. Voting is like fence maintenance. It is what villagers do as a consequence of political membership.

The second criterion of political membership to a village is the payment of taxes through the local headman, the acceptance of decrees the headman may promulgate, the passing of the member's demands on government through the headman in any dealings with officials above the village level. This second dimension defines the political unity of factions of the community. A villager has the option to bypass the headman and pay his taxes (chiefly on matured crops, a sort of agricultural income tax) directly to the township officers. This is an act of hostility. Not only does it deprive the headman of his percentage of tax collected, but also it announces withdrawal from the headman's power and the possibility of political opposition. If many people bypass the headman in tax paying, if they take their demands to higher officials or to politicians, a community is riven by internal dissent and probably has factions based on the political parties.

Village Administrators. In Nondwin, the *thugyi*, as the headman is called, was in a peculiar position, and the particularity of his position highlights the dynamics of village politics. The office of thugyi is made up of a combination of political and administrative roles. The thugyi is elected as a representative of one of the national political parties and is viewed as an agent of government; at the same time he is the lowest link in the civil service and thus regarded as part of the administration. In Nondwin, most villagers make a sharp distinction between administration and government. This distinction is deeply rooted in Burmese experience back to the days of kings and courts. Government is one of the five traditional enemies, along with fire, famine, flood, and plague. The putting of government in the class of natural, unforeseeable, and uncontrollable disasters categorizes its meaning in Burmese political history. From the days of arbitrary demands from the royal city to the British colonial administration, through the Japanese occupation and the civil disorders following independence, political power in the shape of government has been something alien, demanding, and usually capricious or enigmatic. Government is identified with the unrestricted use of force. Nondwin villagers seek means to avoid or subvert the force of government, except when there is a local man who also has the kind of power that governments are thought to have. Administration, on the other hand, is seen as a necessary burden. It is a formal way of getting certain essential things done, and it is sometimes the source of service. This duality not only affects the headman; it also touches the assistant township officers, the township officers, the mass education officers, the agricultural extension people, who are the kinds of government agents who most commonly have direct dealings with the villagers. The police force, the constabulary, the judges, deputy commissioners, and the commissioners are squarely in the category of government, "force of nature," and villagers see them only occasionally and under very formal, defined circumstances. Toward what is seen as a mixture of government and administration, or just administration, the villager seeks to further his advantage, to find out what he can get out of it. Toward what is seen as government, villagers take a stance akin to what they take when dealing with nats (the animistic beings peopling a good part of the village conceptual world): They try to ward off or to minimize this potential evil.

Nondwin's thugyi is both government and administration, and the blend of these elements in any concrete headman is a feature of historical and social circumstance. The duties of a headman are clearly laid down in the manual of village administration. (This manual, the *saokkyi*, means literally the big book used both for administrative procedure and includes the legal codes. For villagers the saokkyi means a set of rules people have recourse to when they cannot settle disputes by internal means or through the use of force. The saokkyi is also conceived of as a weapon one man might use against another.) What a headman actually does is determined by his place in the local social structure and how he in fact got the post of headman. Headmen are of two types, the hereditary and the purely consensual. In Nondwin, the same family line provided headmen for the village for four generations. The headman may go from father to son, from father-in-law to son-in-law, and from uncle to nephew. These lines of headman inheritance are all considered in the family. The headman, if successful in his job, usually holds it for life, and then he names a kinsman who is related in any of the three ways above as his successor. If the village is a united one, without factional disputes, the headman is unopposed and elected. The Nondwin headman was elected by a margin just over 95 per cent of the eligible voters of the tract. He was the son-in-law of the preceding headman and, hence, a legitimate hereditary headman. But he did not have the attributes necessary to make him very effective. He had only administrative functions and carried out the barest, minimal requisites of his office. He did not command, his authority was couched in terms of what superiors asked of him, and he was marginal in settling any internal village squabbles.

This particular thugyi lacked the attributes of a man of power. The village Burman has a trinity of concepts about personal power, and these ideas are the key to understanding the political organization of villages in Upper Burma. Three concepts pon, *gon*, and awza define relations of power, influence, and authority among villagers. Pon, in its secular meaning, is the power to carry out plans, to bend others to one's will, to move destiny to one's advantage. If a person has pon, as a corollary he necessarily has awza. Awza is the authority to command. Officials have awza, but this authority rests in law and must be backed by the coercive apparatus of the police and the courts. The awza of a man with pon stems from his personal powers, his marked and conspicuous abilities to succeed in this world. The notion of gon is akin to the English idea of virtue. It connotes a sterling personal character, special religious learning or piety, or even the trait of impartiality in dispute. Pon and awza are the power dimensions of social relations; gon is the moral content.

Pon is a matter of personal achievement, and in the village there are tides of competition to define a man of power. The idea of pon is mystical; it is close to the idea of grace, charity, election, destiny. The presence of great amounts of pon (all males have some) is a fact of social inference. It depends upon the meshing of community opinion, on the one side, and the mundane success and power of a man, on the other. The bases on which villagers judge pon are multiple, but these aspects are minimal. A man must be successful in what he undertakes, the most evident mark of success being wealth. A very poor man is unlikely to be seriously considered as favored by the disposition of forces. A man must attain moderate wealth at least. Pon is also inferred from a man's demeanor. The qualities of a leader according to village standards are: industry (he is a hard worker), alertness (he does not appear sleepy or slow in movement; his speech is quick and pithy), mercy (he does not push his power to the limit), patience (he does not rush into things, but awaits the propitious moment for action), judgment (his decisions do, in fact, turn out to his benefit), and perspective (he sees events from the right angle; he can tell more than other people about the meaning of events). If a man has these six attributes he is *nayaka,* a leader, and he has *Nayaka gon chaukpa,* the six qualities of a leader. These qualities are but indices to the presence of pon. Pon rests eventually in the moral nucleus of a person. It stems from his *kan,* the summary of all of his past deeds and misdeeds. Such a mystic power is not a continually present thing. A leader must continually show his credentials to pon by being successful in this life, by being heeded by his fellow villagers, by getting respect from people outside of the village, and by being consulted by persons higher in the official structure of political power.

The expression of pon is a delicate social matter. There is a thin line between, on the one hand, being accepted as a man of pon, when your fellow villagers always address you with the U prefix, use respectful forms of personal pronouns, and even give the *shikko* (a bow of respect) when entering your house, and, on the other, being regarded as a false claimant to power. A false claimant is called the equivalent of a domineering man, or *hangyi pangyi,* prideful and haughty without right. Villagers must agree widely on the presence of pon and its underlying source, kan. They say in one of their many proverbs: "You can see a man carrying a spear on his shoulder and walking around, but you cannot see a man carrying his fate on his shoulder." Power must not be obvious, nor used in a forward manner.

The man of pon in Nondwin is U Sein Ko, the village's richest man. Besides wealth, he exhibits his indices of pon in the following ways: he keeps a large extended family under his control, and he groups his relatives and his wife's relatives around his compound; he has good organizational abilities in making arrangements for the apportioning of sentry duty among the household heads; he is regarded

by supra-village officials as the *lugyi*, the big man. When party officials from Sagaing come to talk to someone in the village, they come
to see U Sein Ko, not the headman, who does not have pon. Even when
I came to live in Nondwin, the Deputy Commissioner of Sagaing
district, who accompanied me for purposes of introduction, talked to
U Sein Ko about the possibility of my settling there, not the headman.
In settling village disputes about marriage, adultery, land, and neighborhood fighting, U Sein Ko is always on hand with the elders and the
thugyi. Even if the thugyi is absent, the dispute can be settled if
U Sein Ko is present. Officials of the Agricultural Redevelopment
Agency, the Agricultural Loan Service, and the health services always
get audience with U Sein Ko if they want to make a speech or do
something in Nondwin.

U Sein Ko has his pon validated by his material success, his demeanor, his control over his family, and his recognition by outside
agencies as a broker and as a liaison between political power levels.
He does not, however, rest on these laurels. He acts to increase his
pon, for he, like the ordinary villager, is aware of the fleeting nature
of pon, the need for continual reinforcement of the image of pon, the
possibility of competition from other seekers of power, and the dangers
of failure. He acts out the self-fulfilling notions of pon in many
spheres. In his economic activities, he takes risks and acts on a scale
beyond any other farmer in Nondwin. He carries out alchemical experiments in search of the eternally youthful body and the marvelous
powers that come from converting mercury into the magic metals.
He knows a bit of astrology and can prepare some of the cabalistic
in to ward off evils. He commands a fair amount of the curing knowledge of a village doctor, and he is an ex-monk and can quote scripture,
proverbs, and parables with the best of the villagers.

Like other villagers, he sums up the ephemeral quality of his pon
in common proverbs.

> This piece of wood once crowned the palace, now it is firewood.
> In the rainy season grass grows over the tree, in the dry it withers.
> When the iguana comes out of the ground, one sees it is not a pagoda.

Or he can tell many of the stories that refer to the elusive nature of
pon. Two of the most common tales are about former kings who lost
their pon and hence their lives and kingdoms.

> Doktabaung was the king around Thaton. He had the third, celestial eye.
> The third eye (*natmyetlon*) gave him great powers to see into the future, into
> men's minds, into the plans of his enemies. The third eye, placed between his

two natural eyes, never closed. Close to his realm, was the domain of a very powerful Queen called Peikthano Mibaya. The King wanted to expand his kingdom and so he offered marriage to this great Queen. She refused him. So he sent an army, but it was repulsed several times. At last he prevailed and captured the Queen. She married him, as she had to, but she never got over the loss of her power and kingdom, although she still was a queen. She could only overcome the King if she could rob him of his celestial third eye and his pon. But, since the eye never closed, she hit upon a plan that the King would not see. She summoned a weaver to make a towel for the King. And she gave the weaver some thread from her longyi to use in the towel. The towel with the longyi thread she presented as a gift to the King. He used it, and this blinded his celestial eye, cost him his life and his kingdom.

Manuha was King of Thaton in the time of Anawrahta. Manuha had great power, great piety, and the great gift of speech. When he spoke golden rays poured out of his mouth. But Anawrahta's army defeated him. The King of Thaton was put into prison. One day some rice that had been offered to the Buddha was served to Manuha. He did not know about the rice. He ate it. And his gift of golden rays disappeared. He died an ordinary man.

Power is always in danger of being confronted by counter-power, and a man of pon is not sure that mere possession of it will continue to allow him to make politically relevant decisions. He must always be alert to challenge, aware of the transitory nature of dominance, and sensitive to the people around him.

The presence of pon cannot be institutionalized. It always is the possession or attribute of a concrete, living person. When he loses it, it is gone; when he dies, it dies. In the political sphere a man of pon does not build an organization; he builds a clientele. The power structure of Nondwin is a series of dyadic, interpersonal relationships having its center in U Sein Ko. His clientele share in part his success; they bask in the aura of his pon. If he should lose pon, they would switch to the next manifestation of power, if there were one, and, if none, the dyadic network would dissolve.

With a single man of pon in this community, there are no factions, no political splits, and no disputes outstanding among villagers. The village is a unit and acts as a political unit because its power structure is centered in a man of pon. The unity of political operation can best be seen in some actual case of dispute settlement, in the response of the village to national party solicitation, and in the way villagers handle the administrative agencies that impinge on their lives. But first, the rest of the formal political arrangements of the community need to be sketched.

Below the thugyi (the nominal but not actual power of Nondwin) are the *hse ein gaung*, ten house heads. Each member of the hse ein gaung has under his jurisdiction at least ten households. In Nondwin there are only nine holders of the ten house headship, so the designation is not strictly accurate, for some of the ten house chiefs have more than ten households under their aegis. The ten house group is territorially compact. It is made up of adjacent or contiguous compounds. The ten house head is chosen by the members of this group. And, unless there is some unreconciled, bitter dispute among these neighbors, the job is a lifetime one. The member of the hse ein gaung is supposed to mediate minor disputes among his group. He has no power to enforce; he merely tries to settle quarrels and to keep them from coming to the attention of the whole village. It is a principle of local politics that the more people involved in a dispute, the harder it is to settle. So a dispute is easier to handle at the ten house level, and the parties to it do not become so publicly committed to a stand that reputation, honor, and prestige become involved.

These hse ein gaung are not chosen on the basis of wealth. Among the nine in Nondwin, three are in the poor category, four are medium in wealth, one is moderately wealthy, and one belongs to the big rich. The chief characteristics for a hse ein gaung are trustworthiness and reputation for being even tempered. These are the qualities neighbors can accurately gauge, and they chose their ten house heads on their experience with them in contexts where these desirable attributes cannot be simulated. The ten house heads do not really do very much. If there is a real point at issue, it goes up to the thugyi. But the testimony of the ten house head, when the case is heard, is of foremost importance and frequently swings the decision one way or another.

Coordinate with the thugyi is a council of four elders, or the village committee. This five-man group makes up the village council. It is this group which has the minimal fining and jailing powers. They do not handle rape, murder, or theft. They will turn over suspects in these crimes to the police officer, or to the magistrate in Sagaing. If it is a stranger who commits any of the above crimes, they are just as likely to kill him on the spot as turn him over to higher authority.

The fines and punishment meted out by the village council are small, ranging from 5 to 50 kyats. Their main function is not to inflict punishments for law or custom violated, rather it is to restore amicability between the parties to a dispute. They do not seek justice; they aim at equity between parties. In the half dozen or so times I saw the council handle internal disputes, the procedure was virtually the same.

It must be mentioned, again, how little internal squabbling there is, how little litigation, how little overt enmity between neighbors, and how few the times when the case even gets to the village council level. In case of a dispute, husband-wife troubles, adultery, verbal insult, marriage runaways, and fighting between men are virtually the only causes. Occasionally theft between villagers does come up, and less frequently malicious witchcraft is a cause. The parties will be urged by their neighbors to settle. The high value on peaceful coexistence in a neighborhood, the fear that a slight breach may swell into great trouble are informally used coercively on the parties by friends and neighbors. But there are very severe limits on how much urging neighbors can do. Each person sees himself as responsible for his own actions, and the village's moral code is underwritten by this feeling. A wrongdoing, trouble, dispute, or immorality does not affect others; it affects the person involved. "Each heads his own world," villagers say. Every man gets the good and the bad that he earns. Villagers do not go in for censure or admonition, for each man is responsible on his own. "It is his fate, let him handle," they will say. "Do not meddle and you will have friends." "Do not argue with an angry man." "When the mad dog and the sane dog fight, the mad dog wins." "Nobody knows how to play another's harp." These expressions define, in part, the limits of offering advice, of actively trying to settle disputes among neighbors.

If the dispute is one in which there has been violence, for instance, a man cutting another with the dah (field knife, also dagger, which most villagers carry at all times), or a woman exhibiting her genitalia as a street insult to another woman, the disputants will be asked to come to a village meeting at night. This meeting usually follows a pattern. There are always several small boys around the compound of U Sein Ko, and any of them will serve as messengers. The meeting will be held at one of the elder's compounds or at the headman's. The elders (including U Sein Ko) and the headman will, at the appointed night, be seated on benches which are covered with a straw mat. Villagers will drift into the compound and seat themselves where they like. Tea will be served in plain shan cups. A betel box with the nuts, leaves, and spices needed for making a wad will be in the center of the table. Cheroots of the homemade (hseiholeik) kind will fill a lacquered tray. The elders and the headman will sit in the light of the fire. (When I attended they sat in the light of my Coleman lantern, and, later, U Sein Ko, following my example, bought for his compound a pressure lantern. But still, even in this white light, the fire flicker is a necessary background.) Children will be playing games beyond the bright rim of light. The setting duplicates many another evening in Nondwin except that all the elders and the headman are on hand. Conversation is casual. Talk turns on the usual topics, not on the case. Then one of the disputants comes in. He goes up to the seated elders and gives a shikko, and he seats himself in a respect posture, soles of the feet away from the elders, his head lower than any of theirs, and facing to the West or the South, for the elders are in the mingala (grace or auspicious) directions of either East or North. He drinks his tea and lights his cigar. In Nondwin there are people who are not smokers habitually, but in situations like this everybody smokes or chews betel nut and drinks at least a cup of tea before the proceedings.

The disputant begins his tale. He and this other man had an argument about the fidelity of his wife. He suspected this man of making advances to his wife. The wife, without being asked, says her husband is a jealous man. The neighbors also speak up. "He is not a man of cool mind," they say. "He is given to anger." The accused says he is like anybody else, but he was provoked. "How?" the elders ask. And he tells them of the things this man said about his wife. The husband confronted the man and told him to stop saying these things. The man did not reply. The husband lost his temper, pulled his dagger, and in the scuffle cut the other man's arm. The elders give some homilies and proverbs about the loss of temper, about acting before you have evidence. The accused listens and nods his head, and the tension point is over. He asks for forgiveness, and he is granted it. He is also fined five kyats. Then U Sein Ko begins a jesting routine about husbands controlling wives, about family authority, and about satisfied women giving no cause for worry. Others join in the jesting, and even the recently fined man can summon a joke or two about the dangers of male and female attractions when a husband is not as dominant as he should be. The man takes another cup or two of tea, excuses himself by a shikko and leaves the compound. His wife follows immediately. Onlookers murmur approval in the saying that the "side knot follows the top knot." (Women wear their hair, in dress fashion, with a knot to the side or top, and many men wear long hair with a top knot.) The expression indicates the proper authority relations, for in this instance not only did the knifer express his accord with the rule of community harmony, but the wife also accepted that she had been remiss.

The rest of the group stays intact, and eventually the injured man comes into the compound. A couple of small boys have gone ahead to ask him to have some tea in the headman's compound. He repeats the respect gestures to the elders. Then he starts his tale about being accosted, insulted, and stabbed. The elders ask him why he wanted to aggravate a neighbor. He denies that he did. Some of the people in the crowd say he has a rapier-like tongue. He teases women by his punning and innuendoes. An elder says that, "A good cook knows when enough pepper has been put in the soup." The injured man hesitates a moment and says, "A wise man knows that too much food is poison." This agreement via proverb exchange breaks the small tension. He has admitted that he was unnecessarily provocative. He continues to drink tea. Later his attacker turns up, pays no special attention to him, drinks a cup of tea, smokes, then says, *"Thwabaonme,"* "I will be off now." The elders say, *"Thwaba,"* "Be off." He goes. The other party does the same. The breach is healed. People drift off. The fire dies down. Nothing will be left of the case except gossip.

This at least is the formal and public manner of settling disputes. How much private discussion, pressure from relatives, and appeal from friends goes on before the reconciliation is difficult to assess.

The above description makes clear some of the principles involved in both customary law and in the exercise of political power. The major reason for settlement of intravillage troubles and disputes is the restoration of neighborly and harmonious relations between parties. Everybody has a stake in peaceful relations, for a person nursing a grudge may turn into a community menace, or he may set off a chain of violence and trouble. The participation of all the villagers who want to speak up is a recognition of this ever-present potential for a neighbor to turn into a *luzo,* a really "bad hat," and an acknowledgment of the fact that a person pushed to extremes will act in extreme ways.

Restoration of "cool minds" among neighbors can only be done if a direct confrontation between the contestants is avoided. A direct confrontation means that a quarrel is pushed to the point at which somebody must clearly be the victor and somebody clearly the vanquished. If this comes about, the vanquished will seek revenge, and a cycle of acrimonious interaction is thus initiated. The procedures of settling a dispute follow the dictate of making a clear issue out of the case. The process allows each person to keep his dignity, to compromise indirectly, and to indicate subscription to the norms of peaceful interaction. The settlement is phrased as though it were a voluntary act, freely given by the parties involved. This is the idiom of personal relations, but the facts are otherwise. The elders and the man of pon did have real sanctioning power. They could have turned the attacker over to the township officer for a court trial, and they could have fined him 50 kyats on their own power. They did not invoke their powers because their powers were not challenged. If the attacker did not ask forgiveness, they would have exhibited their strength. But, since he accepted their power and seemingly figured out what they wanted of him, there was no need for displaying power. Power is always kept latent, if at all possible. Both parties recognized that the community wanted them to patch up their troubles, so they obeyed the common will. They did not have to, of course. But, if they had not, they would have defied the man of pon and the diffuse sanctions of the community. Both the aggrieved and the aggressor would have suffered unfavorable consequences. The knifer would have gone to jail, and the victim would have been placed in a position of defiance to the man of pon, who would, in time, have found a way to publicly humiliate him.

The elders, in these procedures, are men of gon. They are the embodiments of the moral code and have the virtues of a good man. Their social attributes are those of persuasion, conciliation, and admonishment. The elders are men who have lived fairly good lives, who have exhibited abilities to get along with neighbors, to be temperate, to be pious, to grow increasingly detached from the search for wealth and power. They stand almost as "special uncles" to the whole village reminding it that the life without rancor, without conflict, without strong desire for dominance, is after all the best life.

There is one other mode of settling internal village troubles. The case of a marriage against the parents' wishes will make this other method apparent. Here, no crime or breach of custom at the community level has been committed. Rather, familial authority has been challenged, and there is the possibility of a rupture between two families. In cases like this, the elders will visit the compound of each of the families in turn. They will give informal advice and counsel, hoping to reconcile the families to the facts of the case. The man of pon will not act in his capacity as a power. No authority will be invoked. Only the diffuse moral code of harmony, cool mind, and reduction of friction will be invoked. This usually works, but sometimes the rupture is permanent. In Nondwin there are parents who do not ever speak to a son or daughter who married against their wishes, or married the wrong person. Such family breaks may endure a whole lifetime, and this means that the range of interaction for the parties is cut down to that extent. The fragility of interpersonal relations is manifest in the extreme in these cases of putting aside a son or daughter and a neighbor's family as forever beyond the bounds of social recognition.

In this political structure of thugyi, elders, ten house heads, there is no clearly defined political process. The whole range of nominal offices like fire brigade, village sanitation, education, agriculture, security, road, water, and reception committees are just 170 names on paper. They are never operational, but are only to show, if an official asks, that the offices are filled. No official is naive enough to ever ask. It is the man of pon who turns a collection of offices into a political structure in Nondwin.

At the first level of exercise of power, the man of pon is the one person fellow villagers will take their complaints to. Some individuals complained to U Sein Ko about the apportioning of sentry duty among the villagers. He told them he thought it was fair enough. That ended the complaint. A single complaint, or series of complaints, are handled at the whim of the man of pon. A widespread complaint may be handled differently, but not necessarily, for the man of pon does as he sees fit, so long as it does not alienate his clientele. People stay with the man of pon because he has power and because they derive something from his exercise of power. U Sein Ko lends money, arranges for government loans, smooths interaction between villagers and higher level politicians, and works out the ties between Nondwin and national political parties. Still, at this level of the exercise of pon, U Sein Ko can commit the village to participation in minor things without much consultation. For example, he arranged for a troupe of Nondwin boys to do the elephant and monkey dances at a pagoda dedication in a nearby village. The pagoda committee came to U Sein Ko and asked him. He agreed and afterwards told the troupe, who were willing to go along for the frolic. If U Sein Ko had decided not to send the troupe, they would not have gone.

At the second level of the exercise of power, the man of pon legitimizes the distribution of community tasks. He certifies that the work in fence building, canal cleaning, sentry duty, road maintenance, well cleaning, and provision of water and food for visitors and travelers is just and fair. He takes into account the relative abilities of families and individuals to carry out or complete these tasks. But when he reviews and approves the lists (almost every job is drawn up in handwritten lists and posted outside the thugyi's house, with a copy for his files), there is little room for argument or complaint. To complain is almost to challenge his pon. In Nondwin these tasks were smoothly and easily carried out with little complaint and little shirking. The second level of pon operates to keep the autonomous families from bickering or from polarizing into factions or cliques.

At the third level of pon, the community is aligned with the national political parties. In a community like Nondwin, with its high rate of literacy, national issues are part of daily life. Newspapers come into the village although there are only three regular purchasers. Many men and women read the papers, and some of the news is discussed. Handbills, pamphlets, and propaganda tear sheets from political parties in Sagaing and Mandalay also find their way into Nondwin. Also canvassers for political parties sometimes visit the village. Political information is not scarce, but it is not very relevant, either. The activities of national leaders, the policy debates reported in the newspapers, the claims and counterclaims of politicians are viewed as things the villager can little affect. This level of political information is sensational. People talk about it, but as an event they do not handle, or a thing that means little in daily life. At the time, the chief national political contenders were U Nu of the newly formed Union party and the Ba Swe–Kyaw Nyein coalition in the Stable AFPFL (Anti-Fascist People's Freedom League). Parties like the NUF (National United Front) or the BWP (Burma Workers' Party) were not in the ken and vocabulary of the people of Nondwin. The special conditions of political sophistication which made these smaller parties have some appeal and following in places such as Patheingyi, or Paleik, or among the students at Mandalay University apparently did not exist in Nondwin.

Nondwin opinion was in favor of the return to civilian government and the end of Army rule, but not on ideological grounds. The consensus was that the Army made too many demands (cleanliness, prohibition of betel nut sellers, replacement of rickshaws by pedicabs, dog poisoning, and elimination of beggars in the larger towns) and had done its job of restoring security and relative peace in the countryside. The Army was seen as an interlude to set the countryside in order, drive the insurgents back into the hills, and allow the democratic process to begin again. In the political jockeying between U Nu's Union party and the Stable AFPFL, the issues were not sharp and clear. For people in Nondwin, they were both heirs of the independence movement, mildly socialist, anti-colonial and neutralist in foreign policy, and committed to democracy and economic growth. The minor differences, within this broad agreement between the parties, were not of interest either in ordinary conversation, or when I tried to find out what the elections might be about, or where the major parties differed. This proverb was invoked in the place of political analysis: "When the buffalo fight, the grass gets trampled." In power struggles between giants, this means that the small man, the villager, is always victim. The political battle over government is still remote from the villager, still seen in terms of a battle between contending men of power. Yet it is grasped under the rubric of leaders and clientele, so that the people of Nondwin do not want to be counted as politically visible.

But they cannot ignore the national party organization and its city and town branches. There was talk about tax raises on cultivators, threats of stopping loans, hints of harassment if the community did not line up with the victors. Not to participate in an election means to be outside of the potential benefits from a successful candidate, while to be on the losing side means to pay some price in favors, in government attention, and in services. To be on the winning side is to receive whatever small attentions and services the government can bestow on villages. At this village level, the political process is a paradoxical mixture of naked and veiled force. The party organizations make appeals to the villagers in terms of barely concealed threats and promises about what can happen if villagers do not vote for them. Inside Nondwin people gravitate to U Sein Ko before expressing a political stand. The national issues are not relevant for them; they are trying to find an advantageous stance in a power struggle in which they believe their chances for being victim are much greater than those of being beneficiary. At this time, the precrystallization period, the topic of local politics is a touchy one. And whatever villagers said to each other, they would not say to me. I could only inquire very indirectly about how people were going to line up, or if they would line up at all, with a national party.

As I lived with U Sein Ko, I could see the external beginnings of the formation of a local party organization. I could watch the enrollment of people into the Clean, Union party, household by household, but I could not find out why. It was only after I had been in the village several months, when my field census was complete, and when the electioneering was over that I could get the social facts of political choice I now report. In the first stages of political organization, before the outcomes were clear, the risks of poor alignment were to villagers sources of great potential trouble. So, at this time, an opaque veil hung over what is basically a process of handling the community adjustment to forces seen as natural, uncontrollable, and, if improperly accommodated, malevolent. It is a time when the scale of interpersonal relations, which also stress accommodation, resolution of conflict, and unwillingness to engage in direct confrontation, is projected by national political demands to a national importance.

In Sagaing and Mandalay campaigning began about the first of October, with the setting up of party offices and the distribution of party literature. On the 10th of October, U Sein Ko and the thugyi were invited to Sagaing to attend a party rally of the *Pyidaungzu* (U Nu's Union party). This was a first important move. The headman was already committed to this party, but he came to U Sein Ko and asked him if he was going to the meeting. U Sein Ko had thought about the invitation and had decided to go. He told me he decided to go, which was a public commitment to U Nu's party, not just the agreement of a man to listen to a presentation of issues, on the following grounds. First, he thought U Nu would win, and that he and Nondwin would be in the correct camp; second, he knew that the Pyidaungzu controlled most of the Sagaing district and he did not want to fight against that; and third, the personality of U Nu and the peasant-oriented campaign seemed to him plausible. U Nu's strong stand on Buddhism, his obvious piety, his great ability to use the symbols of peasant values, his apparent sincerity, and his great devotion to the idea of Burma all struck responsive chords in a man like U Sein Ko, who viewed himself as the local version of what U Nu was on the national scene: a man of pon.

The thugyi and U Sein Ko returned from Sagaing. U Sein Ko had a book of blanks for enrolling party members in the Union party. The cost of joining was minimal, and not beyond the means of a single villager. So, whether or not people joined depended on the play of political forces in the community. The party book was kept in the house of U Sein Ko, and he was the first man to join. The whole community knew by word of mouth that a political drive was on, that U Sein Ko had joined the Pyidaungzu, and that the thugyi had also done so. The party-building drive lasted until December 1. From October 1 to December 1, solicitations to join the Union party were open in Nondwin. Never did I see any active canvassing for party members. People just drifted in, one at a time, to U Sein Ko's compound and, after the usual hospitality routines of tea drinking and smoking, joined the party. During this three-month period of party recruitment only 55 persons joined the Pyidaungzu. They came from 40 different households. Well under half the households in Nondwin openly pledged allegiance to a national party, and under 20 per cent of its voting population became party members. To my knowledge, no one joined any other party organization. The only formal political apparatus centered around U Sein Ko and his adherence to the Union party.

As I observed enrollment I was able to place each new joiner in the proper household, in the correct wealth category, and locate him generally in social space. The matching of party adherents against the relevant gross social facts reveals little about the underlying dynamics of who joins a national party and for what reasons. It shows that the following categories are of moderate significance in disposing a villager in Nondwin to join a national party:

1. Wealth: Only three poor households were represented. Of the 37 remaining, 18 were of the rich, a high proportion, and the rest moderate.

2. Age: The age distribution of party joiners placed most of them in the 35 to 45 bracket, with the next largest group in the 20 to 30 year category.

3. Location: Joiners tended to be clustered in neighborhoods. A glance at the Map of Nondwin Village, where the order of joining is plotted by number, shows four clusters of neighbors dominating.

4. Kinship: Relatives of U Sein Ko and his wife all joined. If a man joined, his brother was likely to, if he lived in a separate household.

5. Clientship: The three poor families were either tenants of U Sein Ko, or habitual borrowers from him.

Turning these factors, the grounds for and the actual decision to join, into social process gives better insight into the meaning of politics for villagers.

Wealthier villagers have a larger stake in coming to terms with the national powers. To them the threat of higher taxes or new government impositions has tangible meaning, and they seek to align themselves with the possible victor. But in a village like Nondwin, where a man of pon is physically present, they take their cue from him. To go against his choice is to lay the basis for factionalism, to compete for adherents, and possibly to be subject to retaliation if found on the losing side. Since Nondwin is not now marked by factions, and a disunited village (about which the people know from experience and observation of other villages) is regarded as undesirable, as an invitation to dacoity and murder, fraught with explosive opportunities in interpersonal relations, and as subject to all sorts of manipulations by outsiders, the wealthier families do not want to take political initiative. They merely seek to shield themselves from calamity and to preserve public harmony.

The age distribution of joiners represents the cultural division of a man's life. In childhood he learns, in young adulthood he works and saves, in adulthood he takes over control of a domestic unit and consolidates his wealth and power, and in full maturity he begins to detach himself in order to build merit and prepare for a propitious rebirth. Politics, then, is the concern of people in adulthood. The younger group is just coming into social responsibility, while the older group is just going out of it. At about 45, most men and women give up thoughts of pon and awza, if they ever entertained them, and turn toward the cultivation of gon, through meditation, pagoda visiting, and pongyi kyaung attendance. They cultivate *thila gon,* the virtue of exemplary conduct and moral thoughts. They are virtually lost to the political process for they focus on internal refinement or on the building of merit. Secular appeals touch them less than the active 35 to 45 group.

The location component of party joining is an instance of neighborhood solidarity and is the diffusion of a political position by means of a network of interpersonal relations. Since people who live close to each other in Nondwin have adjusted their behaviors about many tasks, the act of joining a party when a respected neighbor does is merely the extension of an already existing social solidarity. The order of joining clearly reflects the facts of localized discussion of parties, of the face to face decisions to join, and that the act of joining is a reflection of a cooperating or harmonious neighborhood group.

If a man is in a strong economic position in relation to his near kin, his actions will be signals for theirs. Clearly U Sein Ko's wealth and pon meant that his relatives would join the Union party after he had. And brothers, who have worked out previous common understandings, would reinforce them by a similar political commitment. The previous position of the joining person in terms of his wealth and power and co-activity with kinsmen were the features that made or did not make kinship relevant to the act of party enrollment.

Clientship is a dependency relationship based on social and economic inequalities. The inequalities in status in a community like Nondwin stem from personal or familial life histories, not from systematic disprivilege in a caste or class system or from inherited sets of power relations. The poor households who joined the Union party were direct dependents on the man of pon, but others in the moderate wealth group had borrowed money from him or wanted to place themselves in a position to do so if the need arose. The dimension of client-patron relations was hard to assess in Nondwin, for actual full dependent relations were few and rare, but the potential was always there, and many of the moderate households wanted to be in a position to have even this slim claim on U Sein Ko.

The party structure did not take public shape until after the enrollment drive was over. When the enrollment of the 40-household and 55-person membership in the Union party was completed, a local party branch was organized. Three district organizers from Sagaing jeeped into Nondwin and came to see U Sein Ko at the end of the enrollment campaign. At eight o'clock in the evening, word was passed out that a meeting to elect officials for the party organization would be held in U Sein Ko's compound. Anyone was welcome to come. All of the people who had joined came, and about a dozen other onlookers sat just beyond the glare of the pressure lamp. One of the organizers from Sagaing explained that the election of local party officials was strictly voluntary. He made a short speech about independence, democracy, and a free Burma, depending upon an active citizenry. His speech echoed the general sentiments of villagers. The parts of the political process that have substance and meaning to these villagers are the tangible facts of independence and the palpable business of voting in elections. The political process is not shaped for villagers by their judgment among real competing interest groups, striking ideological differences, or authoritative sanctioning of one or another program. They are expressing by voting their Burmese solidarity, their sense of pride in their cultural tradition, and their sense of accomplishment in being a free and independent nation. The empirical grinding of interests into a rule bound governmental machine has not yet been achieved for villagers of Nondwin.

Apparently, of all the audience to the organizer's speech, I was the only one impressed. His straightforward exposition of why parties were necessary, his understanding of how votes influence policy, and his willingness to answer in plain language any question seemed to me to be the very stuff of local democratic institutions. This man's devotion to representative politics, and that of hundreds of others like him in Upper Burma, does not stem from great reward, or even salary, and only slightly from the promise of political office. It seems, rather, to come largely from the hope of turning an uncivic population, filled with ideas of resentment and suspicion against government authority, into an organized segment of a polity.

Of course, the notions of political culture in the ideas of pon, gon, and awza, the sense that government is still an uncontrollable natural force, the troubles consequent upon taking a losing stand, the veiled hints of local and national pressures for a misdiagnosis of the distribution of power, and, finally, the personal unwillingness to become visible on controversial subjects, all militate against the textbook version of democracy as expounded to villagers by the party organizer. What modifications of local societies, together with supralocal notions of political process, give a new nation like Burma a regime of representative institutions and civil liberties and yet speed the processes of social and economic modernization is a puzzle only the Burmans and time can solve. There are no ready-made solutions for import, and no traditional forms viable enough for adaptation to these needs.

The way the Nondwin party organization was formed that evening gives some more empirical substance to my diagnosis of the nature of local political life. After the organizers had made their talks, they suggested that nominations were open. Immediately, U Sein Ko was named by someone in the audience. U Sein Ko said he was too busy to take on political jobs. Everybody knew just what he meant. He did not need the office to be the power in the community; the selection of somebody who would do the detailed work (that turned out to be virtually nothing) and who was directly connected to U Sein Ko was in order. U Sein Ko's son (resident in another compound) was then named and, by the unanimity of a murmured vote, elected as chairman of the local party organization. A second chairman, two secretaries, a treasurer, and 10 delegates were speedily elected in the same manner, through voice vote of consensus. Only one name was brought up to which there was a muttered demurrer, and that name was dropped. The men elected were those closely tied to U Sein Ko and were not competitors for power in the community.

The organization of the party reflected the internal distribution of power and the interpersonal networks of influence. It never functioned as an organization. No votes were solicited by the committee of the Pyidaungzu, no posters were nailed up, no election speeches made. This community, organized around a man of pon who had no challengers, was clearly delivered into the hands of the Union party. It delivered above a 90 per cent vote, not because 90 per cent of the people had a stand, or even a perspective, on national issues, or a positive view of the candidates, but because of its political culture and the organization of that culture into a series of dyadic relations around a concrete man of power. The vote, for the villager, is a dual thing: an expression of his pride and joy in Burman sovereignty, on the one side, and an allegiance to the current organization of local power, on the other. It is an act mixed with nearly equal proportions of participation and protection. Participation in victory is a means of protection against greater governmental powers. Villagers seek protection against policy, rather than a hand in its formation.

Ties between the Village and the National Government

So far, I have not given in any detail the myriad ways in which a villager's life is affected by government and administration, or ways in which government attempts to affect village life. The ties between villages and other levels of government are many and diverse. The most obvious connections are through taxes and police and court agencies. Tax officials, policemen, and soldiers come to the village in the normal course of business and deal with villagers either individually or through the thugyi and the council of elders. These connections are unproblematic. Everybody pays the proper rate on his matured crop with surprisingly little grumbling. They have paid such a tax for generations, and they would rather pay it to Burmans than to imperial masters. They get, from their point of view, just about the same services in return from the Burman government, and maybe even a bit more, for Burmans, not Britishers, draw the salaries of the civil service. Police and army and special constabulary have stabilized the area around Nondwin fairly effectively. Robberies are few, dacoity in daylight is practically unknown, and the marauding insurgent bands are pushed far enough from village borders so that the community does not have to pay a tribute to these political, paramilitary forces. The tax codes, the law codes, and the police habits are still largely those of the recent colonial regime. They were never strongly unpalatable as such to villagers like these. What was disliked was the fact that the *Thakins* (masters) were English rather than Burman, and when the first leaders of national independence called themselves Thakin, they did not mean master over the Burman, but, rather, "master in our own house."

Public and welfare services also tie the villager into a larger political network. The departments of roads, forests, and agriculture provide the services appropriate to their domain, and villagers give some time and labor in road repair. The villagers must get permission to cut certain size trees and, sometimes, get seed loans or money loans from an agency of the agricultural department. The SAMB (State Agricultural Marketing Board) sets agricultural prices, but a farmer is not required to sell to it, and since rice, the main activity of the SAMB, is but a small part of the product of Nondwin, the hidden levy in the internal price of rice (with the government taking the differential for meeting national planning objectives) does not bear heavily on Nondwin farmers.

The government also provides some minimal medical services which the people frequently use. There is a medical visitor who prods his coughing motorcycle along the rounds of his 30 or so villages. He charges minimal prices for injections and drugs and does some treating of the sick beyond the level of cleansing, massaging, and pill dispensing. He makes weekly visits to Nondwin, and, as might be expected, he parks his motorcycle in the compound of U Sein Ko and does a good part of his medical trade there, only visiting those who are too sick to come to the compound. Since these villagers continually doctor themselves with both traditional and modern medicine (at least as much of it as they can afford), the medical visitor does a fairly brisk trade. In addition there is a permanent medical post in a village about eight miles from Nondwin, and emergency cases (cuts, burns, and contusions, for example) will frequently be taken there for treatment. Midwives are also provided by the government, and most babies delivered in Nondwin use the services of these paid, partly trained midwives. The midwives make trips to Nondwin to see their clients.

The education of the youth of the village is now largely in the hands of the state agency. The school itself is held in a pongyi kyaung (Nash, 1961). There are no public buildings in Nondwin proper, and the school is conducted in one of the two pongyi kyaungs which lie about a mile beyond the village fence. In the monastery, in a wooden structure raised high on stilts, the *koyin* (religious novices) and *kyaungtha* (students) mix and work together. The classroom is on a concrete floor below the building itself. It is open to the four winds. A score of wooden desks, spaced out, facing a blackboard, complete the physical plant. In the main classroom several grades (or "standards" as they are called in Burma, following British usage) are grouped together. Only the younger, first standard students, are kept apart in another open classroom. In the state school are 70 students, 15 girls and 55 boys. In the kyaung, under the pongyi, are 21 koyin, 18 of whom get only religious education. The other three younger boys take some work with the primary school teacher. In the other monastery, to the west of the village, are 15 students, taught only by the monks. The whole school population of Nondwin is thus 106 students. This includes nearly everyone who is eligible to go to school, despite the fact that education is not compulsory. Education for the Nondwin boy or girl usually stops at the fourth standard. In the last two years, only four students (two boys and two girls) have gone beyond. The pongyi school and the state school have minor differences in the content of education, none in method or aim. The state primary, besides reading and writing, teaches some history, arithmetic, geography, and general science. The pongyi kyaung teaches only reading and writing, a bit of *Pali* (the language of the Buddhist scriptures), and some bits of Buddhist cosmology and the life of the Buddha.

Although education, in the abstract, is highly valued by Burmans, support for schools and teachers is meagre at the local level. In Nondwin, books are few, benches and desks in short supply, and even a simple building for the school is lacking. The teacher has tried unsuccessfully to get the people of Nondwin to make contributions to buy or build these things. They say there is a national government to provide these things, that it is not a local concern. They have no social sense about government projects, and will not voluntarily donate time or money toward them. A school and its equipment needs leave a villager unmoved, as does any project for which the national or district government has a major responsibility. The sense of *civitas*, in which citizens interact to implement their ends through political organization, is absent from Nondwin.

Education, like politics, administration, or any development project, must bear on the villagers' chief immediate ends, such as the mundane business of making a living, getting along with relatives and neighbors, earning respect and honor, and the religious activity of laying up *kutho* (merit) so that a favorable rebirth may come in the next life. If education or politics or development do not bear on these concerns in a palpable, empirically recognizable way, they do not mean much to a villager.

In Nondwin, the teacher and his sister, who is his assistant, are not native to the village; they come from a nearby community. This fact may, in part, account for their inability to raise local support for school equipment, but it cannot account for their lack of success with the national authorities. The village teacher is the lowest rung of the educational hierarchy. He must go through the channels of headmaster, supervisor, inspector, and so forth, to make any sort of demand. The Ministry of Education is swamped by local demands and cannot accede or even pay attention to most of them. The teachers belong to an organization of village teachers with district headquarters in Sagaing. Here they join in discussion of common village problems, air their grievances before superiors, and hear the government answers and plans. But the village school teacher is like the villager, he feels powerless before the authority and might of the government. There is only one way to cope with it: compliance in the official context of role as public employee. If he wants to make himself felt, he must join a political party and get the party to do something about education. But teachers are not important enough politically to have much impact. So, like the farming villager, the teacher watches the political contest among men of power at the national level and tries to figure how he can place himself in the chain of strength without making enemies.

The school, as the education agency of the government, is a good place to see how some of the aims and goals of the national political and social leaders actually affect the local society. For the Burmese education planners like those who planned the Pyidawtha or "Burma road to socialism" program of Ne Win, the object of education is not in doubt: Education is to serve as one of the means of transformation from a raw material producing society, where the bulk of the people had a narrow, peasant, traditional view, to a diversified, somewhat industrialized society able to absorb and use the most modern scientific knowledge. Education is to build a modern nation, a socialist democracy made up of responsible and informed citizens. These lofty aims, these urgent goals, are not what villagers see in the performance of the school. The school, to them, should implement their ordinary concerns; education should lead to economic success (the village boy will go beyond the fourth standard to be a clerk, teacher, or civil servant); it should lead to a display of refinement, of common knowledge (for that is how an educated man earns gon and respect); and it should help get kutho. For the villager the school is not an agency of transformation, rather it is the contrary. He sees it as an extension of all those agencies of enculturation that teach the young to be well built-in members of society. The school in fact does not have its own ethic, its own dynamic, and it is not opposed to all the other parts of local society that make for continuity and stability rather than for innovation and change (Nash, 1961).

The relation of the national education program to actual school operation in Nondwin exhibits one meaning of the concept of a multiple society. The multiplicity exists in a divergence of goals between the national segment and the locally oriented members of society. The villagers of Nondwin see the activities of the national leaders, the government, and administration as adjuncts or means of implementing their locally derived needs and goals. They do not think of village activities as promoting a kind of culture and society envisioned by politicians and planners, but as extending and consolidating positions in local and regional networks of economic and political power. Multiplicity exists as a difference in horizon, spatial and temporal. The villager holds an image not of an abstract Burma but of a series of real, connected interests with people not in his daily life. He does not orient his activities to bring about a future for something transcending the existing networks of relationships in which he is enmeshed. For the villager Burma is a culture, a style of life, and a history. It is not, as it is for the national leaders, at least at the program level, a task force designed to make a certain kind of Burma. The often quoted slogan of U Nu, that "Our true history lies ahead of us," evokes in villagers neither a transformation of society and culture, nor a concentrated effort to become something they are not. Rather, it means an extension, on hopefully a higher material plane, of the culture and society they now have. It is this multiplicity, this divergence between the aims of the national segment and the bulk of the peasantry, that places the government in the relation of agent and agency to recalcitrant and reluctant raw material.

This fact, of conscious, ideological persons with images of Burma in the making, exhorting, cajoling, persuading, or coercing persons oriented to the maintenance and extension of a way of life, marks most of the interaction between the government and the peasantry it governs. In a description of the attempt to bring social and economic change to Nondwin through direct national agency, the dichotomy can be again exhibited.

The national government has a series of programs and of agencies designed to help raise the economic performance of villagers like those of Nondwin. It also has some agents and agencies dedicated to the diffusion of a sense of national being into villagers and to the spread of what it considers aspects of modernity congruent with Burmese cultural tradition. One program which reaches many in Nondwin is the agricultural loan. This is under the agricultural welfare department and is designed to provide cheap funds to cultivators at the beginning of the agricultural cycle. In 1960–61, the government loan program provided 4,300 kyats to 43 family heads in Nondwin. The loan of 100 kyats per cultivator carried an interest rate of 50 pyas (pya = .10 ky) per 100 kyats. This is less than a quarter of the commercial interest rate. The loan is a clear boon to the villager when compared to nongovernment sources of funds. But, the government is not as efficient in getting loans into the hands of cultivators as were the Chinese and Indian moneylenders, nor does it provide anywhere near the flow of funds these alien middlemen afforded. Furthermore, the supply of funds depends upon the ups and downs of the national budget and is partly contingent upon the political relations of Nondwin to the national government through village performance in elections. Without political factions in the village itself, the internal distribution of loans did not take the acrimonious tack of bickering and favoritism that it did in some neighboring communities.

Villagers wanting a loan apply to the headman and he forwards the applications to the agricultural bank in Mandalay. The bank approves the loan ostensibly on the basis of its budget for the region. Swings in available funds are reflected in loans to Nondwin farmers in 1959 when 68 families received 100 kyats each, and in 1958 when 43 families got 300 kyats each. The community as a whole takes responsibility for the repayment of the loan. It underwrites the repayment, but the individual farmers are actually responsible. The headman and the elders form the "village loan committee," and they make monthly collections (1.50 kyats per debtor) until the loan is repaid. They then pay the lump sum to the agricultural bank. When this is done, applications for a new loan will be considered again at Mandalay. In the past three years Nondwin paid off its loans on schedule. In 1960 they were behind, and the government levied an interest penalty on the community loan. The failure to meet the payment date was the fault of the accounting system of the headman and the elders. They thought they had collected enough from each debtor to repay the loan, but in fact they were short 3 kyats per borrowing cultivator. A meeting (siwe) was called in U Sein Ko's compound and the borrowers met with the loan committee, and after an evening of reconstructing payments to the committee, everybody was satisfied that it would take two more months to pay off the current loan, and that a mistake in bookkeeping rather than venality was involved. The public review of the state of the loan funds is typical of how community problems are solved. Like any dispute or litigation all of the parties must be heard out and the differential power among them must be veiled; the decision must appear to be the voluntary assent of free agents who have the option of contracting out. The consensus-run community is the ideal image. The fact is that consensus polarizes around holders of pon.

The government loan service can be used as a political weapon, but, since Nondwin backed the (then) regnant Union party, administrative delay or outright withholding of loan funds did not occur. In Nondwin, most of the borrowers used the money for its intended purpose—to buy seed. Only a few families borrowed government money for consumption rather than agricultural production. The loan funds went to the poor and moderate farmers, not the rich. The rich farmers of Nondwin, especially the big rich, are themselves moneylenders, and it would strain the consensual nature of political life if they borrowed money at government rates and reloaned it at market rates. A community member, as against a Chinese, Indian, or unknown Burman, could not so flagrantly ignore the local, sentimental and moral bonds of daily interaction.

The loan program is in part an attempt to fill the gap left by the flight of small private capital and, also, to lessen the continual burden of small holder debt. It is not a program designed to spur innovation, to demand new behavior from villagers. It is only a modest underwriting of the usual agricultural activity. The possible political tinge is passed here by the alignment of the community with the national power through delivering the vote. The "mass" programs of the Burmese Government are of a different character than the loan, health, or seed distributing programs. There existed in the charter of the Office of Mass Education a vague mandate to modernize the people of Burma, to educate them as citizens, to provide and create welfare services, to promote democracy, and to preserve and enrich the viable parts of the cultural tradition of the Burmese. The Office of Mass Education with headquarters in Rangoon had an organization of Mass Education Officers down through the districts and reaching most of the villages of, at least, Upper Burma.

The Mass Education Office, with its mixed bag of motives, its autonomy from the other national agencies providing information and welfare services to the towns and villages, its idealistic and untrained field workers, and its paucity of funds, was an unwieldy and ineffective organization. It was abolished and a Department of Rural Welfare replaced it. But in Nondwin the title of Mass Education Officer still stuck to the Rural Welfare Officer.

From what I could see in Nondwin, the rural welfare program was chiefly hortatory and symbolic. It did not have the resources, the personnel, the tools, or the vision to significantly affect, let alone transform, the life of Nondwin villagers. Its program shifted as the winds of national politics shifted; villages got attention as they could or could not get political audience, and particular field level workers were shifted about at the whim of the national bureaucracy. The welfare program, in short, was not massive enough, not sustained enough, not placed enough in villagers' hands to make any sort of impact on the economic structure of the community or its image of the modern world. Its chief yield to the peasants of Nondwin was symbolic; there was in existence a national government of Burmans, dedicated to the welfare of Burmans, and perhaps, with luck, it might even be really useful.

A description of the most intensive two-day visit of Rural Welfare Officers to Nondwin will make clear some of the assertions made above. It will also describe one of the dimensions of political and cultural multiplicity by indicating how disparate the organizational and goal structures of villagers are as compared with those of agents of the national bureaucracy. The Welfare Officer came to Nondwin bearing gifts. He gave out a few packets of golden sweet corn seed (provided by the Asia Foundation) and some seed packets of radishes and carrots. For U Sein Ko, known to him as the lugyi here, he brought two pounds of sample fertilizer. The Welfare Officer walked around the village, talking easily with the villagers. He stopped in compounds, drank tea, smoked, chewed betel, and exchanged pleasantries. Since he had no awza and no coercive sanctions in the political structure, the Welfare Officer was almost in the role of guest. And since the gap between lower civil servants and villagers is not great, he gave himself no airs. The absence of great status gap, lack of class or status pretension, and political noncoerciveness make it easy for informal personal communication between local Welfare Officers and ordinary cultivators. The break in communication occasioned when the informal, intimate atmosphere is violated does not devil the efforts of welfare workers I have seen.

The multiplicity is not evident in the kinds of persons who come to see villagers but in the sorts of ideologies and programs they bring. Following standard bureaucratic procedure, the Welfare Officer asked that a committee for village welfare be organized. A meeting was called, of men only. The meeting was held in the thugyi's compound just after the evening meal. Men who attended ranged from the young to the old. Additional welfare organizers came from town, so that three Welfare Officers were on hand. It was an occasion for speech making by the outsiders. A committee was elected in short order. It had exactly the same membership as the political party committee. Since these men were in fact never going to do anything, they might as well double their inactivity. Then subcommittees were elected with the titles of Education (headed by the school teacher), Health (by a part time *hseihsaya*, or Burmese physician), and Cooperative Head (son of the man of pon). Then a standing committee was elected of eight men, six of them from the rich and two from the moderate wealth division. The elections were quick, unanimous, and by voice vote.

The speeches of the welfare organizers were excerpts from national programs, speeches of U Nu, and other familiar phrases from the welfare movement. No concrete funds, programs, assistance, organizational connection, evaluation, technology, or advice was given. The speeches were listened to with the patient tolerance that Burmans show on such occasions. The themes of freedom, democracy, socialism, equal wealth distribution, peace, and plenty that recurred in each speech were familiar enough. The exhortation of improved economic performance and national loyalty were old refrains. But concrete, empirical steps to any of these goals were not presented.

The Welfare Officers asked me to make a speech, too. I obliged with the help of a bilingual officer from Sagaing. I asked the villagers what they wanted to make their work more productive. What, in the best of all worlds, could their government give them? The suggestions that came from the audience were: a tractor, chemical fertilizer, artesian wells, and a water pump. The list is instructive. These farmers know fairly well what they need and are willing to take it from government. But the government has not made available, on any scale, these first simple aids to production.

During the year the village welfare committee made a few requests to the Welfare Ministry, but nothing happened, and the program fizzled out in a few colorful communications from Rangoon and Mandalay on the need for villagers to get behind the program of the ministry.

THE GAP BETWEEN SOCIAL AND POLITICAL ORGANIZATION

The gap between villager and government program is patent, and the source of what I have called multiplicity equally apparent. A village community, with a network of regional social relations, a local power structure, and a household level economy has a piecemeal, case by case, cycle by agricultural cycle, election by election view of its economic and political possibilities. Most people cannot be committed to plans and programs over which they have little control, whose implementation and direction depend on powers they little influence. They must exhibit the peasant caution for long-range schemes; they must see first the immediate benefit to themselves; they must be involved in plans and activities that further immediate, not remote, goals. They are pragmatic in the context of their relations with government and grasping in their relations with administration and services.

On the other side, government and politics are mixtures of nation building and personal aggrandizement. The symbolic content of most programs is the outcome of a real search for the meaning of a modern Burma, the urgent drive to find a political and economic system expressive of Burma, the swaddling nation. Much of the message of political talk is, then, the mere communication of confidence among Burmans that they will make a sort of society that will be the "happy prosperous land," worthy of their peculiar genius. As deep as this appeal is to both peasant and cosmopolitan, no society is greatly affected by the mere exhalation of breath or the circulation of symbolic currency. Action must ensue from these. And in Burma, most of the political action follows the route of self-aggrandizement. I do not know, nor can I judge from what I read, just how much of a factor this is on the level of the nation, but it certainly is the motive force for local politics. Villagers act as though it were also the motive of all politicians they meet.

This multiplicity of organizational structure and goal orientation is not irreducible. Continuing programs aimed at real, achievable village goals would reduce it greatly. But the major task is the achievement of continuing sets of legitimate political relations, independent of the concrete individual at the center, and relying on the conventions of citizenry rights possessed by individuals, irrespective of political allegiance.

The bases for these transformations are not immediately apparent, and their course is something Burmans will have to work out for themselves as they make their history. But some of Burma's real assets in working toward a regime of civil liberties and representative institutions capable of promoting modernization cannot be overlooked. They include: a real dedication to nationhood, the absence of a hereditary caste or class system, the easy political and social mobility, the communality of culture (at least for the two-thirds who are Burmese), the religious orientations in Buddhism, and real pride and delight in customs and things Burmese. The optimism of the peasant, his ability to solve many of the problems of his daily life, and his abilities to weather tyrannies, could also be counted as strong positive assets.

Burma's course toward modernization in politics and economics is uncharted, hazardous, uncertain, but it is not a course of complete darkness, without hope of success.

4

Buddhism, the Meaning
and Organization of Religious Life

Buddhism is a pervading force in Burmese society. Even to the casual eye, the hillsides dotted with pagodas, the hosts of saffron-robed monks, and the innumerable monasteries proclaim the strength and depth of Buddhist belief and practice in Burma. In Nondwin, everyone is a Buddhist, and as far back as memory and record go, its people have always been Buddhists. The distinction made by literary scholars and philosophers between the so-called Hinayana (little vehicle) and the Mahayana (great vehicle) forms of Buddhism is absent from village vocabulary. The term Theravada (religion of the elders) is known to some of the monks, but is not part of common parlance. The Buddhism of Nondwin is the most general framework for the interpretation of the world, the explanatory device for understanding the flow of events, the symbolic system for attribution of ultimate meaning to life and death, and the standard and guide for moral action. Buddhism is not a separate compartment of belief and practice, but a system of symbols, psychological attitudes, and ritual behavior forming the warp against which the woof of daily life is woven.

For the villager, there is no single word or idea corresponding to religion or to Buddhism. If you ask, as I did, people what they believe in, or why they do what they do in devotion and ritual, you get the manifest designation of the religious sphere. A villager replies *"bokda batha"* to the question of religious belief. This means that he tries, within the limits of his knowledge and temperament, to follow the path that the *Shin Hpaya* (Lord Buddha) taught. There are, of course, great differences among villagers in knowledge and in devotion to the middle way to salvation. But there is no public disbelief, and, so far as I could learn, no scepticism. Everyone appears to subscribe to, and honor, and hold convictions as to the truth of the teaching of the Buddha, and hold that the following of this teaching is the moral path, the aim of existence, and the highest unquestionable good. I do not mean to convey the notion that the villagers of Nondwin live with a spiritual consciousness that is forever honed to a razor's edge, or to give the impression that the mundane, ordinary business of living does not consume most of the time, thought, and energy of the people of Nondwin. I mean to say that Buddhism, as the villagers understand it, is the master artifice for giving unity, coherence, and meaning to their personal lives and to the world in which they live.

The consensual elements in village Buddhism are the pieces of knowledge, belief, ritual, and practice that every villager shares. It is these elements which are Buddhism at the village level. There exists, among some monks and some adepts, specialized pieces and bits of lore and knowledge, but these are in the realm of expertise. There is the great tradition of the Pali Canon, the learned monks and abbots in nearby Sagaing and the famous teaching centers in Mandalay where the *Tipitaka* (the three baskets of the Pali Canon of Theravada Buddhism) are conned and expounded. But this great tradition of scholarship and knowledge hardly touches the village monk or the villagers. It forms the backdrop and historical continuity against which village Buddhism is formed, but it does not directly nor immediately influence village belief and practice. This lack of impact comes about from the ordinary Buddhist's position in questions of belief, and, more importantly, from the way the *sangha* (the brotherhood of monks) is organized. This I shall explicate later in this chapter. Now I want to describe the religious thought and action that make Burmese Buddhism a part of day to day living, a feature of ordinary life as distinguished from a body of precept and dogma found in the palm leaf books of the monasteries or in the stone at the shrines at the foot of Mandalay Hill where Mindon had the entire Tipitaka chiseled into rock slabs as the crowning achievement of his reign.

THE MEANING OF RELIGIOUS LIFE

Kan and Kutho

Elsewhere (Nash, 1963) I have sketched the form and content of village belief and practice in Upper Burma. The major ideas of village Buddhism rest on three pieces of knowledge: first, the ideas of kan and kutho; second, the notions of the precepts and their observance; and finally, the folk version of the levels of existence and bits of cosmology that are entailed. Each of these ideas is complex, made up of many stranded assumptions and assertions, and deeply involved with philosophical and ontological nicety. But for the village they are the matters of fact which define and map the nature of religious reality and the human condition. Kan is the bundle of ideas tied in with destiny, fate, luck, and life chances. It means to the villager the whole sum of his past deeds, the moral balance of good and evil which goes on from existence to existence, now taking one corporeal form, now another. A person's kan is strengthened by adding kutho and weakened by accumulating *akutho*. Kutho is merit, and akutho is demerit. Some people have *kuthokan kaunde*, a good destiny and proper moral balance, while others have *kuthokan makaumbu*, a bad fate or a preponderance of past bad deeds over merit earning activities. Kan and kutho are not esoteric to the people of Nondwin, and expressions like kan makaumbu, not good kan, are used frequently to explain a misfortune or ill luck. For many outcomes to uncertain ventures, the jingle *kan ame, kan aphe*—kan is the mother and father of what befalls us—is the usual motto.

Kan is the product of individual effort. Every person has built his own store and quality of kan. Only he can add to or subtract from it. His own spiritual state is his own work. This particular life is the result of all previous lives, of all previous good deeds and misdeeds. And this particular existence is an opportunity to add to or subtract from the individual moral nucleus which will be reborn in some form in another existence. So everyone in Nondwin knows that he is responsible for his own state and his future states. But this does not weigh heavily on a villager. First of all, this life is but one wedged in among countless past lives and unimaginable future ones. There is not very much that can be done in a single existence to really shift drastically the amount and quality of a person's kan. Second, getting kutho and building kan do not require heavy interior strain or special devotion, but, rather, straightforward activity and simple observance. They do not require special insight, knowledge, or religious experience. Third, kan, in this life, is not a steady single force operating in an unremitting direction. People's fortunes and luck fluctuate, and so does their kan. Sometimes the good predominates and sometimes the evil does. Whichever is ascendant, only time and the actual course of events discloses, and the discovery of one's full destiny is hardly worth losing sleep over. It is much more fruitful to build and determine kan. Kan, then, is inscrutable and invisible, but individuals determine what sort and how much of it they have through the things they do, say, and think, while they are alive. Everyone who is a human being already has a considerable amount and a favorable sort of kan. Being born in the human state means that the kan has been auspicious enough to avoid the nether worlds of the Buddhist hells, the animal states and other lesser rebirth possibilities. The saying of the Buddha, that it is easier for a needle to fall miles from the sky and land point upright in a heap of grain than it is to be born in human form, gives some idea of the favorable condition of those already human.

The villagers do not hunger to be reborn in the higher states of Buddhist possibility. The thought of the final stage when rebirth no longer takes place—Neikban, as the Burmese call Nibbana, the blowing out of desire that causes rebirth—is remote from villagers. Mention of it as a possibility only elicits smiles. Nibbana is something that the Buddha (three previous Buddhas, Gotama the fourth and historical Buddha, and the fifth one Arimittiya now in the Tusita heaven awaiting the right moment to become manifest) only has achieved. It takes millions of years, and a movement through all the possible states of existence. It is beyond the active desire and the expectation of any villager. When a man dies or is dying, however, he should hope for these exalted rebirths: (1) to be a Buddha, (2) to be a "right hand saint" of the Buddha, (3) to be a "left hand saint" of the Buddha, (4) to be a "saint," and (5) to be a "small" (nonpreaching) Buddha. These are not considered as being in the realm of probability for anyone; they merely declare the hierarchy of moral attainment through the human, to the *devas*, to the approximation of the full enlightenment of a Buddha. The converse of the exalted births, the hells, the suffering monsters, and the animals, are asked to be avoided. These too are not active probabilities for most villagers, although the animal state is a strong likelihood for confirmed and continual takers of life—human and nonhuman.

The understanding of how kan is built, how kutho is earned, is the direct route for the interpretation of belief and practice of village Buddhism. But before this is described more must be said on the cosmological notions of the villager so that the activities and beliefs are in perspective. The cosmology and cosmography is a Burmese Buddhist version of an older Hindu set of beliefs. The villager does not refer to the written word for his version of the world, nor does the monk. The notions I give here are the common ones that every adult can give, not those set out in parts of the *Abhidhamma,* the books of higher learning, literally, after or beyond the *dhamma*, the teaching. The parallel with the English word metaphysics is virtually exact. Aristotle, when he finished writing *Physics*, added a book after or beyond *Physics*, and the *Abhidhamma* is to the teachings of the Buddha what metaphysics is to the natural sciences. When there was a misunderstanding on my part whether the worlds of existence were 31 or 32 in number, no villager could say which was correct. I went to talk with the pongyi. (The word *Bhikkhu* I never heard all the time I was in Burma, and when I mentioned it to some pongyis they said it referred to "old time" pongyis in the days when the Buddha trod the earth.) The pongyis did not know either. We consulted some books a pongyi had, and we saw that according to them there were 31 states of existence.

What villagers do know and what monks do teach are that there are three different worlds of existence. These *lokas* or worlds have their characteristic kind of life. The upper loka has 20 levels of *byama* (Burmese for Brahma: gods). These devas can never be reborn into the world of men. They are beyond that because of moral attainments in countless earlier existences. These devas spend lives of varied sorts of enjoyment, eating luxury foods, appropriating the young maidens that grow on trees for their sexual gratification, and generally indulging sensual appetites. They do not concern themselves with the mundane world of human affairs and are beyond entreaty or appeal. Sometimes, however, at certain rituals they are offered some food and respect by human beings. On the whole, however, they are seen as spending countless eons in joyful pursuits awaiting some slight chance to better their merit and move upward to the Buddha level, the level beyond, above, and without the world or, to say the same thing, encompassing and embracing all.

Below these 20 different grades of byama (which no one can name without consulting a book, and there is never need to make such consultation unless a curious foreigner like an anthropologist asks irrelevant questions like the levels name by name), there are six levels of nats. These are the so-called "Buddha nats" to distinguish them from a set of nat spirits which do play some part in the lives of the villagers. These spirits can be reborn as men or they may ascend to the levels above, but they have no contact with the world of men while they are nats. Sometimes they, too, get hortatory praise at shinbyu. Below these 26 levels, which together are the loka of the spirit or deva world, is the level of men, the world in which villagers physically exist. This is the level of existence, of birth and rebirth, the plane on which kutho and akutho are accumulated, where kan is formed. And lastly, there is the loka of the hells, where there are suffering animals, monsters, people in flames, and many sorts of punishments and inflictions to bear. This is the place of expiation for the lives badly led, and this is a possibility for those now in the loka of people. Among these various planes of existences the kan of a person may shift him, and he can spend countless existences in any plane. The hierarchy of existence is geared to moral attainment, to the state of kan.

In this sense, kan is closer to the English consciousness than it is to the idea of destiny. Some sort of consciousness goes from material embodiment to material embodiment. This is a puzzling idea to a non-Buddhist. Villagers claim, and the local monks support them in this, that no one remembers his past lives, that there is no individual continuity in the flux of birth and death. Only the Buddha is supposed to have full recall of previous lives. Yet, in Upper Burma tales are told of people who do recall their former lives, and I met a woman who claimed she knew me in a former life. When these tales of remembrance of lives past are told to or by the people of Nondwin, there is belief, not incredulity. When they are confronted by earlier statements that past lives are not open to memory, they shrug and give an explanation of "rare occurrence," a "phenomenon" entirely out of the ordinary. They do not trouble to reduce to consistency what appears to me, but perhaps not to them, as a glaring illogicality. So for villagers kan has the notion of consciousness attached to it, and there is a penumbra of ambiguity surrounding the idea of awareness. For on the manifest level they give the idea of anatta, no self, in the sense of no individual continuity with a time spanning awareness or consciousness, but in many acts and statements they behave as though some essence of awareness with temporal durability and a history goes on from existence to existence. The pure notion of no self, a difficult philosophical notion at best, is worked over by peasant experience into an idea containing possibilities of self and self-continuity. But the matter is not pressing and debate on it cannot be long sustained. For as each individual is the maker of his own kan (destiny and consciousness) so each person has a given ability to understand Buddhism. Not everyone has the same amount of understanding, or temperament, or knowledge. An individual understands or comprehends just so much of the profound words of the Buddha as his previous experiences and his moral state permit. If people differ on meanings or interpretations this does not give rise to theological debate, rather it is merely an indicator of the fact that people have different capabilities for absorption and comprehension of the teaching. This of course makes village Buddhism the sort of religion where factions, theological debate, questions of orthodoxy or heterodoxy cannot and do not arise. It is not so much that each man is his own temple, although this is surely true, but rather that each mind, each kan, each temperament is a particular sort of instrument for the refraction of the truths the Buddha enunciated. And because the individual prisms diffuse different parts of the spectrum, no one believes that there are many different truths and teachings, only that there are necessarily many sorts and grades of approximating the truth. What I have said here in abstractions, the village puts in proverbs and pithy sayings: "Each head its own world," "You cannot see the effects of kutho, for it follows you like a shadow," "Though you build a house with posts of iron, if your kan is not good it will collapse," and many others.

A world of unremitting account, where kan is the balance sheet of moral attainment, is summed up in stories like this about Duthana-thaw.

There were four rich young men. They were rakes. They spent their time and their money in the continual pursuit of women. One day they met a bullock cart driver, and they asked him to procure them a beautiful woman. For this they would give him 1,000 kyats. The cartman found them O Ma Dan Di. When they saw her, they fell madly in love. But she was virtuous and would permit them nothing. O Ma Dan Di had been very good in her former lives, so she had the gifts of great beauty (described as eyes like a deer, slender body, firm thighs, good teeth, and hair that glistens), modesty, and moral behavior. She would not give in to the four rakes. They, for their chasing of women and especially for trying to debauch O Ma Dan Di, went to hell. There they burn for their lust. And even their greatest sexual desire was never gratified, yet the flames scorch them below.

A story about Ananda is also current and common and illustrates again the levels of existence and the implacable universe taking accurate account of what a man is, does, and has thought.

When Ananda (here called younger brother, not cousin of the Buddha) was a man he worked as a goldsmith. A woman came to his shop to order a gold chain. Ananda was smitten by her and fell wildly in love. He knew she was married, and that she was virtuous and would not willingly lie with him. He planned to rape her by devising a ruse to lure her into his house. He told her the chain she ordered was done and to come to his house to get it. When the woman came he told her the chain was upstairs in a locked box, and he gave her the key and told her to go upstairs. She went. He followed and assaulted her. For this act he went to *ngaye* (the bottom layer of hell) for many years.

He returned to the human world as a woman, then he was reborn a man, then he was reborn a neuter. Then he became a being that had to kiss other men's anuses. Next, he was a leper, and a madman. After all of these sufferings he paid, and he was reborn Ananda, brother of the *hpaya*.

The hierarchy of states of existence governed by kan is set into a physical geography, having as its ultimate source the same Hindu background as the levels of beings. On earth (*pahtawi*) are the living things, plants, animals, men, all of the metal bearing rocks and soil, and the hells. On this flat earth are four continents. Above the earth rises a high mountain, *Myinmodaung*. Above this mountain are the levels of existence higher than human. The four continents spreading out from the base of Myinmodaung are the East, West, North and South continents. They are also called in speech right (South), left (North), front (East), back (West) continents. The front and right continents are where there is mingala (auspiciousness), and so East and North are preferred directions in ritual and in sleeping and in other more important activities, while West and South are not auspicious and are associated with death, cooking, and other lesser activities. The sun and the moon rotate around the middle of the high mountain, while the earth is stationary. Night and day are caused by this rotation around Myinmodaung, and the phases of the moon occur from the shadow the mountain casts. The stars move in an orbit at right angles to the sun and moon. They go over and under the mountain, and that is why they are sometimes visible and sometimes not. The South continent is the abode of living men. In the North continent are living beings, nearly as powerful as nats (of the upper levels), for these beings need only ask or wish and they have granted to them their desires. This is known because there is a tale of a girl from the South continent who married (in mythic times) a *Zawdika* (man from the North continent). Whatever she wanted, she merely asked for and received, such as a house of gold, studded with precious jewels. In the North jewels are in such abundance that they use them to make light, and the weather and temperature are under Zawdika control. Nothing is known for sure about the East and West continents.

In the continent of people (South) are five big rivers and they all flow into the four oceans that surround the continent. Five hundred smaller rivers flow into the oceans, which are filled with crocodiles, fish, prawn, snakes, and seven kinds of precious stones. Each of the four continents has its complement of four oceans, five rivers, and five hundred lesser streams.

This cosmology and cosmography is the setting for understanding much of what goes on in Buddhism, in nat worship, in medicine, in divinatory and predictive systems, in choosing directions of travel, and in distinguishing auspicious from inauspicious occasions. It will be seen in fuller play when these systems of behavior are later described.

One further thing caps the cosmology of Nondwin people. This is an apocalyptic vision. The apocalypse is the end of the present world and the coming of the fifth Buddha to begin the next world. The next Buddha, Arimittiya, is now in one of the levels of nat (upper) country. The present Buddha, Gotama, founded an era of 5,000 years' duration. It is now just about half over. At the end of the historical Buddha's reign, there will come increases in immoral behavior and increasingly bad times. People will start to die younger and younger. They will fall away from the teaching, and finally they will live no more than ten years of age. Then they will begin to live longer, to be more and more moral; prosperity will become the norm again. And then the next Buddha will arrive and his virtue or reign will sustain the world for one million years. Then the cycle of falling away from the morality of the middle way, decreasing span of life, and bad times will begin again, and there will appear in the sky seven suns at once and the world will forever end. Every living thing will at that time be born for eternity into the level of existence it merits. This vision of the cycle of the world and its ultimate disappearance does not affect behavior in the way that other parts of the world view do. It is much less like the Christian notion of the Second Coming, which at times can and does flare into an active hypothesis, than it is like the second law of thermodynamics, where the tendency to entropy makes no difference to plans, hopes, or activities.

The whole world view, in its bearing on activity, can be summed up in the continually heard refrain: *aneiksa, dokhka, anatta*—change, suffering, no self. This is a shorthand for the truth of the middle way; it sums up what the Buddha discovered at his moment of enlightenment beneath the Bo tree. For the idea of change, the villager can give a host of examples and analogies: the wearing out of houses, the facts of life and death, the shifts in fortunes of men and peoples, the decay of some, and the growth of others. For suffering, he can tell of pain, of death, of frustrated desire, of money lost, of hope unfulfilled, of meanness, and of murder. And for no self he has the analogies from the *suttas*, especially the tale of the wheel and chariot, from the questions of King Milinda, which is a popular exposition of this point. Most villagers have a string of 108 beads (tied to the 108 marks of the Buddha) or a shorter string of 32 beads (for the 32 teeth of the Buddha) which they finger, bead by bead, mumbling half aloud or silently, aneiksa, dokhka, anatta.

The middle way, bokda batha, the true wisdom, is a means of ultimately breaking out of the cycle of change and pain and false attachment to an ego. But it is proximately the chief guide to morality and the bench mark against which the building of kan, the unending accumulation of kutho and akutho go on. The main teaching is embodied in the *Mekgin Shitpa*, roughly translated as the Eight Virtues, and more commonly called by non-Buddhists the Noble Eightfold Path. The full eightfold path cannot be given by some villagers, for knowing it verges on specialist knowledge of monks and those who have spent some time in monasteries. The noble truths are embodied in the aneiksa, dokhka, anatta formula. The eightfold path of virtue is: right belief, intention, speech, conduct, livelihood, effort, mindfulness, and concentration. It is a virtual waste of time to speak to the ordinary resident of Nondwin about what these entail. He will only parrot what a monk has said in a sermon, or what he has learned as a novice, or perhaps read in a book like *Popular Heresies in Buddhism*, or *The Philosophy of the Abhidhamma*. These books in fact are present in Nondwin and nearly ubiquitous in the Mandalay region, for they were authored by monks in Mandalay.

The action aspect of the Mekgin Shitpa are the five precepts. The precepts, not to kill, not to steal, not to engage in sexual misconduct, not to lie, and not to cloud the brain with intoxicants, constitute the minimal code not to be violated. Violation brings in its wake akutho, and breaking the first precept is the worst form of getting akutho. If a villager does not observe the precepts, he does not sin, for these are not divine commandments. What he does is to move his moral balance in the wrong direction, making it more difficult for him to find the perfect peace. Observing the precepts builds good kan and also has the daily life effects of making one generous, without strong craving, respectful of elders, attentive to pongyis, and generally well regarded by one's neighbors. The five precepts are binding on daily life, and most of the people of Nondwin say them aloud once a day, as a sort of vow to observe them. The precepts are usually taken in front of the house altar and said aloud. They need not be said at all, just thought of, and there is no particular place where the vow is more or less binding. On special duty days (*ubonei*) tied to the phases of the moon and occurring four or five times in a calendrical month, some of the people of Nondwin take the eight precepts, and some even make a tenfold vow to themselves. The eight precepts add these three to the daily five: a vow not to eat after noon, to abjure cosmetics, flowers, perfume, music, and dancing, to refrain from sitting on high places and to avoid sleeping in a luxury bed. These added precepts are binding only for the day they are taken. In the seasons of heavy agricultural work, few people go to the kyaung on ubonei, and fewer still take the additional vows. In the many times I went to the kyaung on duty day for a short visit, I never saw more than a handful there to take the added vows, and these were chiefly the older and economically inactive villagers.

In addition to the five precepts which all the villagers, or nearly all, say daily, there is a common devotional said either before retiring or upon arising. The chant that usually opens all gatherings of Buddhists, whether or not pongyis are present, follows. I give my translation here because it is a tidy way of presenting some of the basic symbols and beliefs of village Buddhism. The *Awgatha* (from its introductory words asking permission to offer respect and devotion) is often called by villagers the "wheel of life," or whole world prayer.

Awgatha, Awgatha.

In words, deeds, thoughts, in these three things I have erred. Let me be rid of all the angers and passions. I take refuge in the Buddha; I take refuge in the monkhood; I take refuge in the teachings. To the Buddha I am offering respect with hands clasped, bowing, adoring, humble in devotion to the Buddha.

As I have adored spare me the fourth level (of hell in which rebirth is in the form of a monster), spare me famine, killing, disease; spare me the eight calamities (being mute, deaf, stammering, blind, mad, crippled, lacking concentration, and feeble-minded); spare me the five evils (flood, fire, kings, thieves, and enemies). Let the four lacks of virtue (failure to carry out precepts, to know the noble truths, to do one's duty, and to spend money foolishly) be behind me. From all these harmful things may I be protected. Rather let me walk on air, believe firmly (that I can work out my salvation with diligence), be free of desire and reach Neikban (the blowing out of desire). O may Lord Buddha grant that I avoid evil and seek Neikban.

This devotional utterance, plus some repetition of the well-known *Mingala Thok*, some parts of the heart and diamond suttas, some of the *Jataka* tales, analogies and explanations from part of the Pali Canon, and the omnipresent intonation of the Triple Jewel (I take refuge in the Buddha, I take refuge in the monkhood, I take refuge in the teaching), encapsulates the cosmology for the villager. They are the true collective symbols which enable one to encounter and think about Buddhism.

Buddhist Giving. But the chief activities involved in being a Buddhist are those concerned with giving, with observing the annual ritual round, and with sustaining the monkhood. The building of kutho is tied to the act of giving food, alms, help, hospitality, buildings, time, and thought. Kutho is also accrued from observance of the precepts, from meditation, from devotion, and from pilgrimages. But it is the first agency and activity, the voluntary gift without ulterior motive or immediate advantage, that for the people of Nondwin is the fount of kutho. Meditation is too specialized an activity, except for the old who have few duties, or those in monasteries who have that as a duty, or sometimes for a person in trouble who may take a few days to meditate. The full form of meditation, involving seclusion, the use of a *kasina* device to focus concentration, the breathing exercises, and the achieving of "one pointedness" of mind, is beyond most villagers. Devotion is ordinary, takes place before the house altar, and gives some bits of kutho. The giving of cooked rice to the Buddha image or picture, the recitation of the devotionals, the fingering of the beads, the chanting of aneiksa, dokhka, anatta, the Triple Jewel, all do their part in building kutho. But these things act almost to keep the kutho in what a villager thinks of as nearly a "steady state." They keep him from backsliding, from accumulating akutho, from turning to evil words, deeds, and thoughts.

It is the act of freely offered giving that positively adds to kutho, that makes the increments of morality into a heap of goodness, an engine of destiny that can move a person into a better plane of existence. Now both giving, meditation, devotion and even pilgrimage have the same kind of ultimate effect. By sacrificing something of the self, by concentrating on something other than the self, the bundle of sensation and desire that is the self is purified, made less demanding. In this sense kutho is a refining process of smelting out of the person those elements that tie him to mundane concerns. The villager tends to think of kutho in amounts, in heaps, in quantities, but it is a sort of negative thing: the more kutho, the less the self is that sort of self which has the attachment to those things appealing to the craving for the fruits of the phenomenal world.

Giving, then, can be seen as the means, the positive volitional acts of building kutho, of refining the nature of the self. The act of freely giving is in a strict sense the Buddhist rite of sacrifice. For I view religious sacrifice as nothing other than the offering of one's self in exchange for religious fulfillment, for that sense of unity with whatever it is that makes the universe what it is. Sacrifice need not be total;

one can give parts of the self, or things the self is attached to, or even the dreams of the self, or intermediaries for the self. In this sense sacrifice is a graded system of merging identity with a cosmic consciousness. Both the temporal duration and the amount of self that can be merged, of course, differ from world view to world view. In the end the successful Buddhist makes a complete and total, everlasting merger in Neikban. Giving is the lowest rung, but it is an absolutely necessary one in this process of sacrificial merger with the universe. It is the activity supremely open to the householder, the ordinary Buddhist, and by itself, in Nondwin view, may inch one along the path to Neikban.

Kutho garnered from any act of giving cannot be, and is not, calculated in actual units, but there is a hierarchy for the act of giving and a hierarchy of persons given to. The hierarchy of meritorious acts of self-sacrifice is:

1. to build a pagoda
2. to give a shinbyu (act as sponsor for a novice monk)
3. to build a monastery (and donate it to a monk)
4. to donate a well or bell to a monastery
5. to give a hsungywe (to feed a group of monks)
6. to feed and give alms to monks
7. to feed and give hospitality to laymen

In order of merit or kutho accumulation these are the ranked statuses:

1. presiding monk of a monastery
2. pongyi
3. koyin (novice)
4. nun
5. lay person

Exploring the acts and statuses in giving will make clearer the role of volitional self-sacrifice in a village like Nondwin.

Building a pagoda is the highest act of sacrifice. The Burmese word for pagoda (they do not know the form pagoda) is hpaya. Hpaya also refers to Buddha, with the prefix Shin for lord, and may be used in address to an absolute superior like a great monk or a very high government official. Hpaya carries then the connotation of the highest act of self-abnegation, while it honors the sacrificer by allowing him to contact the most exalted embodiments of the sacred. To be the sponsor of a pagoda is such a great act of kutho, in addition, because it implicates most of the other acts of giving: it requires feeding of monks, it requires feeding of laymen, it is preceded by several hsungywe, and only a man who has already sponsored several shinbyu would do it. Further, although building a pagoda is an individual act, it entails wide cooperation in Nondwin. The cooperation is in the upkeep of the pagoda (perhaps the family will be involved, or, in pagodas larger than any Nondwin is ever likely to build, a board of community trustees), in the celebration each year of the pagoda festival, which is community and supracommunity wide, and in the constant repair and gilding of the pagoda as wind, sun, rain, and time erode it.

The countryside of Upper Burma is heavily dotted with pagodas in ruins or in advanced states of decay, untouched for generations. From the knowledge gained in Nondwin of what the building and upkeep of a pagoda means, I can understand why so many towering heaps of brick, mortar, and rubble are allowed to gently slide into shapeless mounds. A man will be the builder or sponsor of a pagoda only at one point in his life: when he believes that his kan is at its peak of strength, when he can give this greatest offering at the height of his secular and spiritual power. Although any kind of pagoda will do (from wood, to the stone and gilt of the great ones like the bell-shaped pagoda outside of Sagaing, or the Arakan pagoda, or the *Shwe Dagon*), the actual hpaya built reflects a man's estimate of the height of his pon, his kan, and his wealth. So people hold off until the right combination appears. It was even so in the courtly period when kings built pagodas. They always conceived of projects larger than they could handle. The rationale was that their pon, kan, and the prosperity of the kingdom would grow to meet the demands, and the given monarch considered himself as on his way to being the always hoped for universal ruler, or the Buddha to be. This accounts for many of the partially finished acres of royal efforts to build virtual cities of pagodas.

Furthermore, a pagoda is conceived of as an individual act of giving. It should be tied to a name, to a person. So if a man in fact has the funds and the feeling of pon and kan, he is not likely to want the lesser merit involved in repairing someone else's pagoda; he will build his own glory. And, finally, a pagoda needs some sort of social group to give it continuity. Its care must be laid on either relatives and the community at large (the only feasible means in Nondwin), or, as in the earlier days on pagoda slaves tied to its maintenance (there are still descendants of such slaves in attendance at the Arakan pagoda), or in the larger communities on a board of trustees who see that the pagoda is kept up.

Because pagoda building is tied to an individual at the height of his pon, kan, and wealth, because he wants his name attached, he builds new ones rather than care for old ones. And because the care of a pagoda requires some sort of continuous social entity, and social groups die out over time (like dynasties, families, and communities), many pagodas have no one to keep them up.

In Nondwin there is a single major pagoda, built four generations ago. There is one smaller pagoda built by U Sein Ko about eight years ago. His smaller pagoda cost for the actual building 6,500 kyats and another 1,000 kyats in the hsungywe and upkeep. It is not yet topped with the final hti and so is not yet a finished pagoda. U Sein Ko, like the kings of old, leaves himself some room for the burgeoning of greater fortune. And since it is not in a finished state, it has neither an annual celebration, nor does the community pay attention to it, nor does anyone but those U Sein Ko hires from time to time do anything about its upkeep.

The pagoda, to the East of Nondwin, is both a community and a family responsibility. There is, in Nondwin, a Buddhist Association. This Association plays a part in all the rituals and ceremonies in which more than relatives or neighbors are involved, in rites and celebrations that draw on funds from all the households. The Association is organized with a president, a second president, committee members, and a treasurer. The treasurer of the Association (one of the big rich of Nondwin) is responsible for the gathering of personnel and funds for the celebration of the annual pagoda festival. This year (1960) the pagoda festival fell on the 17th of November, but it always falls on the "dead" moon of the month of Tazaugmon, whatever its calendar date is. On the day preceding the actual pagoda festival, a hsungywe is given in the name of Nondwin. The treasurer writes letters of invitation asking 12 monks to this hsungywe. The monks are invited from Legyi, Nyaungbinhla, Mondaw, Nyanbintha, and Nyaungbinwin, in addition to Nondwin (where there are only two, one in each of the village monasteries). This is the inner "circle" of about a seven-mile radius from which the people of Nondwin usually invite monks to hsungywe. The outer "circle" is about 20 miles in radius and does not of course reach the exalted abbots of Sagaing or Mandalay. The monks, if they are well, without previous engagement, and able to move, are obliged to attend a hsungywe when they are summoned.

The monks come to Nondwin to take the morning meal at about

11:00 o'clock. They assemble in the house yard of the Association treasurer, and they dine on food that had been collected earlier from the villagers. This small hsungywe is a miniature of all the larger and smaller feedings of monks in a group. It is a standardized hsungywe, and the only differences from one to another lie in the number of monks and their accompanying koyin or kyaungtha, the elaborateness of the food offered, and the number who stay to hear the final sermon.

The monks are seated on boards, on a raised dais about three feet higher than the laity, who sit at the monks' feet, on the ground. The monks are in the East (mingala or auspicious direction) and face West to the villagers. The men sit in nearly even rows close to the dais, and behind and to the sides of the men sit the women. The courtyard is virtually covered by straw mats, and people sit about drinking tea and chewing some of the fried beans or peanuts or pickled tea that are being served. Betel nut is chewed and cigars, of the country variety of *hseiboleik*, a cheroot made of tobacco and chopped parts of a tree, wrapped either in a corn leaf or a tobacco leaf, and plugged at the smoking end with a rolled corn shuck, are smoked. (This cheroot drops large pieces of lit ash, from the wood fiber, and smoking can be dangerous for a novice, who may, as I did, frequently burn holes in his clothing. The villager may carry around with him a used sardine can as a protective ash tray or use one of the small bowl-like Shan teacups for resting his cigar.) A few *hseibyinleik*, the full tobacco cigar, are available. For the monks soda pop is served as well as tea, and they may even get a few cigarettes. Since about 7:00 A.M. when the first monks arrived, people have been drifting in and out of the yard, drinking tea, chatting, smoking. At least one representative from every household comes. Nobody can, or wants to, opt out of this communal ritual. The villagers mainly talk among themselves, and the monks carry on among themselves with equally light-hearted and desultory conversation. As each villager comes into the compound he walks up to the dais, where the monks sit cross legged, one shoulder uncovered, and gives from one to three shikkoes. This the monks do not necessarily acknowledge unless they are spoken to. On leaving, the villager also approaches the dais to give a shikko.

There is in Nondwin an old man who is devotion leader. He is called "Neikban Pointer" in his official capacity. At about 11:00, standing to one side of the dais, he calls out "make ready." The bustle of tea-cups and the hum of chatter subside. The monks arrange themselves in a line facing the congregation, the elder and more venerable monks in the center, the younger ones at the flanks. They cover both shoulders and stop speaking and laughing. The congregation faces them in a kneeling position. The Neikban Pointer shouts out "Awgatha, Awgatha," and the congregation recites this devotional. Then there is a chant and response between the monks and the laity. First comes the Triple Jewel, then the five precepts. The *gadawbwe* (basket-like arrangements of banana, coconut, flowers, and fruits), placed earlier in front of each monk, are moved to one side by the koyin. The water blessing is offered. The Neikban Pointer (as community representative) gets on the dais with the monks and slowly, drop by drop almost, pours water into a brass bowl while the monks intone in unison the blessing that ensures merit from life to life, and gives some kutho to all who are present and all who have participated in this hsungywe. There is a short blessing given by the senior monk for all living things. He then gives a short sermon, most of which, like most sermons, concerns giving to the sangha, respecting the sangha, remembering that the sangha is the custodian of the dhamma and gives an opportunity to see the teaching being lived. With a series of *Thadu, Thadu, Thadu* (amen, or so be it), the hsungywe is formally over. The monks then eat their special festal curries, and those of the laity who stay on also eat. Ease, casualness, and informality quickly return to the courtyard.

The food for this hsungywe, as well as for the one the day after at the actual pagoda celebration, was donated by the households of Nondwin. The donations were scaled to public knowledge of the wealth of given households. There were three divisions of giving: the rich give food and bananas; the moderately wealthy supply food; and the poor supply bananas alone. The cost of food and bananas was 7 kyats: food alone 5 kyats and bananas 2 kyats. The total collected then was:

Rich 33 × 7 ky	231
Moderate 33 × 5	165
Poor 26 × 2	52
	448 ky

This was the first year that the costs of the pagoda celebration were apportioned among households. Hitherto, it was borne by a single household. This family was descended from the original builders of the pagoda and was in the category of *hpaya dayahka*, temple supporters. The genealogy that villagers give for the temple supporters follows. The pagoda then is four generations old, and, through all of the

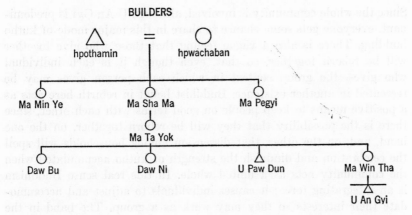

possible kin links, nearly 70 persons in Nondwin could be traced who fall in the category of temple supporter. But the responsibility falls on a brother-sister pair, and, since U An Gyi is in the rich category, whereas his other relatives are not, the burden and honor falls chiefly on him. The founders of the pagoda did not have Burmese names, and village opinion is divided as to whether they were from the Arakan or from the Shan plateau. Historical records are lacking, though my guess, on the basis of proximity of the Shan region and from the fact that Shans did from time to time in the past hold dominion over this part of Burma, is that they were probably Shans. They cannot say why the care of the pagoda descended through female links, and I do not know. U An Gyi's sister, responsible for the provision of tea, spent an additional 25 kyats for the celebration, so that the cost of the celebration was, in total, 473 kyats.

The food for the celebration was collected by the Buddhist Association. The young men of the Association with their musical instruments assembled in the treasurer's house for a march down the main street where each household would give its apportioned amount. For this march they assembled: a large gilt offering bowl (*hsundawgyiok*) carried by a cross stick on the shoulders of two young men, a large gilded betel box carried by one youth, gilt ornaments in the shapes of birds and flowers each large enough to necessitate being carried by one person, two gilt fans, and two gilded umbrellas. These things are the property of the East Pongyi Kyaung and are borrowed for the occasion. The paraphernalia are royalty and power symbols, and they express the royal style and the feeling of a major increment of kutho.

Since the whole community is involved, although U An Gyi is predominant, everyone gets some chance to share in this major mode of kutho building. There is also a vague feeling that those who give together will be reborn together, so that, even though it is each individual who gives, the group context in which each person gives may be recreated in another existence. Buddhist belief in rebirth here acts as a positive means to keep people on good terms with each other, since there is the possibility that they will be reborn together, on the one hand, and, on the other, that dissension among households will spoil the celebration and diminish the strength of kutho accumulated when the community acts as a united whole. In this real sense Buddhism is an integrating force; it causes individuals to adjust and accommodate their interests so they may work as a group. The band in the procession is made up of a heavy, triangular, brass gong, which is turned up at the corners and needs two men to carry it on a cross shoulder pole, a skin-covered drum, cymbals, a portable xylophone, wooden clapping blocks, and bamboo split clappers. This band, with its ornaments and a white banner with Buddhist Association written on it, moves down the street, and each housewife waits with her uncooked rice or meat or bananas and puts it in the large bowl. Nobody is asked; the band procession moves at its own rate and disbands at the end of the street.

As part of the celebration a group of women, in the household of a first cousin of U An Gyi, are cutting paper into flower-like patterns and are putting these ornaments on bamboo poles, to be later placed on the pagoda grounds. Some men come in and help with the making of decorations; they are distant cousins of U An Gyi, in the category of temple supporter. (No one will bother, for my benefit alone, to trace out the long links of bilateral kinship which put them in that category. It is enough, for them, to know that they are kinsmen and should help out.) The decorations add about 10 kyats to the celebration costs.

The pagoda itself sits at the eastern margin of Nondwin. Since it is in the basic form of most pagodas in the region, its features are worth noting. There is on the pagoda grounds a *tazaung*, a raised platform for placing images (none are in fact here) and a *zaiyat*, a covered pavilion for the congregation and the monks. The form of the pagoda, villagers say, comes directly from the words of the Buddha. They say that when the Buddha was leaving this existence, Ananda asked how he should be remembered, and the Buddha said, "Recall me this way," and he turned over his begging bowl and placed his staff atop it. The

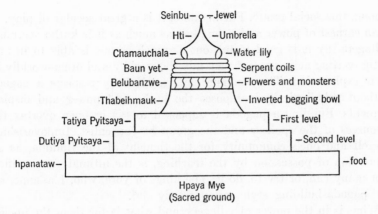

Hpaya Mye
(Sacred ground)

additions of the lotus motif, the monsters, flowers, and the coils representing serpents are elements plainly derived from the cosmology sketched earlier.

At the pagoda itself, the ceremony repeats the hsungywe held the day before when the monks arrived. At this event a few dances are performed by the dance teams of Nondwin. The dancers of Nondwin have costumes for the elephant dance and a sort of bird dance. The first are papier-maché elephants moved by dancers. The bird dance has a series of splendid gossamer costumes of various mythical birds. This dance group often goes to other villages for pagoda dedications or similar celebrations, when invited. They, for example, went to Nyaungbinwin and danced for a pagoda dedication. The village of Nondwin also contributed 60 kyats toward the placing of the umbrella and seinbu atop this pagoda.

This act of giving, the building of a pagoda, has been described at such length because it opens up some interesting paradoxes in the notions of sacrifice and of giving to get kutho. In the first place, for villagers, pagoda building is rarely a possibility, yet it is clearly at the top of the hierarchy of volitional giving. It is to be undertaken only at the height of one's kan, pon, and secular prosperity; it is a token that an individual is willing to give all for the act of remembering the Buddha, and it is a sign, or supposed to be a sign, that one is filled only with thoughts of the Buddha and his teachings. Building a pagoda is clearly the "royal style," the expression of kings and powerful men that they are approaching the fullness of the Buddha. But even this singular act of individuality requires the participation of a social group, and the kutho is shared out among, or diffused among, this social group. Furthermore, it is a great secular display. It is an earnest of power and strong kan as much as it is kutho accruing. Villagers say it is good to put out as much as one is able to in any kutho-getting activity, and they mix the worldly and other-worldly in their explanation. The common saying, "Nobody respects a pagoda without gold," nicely juxtaposes the kutho and power and display elements. Building a pagoda is supposed to tax or even overtax the resources of the sponsor and the group he can enlist. Impoverishing oneself and one's community for the thought of the Buddha, as an expression of possession by the teaching, is the ultimate in sacrifice. Not many can, or try to, do it. The kings of yore, who, I assume, set the pagoda-building style, often nearly did.

What is in the power of villagers, and what is for them the apogee of giving, is the shinbyu. The shinbyu is the ceremonial for the first induction of a young man into the monastic life. Every Burmese male in Nondwin has spent some time in the monastery as a koyin, and all have passed through the role of *shinlaung* (lord to be), as the boy is called when the shinbyu ceremony is underway. Shinbyu can be given at any time of the year, except during *Wa*. Wa is the rainy season, a period of three months, and is a holy time of the year. During this period, no celebrations are held, no marriages made, no plays given; monks are supposed to confine themselves to their kyaung, and pious laymen often go into retreat. When a boy is initiated into the novitiate, the time he actually spends in the monastery varies considerably. Sometimes it is no more than the minimum requirements of a single night or two. The older idea was to spend three Wa (a total of nine months) in the monastery—one for the Buddha, one for the father and mother, and one for the teacher. In Nondwin this idea was recently operative, for more than 85 per cent of the men in the village above 25 years of age had in fact spent three Wa seasons in the kyaung.

The village rationale for the shinbyu is both in the sacrificial and the mythological idiom, and these two meet, as do most Buddhist ceremonies, in the secular display attendant to kutho building and kan demonstration. The shinbyu also implicates a community as well as a particular individual (or more likely a married pair) in a common kutho-building activity. Shinbyu is held because it is the greatest giving a household can muster. It is the dedication of a son to the "homeless" life and thus makes the shinlaung much more eligible for higher existence. But, more importantly, it expresses the sponsor's willingness to sacrifice a very dear relationship for the sake of the propagation of the dhamma and to spend his resources to the utmost for this end. The community is summoned (and friends, acquaintances, and relatives from the outer circle of interacting villages) to witness and validate the giving, the devotion, the display, the wealth and power of the sponsors. Monks are invited to be fed, before, during, and after the shinbyu. All in all, it is the greatest event in both the religious and secular life of a family in Nondwin. These sets of meanings, these combinations of piety, display, vanity, and communal kutho, tell why the bare, simple, but totally acceptable sort of shinbyu has never been undertaken in Nondwin. A family or sponsor could make a shinbyu by the simple act of taking the shinlaung to a kyaung, having the monks carry out the ritual of shaving the boy's head, clothing him in monks' garments, and by leaving him there. Theoretically this is enough, but it does not contain the elements that, for the ordinary villager, make the shinbyu the climactic religious and secular event that it is. I only know of one case, that of a poor widow, in another village, without relatives to sponsor a shinbyu, where this minimal, if not inglorious, mode of holding a shinbyu was taken.

The content, as against the reason for the shinbyu, is dictated by the legend of the Buddha, and by another approximation to the royal style. Villagers in Nondwin have this much of the story in common (some people have many more elaborations on the basic plot and elements).

When the Buddha decided to take up the wandering, homeless life in search of salvation, he stole away from his palatial home in the dead of night. He took a gilded saddle and mounted his favorite horse. His faithful groom followed him on another horse, begging him to return. They rode together to the Kandiga river, and then Gotama sent both horses back with the groom. His horse died of heartbreak. The groom took the gilt saddle, but on the way back he decided too to take up the homeless, wandering life. Prince Gotama then thought about being an anchorite, and he thought that he did not need his hair, for it was only vanity and trouble.

If he became hpaya he would not need his hair, so he cut his hair off (this is why monks are bald of pate today). He made one condition when he cut off his hair. If he threw his hair into the air, and it stayed up, he would indeed become hpaya. The nats heard him, and when he threw his hair into the air it rose up into the sky. Now up in the sky the Sulamani pagoda houses the Buddha's hair (and it is to this place that the Thadingyut balloons released by villagers on this festival of lights are supposed to float upward to).

This shinbyu will be accompanied by a *nahtwin* ceremony. Like boys when they are inducted into the monastery, girls reach their ceremonial zenith in the nahtwin, or ear boring, ceremony. This is of much less religious importance than a shinbyu and is an accompaniment to the shinbyu. While her brother is shinlaung, her ears are bored, at the same ceremony. The shinbyu described here did not take place in Nondwin, but in nearby Ondaw. People from Nondwin were invited, and many went, as I did. I describe it here because U Sein Ko and others who went along with me to nearby Ondaw could tell me just what about this ceremony would have happened in Nondwin or not happened there, if a shinbyu had been given that year. And it will serve as a contrast to the shinbyu I saw in Yadaw, the rice growing community as contrasted with Nondwin, so that the extremes of rural society and culture in Upper Burma may be charted.

This particular shinbyu is rather larger than any likely to take place in Nondwin. In Ondaw (south) a certain Ko Aun Pe and his wife Ma Tin Nyunt are inducting at one time three of their sons, one nephew, and paying for ear borings for two daughters and two nieces. The nephew has been a koyin before at a very early age, under his own family's auspices, but it adds kutho to the sponsors to induct him again, although not nearly as much as at the very first induction and not nearly equivalent to that of their own sons. The lending of nephews and nieces for the shinbyu is common practice, and is done reciprocally, everybody involved getting some kutho from the transactions. Having the girls' ears bored under a rich man's aegis saves a family money, expresses solidarity with a powerful man, and loses no kutho for the girls' parents. The man and woman sponsoring this shinbyu are rich and well-connected. He is a rice mill owner, and friends and relatives came from Mandalay, Sagaing, Nondwin, Legyi, Ondaw, Ywama, Ywathagyi, Shanta, Konywa, Bagyi, Yedwingaing, Maledaw, Wethabot, Yaungbingaung, Nakayaing, Natayaw, Sadang, Yimagin, Chatmingyi, Ywathi, and Kyause. The outer circle of Ondaw is larger, spatially, than that of Nondwin. He spent 5,000 kyats, about 1,000 kyats more than the best that Nondwin had done (U Sein Ko had laid out roughly 4,000, he says, for his son's shinbyu and daughter's nahtwin). The settlement of Ondaw is welded into one cooperating unit for the shinbyu. Neighbors, relatives, coresidents take on the tasks of preparing food, serving tea to the guests as they drift in, setting the places to eat, laying out mats, putting up lean-to temporary shelters, and even housing visitors for a night or two.

The guests, from the outer circle and from Ondaw itself, are fed the best of Burmese festal cooking: *monhsikyaw, monlehgwin,* and tea (cake and tea served at odd times during the day), and a meal of dry fish, curry with coconut oil, and milk, dal soup, preserved bean stalks, chili powder, rice, ngapi, some pork curry, and some mutton curry. All this is washed down with "rough," or Shan, tea. The 21 monks who were invited get all of this plus some chicken curry, soda pop, and coconut rice. There are also, in abundance, garnishes and snacks of pickled tea, peanuts, roasted broadbeans, toasted sesamum seeds, bananas, and other fruits. With the noise of the crowd, the abundance of food, the music from the amplifier playing records, the hired band, the gay longyis, the flowers strewn about, a great illusion is created, a believable facade presented. This is the abode of royalty, truly a prince will be presented to the sangha, and everyone here swims on a high tide of kan and kutho.

This subjective impression is just what people strive for. The sponsors come over to U Sein Ko and ask him, point blank, if this shinbyu does not feel like a king's and is it not the height of fortune, of kan, and kutho.

For the ceremony itself, a *mandat* was built. The mandat is a cardboard and wood imitation of a palace. It was hired from Mandalay, and a *mandat hsaya* (mandat master) and his crew erected it on order from the sponsors. It is all gilt on the outside and studded with glass to resemble diamonds and rubies and emeralds. To enter it one passes through the wooden gilt open doorway. Inside, the mandat is divided by wooden posts into square sections, representing rooms off of the main throne room. At the end of the throne room is a dais, backed by a series of full length mirrors studded with the imitation precious stones. The compartments running off of the main room are seven on each side, each seven feet square, and the whole mandat is 49 feet square and about 13 feet high. Around the inner walls of the mandat, where the roof meets the walls, are a series of murals painted on cloth. These murals depict scenes from the legendary life of the Buddha, especially the procession inducting him into the homeless life. The floor is covered by straw mats, and everyone who enters removes his shoes and is greeted at the door by young village girls, wearing the flowers of fortune in their oiled, glistening hair, and is given a cheroot. The whole scene is an elaborate imitation of a royal palace set for the going away of a prince.

What I did not see this time, but what I know from informants and other shinbyus, was the part of the divination that preceded the ceremony. Astrologers were consulted on the basis of the horoscope of the shinlaung and the sponsors for a propitious time; a nat pole was erected before, on the spot where the mandat stands. These protective and divinatory systems I describe more fully in Chapter 5. The splendor of this occasion is paraded through the village, around it, and down the main road near it. The procession, for sheer display, is assembled in this way: a line of women carrying gadawbwe on their heads in porcelain pans, boys carrying gold umbrellas, the shinlaung on small ponies decked out with gilt harnesses and draped with brocaded cloths, a band of gaily dressed clowns beating loudly on bamboo clappers, a dancing girl with a band consisting of an oboe, gong, and xylophone, a clutch of girls in best clothing and with oiled tresses, carrying trays of flowers, two ox carts, decked with flowers, carrying the nahtwin girls and their friends, another band, and the villagers and friends bringing up the rear.

The procession, noisy, colorful and serpentine, winds through the village and around it. As we pass houses, people remark that it is good that a rich man spends his money this way, that it would be a scandal and a shame if he had been frugal with this aspect of display. At this point the shinlaung and the nahtwin girls are but pretexts for the splendid display of the power of the sponsors. The religious moment comes on the following day. In fact the shinlaung and the nahtwin girls look slightly bored or startled by the whole thing, and nobody pays much attention to them.

To add to the festivities a hired band arrived. This one is a typical Burmese festival band of the heavy cowhide drum which hangs from the patron monster of music, the *pyinsaupa* (a five-bodied animal welding together in one carving, the elephant, snake, buffalo, bird, and fish), the circle of talking drums, 21 of them of different sizes, a circle of cymbals, two bamboo clappers wielded by men who also double in shaking bells, a man with small bells who also clangs small cymbals and sometimes blows a whistle, and a *hne* (Burmese oboe) player. This band plays all day, most of the night, and through the actual ceremony the following afternoon. All this costs 350 kyats. The band plays inside the mandat; the loudspeaker blares nearby; and the noise, the movement, the chaffering, the dust, the crowds make it, for the Burmese, a truly happy time.

On the day of the actual shinbyu, the invited pongyis come at 5:00 A.M. They have hsungywe in the mandat, and they depart. The shinlaung are driven on their horses, accompanied by a bit smaller procession than yesterday, to the pongyi kyaung. They ride around the kyaung twice, while small boys from the kyaung cheer and sing out a poem. This ceremony is to keep away evil nats, who might be envious, and the Buddha himself, they tell me, is supposed to have performed this very ritual. The shinlaung dismount, enter the kyaung, and give gadawbwe and shikko to the two resident monks. This means that even a prince must respect a monk. The boys remount and ride in stately procession back to the mandat. The sponsor then carries a black begging bowl and a palm fan as he walks, in pride, holding the bridles of his sons' horses. The bowl and fan he presents to the shinlaung when the induction is completed.

At the mandat, the guests assembled, facing the dais on which the shinlaung and the *nattha* girls are seated with the band. Two *beiktheik hsaya* (Brahmins, or special talkers, masters of ceremony, court attendants) have come to officiate at this shinbyu. They are dressed in the Burmese version of a Hindu and wear in their gaung-baung gaudy imitation diamonds and emeralds, and from their necks hang imitation gold chains with paste diamonds and rubies. All this equipment is part of their trade, and they, not the sponsor, provide it. Behind the Brahmins are plates set with the offerings that are to be soon used in the ceremony. The offerings are cake, fish, betel, and dried fish mounds in the shape of small pagodas. Just beyond the offerings are the male and female sponsors, and off to one side of them are the grandparents of the shinlaung. The audience is distributed on the mats. The children are shunted off into the side sections.

One of the Brahmins prepares a sacred thread of seven strands of cotton. These they place around the necks of the boys and girls on the dais. Then they recite the chant to pacify evil nats, to lay envy to rest, to bring the witness of good guardians. The chant is loaded with extravagant metaphor, praise, and unction for the sponsors, the boys, the village, the guests. The Brahmins are hired because they have this smooth, flattering line of patter, because they can inflate the egos of the audience to equality with the facade and display where the shinbyu is being acted out. They are rewarded for their ability to be successful flatterers and rhetoricians. The chant they gave can be translated. (Translated roughly, that is, with some parts left out, for parts of what they said were swamped on my tape recorder by the band, by the loudspeaker. Since each beiktheik hsaya is a bit of an improvisor, no performance is exactly like any other, for like all good performers, they often get carried away by the performance. But what I give here is fairly standard, my informants assure me.) They call on the "most magnificent thing (Buddha), the golden complexion, the shining throat of the Buddha to fight off evil nats, the guardian angel of Neikban, the guardian angel of the earth, the guardian angel of the sun, guardian angels of the moon, guardian angels of the planets, the elephant nat." They then give thanks to the "owner of the elephant (my informants are not sure whether this is the king or the Buddha or both), the guardian nats of the world and the oceans," for whom they do these things. These are mingala repositories. "May all of you bless the shinlaung, the nattha, the sponsors, the guests, and keep away evil from them for ever. Thadu."

Then, there is a switch in mood; the serious is replaced by pure play. The Brahmins clown with each other and tell jokes; the laughter of the audience is their reward. They then turn to the circle of 21 drums and carry on a "conversation" with them. This is all standard. The beiktheik hsaya ask questions of the drums or make extravagent claims, or tell jokes, and a stereotyped roll or beat on the proper drum or drums is a response. To this the audience responds with hearty, punctuated laughter.

Then comes another shift in tone. The drums roll for quiet, and the Brahmins ask the boys and girls honored to remember to respect and thank the five important things: hpaya, dhamma, sangha, parents, and teachers. The shinlaung and the nattha are asked to *gadaw* (respect) and shikko to hpaya, father, mother, and grandparents. The Brahmins fill a conch shell with water and place a flower in the water. Bit by bit, they drip some water over the heads of the shinlaung and the nattha. The conch shell is the symbol of royalty, and the flower is the emblematic lotus for the perfect unfolding. The sacred threads are placed on each boy and girl. They are each offered a token spoonful of rice and curry. This they twice refuse. The Brahmins again call for honor to the parents and sponsors, fortune for the village. The boys and girls shikko once more. The Buddha and the nats are called to witness. The drums roll—end of shinbyu. The children in the wings scramble out, on the signal of the drums, for the food heaped near the Brahmins. The boys and girls leave the dais, the boys to ride in last splendor to the kyaung, the girls to melt with the crowd (they at this particular shinbyu did not get their ears bored, for they already had holes in them. They were part of the trim, the ornamentation of the ceremony).

People stay around drinking tea and being served, both in the mandat and the temporary shelters, the festal meal. The shinlaung return in about an hour. At the monastery they had their heads shaved; they were robed in the monks' garments and formally received by the presiding monk as koyin. They come now to sit on the dais for about 20 minutes. Then they are escorted, this time on foot, back to the kyaung, where they spend at least this night. The sponsor plans to leave them there only one week.

The following morning they return once more to the yard of their parents, where the monks of the village are at hsungywe, and the koyin receive their monastic names, used all the time they are in the kyaung. Most of the guests have dispersed; the band goes; the mandat is taken apart; the loudspeaker and records are gone; and ordinary life resumes. But before this, the hired photographer takes his pictures of the splendid display, of the assembled people in front of the mandat. The pictures will be part of the upper east room of the house, where the valuables, the Buddhist altar, and honored guests are kept.

At this shinbyu, each guest who came signed into a book kept by one of the villagers. Each guest contributed some money, from one to 25 kyats, and this was duly entered into the book. This money goes to the sponsors, and the nearly 1,500 kyats collected from the 250 registered guests go to offset part of his expenditure. For the guests, this is a chance for them to participate in the exalted shinbyu, to get some merit. For the host it makes for him a kutho community, as well as helps to pay off some of the costs. The book of guests is kept, and when these sponsors are invited to a shinbyu given by any of the guests, they will look into the book and see how much that guest contributed. They will reciprocate exactly, for to give more is to place yourself above the guest, to give less is niggardly and disprizes guest.

There is, I think, little need to recap the themes in the shinbyu, for the expenditure makes clear the notion of sacrifice, as does the presentation of a son; contributions, time, and help define the kutho community, and the actual ceremony calls on almost everything in the village pantheon: the Buddha, the upper nats, the lower nats, the world guardians, the dhamma, the sangha, the honored things, the moral behavior, and the proper conduct. All of this is set in a mixture of the sacred and the secular, the humble and royal, this world and the next; kan is built, secular honor earned; and the Buddha is served.

In the time I spent in Upper Burma, I never saw or heard of a bell or well or a monastery being given to the sangha, so my meagre report on these activities comes from informants who have witnessed, but not performed, them. These major gifts to the monastic order also need the flavor of strong kan, pon, and prosperity. One does not give a little bell or a shallow well, for the same reasons that a wooden pagoda is not built. The hsungywe, at least one, is always part of the donation, and a dance team with music provided by the battery-run loudspeaker may be affixed to a building on monastic grounds when the donation is made. These gifts share with the pagoda and the shinbyu the idea of total expenditure—the property goes to the monastery and only the name of the donor may linger; kutho is the chief yield. A community element is involved in the numbers of persons invited to a hsungywe, in the help given in cooking and cleaning accompanying the meal, and in the attendance at the kyaung when the donation is made.

So far, I have written of the occasional and spectacular acts of giving—those that may properly be undertaken when the donor feels the competence and devotion and has the means to initiate them. But giving is woven into the daily life of the community. This giving is tied to the upkeep of the brotherhood of monks. There is one spectacular giving for the maintenance of the sangha, called kahtein. Kahtein is the time to present to monks the necessities they need in order to live the monastic life. Kahtein can be individual, but there is usually a community organized kahtein. The Nondwin kahtein is held at the end of the first week in October, just a few weeks after the end of the Wa season, and it marks the opening of the secular part of the year. The feeding and equipping of pongyis is the proper thing to do before the cycle of pwes and worldly concerns come to dominate activity. This kahtein was organized by the Buddhist Association that collected money and rice from householders. The band, with the banner of the Association, marched down the main street. Four boys carried a large pole-slung basket in which they collected uncooked rice from those who could not give cash. The rice collected sold later for about 200 kyats. With the proceeds from the rice and with the cash collected, the committee for the Buddhist Association bought in the name of Nondwin some of the monks' necessities—the robes, straight razors, begging bowls, umbrellas, water filters, mats to sit on, sandals—but they also bought items that are not, in the strict sense, part of the eight items a monk must have. For example, they bought packets of tea leaves, notebooks, brooms, plastic colored tablecloths, and bars of cheaply perfumed soap. The whole outlay on the items purchased by the committee came to 225 kyats, plus another 5 kyats for the travel expenses of the committee, making this communal kahtein cost 230 kyats. The list of items and their prices was posted on a tree about midway up the main street of the village, and it was open to inspection by the people of Nondwin.

The goods purchased for donation are displayed in the yard of the treasurer of the Association. Volunteer children have built bamboo-lashed stands on which the goods are exhibited. Paper and real flowers and bits of colored ribbon and paper decorate the gifts and the stand. From time to time a gong is struck to summon villagers to come and look at the gifts they are making to the sangha. The loudspeaker plays records all through the night, and from time to time, all through the night, the gong is struck. On the day before any ceremony or celebration, villagers get little sleep, and the loudspeaker cracks out its loudest noise at daybreak of the celebration, so that the whole community will be up and doing what is needed for the ceremony.

On the day of the kahtein, the village goods are brought to the kyaung and displayed inside. There they are arranged on bamboo racks, some of which are shaped like trees, others more rectangular. In addition to the goods carried to the kyaung, villagers bring other individual gifts, and the monks' necessities now are swelled to include biscuits, towels, blankets, and kyats pinned to a "money tree." Although monks, in strict accord with *vinaya* rules, are not to receive, handle, or possess actual money, the kyat gifts have been common for more than a decade, and the monk with his purse is not an uncommon scene in the Mandalay market. The display at the kyaung is further accentuated by the addition of bananas, packets of sweet flour, and banana leaves arranged to simulate large floral designs. At this kahtein, about 150 villagers from Nondwin came to the kyaung. Again, the representation of at least one person from each household underlines the communal nature of individual giving. There is a hsungywe accompanying the actual turnover of goods to the monks. The goods are turned over by the Association representatives in the name of Nondwin. The laity thank the monks for accepting them and the monks make no reply. The meaning is clear; the monks do the villagers a favor by accepting gifts from them. They give the laymen an opportunity to sacrifice to a wholly worthy object. The monks, by receiving from villagers, acknowledge that the villager is trying to follow the Eightfold Path and endeavoring to refine himself through the act of volitional giving. In turn, the villager asserts, by giving, that the pongyi is the exemplar of the middle way, that he lives in accord with the highest strivings toward the total merger of self with the universe, and that he is worthy of the respect and honor of those who cannot, or do not, achieve this road to salvation. Together, the monks and the laity, in their give and take, reaffirm the teaching of the Buddha and give it a human and material base for continuity.

In inviting the monks to kahtein and hsungywe, villagers express their ranking of the virtue of a given monk and their estimate of his piety, learning, and mystical power. They will not invite, either to individual hsungywe, to kahtein, or to communal honoring of pongyis, any monk they do not respect, any monk they know not to be dedicated to the prescribed life, or any monk who has been involved in a public scandal. The frequency with which monks are sought and invited is an accurate barometer of village estimation of their status. A villager will treat any wearer of the saffron robe with the outward forms of deference (using the special language in addressing pongyis, giving the shikko on approach or leaving their presence, keeping the head lower than that of the pongyi, never showing the soles of the feet to a pongyi, and sitting in the proper direction when facing a monk), but his option to honor and to sacrificially participate in the upkeep of the sangha and, with it, the dhamma, he exercises in the business of inviting monks to special giving occasions and in the act of kahtein, in giving to a monk the wherewithal to carry on the homeless life.

Even though it is individual, particular monks who are invited and honored, the idiom of sacrificial giving demands that the gifts be to the sangha and not to particular members of the sangha. The fiction that the corporate group is recipient from an anonymous and grateful body of householders is maintained by a simple device at kahtein giving. All of the gifts on the bamboo racks and trees have numbers attached to them. The monks put their hands into the begging bowl provided, draw out numbers, and get the corresponding gift. When they take these things back to their monastery (the visiting monks from the outer circle all come accompanied by either koyin or kyaungtha, for it is unfitting for a monk to tote parcels or carry burdens), the presiding monk decides who shall receive what, and any maldistribution (like seven towels or three begging bowls or four razors for a given monk) is worked out in the kyaung.

The kahtein, after pictures are taken (some for the monastery, some for the village), is completed by the ordinary Buddhist devotional sequences: the precepts and response, the Awgatha, the sermon, the water blessing. Only the raffling off of gifts in public is novel. The monks then take their gift meal and depart, and the villagers and guests return to their homes.

The kahtein of Nondwin, although loaded with display elements, still has the feel and flavor of a sacrificial giving for the sake of kutho, for the display is mainly mirror-like; villagers see themselves giving and are doubly pleased by the image. In some larger communities, the secular display elements, the facade itself, has come to outweigh the meaning of the kahtein. In Ondaw, for example, the kahtein display was set up at a crossroads for a week in advance, for the passing world to see, and the vanity and ego of the people of Ondaw was set out for indiscriminate flattery.

In addition to this communal kahtein, four of the rich households of Nondwin gave individual kahtein to the monks in the following two weeks. The largest of these involved six monks (meaning four were invited from neighboring monasteries). My estimate of the costs was about 800 kyats for the four private kahtein.

One other element involved in kahtein is the marathon of *matho yekchin* or *matho thingan* (the early robe, or early weaving ceremonial). This is the drama of making five yards of orange cloth (sufficient for the upper part of a monk's robe) between nightfall and dawn, by weaving all night. In Nondwin, they must finish before 3 A.M., which is the conventional hour for dawning. The story accompanying matho thingan explains that the woven cloth, left in the center of the village, will be transported by an "angel" to the monastery, and, on opening his eyes, the recipient monk will see, first thing, this earnest of the piety of the community.

The drama recapitulates the activities that go into making a monk's robe. A mock planting of cotton, harrowing, tree growing, plucking, and ginning of cotton are performed in the afternoon. That evening, the cotton is brought to a large compound (at this time, that of a man who was not especially devout, but who happened to have a centrally located yard with plenty of room). Spinning wheels and a large loom are set up in the compound. Firelight and a pressure lantern provide the illumination. About 30 girls tend the spinning wheels and the loom. Girls take turns at the spinning and weaving. Every household that has an unmarried girl sends at least one representative. The unmarried girls, by their purity and innocence, add to the merit of the robe. The girls involved range between 13 and 20 years of age, with the preponderance about 14 to 16 years old. (Most of the girls, in fact, still wear the little girl's or maiden's hairdo with the front bangs, rather than the married or older woman's knot at the rear or side, and many still have their hair arranged in the tierlike partings that indicate prepubescence.)

The girls work in good coordination and without any visible supervision. They rotate jobs about every fifteen minutes, since they want peak performance. They pride themselves on the belief that they are the only village in their outer circle who will, in fact, complete the weaving of five yards of cloth before daylight. There is no such thing as an "outsider," and every girl present takes her turn either at the loom, the wheel, or over the large bonfire, where the starched thread is being dried (it is normally sun-dried).

Elders from the community are on hand to help, by giving preserved tea leaf snacks to the girls (this is supposed to fight sleep), by serving tea, and by roasting ears of corn (gifts from the villagers). There are a few boys about, on the peripheries of the firelight, but they do not flirt, or tease, or annoy the working girls. The loudspeaker is blaring, and I suppose that no one in the village is actually sleeping. The girls work all night and finish the cloth, and the following day it will be sent to the monastery. The cost of this ceremony is about 50 kyats, most of which (30 kyats) goes to pay for the loudspeaker.

This ceremony again shows the territorial and communal aspects of kutho, in the whole village participation, and reminds people that, for maximum kutho to be in their reach, they need each other, even though kan and kutho are individual affairs.

This ceremony comes at the time of the Buddha's day (November 2, 1960, described above) and is accompanied by other individual and communal gifts or expenditures. The pagoda is lighted with candles, each person bringing a few or many. But one man (the rich son of U Sein Ko) spent 100 kyats on candles and got his whole family to come to the pagoda and spend a few hours that night in the lighting of them. He was honoring the Buddha, the pagoda, and also building kutho. He needed a special increment of kutho, for his wife was pregnant, and she had had two miscarriages, so he wanted to build kan and kutho on her behalf to tide her over the coming birth. This notion of "instant" or, more properly, "emergency" kan and kutho is widely prevalent in Nondwin. It is a magical element villagers find in their Buddhism. The purely rational cause and effect, slow build-up of moral fibre and exalted consciousness cannot meet the upsets and problems, misfortunes and risks of daily life. So emergency kan or attempts to change the influence of kan are resorted to. Everything from an emergency hsungywe,[6] prior to a venture, or when calamity is suspected to be in the offing, to special gifts, increased devotions, pilgrimages, vows to give, vows to abstain, and even special mediations is a means of getting emergency kan or a shift in direction of kan. Besides Buddhist elements used in this mundane, emergency manner,

---

[6] There are only seven obligatory times to hold hsungywe: The full moon of Kason, the beginning of Wa (the full moon of Wazou begins the Wa season), the ending of the Wa period in Thadingyut, the lighting feast of Tazoungmoun, during Thingyan, seven days after a death, and on the anniversary day of a death.

other systems are invoked, but I shall treat them under the rubrics of divinatory and predictive systems.

The way of building kan and kutho every day, however, is tied to the feeding of monks, the taking of the precepts, and the repetition of the Triple Jewel and the aneiksa, dokhka, anatta formula. Monks are supposed to beg daily for their food. With a begging bowl slung over the shoulder, they are to wait, eyes downcast, looking neither at the householder nor at the food, and then shuffle off wordlessly to the next house. They are to eat the contents of the begging bowl without regard. The villagers tell the tale of the Buddha, who, on finding a leper's thumb in his begging bowl, ate it without flinching. On the other hand, they also tell why it is good and needful to give the best foods to monks. This story sums up the tension in daily giving between the purported simplicity of the monastic life and villager's drive to give the best for sacrificial ends.

In a country there were a prince and a king. The king was elder, the prince junior. One day the prince went hunting and he saw in the forest a deer eating the rich grass and then chasing after a doe. On seeing this he was reminded of the rich food his brother the king sent daily to the monks, and of the active sex life his brother led. So he returned to the palace and gave orders that the delicacies his brother had prepared for the monks be removed. The king saw this and became angry. He ordered his younger brother the prince to be jailed without food for seven days, and on the eighth day to be given anything he wanted of food or of women, for on that day the prince was to die. On the eighth day the king went to see the prince. The prince, who knew his sentence, had not eaten any luxury food nor had he availed himself of any of the beautiful women. The king asked him why. The prince answered, "Because I die on this eighth day it is useless to seek enjoyment." The king replied that is just the way it is with monks. "If they do not eat they cannot carry out their duties, so I give them delicious food. Now as you have seen death you can no longer think of enjoyment, so it is with a monk. They do not eat for enjoyment, just to sustain themselves, for they, too, have thought about and seen death, and they know that the search for enjoyment is futile." He released his brother from jail and said, "Now you can live among rich things and not become attached to them; you can have a beautiful wife and not be attached to her. Now you know what the monks know: aneiksa, dokhka, anatta."

The householder gives the best of his available food to the begging monk. This requires some preparation on the part of a woman. She must have available cooked food, for one cannot give uncooked food, especially uncooked rice, to a pongyi. The begging monk comes roughly at the same time each morning, and the woman knows when she is to have the food ready. If she cannot, for some unforeseen reason, have the cooked food ready, she borrows some from a neighbor in order not to miss out on this kutho-building time. Not only she, but her whole family would lose kutho if the gift of food were not made to the monk each day. Usually a bit of special food is prepared to go into the begging bowl.

Now, although it is incumbent upon every monk to go his daily rounds, to earn his rice "with his feet," as the villagers say, I never saw any of the Nondwin monks actually making the begging rounds. In fact, the koyin and apprentice monks do the food begging for the two monasteries of Nondwin. They follow a path which takes them to each household, where they accept the offerings of villagers in the proper manner, silently, shoulders covered, eyes averted. It amazed me to see frivolous 7- and 8-year-old boys turned into serious, stately representatives of the sangha, and to see the villagers treat their sons and their neighbors' sons with such quiet, evident respect and deference when they were on the begging round.

Furthermore, the food collected by the boys is not eaten by the monks. They eat it, the kyaungtha and guests or visitors eat some of it, and the village dogs, the birds, the ants, and the flies will have some. The koyin are stand-ins for the monks, and the food is chiefly symbolic, for it represents the chance to give, to sacrifice, to a worthy object. And no villager resents the fact that the monks themselves do not make the rounds; they say it is the same thing when the koyin do it for them. The monks themselves eat an ordered, course by course, Burmese meal at about 11 A.M., which is prepared piping hot for them in the kyaung, either by some of the more reverential villagers who come to do this, or by an old man who serves at the East Kyaung in the capacity of steward, general servant, and helper in lay affairs for the monks.

The daily giving to the sangha then is a ritual statement of the relation of the laity to the sangha (and reciprocally) and of the relation of human beings to the teaching of the Buddha, all placed in the sacrificial idiom of continually giving to purify the self, until that too is finally given. The daily acts of putting some rice out for "other living creatures," the placing of cooked food on the Buddha altar, and other giving of cooked food all, to greater or lesser extent, say and mean the same things.

From giving to monks, the power of the act of free offering dribbles down to hospitality, to gifts to nuns, beggars, visitors, and strangers. The nuns (none of whom are in village monasteries) come, usually on ubonei, from Sagaing to beg for food. These shaven-headed women wear a peach-colored robe and are lesser exemplars of the middle way. When they come for food, they get uncooked rice, a much less prestigeful offering than the cooked food given to a pongyi. The nuns may go from house to house, or they may station themselves in a central compound and await householders who come and pour rice into the begging bowls they carry.

There are other beggars who visit Nondwin regularly. There is, about 30 miles away, a cluster of keba, outcast or beggar, villages. These are hereditary begging communities, and everyone in them must, at least a few days in the year, whatever his wealth may really be, go forth to beg. The people of this cluster say that they have the curse to beg because in days of old a beggar came to their village, and they laughed at him and refused to give. The king heard of it and laid upon them, forever, the burden to go forth and beg. They are the descendants of those who had this charge. They still beg. They are largely endogamous, and most of them live in poorer conditions than surrounding villages. When kebas come to Nondwin, they stand in U Sein Ko's compound with two sacks slung from a cross shoulder pole and call out for donations. To ask for alms is especially demeaning, and this calling out is a form of punishment. Actually asking almost violates the whole notion of volitional giving, except that the villager is not constrained to give just because he is appealed to. The kebas get their uncooked rice and go on to the next village.

Hospitality is part of the theme of giving. At least tea and tobacco and betel are offered whenever two or more Burmese sit down at a person's house. Depending on the status of the visitor and the wealth of the household, other things, food and delicacies, may be added. For people who are neighbors and friends, the giving idiom is the street greeting. When two Burmese meet they do not ask each other, "How are you?" unless one has been recently ill or looks very sickly, for that, in Burma, is a literal inquiry into the state of one's health and demands a quasi-clinical response. Rather, they use the conventional greeting and standard rejoinder, derived from food and giving. Burmese do not interact, in the homes of others, without taking at least tea, and conversation does not start until some food and liquid, betel or tobacco is given to the visitor. This form of giving is meritorious, not so much in building kutho as in not building akutho. Not to give, not to offer in these instances is ignoble and a source of akutho.

The final and lowest level of giving is expressed in things like the continually filled jugs of water placed outside the village gate for the use of thirsty travelers, the bits of rice scattered for the birds to eat, or the food thrown away for dogs. This is generalized, impersonal giving that keeps the impetus to give ever green, ever ready. It is a sort of continual reminder and discipline that to give is to live the teaching of the Buddha, to prepare the self for the state of extinction which is the highest good. Giving is the sacrificial idiom of village Buddhism.

The exemplar of the virtues of the middle way is the pongyi. The word pongyi in its religious sense means literally, the great (gyi) glory (pon) in the estate of man. A pongyi is a man who is self-dedicated to the homeless life, to the monastery, to the Buddha, to the preparation of other monks, to the perpetuation by teaching and by example of the dhamma, and most importantly to the conscious movement of the self to higher states and to more glorious rebirths. Monks must live in kyaungs. The Buddhist innovation over the wandering ascetic orders of Indian anchorites is the invention of the cenobium, and members of the sangha always live in a monastery. (There are some hermit monks living in caves in Upper Burma, but I did not see them.)

THE ORGANIZATION OF RELIGIOUS LIFE

In Nondwin there are two kyaungs at the outskirts of the village. The kyaungs are placed in accordance with a saying attributed to the Buddha, that monasteries should be built beyond the sound of women's voices when they come to the well to do their washing. The East Kyaung, according to the pongyi who says he knows because of "oral tradition," is 300 years old, and the small pagoda on its grounds is nearly 500 years old. The kyaung has a name, *Thanbukya*, roughly "emissaries died here," but it is called the East Kyaung since nobody can say what legend or fact the name refers to.

The kyaung is a large wooden structure, set on high piles. The wood has been mellowed to a soft, deep, rust color by sun and rain and applications of "earth oil" (crude petroleum), which also protect it against termites. Below the kyaung itself is a concrete floor, put in about 40 years ago. This is used for both a state school and, later in the day, for monastic students. The kyaung overlooks a small, still body of water, and has nearby a copse of trees. The grounds are partly fenced in, and the area in which shoes must not be worn is clearly demarcated. The monastery also has a well, along with the older hand-dug lake. In the old days people came here to get their water for drinking, since there was no other supply, and thus used to regularly visit the monastery and the monks, which they no longer do. The concrete floor opens into two covered verandas, and out toward a bell given about 30 years ago to the monastery. On this lower floor, beside the students, laymen come and sit, and the presiding monk receives and talks to them. He usually receives lay visitors as he received me, with tea and two kinds of sweet breads (one made from arrowroot, the other from wheat flour) served by one of the koyin. As we drink tea, we can see some of the usual morning activity. The older koyin are leading the younger in chants of mixed Burmese and Pali. All are reading or have memorized from paper books. The chant and response place a premium on rote learning, and full memorization of the texts is the highest intellectual good. Both koyin and monks spend their time in memorizing, rather than in interpreting the texts. Writing is mainly taught by copying out sections of the texts. What are most studied are the 227 rules of the monastic life. Most of the younger boys' time is spent with these rules, and even a junior monk here for more than three years is still involved in conning the vinaya rules and the commentaries on them.

Above the concrete floor is the main room of the kyaung. The room is dominated by an altar at the mingala end. On the altar are several small, gold-plated images of the Buddha. These are placed between decorative, round, gold-plated gongs and upright flower-filled vases. In front of the altar are straw mats on which devotees kneel when they come to contemplate the Buddha and the teaching. Beyond the straw mats are four thick teak posts running up into equally heavy teak beams. The beams sport antlers of deer and heads of other animals that were gifts to the kyaung. Also on the beams are three large clocks, all ticking. At the base of the pillars are the palm leaf books of scripture wrapped in cloth. These neat piles make up the kyaung's library and are the books the monks study. The books are lacquered palm leaf, 5 inches across and 2 feet high. The black Pali lettering is sometimes bronze coated at the edges of the leaf. The leaves are bound together by pieces of red, lacquered wood. The pongyi tells me that these very books were a gift from *Alaunghpaya*, the founder of the Shwebo dynasty more than 300 years ago. There are other similar books about 100 years old, but the monastery has not collected any more during the last century. There are also some pictures of the former presiding monk, some bedrolls of the koyin, the sleeping pallet of a monk, and some bundles of possessions of the residents that complete the furniture, and off to one side there is a small desk and chair for the monk's use. All of the things needed for preparing and serving food are kept on the lower level, and the kyaung has many sets of china dishes, teacups, and silverware, in case there is need for serving in the kyaung.

Like the other, smaller kyaung, this place exudes calm and quiet and a feeling of withdrawal from the affairs and troubles of the world and of the village nearby. This kyaung is of the kind given to a particular monk. The other sort of kyaung is built by a community or an individual for any worthy monk. When the monk himself is given the kyaung, he may take some liberties in it that a pongyi in the other sort of kyaung cannot. This kyaung, then, has its donor, its *kyaung daga*, a sort of patron for the monastery and for the chief pongyi. From time to time the patron will give special gifts to "his monk," and see to it that he is well clad in the best robes, sandals, and umbrella. In return the daga may get special attention from the monk and special opportunities to gather kutho. The particular daga of this kyaung now lives in Rangoon, and the monk has just returned from a visit there. The daga's family rebuilt the kyaung about 40 years ago (when the concrete floor was laid). All kyaungs have some sort of patron, even if not the builders. Some village family or families will undertake to specially supply the monk or keep up the kyaung. The smaller kyaung in Nondwin is the responsibility of the thugyi's family, and has been hereditarily so. In a kyaung given to a particular monk, that monk has the right to name his successor and thus passes on the privileged sort of monastery. In the community kyaung, or kyaung given to the sangha in the abstract, the villagers invite successor monks, if the presiding monk has not trained a worthy successor.

In Nondwin, there are only two full monks and only one apprentice monk at the East Kyaung. There are 19 koyin, none of whom, at this point in time, are considering becoming pongyis. Going into the sangha is not necessarily a lifetime commitment. One may leave the order at any time there is a desire to do so, by summarily announcing his decision. Conversely, a man may enter the order by just deciding to do so. He needs no special training, only the permission of some monk to live at the monastery. He has to observe the monastic rules and schedule only while he is resident in the kyaung. The grades of the brotherhood are these:

1. Koyin. (Koyin are junior and senior; one over 19 is a senior novice.) Novices usually are boys who have just been through shin-

byu. There is no commitment to stay any length of time, nor to pledge
to the monastic life.

2. Upazin. A upazin is an assistant or junior monk. He works under the presiding monk of a kyaung. He has been ordained by the
standard ordination ceremony. I did not see in Nondwin any such
ceremony, but those I saw in another village are virtually identical
to that described by Scott (1882).

3. Pongyi. A pongyi is a monk; it is the most general term of reference (the term of address is Shin) to a member of the sangha, and
includes upazin, this grade, and the next higher grade. A pongyi has
his own kyaung or is attached to a particular monastery. His is not
necessarily a life commitment, but a "real" pongyi in Nondwin is a
man who has spent at least 10 years in the order and who intends to
make it a life choice. It is this sort of pongyi who is the appropriate
symbol for sacrificial giving. He is the exemplar, the great glory, the
embodiment of the dhamma. Pongyis in this genuine sense are to be
distinguished from rogues, fakes, or spongers, who temporarily take
up the homeless life. The general term in Nondwin is *khit pongyi,*
meaning literally modern monk, not worthy of respect. In this category they place those monks in Mandalay who work part time at
learning trades, or those arrogant wearers of the yellow robe who are
seen at football matches, pwes, or with women.

4. Hsayadaw. Like an abbot, he is the head of a group of pongyis
or is a very learned and respected pongyi. The hsayadaw is already
committed to the order for life. He may either be the presiding monk
of a kyaung, at which there are other pongyis resident, or he may
preside over a group of kyaungs. An hsayadaw is mainly a teacher
of other monks, and his attention to the laity is much less than that
of the usual pongyi, although he accepts invitations and is greatly
honored at hsungywe when he attends.

These grades of monks give some clue to the organization of the
sangha. Each kyaung is virtually an independent entity, and each
hsayadaw is of the highest rank. At the village level, this is certainly
the case; each kyaung runs itself, and each of the presiding monks
is a self-sufficient authority. There is, however, a vague notion of *taik,*
a group of monasteries tied together by the authority of an especially
venerable monk. The most venerable hsayadaw in the outer circle of
Nondwin is in Legyi, and he has authority for about 20 villages. His
authority has to do mainly with internal affairs of the sangha, not
with the laity. If there are disputes that cannot be settled by a given
presiding monk, he may be consulted. Or if there is a case of disci-

plining a monk, or even of expulsion, which takes a set quorum of monks, he would convene and preside over that. But, in all the time Nondwin villagers can remember, no one has ever been expelled from a monastery in the region, and the taik has never formally convened. The only organizational reality it has is that when the 21 or so monks from the region are assembled, they sit in rank order descending from this venerable hsayadaw.

The Nondwin monk tells me that, when he took his training in Mandalay, he was part of a taik which included 30 kyaungs, under one hsayadaw. It was teaching monks under him, and upazin under them, and training the upazin to take up various posts in villages. When he was in this taik, he was the "school seated monk" (*kyaung htain kodaw*) and had no duties with the laity, only the tasks of absorbing wisdom and knowledge from the learned hsayadaws of Mandalay, the region which still has the reputation of expounding the purest, deepest, and wisest Theravada in all of Burma.

Above the level of the taik is an even vaguer level of organization called the *gaing*. Gaing variously means party, or sect, or group, or followers of a given leader or doctrine. To village monks, like this one, the gaing means chiefly the doctrinal divisions in contemporary Burmese Buddhism. He speaks of the differences among Thudhamma, Swegyin, and three lesser sects he could name. He says (and other monks in other villages I visited and the laity of Nondwin concurred) that Thudhamma accounts for 90 per cent of Burmese pongyis. The differences are in minor interpretations of the vinaya; for example, the Swegyin monk cannot smoke or chew betel after his main meal, and the Thudhamma can. The differences between gaing cannot be seen in the arrangement of a kyaung, the texts studied, or the dress of monks (all of whom are similarly clad, though the color of robes varies from a darkish brown to a bright orange, depending on the dye used and the age of the garment). The other sense that village monks give gaing is for the group of followers of a given hsayadaw. Such a following may include both laymen and monks. But the persistent theme always returns: each monk is self-sufficient; each monastery is self-regulating; there is not a real enforceable hierarchy in Burmese Buddhism. It is as Mendelson (1961) reported. Even at the national and urban levels, a series of autonomous monks and monasteries without an organizational format exists. Whatever organization there is results from the charisma of a given monk, not from the structure of Buddhism.

Monks, then, are voluntary members of a loosely organized brotherhood, whose aim is the perpetuation of the dhamma and living of a sort of life that allows the maximum of self-purification and affords the best earthly means to overcome the cravings of the world. In this context monks are not related in any territorial or parish sense to a congregation. They are not shepherds of the laity, and they are not responsible for the morality of the laity. Each man, monk or not, is engaged in seeking his own salvation by whatever means he can muster. And the monk is only one point on the continuum of laity to Buddha, a constant living reminder of what others could be if they had the kan, the temperament, and the discipline to live the monastic life. The monks are detached from daily life, and they do not meddle in it unless they are asked for advice, or to ward off an evil, or to prepare a charm, or to do some tattooing with magical overtones. They do however take two tasks in relation to the laity with great serious-ness: the attendance at hsungywe, where they expound and sermonize, and the monastic schooling of the young. Pongyis do not have, nor in village life do they seek, secular or political power. The village monks have sanctions in the sense that they are able to refuse to attend a layman's hsungywe, or to stay away from funerals, or to refuse to accept offerings and alms. These sanctions have, according to remembered history, never been applied against any villager in Nondwin. The use of such sanctions would not be to discipline an individual, to move him to moral behavior, or to censure him for an infraction of the precepts. These sanctions would be used in a political and power battle in which the sangha had a stake against the civil regime. One instance, involved with the Mandalay bus transport sys-tem, will make this clear. This case I discussed with villagers and with pongyis, and, from it, I came to the understanding that when monks feel that the sangha is being infringed upon by the state, or that dis-respect is shown to the wearers of the robe, they will take action and invoke sanctions. It is the practice, in Mandalay, to permit beg-ging pongyis free passage on the buses until 10 A.M. The monks pour out of their kyaungs and take the bus to the point where they begin the round of begging food. They sit or stand in the front of the bus. On one line (called the blue bus line) the monks rode the buses at the time of heavy passenger use. These buses passed through the zeigyo, the main market of Mandalay, and up to the Arakan pagoda, behind and around which are a host of monasteries. The driver on one of the blue buses refused to accede to a monk's request to stop in the middle of the usual route. The young monk was not content with getting off at the regular bus stops but wanted to be let off exactly at the beginning of his route of alms and food begging. The monk and the driver had been arguing about this for several days. Finally, the driver agreed to the pongyi's demand. But on the day he agreed, when the pongyi was getting off the bus, with one foot on the step and the other on the road, the driver started the bus with a jerk. The pongyi was thrown to the ground, his bowl flew from his grasp and cracked, and he was slightly bruised. This was the actual incident.

The consequences indicate how pongyi power is mobilized. The monk took his broken bowl and story back to his taik. Immediately pongyis swarmed into the zeigyo and began to stone blue buses. The police tried to intervene, but they received their share of abuse and rocks. They could not, or would not, reciprocate, against robe wearing monks, with physical force. The blue buses were driven from the market. The news spread among other kyaungs, and all over the city pongyis stoned blue buses. The bus line was forced to suspend service at great inconvenience to traders and workers in the bazaar. Finally, after two days of keeping blue buses off the street, one of the senior monks presented his demands. He wanted a full public apology from the owners of the bus line, dismissal and imprisonment of the bus driver, and a promise of more courteous treatment of passenger monks. The owners of the bus line were forced to accept. They gave a hsungywe for more than 150 monks in the taik of the offended pongyi, they fired the driver (he was not jailed), and they made public apology and praise to the sangha. The rioting monks returned to their more sedate pursuits of study and begging.

Here the indirect but great power of the sangha when aroused is manifested. Their special position and their near unity when they feel the brotherhood is slighted or threatened give them secular and political weapons. The laity is virtually powerless even if they do not support the efforts of the monks. One can see from this small incident how monks got involved in and rallied laity to the cause of Burmese independence, and how sangha in politics may tear down a political order, even if it does not have the capacity to build one. The troubles in South Vietnam in the old sacred city of Hue show again the stubborn power of the sangha in conflict with the state, there more exaggerated because the state is not, as it is in Burma, nominally and emotionally Buddhist.

Village monks in Nondwin and surrounding communities understood and approved of the action of the Mandalay monks although the pongyi here deplored the throwing of rocks. (He favored a human wall under the bus wheels.) The sangha then has no direct political role, but it is jealous of infringement, and, on higher levels than the village, it seeks to vest its rights and to get secular and political support for privileges. The examinations and the riots in Rangoon are another example of this tendency, and the pongyi support for U Nu's state religion is yet one more. The local monks who had heard rumors of pongyi registration and identity cards were strongly opposed to any state regulation. What they sought was support and privilege from whatever sort of state there was.

However, such questions of politics, the position of the sangha, the role of the state in religious affairs are generally remote from both the people and the pongyis of Nondwin. The life of a village pongyi, with its busy routine, leaves little time for him to pay attention to such abstractions. The ordinary day of the ordinary village monks starts when they arise at about 4 A.M. They go to the Buddha altar and gadaw hpaya and say prayers for the four continents and all the people who live there.[7] After this a monk paces the kyaung compound reciting the aneiksa, dokhka, anatta chant while he fingers the string of 108 beads. This leads to meditation on the five senses, to empty the mind and to control the passions and desires.[8] At 5 A.M. they take the morning meal, usually a vegetable soup called *gangyi*. This is cooked by the koyin. Then they read texts in Burmese and Pali and prepare lessons for the koyin. The koyin return from the begging rounds and the main meal is eaten. Classes are held until about 1:30 P.M., after which is a rest for about an hour. Teaching resumes until about 4 P.M. Then resting and meditating during the heat of the day take place. From 6 to 7 P.M., they recite chants and devotionals before the altar. At 8 P.M. they gather the koyin and stay with them for about two hours. They go to bed at 10:30 after more meditation on suffering, impermanence, and vanity of self.

The routine is only varied on ubonei, when villagers come to take the eight or ten precepts, and on special days when the Buddha was traveling and spreading the work, when they also go out to preach. And on

---

[7] This is similar to what a householder usually does, and it is this chant of blessing of all living things that is the only expression of *myitta*, universal love. As a rule the village saying that there "is no love like self-love" is closer to daily behavior than is the idea of myitta.

[8] Here the monk and the laity have parted, for this pongyi activity is not for the householder, except in time of crises or when a villager has reached the age when he begins to turn his back on the mundane world and seriously gets concerned with his next plane of existence.

the day of Buddha's enlightenment, which is his birthday also, they go with the laity to water the banyan tree that stands at the entrance to the village in honor of the Buddha. They also vary the routine by attending hsungywe, or listening to troubles of villagers, or doing curing rites, or tattooing. But the aim of kyaung routine is to free the monk so that he may free himself from any concern except that of the diligent search for salvation.

The monks of Nondwin study chiefly the vinaya rules and the book of suttas, and only marginally the Abhidhamma. Conversations about the content of monkish study usually elicits stereotyped lists of the branches of Buddhist learnings, a string of Pali titles, and a summary that a monk is concerned with the literature of the Buddha (the Tipitaka), the life of the Buddha (mainly, but not exclusively, in the Jataka), and the practice of morality and the way. Morality is defined negatively by the 227 rules of monastic living. There are four things, however, that a pongyi must never do unless he is a living "lie" in the robe. He is forbidden to kill anything.[9] He is forbidden to steal and to commit sexual congress with a woman.[10] He is forbidden to claim false powers. This latter danger, the assertion of mystical powers that is built into the nature of the monkhood, is his greatest internal threat.

As a monk proceeds in inner wisdom, in fuller understanding, and in self-purification, there should be some manifestations in his daily life and in his ability to handle the universe. There is precedent for this in the life of the Buddha. All monks (and laymen on special occasions) recite the inventory of the abilities of the Buddha, and monks aspire to these marvelous powers as earnests of their progress along the way to Neikban.

---

[9] The water filter is used to strain his drinking water so that living things will be spared. When, in the interest of provoking theological debate, I asked the East Kyaung monk about the microbes in the water, he shrugged. "We can only spare what we can spare. It is beyond our power to spare microbes. We do not knowingly kill anything."

[10] By extension, he is forbidden any sort of sexuality from concupiscence to ogling. A good part of the discipline that a monk subjects himself to is aimed at repressing the imperious sexual drive. Any monk has, as this one does, a series of particularly effective thoughts, devices, and activities to turn his mind from lust. Women are the great danger to the sangha, and sexual lust is the chief reason for monks leaving the order. For example, U Sein Ko was a pongyi for 10 years, when, one day, Daw Aye walked into the kyaung. He was smitten and nothing could drive her image from his mind. He forsook the robe and became "a man set free" so that he could marry Daw Aye.

1. Knowledge of previous life (that is, total recall of all of his existences and of anyone else's).
2. Power of great sight (not only to see great distances but also to see through, over, and under objects. To see anything in the world at any time).
3. Complete absence of sexual desire (indicating fulfillment and complete satiation).
4. Ability to change his size (to any largeness or smallness).
5. Power of great hearing (to hear any sound anywhere at any time).
6. Power to cause events (if he wants a thing to happen, to will it).
7. Power to be where he wants (by an act of will to transport himself to where he wishes to be).
8. Power to be invisible.
9. Power to walk on air.
10. Power to know all that is known.

These abilities are paralleled by manifest virtues, which always accompany them. The *thilathanwara* (virtues second to none) that come with the powers (or the powers that come with the virtues; it makes no difference—they are indissolubly wed) are: humility, modesty, dignity, exactness of food intake to energy output, good, restful sleep, vigor and health, generosity, a good conscience, wisdom, and serenity.

Claiming these powers and virtues moves a monk into a category of great, makes him respected, and sometimes even brings talk of his being close to a Buddha. This claim to near-Buddhahood is one of the sources of disruption in a sangha so loosely organized as is the Burmese. The means of control is to place false claimants in the same damned position as killers, liars, and sexual malefactors. Yet among the laity of Nondwin there are always tales of monks with some of these powers and shadowy reports of marvels, miracles, and pongyis near the final merger (Mendelson, 1961).

The monks and the pongyi kyaungs are the most conspicuous elements in village Buddhism and are the objects and means for the exercise of the sacrifice of giving. But in the community itself there are a series of perduring organizations—corporate groups deriving from the way villages handle their Buddhism. This is not to say that Buddhism *per se* requires or even fosters groups and group activity. Apart from the territorial aspect of kutho in the kutho group that sacrifices together, Buddhism has a contrary effect. It is individuating.

It places each irreducible nucleus of kan at the center of the universe; it makes each individual responsible for his own spiritual state; and it lays the burden of salvation squarely on the lone individual. What accounts for the Buddhist-derived group in Nondwin is the village insistence on publicity, on display, and on the intertwining of the ideas of pon, kan, gon, prosperity, and play in all concrete Buddhist events and activities. To get the maxima of kutho at affairs like the shinbyu, the kahtein, or the large hsungywe, an organization above the personnel and resource level of the household or the family is required. The community is always mobilized in these events, and, although the events are individually sponsored, they, as earlier described, require community-wide participation. Community participation is organized in two corporate groups. There is a group of *lubyo* (literally bachelors) and a group of *aphyo* (literally spinsters). These groups include all of the unmarried boys and girls 15 years or older. They are headed respectively by a lubyo gaung and an aphyo gaung. These groups do the tea serving and food serving at the large feedings which accompany religious affairs. Nondwin has, in addition, a *htamin chet gaung*, a cooking chief, who oversees the large cooking pots. The lubyo and aphyo groups are custodians of the extra china and flatware needed at these events. They also have the extra seating mats.

These groups are the ushers, waiters, cooks, and dishwashers needed to give the requisite publicity to kutho-making ceremonies. The cups, saucers, mats, cutlery, and crockery that the lubyo and aphyo groups own come from voluntary village contributions, especially for services at a large celebration. These groups are the beneficiaries of a sort of marriage tax, called *gebo*. Gebo is, in part, a compensation to the peer group of unmarrieds, in part, a survival of the custom that newlyweds were stoned unless they paid gebo. The money collected from gebo payments (the payment is higher if the groom comes from another village) is used to augment the supplies of the aphyo and lubyo groups and is a contribution to the maintenance of the unmarried as an organized segment of the village social structure. Wealthy couples may, at a marriage, give to each unmarried boy and girl, such minor things as thanakhka or cigarettes.

Two other groups exist in Nondwin and are derived from its Buddhism. There is a nightly prayer group of girls and young boys, and the Buddhist Association. The devotional group meets in one of the larger two-story houses three or four nights weekly. There they are led in chants of some of the thok, the precepts, the Triple Jewel, and the aneiksa, dokhka, anatta liturgy. Most of the young girls under

18 attend these sessions regularly. When there is a loudspeaker in use for some other ceremony, the chanting is blared through it to envelop the whole village in a babble of devotion. The Buddhist Association, composed mainly of young men under the leadership of respected elders, is the tax collecting agency for Buddhist festivals. It collects the rice, the money, the flowers, or whatever for kahtein, for pagoda lighting, for contributions to other communities, for hsungywe, and for sending its dance groups to perform in neighboring villages. Almost all of the unmarried boys are members of this group.

These groups are the only groupings beyond the family. Politics gives some statuses but forms only client, satrapy groups; economics gives categories of rich, moderate and poor, but it is the facade and display element of village Buddhism that eventuates in a series of perduring groups. It seems only religion, on which there is full consensus, lays the basis for corporate, continuous groups.

Funeral Ceremonies

The meanings and organization of village Buddhism can be seen in full play at the crisis of death. It is not paradoxical that what Buddhism is in life is best understood through what it is at death. The funeral ceremonies of Nondwin summarize and bring out, as does a litmus paper, the core elements of Buddhist belief and practice. For it is death, the movement from one existence to the next, that invokes all of the ideas of the cosmology, kan, kutho, akutho, metempsychosis, and bears home the true sense of aneiksa, dokhka, anatta. Buddhism is geared to make death only a stage in life, and pongyis, who may be viewed as dying daily for glory, are central figures at death ceremonials (whereas they must be absent from marriage, procreation, and birth rituals).

There is a marked difference in the treatment of those who die from natural causes, age, illness, and disease, and those who die from unnatural events, accident, injury, or any violent end. The violent death is especially unpropitious and is called a "green" death, with the notion of prematurity and unwillingness for the deceased to leave the community of the living. There is in any green and violent death a strong probability that a spirit will return to trouble the village and to frighten people in the night. So, special precautions are taken, and special haste made, in disposing of the premature, unnatural dead. In Nondwin I saw only one case of a green death. A young girl, about 15 years old, fell into the creek and drowned. When I tramped with the village elders through muddy fields to the creek, we came upon a scene in which the body was stretched out on the bank, and about 100 villagers were circled around it in various squatting positions. The immediate family of the girl were closest to her, and only her mother was sobbing. Everyone else was subdued, but dry-eyed. The elders only wanted to ascertain one thing—was the death accidental? All felt the need to get the body into the cemetery as quickly as possible. The longer it was in the community, the greater the probability of its being a lure for other violent spirits to congregate. From interviews of the parents on the spot and from the boy who discovered the body, the elders quickly decided that the drowning was accidental, and that they would bury the body that day and forward a report to the police at Sagaing on the next.

The girl's body was not washed or treated in any way, for the spirit had already fled from it, and the usual ceremony was of no avail. It was merely swathed in longyis, toes tied together, hands folded across the trunk, eyes left open, staring and sightless. The simple wooden coffin was brought to the spot, and the body was taken to the cemetery where three of the deceased's relatives had opened a shallow grave. The body was removed and dumped into the grave and covered with earth and rocks. There was, like in all village funeral cemeteries, no gravemarker or stone. There were no followers of the body to the cemetery, and gravediggers came back unobtrusively, after washing off any of the cemetery dirt they picked up in digging. Nothing was done that day for this violent death, but an ahlu was held one week later, and two monks were fed, and people from Nondwin dropped in during the morning to have a cup of tea while the monks were there.

The more usual death ceremonial takes place when passage from one existence to another is considered natural, or ripe, by the people of Nondwin. When a person dies, the whole village is in a state of contamination, and everybody must be involved in removing this impurity. If a person died outside of his community, the body could not, and would not, be brought through the village gates. People do not seek contamination, and death brings it. When the death is announced, relatives, neighbors, and at least one person from every household must come to the compound of the deceased. The body is laid out in the house after being washed from head to toe. The water used for this is carefully kept in a pot and later poured out beyond the bounds of the village; the pot is cracked and left at the cemetery. Someone is always in attendance in the room with the dead person. Outside, the compound is filled with people. There is always some possibility that the ghost of the dead person may linger, reluctant to find its place in the next existence. The presence of so many people has the dual effect of frightening ghosts, who dislike multitudes, and assuring the spirit that this kutho group hopes to rejoin it in the next favorable plane of existence.

Some of the death watch, as the mourners are called, stay in the compound day and night, until the body is taken to the cemetery. Usually two or three days is all the body can be kept, for it begins to decompose and rot in the heat of Upper Burma if kept much longer, and the vapors from the dead are considered especially malignant.

Those who keep the night vigil are usually men. The men stay awake all night, for it is wakeful people who frighten ghosts and reassure spirits. They stay awake by gambling at a game of Burmese dominoes. The game or games (at one funeral there were three domino games in progress at 3:00 A.M., with 24 players involved) are for decent-sized stakes, by village standards, and a man may lose or gain quite a bit during his kutho-gathering vigil of the dead. Women who come sleep the night at the house of the dead as an act of kutho. The compound in the house of a deceased does not look like a mournful or solemn place. It is gay with gamblers, tea drinkers, visitors, with the lubyo and aphyo groups serving and ushering. These people are not in any conventional sense mourners; rather, they are doing an act of kutho and a village duty by speeding a spirit on its way.

There is this dangerous, risky interval between existences when a willful spirit may try to cling to acquaintances, relatives, and territory of its former existence. The death watchers, in part, guard against this, and the monks insure, at the time of burial, that the transition is made, and that accurate account is taken of the balance of kutho and akutho, and that kan is properly weighed for rebirth.

Other things the villagers do before the monks come are: Prepare the "death-carrying house" in which the body will be transported to the cemetery, for a real coffin is not used, and make the ladder for the body to leave the house. This is a symbolic ladder drawn with charcoal from the bedstead of the deceased to the ground. It must always have an odd number of steps. (Seven is the preferred and most common, although five and nine are also used.) The villagers put up to 3 kyats of "ferry money" with the deceased, for there is a belief that a river must be crossed between existences and that the ferryman must be paid. They must also prepare gadawbwes for the monks who are invited. The gadawbwe of bananas, rice, and tea leaf gifts are the way monks are summoned to attend and preside over the funeral ceremonies. And, finally, villagers must perform the ceremony of seeing if the *leikpya* (butterfly soul) has indeed left the body. This is done by putting a mirror before the mouth of the deceased and calling out to the leikpya. Then, with a bit of white string, the invisible leikpya is drawn onto a branch of a tree. In this way it will be carried carefully to the cemetery and set free when it sees that it needs a new material embodiment. It is this butterfly soul essence that goes on from existence to existence, and for the villager it is a material thing, the vehicle of metempsychosis, the carrier of continuous kan. It is the butterfly soul that can be misdirected or lost in transit between existences, to fall in the highly undesirable category of lost and wandering souls.

The ceremony of the leikpya soul is carried out just before the body leaves the compound and sometime after the monks have arrived. The death watchers know what a butterfly soul looks like. It is a small, circular luminosity and can be seen glowing at night if it should escape. It is called butterfly because it makes a noise like the fluttering of an excited, trapped butterfly's wings. It may, during the course of the death watch, come out and circle the house three times and then return to the body. It is in a state of uncertainty and worry about reincarnation.

This view of the soul, of the trouble of transit, of the weighing up of the next form of existence, expresses the villagers' chief concern at a funeral. It is not sorrow for a life ended, a consciousness cut off, but rather a desire to guide the nucleus of kan to its proper destination, to help a soul over the blank spots between existences, to insure speedy transfer, and to keep the chain of being intact, without anomalies like wandering souls or lost spirits that may trouble the village and even bring it calamity.

The villagers do two final things in a funeral: they take the deceased's horoscope (usually carved on a palm leaf and kept wrapped in a cloth in the roof beams in the East part of the house, and never consulted by anyone but the owner) and drop it into the creek where it floats away, thus marking the temporal end of the forces that kept this material body going. Second, before moving the body to the death-carrying house, they rotate the head from East to West and give a seven-time shikko to the Buddha and a farewell to the community. The rocking of the body is taken as assent, that it is ready to go, and that the Buddha guides it in its journey. At graveside it is rotated again; more shikkoes are given, and the body is lowered in, head to the East.

On the day of the burial the monks come. They sit in a line facing the people in the compound. They offer up a blessing to clear the way for the soul, and each of them is presented a robe or longyi for his attendance. The monks arise, walk in silent line, followed first by koyin, then the death house, then a man with the branch supporting the leikpya, and another with the pot containing the water from the last washing of the body, and then the men and boys; women and girls bring up the rear. In this procession, only the women and girls are permitted to wail, and they do it in a very controlled manner of sobbing. There is none of the tearing of hair, the gnashing of teeth, and the extravagant display of grief that I know from my experiences in Mexico and Guatemala.

The procession stops near the pagoda grounds. The body itself is not brought into the sacred grounds but is left nearby at the edge. The death house is dismantled, and the monks begin the ceremony. The monks chant the *Tharanagon* as part of the death rites. Included are the usual elements of any gathering of Buddhists, plus this dilation on the levels of existence, the nature of kan and kutho, and the sermon spelling out that life is suffering, that death is the sure sign of impermanence, and that the heap of bones and flesh about to be put into the ground is not a real entity. The villagers listen with bowed heads as the monks crystallize for them in sonorous tones the meaning of life and death, the utility of the middle way for coping with these problems, and the solemn reminder that life is preparation for death, and death is the chance to earn fuller life. After a water blessing and a devotion to share the kutho and the kan of the living with the dead so that the very best possible rebirth may happen, the monks file away, both shoulders wrapped, eyes down. They are living reminders that the phenomenal world is an obstacle to be overcome in the attempt to sacrifice self for merger with the infinite and all-knowing, and the receding tread of the sandaled monks turns the death ceremony into a full Buddhist commentary on life.

Most of the villagers go back to the village. The immediate family accompany the body to the grave. There, a final wail is permitted before the body is lowered into a common grave, where other bones may be disturbed to make room for it, and the unmarked grave is covered. People returning from the cemetery must wash before they go into the village.

What I have described are the common, necessary, and minimally present elements in a Nondwin funeral. Sometimes, elaborations are added in the form of fancy death houses, or a band to accompany the procession, or an oxcart to transport the body. Another elaboration, the closest imitation of a royal style, is the cremation rather than burial of the dead. Monks are always cremated in a flaming pyre of kerosene-soaked logs, and some rich or especially pious people may be so treated. Sometimes the gifts given to monks are exceedingly expensive or elaborate; the number of monks invited may reach up to 20 or 30, and the guests fed may run into the hundreds. But whatever secular display is added, the funeral ceremony has the same set of connotations, the same direful commentary on life, the same capsule lessons about the meaning and purpose of life.

EFFECTS OF BUDDHISM

Drawing together this description and analysis of village Buddhism will take the form of a series of summary statements intending to characterize Buddhism as a religious system and to indicate its chief effects on the character, culture and social structure of the people of Nondwin. Buddhism, in the economic sphere, has been held by illustrious thinkers like Max Weber to inhibit economic growth, or to make believers insensitive or indifferent to economic opportunity. The otherworldly element of world view and the concern with the spiritual state were taken to be, even if not antithetical to the use of talent and resources in economic pursuits, at least not conducive to the full and rational employment of human and nonhuman resources in economic activity. These common and large assertions about the relation of Buddhism to economic pursuits and growth have stirred students to find empirical modes of checking out what scholars have inferred from the textual demands on ideal-type believers. Pfanner and Ingersoll (1962), in a study of a community in Lower Burma, have reported that Buddhism and economic activity are related in a way so that productive resources are spent in merit making rather than in investment, and that the exemplary role of the monk acts against high value being placed on economic roles. These findings, of course, follow Buddhist belief, but they do not get very close to the solution of the enigma that Weber and others have willed us. The real, central, and researchable questions raised by the Weberian hypothesis on the relations between a given religious orientation and level and type of economic activity have been well-phrased by Singer (1961) and Bellah (1963). Singer raises the problem of the totality of orientations toward the totality of activity in a given society and culture. The question is one of sorting out orientations to action in a graded scale of relevance to particular activities. In this way, an analyst can judge and have his judgment carry conviction: at what point, in what ways, on what activities, and in just what contexts the religious orientation and values determine or shape behavior. Bellah handles the obverse of these questions. He is concerned with the extent to which central religious values are, in fact, institutionalized, how much of the normative elements are built into social relations so that they concretely cut down on options for behavior, on the one hand, and make other sets of options desirable on the other.

The scale of the Weberian hypotheses is such that no single study does very much to confirm or disconfirm them. Holding an intellectual position in regard to these hypotheses is a matter of making a "convergence of inferences" from a host of findings and reports centered around the Weberian notions. My judgments about the role of Burmese Buddhism, at the village level, in economic behavior, while I think they cover the facts I observed and make social science sense of them, cast but a shadow on the Weberian hypotheses. But they are directed toward and aimed at the sorts of empirical stipulations that such assertions demand.

One easily gotten and meaningful indicator of the role of religious values in economic life and activity is the occupational choice pattern and ranking of occupations. In Nondwin most people are cultivators and only the poor, as reported earlier, are driven to take low prestige and religiously condemned occupations. No one in Nondwin, if he could do otherwise, would hold the job of hunter, fisherman, butcher, stock breeder, fowl keeper, or soldier. These are occupations deliberately concerned with the taking of life; deliberately and as a matter of course they involve a person in the daily accumulation of akutho, in worsening his chances for a favorable rebirth. The occupational structure of Nondwin is based on the matter of opportunity, knowledge, and the material and spiritual rewards consequent to following one or another line of work. Only necessity makes some people takers of life, and these occupations do not spread because not enough people are driven to them. Buddhism tempers opportunity by attaching negative consequences to available sorts of economic activity. Those who are in jobs requiring the taking of life are devout bokda batha, and they do not get as much economic return as they could, in part, because they are especially involved in getting kutho to offset the akutho their occupations entail. They give in the sacrificial vein so that they may continue a secular life of violating the first precept. Buddhism, at one and the same time, provides the rationale of penalty and expiation, and this allows people to carry on in jobs that are beyond the religious pale because they are not necessarily condemned to be outcasts (as would, for example, prostitutes or habitual criminals in our society, for whom there is no standard piaculum as sacrificial giving in Buddhism).

I found the positive dimension of occupational choice by asking school children. They are on the verge of a work life; they have a value system uncorrupted by the constraints of making a living; and they have the hopes and dreams of the young, not yet eroded by the weathering acquired in making one's way through a world that is what it is. All of the boys in the third and fourth standards of the village school wrote an essay on what they would like to do, and what they would not like to do, in their coming working lives. Of the 13 essays I had translated, the choices and reasons can be summarized this way.[11]

TABLE XV   Occupational Choices of Third and Fourth Standard Boys

Occupation	Favorable Citations	Reasons	Unfavorable Citations	Reasons
Cultivator	2	Money, security	9	Hard, dull, poor pay
Army officer	3	Happy work, travel, patriot	5	Killing, danger, fear
Army clerk	3	Easy work	—	—
Doctor	1	Money, helping	—	—
Schoolmaster	1	Money, helping	—	—
Timber clerk	2	Money, easy	—	—
Schoolteacher	1	Respect, money	—	—

The flavor of the "reasons" listed can be seen in these two excerpts from the compositions. A favorable response to the job of army officer is phrased:

When I'm old enough I'll be an army officer because an army officer is one who learns war, and it is a happy thing to attack and be in a war, and you can

---

[11] All of the boys came from cultivator families, and a preliminary sorting did not show any difference in pattern of choice related to the wealth of their households, although with such a small number, the relation, if there were one, given the unitary nature of the response, could be obscured.

give orders to all the soldiers under your control. I can eat what I like and go where ever I like. To be an officer means going to war with soldiers, going on picnics with other villagers. This is a part of happiness. I can command civilian people, so I like army officer work.

An unfavorable view of the military life is:

I do not want to be a soldier, because you must do whatever you are told. He has to go into the jungle bushes, and there are snakes, and it is dangerous. He has to kill people, and if he dies in the attack, he will go to the fourth level down (of Buddhist hells).

For farming, the major, real life chance in Nondwin, the favorable is:

I want to be a farmer. On sowing cotton and sesamum and beans I will get much money, and by buying and selling cotton I will get much money. For my bullock I will cut grass every day, and I will put food and water in the trough. I will put cow dung on my cart and take it to the fields and keep fences.

The unfavorable idea is:

I dislike cultivator work. He has to work from the very morning to the very evening with no rest, but at 11 o'clock to 1 o'clock you have time for lunch. After that you take the plow and go back to the field again. The working all year round will make you sick. I would hate to be a cultivator.

In these spontaneous judgments of occupations, among schoolboys, it is clear that Buddhism tips the balance against soldiering but that the role of the army in building Burma has made its impact on the youth. (The mature never give a favorable choice to soldiering and reject it on Buddhist grounds of being in violation of "right livelihood.") But what is more striking is the limited number of occupations that are even conceived of and the clustering of sentiments about them. I am impressed by the fact that most of the occupations are religiously neutral, in the sense that Buddhist values neither promote nor inhibit their choice. The obvious conclusion is that, except for a restricted number of life-taking occupations, Buddhism is neutral in its bearing on economic roles and it does not encourage any particular activity positively. The fact that pongyis are rated as the most respected role does not mean that a large percentage of men will choose this role or that life commitment to it will ordinarily ensue. (In fact, with only two pongyis now and only one in training in Nondwin, its monk population has declined. Prior to "Japanese times" there were usually from four to six pongyis resident in local kyaungs.)

However, the neutrality of Buddhism in respect to most occupational pursuits has some consequences. It does not build up work or industry or craft skills, or competence or honesty in task and work as a good by itself. The true, right livelihood idea makes some gestures in this direction, but, in the main, Buddhism leaves the world of work out of account. This is a mixed factor when considering economic growth. On the one side there is no positive, normative urging to do the world's work with dedication, but on the other there is no religious tradition despising work or fixing one to a small number of ways to earn bread. The Buddhist tradition is neutral, but it provides, I think, good soil for the rapid growth of the division of labor and economic specialization which underlie a dynamic and growing economy. As a religious system, it will not actively promote this, but it will not block any other agencies from providing new economic opportunity.

In the temporal spacing of life as described by villagers, one thing is favorable to high commitment of human resources to economic activity. They say that a man should apportion his allotted span in this fashion: From age 1 to 20 should be spent on learning and knowledge, 20 to 40, on seeking fortune and wealth, 40 to 60, on reducing work and on enjoyment, 60 and on, on thinking of hpaya. This loose life plan, which is nearly followed except that people begin active work much earlier than 20, and most are not rich enough to begin enjoyment on any scale at 40, keeps people in the labor force in full economic pursuit during their most vigorous and productive years. And furthermore, a system of religiously sanctioned withdrawal from economic power and control makes the problem of succession, of conflict between generations, minimal. It opens the way for young men to assume economic power and to bring with them (if they have any) new modes of organizations or production.

Where Buddhism does cut directly into economic life is in the costly business of facade, display, and monument building. Based on the annual expenditure patterns I computed (see pp. 33–42), religious donations are about 14 per cent of the annual outlay of a rich family, about 4 per cent of a moderate family's outlay, and about 2 per cent of a poor family's outlay. This clearly indicates the meaning of wealth— the more it is accumulated, the more it is lavished, at the village level, on sacrificial giving for kutho and on the display and front associated with Buddhist ceremonial. The wealthier a person becomes, the more, absolutely and relatively, he spends for religious ends. This orientation not only uses capital but grades the ends of activity so that merit-making—self-movement toward Neikban—is the highest unquestioned good. If there were real economic investment opportunities to compete with religious expenditure, I do not know how the rich would react. From my earlier description of the economy and technology, it emerged that those who do the large religious spending are, at the same time, those who have filled up the real investment spaces in a peasant economy like that of Nondwin. Buddhism does not get in the way of acquiring wealth, for wealth is needed and desired for accumulating kutho, but it does channel much of the accumulation into a form of wealth whose only future productive use is in the stream of esthetic and religious memories and feelings it can generate. It fixes the form of accumulation so that it is not easily converted to other uses or mobile from place to place. The Buddhist emphasis on giving sacrificially, then, is both a spur to economic activity (to get the wealth to give) and a brake because it freezes wealth in monumental rigidity of the pagodas and kyaungs, or dissipates it in the feasting of kutho groups for both secular and religious ends.

Another double-edged effect of Buddhism on the economy and potentials for economic growth is the extreme emphasis on the individual. Buddhism is an individuating system of belief; it places at the center of moral concern the fate and destiny of a single individual bundle of kan; the kutho group and the territoriality are but minor elements compared to the overwhelming preoccupation with the plane of existence of a given consciousness. The individualism has the effects of inhibiting the formation of groups above the domestic level of organization, of inhibiting the allowance of wide swings in a person's reaction to authority (without force accompanying it), group effort, cooperation, and the formation of organizations not tied to a concrete individual. This indifference, or unwillingness to organize for any end other than that of building kutho (and all of the perduring groups in Nondwin have at their base the same leitmotif of kutho), is certainly a liability when economic growth is so closely tied to effective hiearchical organizations based on functional, task-oriented authority. Buddhism makes it difficult for villagers to participate in these sorts of necessary organizations or makes them apathetic in devising them. At the same time, the positive consequences of the individuating aspects of Buddhist conviction must be balanced against this liability.

Buddhism makes for an equalitarian society, and, except for the dimensions of sex and age, it is the individual achievement of pon, gon, and awza that is relevant to social action. There are no fixed hereditary status divisions, no tight class systems, no places in the social structure to which even the humblest may not aspire. It is a fluid, open system of individual, not categorical, ranking and, as such,

moves people to strive for a place if they wish. The notion that outcomes are closely geared to individual effort is an extremely positive
element in the search for economic potential. Even the notion of kan,
as the principal cause of what befalls a person, is tempered by the
accompanying ideas of *nyan* (wisdom or knowledge) and *wiriya* (work
and industry). Kan by itself does nothing. It is knowledge and hard
work combined with good kan that make a favorable life and rebirth,
but even these two without kan bring nothing. So the only way a man
can truly test his kan (and it is religiously important to have a notion
of it) is to learn from life and work hard at his tasks. The fact that
the individual, in the end, is responsible for what he is and does, of
course, leaves the way open to innovators, deviants, and new modes
of behavior. No one will be sanctioned because he tries some new
way to make a living, or some new gadget, or fertilizer, or idea. It is
his business. So change, if individuals perceive opportunities, is easily
permissible in the individually centered religion with its meagre
prescriptive and proscriptive moral code.

Burmese life has the dual quality of appearing as a series of rather
unconnected, immediate instances without much tie to the past, and
with little concern for the future, and at the same time it is filled with
beginnings for projects of great energy which fizzle out and leave nothing in their wake. I take this quality to mean that the great emphasis
on long, vague time periods in Buddhism, the notions of one passing
existence wedged in among countless others, gives villagers the sort of
time horizon that is not conducive to good planning and to execution.
And without the constraints of meeting a standard at a given time,
plans have an open-ended, unserious sort of vagueness about them.
On the other side of this is the fact that failure is not discouraging;
Burmans bounce back quickly from defeat; they are never long sunk
in apathy; and they have generally a cheerful, optimistic outlook on
the world and their condition. Numerous observers have commented
on the cheerfulness, the even tenor, the capacity for pleasure in simple
things that characterizes the village Burman. These traits I take to
be derived, too, from Buddhism, where each man can repair the damage
to his kan, where getting merit is lacking in interior strain, and where
everyone believes that kan will, someday, take its turn for the better.

I have here deliberately stressed five features of Buddhist belief
and practice: accumulation, career choice, organization, relation to
authority, and time horizon and planning. By scanning what I know
of village thought and behavior, I developed the logical and empirical
consequences of Burmese Buddhism as it is in Nondwin on these aspects

of economic behavior. In my analysis I consciously made paramount the multiplex nature of the consequences of Buddhism, and the emphasis on ambiguity and the treatment of the same features as both assets and liabilities for economic change stems from methodological and theoretical predilections.

My way of work, as exemplified in the chapters on economy and social organization where I was more at home and hence more thorough and detailed than I was in the realm of religious thought and behavior, does not allow the smooth extrapolation from a cultural system or a social structure directly to behavioral events. I need a third category, that of choice. I see people as playing the "game" of social life, with a given command over resources, a given control over actions of others, and sets of ends they develop in the act of living the game and enacting whatever strategy their knowledge and personality allows them to conceive of and execute. I mean to say that Burmese culture and society provide, for their people, human and nonhuman resources and power and dependence linkages in actual role networks. It is only by finding what a role makes available to a given person, and by that person judging as he would judge as role incumbent, that he discovers what he is likely to do in that role. And from wider knowledge of the role network and the sorts of goals that persons typically develop, the observing anthropologist may possibly show how and in what ways culture and society bear on, and form the options that are manifest in, the choices of these persons. It is these choices, or option sets, against the heritage of social and cultural life, as that is distributed among live role players, that account for both the stasis and the dynamics of a given society.

A given religious structure may make the game different from society to society, and Buddhism of the Nondwin or Upper Burma variety makes the economic sphere different from that of a community of Burmese Muslims, with whom I spent a few days. A close, controlled comparison between this community and a Burmese Buddhist community that sits just across the road from it would be exceedingly instructive. These communities share a long common history; they are ecologically identical and function in the same cultural tradition, political environment, and economic field; they differ in the vital single dimension of religious systems. From this comparison, we could clearly see, at least in Burma, how differently the game is structured by a dominant religious orientation, and what kinds of different options are indeed available.

I raise the opportunity of this comparison to underline my theoretical position: Choice in a structured situation is the way to understand behavioral events; it is the key to the functioning and the dynamics of social systems. Sometimes I am not sure that many of my anthropological colleagues do in fact wish to understand behavioral sequences, to make sense of what a society is doing, has done, and will do. I do not go as far as Leach (1961), who sees a good part of the profession bemused by making classifications or collecting colorful specimens of social types. This digression I close with a delineation of Buddhism as a system that bears on choices and action possibilities.

Burmese Buddhism, at the village level, is a system of belief and practice oriented to the condition of the self in future states, with practices designed to further the movement of the self along a continuum of ever more desirable states. The movement is phrased chiefly in the sacrificial idiom of giving. It rests on the process of enculturation, and in that sense is a voluntary communion with limited prescriptive and proscriptive canons. It is centered in the individual, is nonhierarchical, with frequent movement between laity and clergy, and it lays little emphasis on the interior state or the quality of conviction as against the performance of religious works. The structural and cultural concomitants of this religious system are: a built-in need for supplementary systems of handling daily affairs, individuation, monument building, the rise of episodic and charismatic leadership, and the unavailability of religious slogan for secular factionalism.

This system bears ambiguously on the Burmese prospect for economic development. One of the tasks of Burmese intellectuals is the reduction of this ambiguity to make Buddhism come to grips with the prospect of a modern, industrial, and ever-growing society. They have searched in the doctrines of Marx for the key to ideological breakthrough, but the many tracts attempting to show that Marxism is but the secular expression of Buddhism are singularly unimpressive, and certainly they do not have any impact on peasants like those of Nondwin. The ideology that will (if any ever can) guide Burma through the transition to modernity will have to rise from the experience along the route of social change. Living ideologies treat with problems that arise from actual experience. They are the symbolic condensations of the meaning of experience and are the shorthand for coping with that experience. What orientation Burma will produce (and its intellectual and political elites at least are always producing ideological statements like Ne Win's revolutionary council's *Burma Way to Socialism*, 1962) will bear the marked imprint of Buddhism.

What Buddhism will look like in a modern Burmese society only time and the Burmese experience can say.

My prognostication, for whatever it is worth, is that the supplementary system of prediction and divination (see Chapter 5) will attenuate under the onslaught of modern science, and that remote Nibbana will come to be replaced by more proximate religious states of salvation, and that a more austere and puritanical element will come to mark Burmese Buddhism. But, to put aside my own efforts at prediction, it does take more, and a different sort of, incentive to get a Buddhist into economic activity in Burma, as against say a Muslim, or a Chinese Confucian, or even a Sikh or Hindu, all of whom are prominently engaged in the most modern of the occupations, while the Burmese, except for government, army, and politics, are over-represented in the most traditional of occupations.

The Theravada of Burma grew up in a society where structural change was minimal, and it faces the tasks of becoming the ideological harbinger of massive, and of thorough-going social change. It will either be adapted to this end or be as problematic as Buddhism is in Japan.

5

*Nats, Spirits, Predictive,
Divinatory, and Curing Systems*

No account of Burmese world view, religious orientation, and means of coping with crises is complete without a description and analysis of the nats, predictive, divinatory, and medicinal systems. These systems of thought and handling nature are analytical categories devised by the recording anthropologist. To a villager in Nondwin, these systems, together with his Buddhism, make a rather coherent whole, a single set of beliefs and activities to be invoked as instrumentalities, depending on the particular situation he confronts. Just as parts of Buddhism are used as a technology for handling the sacred, so, conversely, parts of the predictive and divinatory systems come in for their share of respect and devotion akin to that accorded to the Buddhist pantheon. As recent students of Burmese Buddhism have agreed, nats, alchemy, magic, and Buddhism form a single continuum, and villagers move, as need and courses sway them, along this integrated view of the nature of reality that is without inconsistency or leaps of logic (Brohm, 1963, Mendelson, 1960, Nash, 1963). It is an error to see village Buddhism as a "thin veneer," covering a host of animistic and tribal, pre– or folk Buddhist beliefs (Htin Aung, 1962). For it is the Buddhist cadre of belief that defines and incorporates these supplementary systems of sacred technology. Village Buddhism requires, as I have argued in the preceding chapter, some set of supplementary activities to handle immediate, day-to-day emergencies, to deal with more mundane threats than the plane of rebirth, to enable men to cope with a world that sometimes baffles, often frustrates, and frequently obstructs their plans and dreams. When I have explored this category of belief and action, I shall attempt to put it together, schematically, with the Buddhism analyzed earlier, so that the whole, as it appears to the persons involved, may be approximated by the reader.

166

THE NATS

Nats are the most important category of the supplementary systems for handling the world. Nats are fundamentally, but not exclusively, anthropomorphic, and many of them have real histories. The core of the nats are the so-called "37," or royal, nats. These nats supposedly stem from the time of Anawrahta and represent his compromises with popular belief as he sought to institute, or reconstitute, Theravada Buddhism in the Pagan dynasty. The stories, the characters, and the provinces of these nats are well summarized by Temple (1906) and Htin Aung (1962). Their interests were cultural-historical and, only slightly, functional and comparative. My aims are almost exclusively the latter, so I will not recount their hypotheses and speculations on why the 37 are who and what they are. The most complete comparative study of Upper Burma nats that I know is that of Dr. June Nash (1964), and I use this work.

In Nondwin, nobody knows the 37 nats, except the pongyi, who gets his list by consulting a book. And nat membership in the population of the 37 varies from village to village in Upper Burma. Most of the 37 nats are, in fact, inoperative or not propitiated in Nondwin. However, the category of 37 does exist, and at some nat rituals the 37 are invoked, and a particular tune is played by the band for each of the 37. But this invocation is the sphere of specialists, traveling nat dance teams or natwives who sometimes come to Nondwin, or people from Nondwin go to where a renowned *natkadaw* (natwife) is dancing or where there is a regionally important nat ceremony.

There are four levels of nats in Nondwin:

1. Territorial nats. Those who are lords of a given region. People in that region must pay attention to these nats, as do individuals who travel through the province of the territorial nat.

2. Village nat. A guardian nat whose job it is to keep other, more malignant nats from seeking abode in the village. The villagers have already come to terms with this nameless and historyless nat in Nondwin. (Other villages may have a "storied" nat.)

3. Inherited nats. The *mizaing-hpazaing* nats are those inherited one from the mother and one from the father. These must be fed and propitiated, too.

4. Activity nats. Those associated with certain realms of action or protection, like the house nat, or the rice nat.

These levels of nat belief reveal a significant and surprising element in what has hitherto been conceived of as an amorphous animism. Burmese nat belief is a *structured* system of animistic belief. Its structure is closely related to the levels of social relations: (1) Activity nats are for the individual and the family; (2) mizaing-hpazaing nats are for the family and kin; (3) village nats are for the community; (4) territorial nats are for the inner and outer circles of social relations. In Nondwin one moves not only along a cultural plane where nat powers are oriented to fairly discrete realms, but concomitantly on a continuum of increasing width of social relations. The propitiation of nats, then, has a social and cultural dimension as well as the individual dimension of need or demand to be safeguarded from evil.

The nats, at all levels, are chiefly evil powers. They can, if angered or ignored, punish and bring trouble to human beings. At the very best they can safeguard an individual against trouble from other nats or malignant spirits. The whole business of nat propitiation has less the feeling of wooing positive good than it does warding off probable evil. The nats to whom the villagers pay deference and attention are individualities, with tastes, preferences, personalities, conceits, and crotchets. Nat rituals take account of the peculiarities of the nat to whom they are addressed. In nat ceremonies the language is the deferential sort used in addressing pongyis and high civil officials. Nat rituals are spaced throughout the year in accord with two different rhythms. First, there is the predominant cycle of Buddhist ceremony, of which some nat rituals form an integral part, and, second, there is the fixed time for some nat ceremonies plus the unscheduled needs for protection or fighting off evil.

Every house in Nondwin honors the *eindwin* nat, Min Mahagiri. This household nat is represented in all the households by a coconut. The coconut is tied to a special post, called *uyudaing*, or nat post, or post of grace. This, like all the sacra, is in the mingala direction of east. Flowers are placed under the nat coconut, and sometimes food (cooked rice) offerings are made to it. The flowers for the nat are not changed frequently (or daily) as they are for the Buddha altar, nor is food offered daily, nor is there any devotional performed near the grace post or under the coconut. Custom as to changing the coconut is varied. About half of Nondwin breaks the old coconut and replaces it at the beginning of the Wa. About one-third of the households replace the coconut every three months or so, and the remainder change when they think the coconut is too dry. Only a handful of households decorate their nat coconut with the piece of red cloth, which is supposed to be especially appealing to Min Mahagiri. (Other Upper Burma villages use this bit of cloth nearly 100 per cent.) The propitiation of Min Mahagiri is supposed to ward off two things: dacoits (armed robber bands that rove the countryside) and disease. If a person in a household dies, the coconut must be changed, or if there is a serious illness in the household, one of the curing techniques used may be a special food offering to Min Mahagiri. Min Mahagiri's day is not celebrated in Nondwin. In nearby Legyi, Min Mahagiri is specially honored with a *natpwe* (as the ceremony is called when there is a band and a troupe of dancing natkadaws, three days after the full moon of *Tabaung*) and many people from Nondwin attend the rite. This is a condensed version of the most common telling of the tale of Min Mahagiri in Nondwin:

There was a very strong and powerful blacksmith, named Maung Tinde. He could forge the greatest amount of iron. He was famous for his strength all throughout the whole Kingdom of Burma. The king heard of the power and the strength of Maung Tinde, and he was afraid that the blacksmith might use his great strength to drive him from his throne. The king sent his troops to arrest or kill Maung Tinde, but he was warned and hid from them in his forest. The king then thought of another plan. He married Ma Lat, one of the sisters of Maung Tinde. He told Ma Lat, "Why should your brother, my brother-in-law, continue to live isolated in the jungle? Tell him I will guarantee his safety, if he will come to court, and I will give him a high post, and you and he can be together again." "If," he continued, "you convince Maung Tinde to accept my offer, I will elevate you to Number One Queen." (It is recalled that Burmese kings were in the habit of having a number of queens, and that the queens often changed position as to whether their offspring were most or least likely to be royal successors.) Ma Lat believed the king, and, as she wanted her brother near, since she was very fond of him, she went to him and called him out of hiding. Maung Tinde came. When he set foot in the royal compound, he was seized and tied to a stake, and a fire of faggots burned him. Ma Lat saw the king's treachery and threw herself into the flames with her brother in repayment for her guilt and her ambition. They became nats and troubled people, but finally people honored them as house nats, and now they live peacefully on Mount Popa (the reputed home of many nats).

This brother-sister pair of nats, of course, are allergic to fire, and one does not cook near them or let flames near them, and they act as talismans against fires.

The nat who guards the village of Nondwin is nameless except for the descriptive appellative of *Ywadawyin*, which only means village guardian nat. Ywadawyin is housed in a small *natsin*, nat house, at the edge of Nondwin. The house is a small, ramshackle structure, not well kept up. Usually it contains some wilted flowers, a pot half filled with stagnant water, and some grains of dry, stale rice. This nat is propitiated once a year. Since Nondwin has no natwives, the natkadaw from Legyi is hired to come over and perform the rite, at village expense. The villagers pay her by voluntary contribution, by contributing to the band, and by paying for the liquor she consumes. Coconuts, cake, flowers, and bananas (the usual gadawbwe of respect) will be placed in the natsin on this nat's day, and then it will be ignored for the rest of the year. At such a small festival, only the single natkadaw comes, together with a few local musicians. The cost of the whole ceremony is about 25 kyats. The natkadaw, like all natwives I spoke to, became the medium for Min Mahagiri unwittingly. Her story, with minor amendments and elaborations, is natwife ordinary. She went to a natpwe, once, for Min Mahagiri. The natwives were dancing. She danced a bit too (as spectators sometimes do to especially honor a given nat). Then she sat down, but she was unable to remain seated; something prompted her to dance again. She got up and, while dancing, was seized in a trance. She danced in semicoma, and while she twirled she heard the nat saying he wanted her for a wife. She fainted, and when she recovered she knew that, on his day, the nat would visit her and, perhaps, in her state of trance speak through her. Everybody believes such a story; it is part of common occurrence, for that is how natkadaws are made. Sometimes, natwives refuse the embrace of the nat, and then they are troubled by horrible dreams; they suffer various bodily ills, lose weight, and are not able to work well. All of these things disappear when they accept the nat and become his vehicle on earth for speech. This Legyi natkadaw also used *Kogyidaw* (the liquor-loving nat) in her ritual. She gulps down a bottle of country spirits (made usually from distilled toddy palm) and then goes into her twirling trance. She stops in the state near somnambulance, and answers questions the villagers put to her about their personal troubles. With each question 10 or 25 pyas will be tossed to her. After about 20 minutes of trance, she snaps back to normal and apparently is sober despite the large amount of alcohol she has recently swallowed. Villagers do not rely very much on the replies of the natkadaw. First, the natkadaw replies to queries are vague and ambiguous, and, second, they are only a minor means for a villager to get information about the future.

The other nats regularly propitiated here are mizaing and hpazaing nats. Not everyone in Nondwin has these nats. About half the villagers have them and pay attention to them, and this half is a cross-section of the population, showing no particular cluster of social and cultural characteristics. Whether or not they have mother- and father-line nats depends on the simple fact of whether or not their parents bequeathed them such nats. If they have them, they observe their day once a year, by placing food out for them and by sometimes hiring a natkadaw to honor them. The placation of these nats is tied closely to the birth and health of the children of the household, and failure to keep up the charge laid on by parents may result in sickly children or an unusual child mortality toll. In a vague way, too, nats are tied to birth. The people of Nondwin know about the relation of babies to intercourse, and they are fairly straightforward about the role of semen and ovaries in forming babies, but that is not all there is to it. For, not only are these, so to speak, efficient causes involved, but there are also formal and final agencies implicated. The final cause of having, not having, or the number had of children is the kan of the parents. Kan governs this aspect of birth and rebirth and material embodiments. The formal cause is nats. Nats collectively, both Buddha nats and the more mundane nats, are the active principles in forming the foetus, or malforming it, in saying whether the birth is live or dead, hard or easy, and whether the health of the child is good or not. Mizaing-hpazaing nats play a particular role in this, and, hence, if one has them, one must propitiate them on this score. The villagers say *nattha gya peide*, the nats give babies, meaning that they are the agency that controls the effectiveness of the act of intercourse, against the larger background of kutho-kan. This sort of information is fragmentary for me. It is women's talk and their province (as the nats generally are), and men are not much informed nor concerned.

The remaining nats propitiated in Nondwin are a mixed bag of territorial and crisis nats. There is *Bobogyi*, the nat in charge of all trees. Before cutting down a tree, the permission of this nat is required. For a small tree or sapling, a tea leaf offering is made in payment. For a larger tree the dah test is applied. The woodsman or prospective tree chopper addresses himself to the nat and asks permission to cut down this tree. He then rests his dah at an angle against the tree. He goes away and returns in 20 or 30 minutes. If the dah is still upright, permission is granted; if it is lying on the ground, the nat has denied permission. Bobogyi has a local nat shrine on the crest of a hill near a ruined pagoda, just at the limit of naked eyesight from Nondwin. Nondwin people do not usually go to his natpwe.

There is also a special territorial tree guard nat, called *Bodawgyi*, who lives in *Bodawgyi nat gyi* (the big royal nat's cave). This nat's permission must be asked in a demarcated region of which he is considered spiritual owner or guardian, if one wants to cut trees or even hunt animals or birds there. The same dah test is used. Failure to get nat permission when felling trees brings trouble to one's cattle, health, and family.

In addition, all large, old trees have their own particular, indwelling, resident nat, called the *yokkazo*. The yokkazo is a nat or spirit who has taken up residence in a particular tree. Some yokkazo, in the form of white wraiths, sometimes come out at night and wander. They do no harm, but they frighten children. The resident yokkazo in an old, venerable tree is domesticated. It is thought that he has lived a long time without harming villagers. If the tree is cut down without his permission, he may get angry and cause trouble (chiefly sickness or even a plague), or he may be replaced by an angry, malignant nat who will cause trouble until he too is domesticated into peaceful coexistence with the villagers. In Nondwin, the most venerable of the yokkazo lives in the banyan tree, near the village entrance gate, and the next most venerable lives in the banyan tree near the village exit gate. The banyan tree is respected because of its association with the enlightenment of the Buddha, but it is also respected because of its resident yokkazo. When the banyan watering ceremony takes place on the Buddha day, both the Buddha and the yokkazo are honored. Even the pongyis who come for tree watering give deference to the yokkazo of the banyan. The delicate feelings of the yokkazo are considered in one's personal conduct near the tree. One should not urinate near it, nor have intercourse or use profanity under its shade. The banyan tree also is incorporated into some of the pithy sayings of villagers. When a man brags about something he will do, and villagers think it is beyond his capacity, they say he will do it when the banyan tree flowers, which it never does. This is a parallel use, of something from the nat realm, with the saying, for similar overestimations of accomplishments, of a man who claims that he is the brick that will top the pagoda. A single brick does not make a pagoda.

The people of Nondwin attend the region-wide, or Upper Burma-wide festival of Taungbyon. There are visitors and believers who come from the whole of Burma, including Shans, Chins, and even a Kachin or two. The Taungbyon brothers' natpwe is the most important in all of Upper Burma. It is a five-day festival beginning on *Wagaun 12*. There are many versions of the tale of the two gold brothers, Shweipyingyi and Shweipyinlei, who are honored and feted at the Taungbyon nat ceremonies. The shortest village version follows.

There were two royal brothers, princes, sons of the king, called Shweipyingyi and Shweipyinlei. They had been generals and had carried the king's armies to victory against the Shans. The king ordered them to stop and build a pagoda as thanksgiving for the victory over the Shan princes. The king ordered all of his subjects to carry at least one brick to the spot where the pagoda was to be built. The two gold brothers did not carry their bricks, either because they were at play or because they forgot. The king, who wanted some excuse to get these popular generals out of the way, for he was afraid that they might revolt and seize his throne, ordered them executed for this infraction of his orders. They were executed, and, since it was both a violent and unjust end, they became nats.

In those days, the king's men traveled up and down the Irrawaddy in the long golden royal boats. Whenever they came near the place where the Taungbyon brothers were killed, the boats were capsized or turned back. They could not sail up and down the river. The brothers were getting their revenge on the king. The king tried many things but finally turned to his ministers and asked their advice on how to appease the brothers. The ministers said the only thing that would work would be to build a simple house and offer food to the nats. The king did this and ordered the people to do this also. He gave them command of the territory, and from this comes the annual five-day festival.

I did not see the Taungbyon festival, but it has been described many times, and, from what informants who had, in the past, attended the natpwe told me, I could add nothing of substance to the published accounts. I did visit the nat shrines dedicated to the two gold brothers. These are the only nat shrines I saw in Upper Burma that had the aspect of a pagoda. They were on sacred ground, on which one could walk only in bare feet; there were a permanent shelter for the tiger statues and other statues, resident full-time nat guardians, and hosts of pilgrims, who came to pay devotions to these nats by placing gadawbwes in front of the images or by offering food and flowers to small nat images. The language of address was deferential, and the approach included the shikko. I even saw, at Taungbyon, young pongyis pay respects to the territorial nats. At the festival for the Taungbyon brothers' mother (also a nat), I saw the full dancing troupes of natwives, mainly from Mandalay, but also from other parts of Burma. These women wore red turbans (a color especially liked by nats), belted longyis (to hold them in place as in a trance they do their whirling dance), and used swords in their dance. These natkadaws drank three or four bottles of country spirits after their trance and predictions without showing signs of intoxication. I interviewed one of these natwives, and she told me a story much like that of the natkadaw of Legyi. Her story had much more of the hysterical in its account of the wooing of the nat, and she had much more trouble before she finally accepted the brothers. The Taungbyon brothers are especially sexually potent and pick out dancing women at every celebration in their honor. She reported former residence in a village community, but recalled that when the communists held her village, they drove out natkadaws, most of whom went to Mandalay, which is now headquarters for natwives. The communists, she also reported, went so far as to kill *sonma* (witch women) but they only drove natkadaws from the community. She, like other women who are in the professional nat media, spends a good part of her time traveling from natpwe to natpwe and earning her living by predicting when she is in the state of *natpude* (nat-possessed). It is obligatory for all the natwives of the two gold brothers to attend their natpwe, as well as the natpwes of his immediate nat relatives. At Taungbyon, then, there is concentrated nat reverence.

The above are the nats that count in the life of Nondwin. They must be propitiated, placated, and appeased in any time of trouble, for they may be involved as causal agents. The bulk of attention to nats, then, is to ward off the potential evil these vain, capricious, and often violent beings have the power to wreak. In traveling, Nondwin people sometimes cross into the territory of other nats, and they take the proper precautions, especially on the way to the hill town of Maymyo, where there is a plethora of nat shrines for Shan nats, under the jurisdiction of the "nine lords." If they travel in a car with nine passengers, they are considered to be inviting trouble from the lords of the nine towns. What the jeeps and buses do, if their passenger load is nine, is to pick up a stone from the side of the road, give it a name, and carry it like a passenger, thus making a combination or total that will not infuriate the lords of the region.

The description of the functional nats in Nondwin may not give an adequate sense of how real and omnipresent these possibly malignant forces are. One good indicator of the hold of nat belief is that Nondwin migrants to Mandalay return to Nondwin on the day of the nat celebration, even if that is the only time during the year they visit. They still feel themselves somehow under the baleful protection of the village nat. They do not necessarily return for pagoda festivals or Buddhist ceremonies, for these things are not so tied to a place, a locality, but are everywhere the same agency for the gathering of kutho.

SPIRITS

The nats are the structured aspect of animistic belief, but there is also the classic jumble of spirits, forces, ghosts, demons, and goblins in the thought of the villagers. These act intermittently in the lives of villagers and are possible cooperating causes in their troubles. They are not regularly propitiated, nor are regular precautions taken against them. They, if seen, or suspected to be in play in a given crisis or emergency, are treated by specific countermeasures, depending on what class or kind of spirit is believed to be involved.

The most inclusive kind of spirit is a ghost called *Thaye* (literally, brave he). Thayes have their origin in the death of a person in cold blood. These ghosts are harmful; they cause falls, spills, bone breaks, and even accidents leading to death of the victim. They operate at night. These ghosts are frequently invisible, but they can take animal, or larger than human, form. Their flesh is cold to the touch (but nobody has ever touched one). If one is deviled by a Thaye, a special ghost-treating doctor (*payogasaya*) has an anti-ghost medicine (either *lethpwet* or *yeimanseiman*), either a powder taken internally or a medallion-like metal worn around the neck. Nondwin has never had a ghost of the Thaye class, but Nondwin people have been troubled by, and have encountered, such ghosts. Currently there is believed to be a Thaye residing in nearby Nyaungbinwin. This ghost caused the headman of Nondwin to have an accident. U Sein Ko and the headman were returning to Nondwin on bicycles, and the headman fell from his bicycle, right at the very spot the Thaye was believed to be. Now, it is true that the headman was drunk at the time, but that is irrelevant for he could have fallen anywhere, but, in fact, he fell at the Thaye-guarded spot. U Sein Ko, adept at these things, knew just what to do. He recited a Pali chant (from the *payeikkyi*) that drove the ghost off and prevented further attack. This chant is one that all the pongyis know, and U Sein Ko learned it during his 10 years as a monk. Monks are often summoned to recite this chant to drive ghosts from houses, deserted places, trees, or dark forests. It is, in Nondwin view, invariably effective when a monk does this. This piece of anti-ghost devotional was given to the sangha by the Buddha, while he was under the banyan tree, and thus its chanting invokes the superior power of the Buddha over the ghosts, who also recognize the dominance of the Buddha and are thus obligated to leave when a monk makes this incantation.

U Sein Ko once met a ghost of the Thaye variety just outside of Mandalay. He and a friend were about to sleep in a deserted hut in a paddy field when the ghost (who was residing in this hut) appeared. It was, according to U Sein Ko, a huge figure, with legs 10 feet long, eyes as big as saucers 6 inches across, and its whole huge body was covered with long, black hair. His friend ran off to a nearby village, where he died of fright. U Sein Ko pulled out his dah and swung at the Thaye, shouting imprecations of defiance all the time. He could not cut or touch the ghost, but his dah and noise kept the ghost from embracing him in a fatal grasp. He kept up the racket until people came running. The ghost fled the crowd.

There is another sort of ghost, less dreadful than the Thaye, called the *tasei*. The tasei comes from the bodies of dead animals, especially dogs, and is expiating akutho from former existences. The tasei is frightening chiefly because of its monstrous appearance. When the tasei has suffered sufficiently, it will be reborn into its appropriate plane. Thaye, on the other hand, spends countless years in that state, for it is the spirit of an extremely wicked person, but even it, eventually, will be reborn in its proper state. There is this strain to reconcile everything with the dominant Buddhist notions of rebirth, although there are evident flaws in these patched world views. Tasei fright is treated by the same sort of doctor and in the same way as Thaye affliction.

One other ghost, who attacks children especially, is the *htamin lon tasei* (rice-ball ghost). If a child steps on cooked rice, he will dream of ascending to and then falling from a high place. This frightening dream often wakes the child in a fit of crying. The point of this ghost and this punishment is to make sure that children are careful, when they are eating, not to spill htamin or tread on it. If rice is dropped, it should be carefully swept up and always handled respectfully. The htamin lon tasei is somehow, but not very directly, related to the *bomagyi* nat. The bomagyi nat is the "rice mother," and she is responsible for the increase of rice stored in the godown after harvest. Some people in Nondwin have a natkadaw and offer bomagyi food in October, but only a few of those who have rice in the godown do this. And these same people with paddy in the godown will light a candle or two to bomagyi at the pagoda festival lighting. But, on the whole, bomagyi is very unimportant (as is growing paddy), and her power is not known here, as it is in paddy economy communities.

Witchcraft

In Nondwin, there are also a host of ogres (*balu*), mythical animals (*galon*), and unembodied forces that can cause troubles. But they are not much considered or worried about. There is also the special possibility of being turned into an unwilling treasure guard. There is a group of pretty young maidens called *oketazaung*, treasure guards. These lovely treasure-guarding maidens have power over the balu, and they always guard treasure in lonely places. The oketazaung are the spirits of misers who have spent their lives in jealous care of their treasures. Turning into this spirit treasure guard is their punishment. The maiden spirits are guarded by the balu, so no one can rob them of the treasure they guard. The oketazaung get out of their punishment by befriending a pretty girl, and then they lure (it is not known exactly how) her soul out of her body. They enter her body, while her soul goes to replace the body the oketazaung have left guarding the forlorn treasure. The oketazaung then must seek out an *ahtet lan hsaya* (literally "above the road" master), white magician, and get permission to live on earth until she dies and can be reborn in the proper plane. This story, while based on evil for a miser, and kutho-kan for the bewitched substitute, is a morality tale. Its moral is plain: Be not greedy if you are rich; do not wander alone if you are young and beautiful.

The oketazaung belief touches on the province of witchcraft and white and black magic as it is conceived of in Nondwin. *Auklan pyin nya* ("under the road" magic, or black magic) is practiced by living people against other living people. The auklan hsaya makes his evil medicine from dead bodies, especially from skulls and genitalia which are robbed from the cemetery. He will light a candle, spray it with the powder made from the dead body elements, and invoke evil against a person. Everytime he lights a fire or a candle, the afflicted person will get hot in his body, and if not countered, this internal heat will eventually consume him. To counteract the black magicians, there is *ahtet lan pyin nya* ("above the road" magic, or white magic) practiced by ahtet lan hsayas. The white magicians usually operate by making in. An in is a special cabalistic charm written on a piece of paper. There are hosts of in, and I have collected about 40 of them, with their special provinces (certain illnesses, witchcraft, childbirth, fortune-getting, protection against knife wounds, bullets, safe conduct passes through strange territory, and love-inducing in). The in against black magicians is supposed to work by being hurled against the auklan hsaya. It results in an explosion which consumes the witch. No one in Nondwin can prepare this particular in, so they depend on a highly reputed monk in Nakayang. The pongyi of Nakayang's reputation rests on tales like these.

Once an auklan hsaya came to the kyaung of Nakayang where the pongyi is an ahtet lan saya. The black magician and the pongyi both had in their possession magic balls of mercury. The black magician said he had come to exchange *datlon* (magic round balls, usually mercury) with the pongyi. The pongyi asked the auklan hsaya what powers his datlon had. The magician answered it had the power to turn 100 kyats into 200 kyats. The pongyi heard a voice in his ear telling him not to make this exchange. So the pongyi refused to make the datlon switch. The auklan hsaya then offered a challenge. The black magician threw an in at the pongyi, but it fell harmlessly at his feet. The pongyi then threw an in at the auklan hsaya, and it burned to ashes the carrying bag of the black magician, who, at this demonstration of the power of the pongyi, fled in great fear.

The sponsor of the East Kyaung in Nondwin, who of course was wealthy, had a tragedy. His son was captured by dacoits and held for ransom. The people of Nondwin knew who the dacoits were, and they were going to tell the police to go after them. But the father was afraid that the dacoits might harm his son, so he went to the pongyi to ask his advice and intervention. The pongyi consulted the stars and planets, prepared an in, buried it, and predicted the kidnapped boy's return at a precise hour and minute on the following day. And next day the boy appeared at the kyaung, unharmed, even though his hands were tied.

A villager in Nondwin suspects witchcraft if his child cries every night, or if he gets continual stomachaches, or if his sight begins to fail. Women get unaccountable fevers and turn into malicious gossips when they are under a witch's spell. If any of these symptoms persist, the afflicted seeks out an ahtet lan hsaya for treatment. A direct confrontation of white and black power is not sought; it is avoided (just like a real power struggle in ordinary social relations in Nondwin). The ahtet lan hsaya will prepare medicine for the bewitched and make an offering of food to the witch on the behalf of the patient. The food offering is to ask forgiveness of the witch for whatever slight or trouble the patient may have, unwittingly, given the witch and to demonstrate, as food offering always does, a position of dependence upon the power of the witch. If this does not work, then the pongyi (local or Nakayang) is asked to prepare an in. This in is burned to an ash, mixed with water and drunk. It is supposed to cure. The pongyi in, in this case, is supposed to drive out a special kind of slow poison that the black magician and his female witch assistant have somehow gotten into the patient's daily food.

Witches (sonma) are chiefly women, although an occasional warlock is spoken of. These women are supposed to learn the essentials of the black arts from the Shans, who along with other hill tribes, are thought to be especially expert in this malevolent magic. Sonmas have all sorts of occult powers. They can, for example, turn into vultures. There was Daw Ni, the famous witch on the nearby Mu river. She had caused much trouble, and a group of people went to challenge her power. She knew they were coming and magically removed their testicles. The men saw that they had no testicles, so they went to the witch and asked her pardon for their challenge. She pointed to a basket where the testicles were, and they each took their own and returned to the village. A sonma could be not only a vulture; she had the ability to be a snake, a dog, or a horse, and the ability to go around making people sick. But even she was powerless against a skilled pongyi.

Once, U Sein Ko recounts, when his eldest son was young, he was bewitched. He knew this because the boy could not sleep through a night for five months, and he cried every night. U Sein Ko knew, from watching, from observing the obvious changes this woman made at night, and from her working alone over medicine making, that a Nondwin woman had cast a spell on his son, out of envy and spite. He invited her to come to his house and eat beef curry. She accepted. She was served by his wife, and, while she was eating, U Sein Ko sneaked up behind her and put a spear through her back. Before the spear came out her chest, she turned into a black dog. He and his brother-in-law removed the dead dog to the outskirts of Nondwin, through the West gate. (I interviewed both men and the brother-in-law vouches for the story. When the story was told me, there were five or six other adults present, and nobody blinked an eye. His wife, whom I know to be a sober, sane, and truthful woman, nodded her assent during the telling of the story.) The next morning they went to look, and the body of the dog had disappeared. The sonma herself, U Sein Ko said, continued to live in another village for many years. The black dog was just one of her extra bodies, which witches use on occasions when they are found out. Since then, he claims and others agree, there have been no witches in Nondwin.

But, one morning, a neighbor of U Sein Ko's came over to borrow from him an ox team and cart. He wanted to take his ailing son over to the pongyi kyaung so that he and his wife could consult the monk about the boy's illness. The child cried every night, and they suspected witchcraft. This pongyi knew traditional Burmese medicine, and he also could prepare an in, if that was required. The pongyi took the child's pulse at the wrists, and the coursing blood beneath his knowledgeable fingers "told" him if the child was bewitched. The pongyi recommended the usual first step. He told the couple to place in the corner of their compound a dish of beef and rice. A dog would come along and eat this. It would be the extra body of the witch, who would take the food and in forgiveness give up troubling the child. But, according to the pongyi, it was not the child who was under a spell, but its mother, and it would be its mother from whom the food offering would lift the spell.

When I spoke to this man after his return from the pongyi, he said that if the pongyi's first advice did not work, he would do some other things before requesting an in from the monk. He would make special food offerings on the Buddha altar; he would make a special gadawbwe to his house nat, and he would offer food to a nat in a large tree. He wanted to be sure, at least, that all of these possible malefactors had not had their touchy pride offended in some way by his wife's behavior. There was, on his part, no feeling of reverence or awe for the nats, just a step-by-step checking out, in the proper ritual manner of appeasing superior forces, the possible sources of his troubles. The transaction was a straight bargain: food and respect for the nats in return for the removal of evil forces. In time the boy recovered without the need for an in. If the pongyi had prepared such a charm, it would have been without any "fee," but some gift, or maybe even a hsungywe, would have been tendered and accepted.

The closest things to an in, and suitable for the same sorts of troubles, are the magical tattoos. In fact, tattoos may be considered as a form of in, except that they are indelibly marked on the skin of a person, and they have a longer lasting efficacy against the particular evil or force they are directed against. In royal days, men were tattooed from navel to knee with the intricate patterns of blue lines. This older form of tattooing was supposed to test the strength and mark the virility of a man. It was exceedingly painful, given the iron prick-by-prick placing of the pigment under the skin, and infection was not a rare occurrence. Nondwin people say that in the old days a woman would have nothing to do with a man who did not exhibit the tattoed thigh. Now, in Nondwin, there are three or four older men who still have the royal sort of tattoo, but the last two generations ignore this mark of manhood, and the custom is on the way to desuetude. The most common tattoo is a *pyithsei* tattoo, usually placed at the crown of the head, and it can only be observed if a man is shaven on the pate. The pyithsei looks like this:

It is a charm which prevents knives from cutting the wearer and bullets from entering his body. Tales are told of its efficacy in turning away dahs and steel, but failures are also known. It sort of functions like the idea of bullet-proof glass in our society; sometimes it works, sometimes it does not, but it is the best protection one has in any case.

Almost everyone, male and female, has a band of blue tattooed on either the ankles or the wrists. This tattoo, with the proper incantation said when applied, repels snakes and is called *mwehsei,* or snake medicine. The villagers do not place complete confidence in these tattoes, for there is still great worry about snakebite, and it is still an unreasonably frequent cause of death. No Nondwin house, for example, is set in a grassy lawn, for this would invite snakes to slither close to home and would increase the chances of being bitten. All houses sit in a cleared, bare, brown patch. In the fields men carry their dahs, and if a poisonous snake comes close, they will kill it. They do not, however, go out of their way to find and kill snakes, for, useful as it might be, that would be non-Buddhist. A living thing, like a threatening snake, or a poisonous scorpion, or a rabid dog, is killed if there is no other resort, because a person does not have the capacity to die a martyr, which, in the abstract, is preferable. A line of three, four, seven, or nine blue dots is a frequent tattoo on both men and women. This tattoo keeps off witch power and makes the work of the auklan hsaya much more difficult. Single blue dots on the palms of the hands or in the web connecting the fingers have the same function. Some men have tattoos of mythical animals, like the galon, the Burmese version of a phoenix-like bird. This is supposed to endow them with some of the virtues of the animal they have on their body. Tattooing, then, is a system of charms, like ins, which has powers to ward off particular evils and, only marginally, in one case, to bring positive good to the person. The tattoos are usually done when an individual is a young adult. Children are rarely tattooed unless there is special witchcraft danger, and then they get the line of dots somewhere on the arms, legs, hands, or even in the middle of the back.

Akin to the meaning of tattooing are all the precautions involved in the cutting of head hair. The head is the most sacred part of the body, and a man's pon is thought to reside in the top of his head. The raising of one's head to a greater height than another's is, of course, a sign of greater status and honor. Striking on the head is virtually absent; even angry parents take care to flail their children in other places. Part of the mystique of the hair is related to the august position of the head, and part of it is related to the stress the Buddha himself made on hair. In Nondwin hair is also considered the best expression of vanity, and the amount and style of hair is also an indicator of sexuality. Hair treatment and cutting bears many of the notions expressed by Leach (1958). Hair style is divided by age and sex. In the ideal and prevailing pattern, small boys and small girls wear the tiered hairdo ending in a top knot. Girls then go to a style with bangs and a knot at the top; boys to a simple knot at top; married women to long hair, drawn straight back with the side knot; full grown men to the long hair tied in a top knot. Later in life, men shave to the pate. Oiling and combing the hair, washing it, and arranging it takes time, and the shedding of hair is a mark that one is turning from the mundane vanities of personality to the inner life of search for Nibbana. Now few men in Nondwin wear the long hair, and only a few are shaven to the pate. Most wear a form of short hair or a crew-like cut. Women still, universally, wear the long side knot style popularized by Thibaw's last queen. And, for a villager, watching a woman comb and brush her flowing hair is highly erotic, and many sexual anecdotes turn on the imagery of long, flowing, female locks.

PREDICTIVE AND DIVINATORY SYSTEMS

With all of this symbolism that hair must bear, it is not surprising that it cannot be cut at will, and that its cutting is surrounded by taboos. Hair cannot be cut on a Friday or a Monday; nor can it be cut on the person's birthday (that is, the day of the week on which he was born); nor can it be cut if he is ill. A violation of these injunctions would result in fever and illness. Everybody observes these haircutting rules, and even the barbershops in Mandalay are closed on Mondays, for there are no customers. Hair washing should take place on a Sunday,

Tuesday, or Saturday for an increase in luck and health. Washing on other days does not bring misfortune or illness, however.

Astrology

The business of attaching haircutting and washing to certain days is also tied to the astrological and planetary beliefs of the peasants. No day is ordinary, no moment in time is without its special conjunction of fateful elements, for the *gyo* (planets) are always exerting their influence on the lives of people, on the fate of the world. Astrology is a system of divination of the disposition of the planetary forces toward an individual or an event. The full rationale of astrology is the province of adepts and experts, who are either called *ponnas* or brahmins (clearly indicating the Indian sources of the beliefs and the Burmese yielding to superior Hindu expertise in this realm of the occult), or who are monks who have studied and mastered the lore and knowledge of the stars and planets.

In the disposition of the heavenly bodies, there are some fixed constellations, about which all peasants know. There are lucky and unlucky days in a repetitive pattern all throughout the year, and this is the way they fall, according to Nondwin consensus:

April:	Lucky:	Friday and Wednesday
	Unlucky:	Saturday and Thursday
May:	Lucky:	Saturday and Thursday
	Unlucky:	Friday and Wednesday
June:	Lucky:	Tuesday
	Unlucky:	Sunday and Monday
July:	Lucky:	Friday and Wednesday
	Unlucky:	Tuesday and Wednesday
August:	Lucky:	Friday and Wednesday
	Unlucky:	Saturday and Thursday
September:	Lucky:	Saturday and Thursday
	Unlucky:	Friday and Wednesday
October:	Lucky:	Tuesday
	Unlucky:	Sunday and Monday
November:	Lucky:	Friday and Wednesday
	Unlucky:	Tuesday and Wednesday
December:	Lucky:	Friday and Wednesday
	Unlucky:	Tuesday and Wednesday

January:	Lucky:	Thursday and Saturday
	Unlucky:	Friday and Wednesday
February:	Lucky:	Thursday and Tuesday
	Unlucky:	Sunday and Monday
March:	Lucky:	Saturday and Wednesday
	Unlucky:	Tuesday and Wednesday [12]

In this annual round of lucky and unlucky days, the pattern repeats every few months, and it does not appear a contradiction that in July, November, and March, Wednesday is both a lucky and an unlucky day. The apparent illogicality is resolved by the particular kinds of things this day is lucky or unlucky for.

In addition to these generalized lucky and unlucky days for beginning and ending certain kinds of ventures, each individual has his own particular set of auspicious or "kingly" days based on his particular moment of birth, and the planetary projections made from that portentous fact. When a baby is born in Nondwin, there is a mad rush to the house of one of the rich men, who has a clock, to ascertain the exact temporal locus of this event. It is carefully noted and will be communicated to the ponna who casts this individual's horoscope. The sada (horoscope) is usually cast when an individual is a young adult, but if there is a serious illness in childhood, the horoscope is cast then. The best horoscopes are made by the ponnas of Mandalay for a fee of three kyats. The actual horoscope is cut into a palm leaf, and shows the distribution of the nine gyo at the exact moment of birth. From this information, extrapolations can be made (by the experts with their books and charts) to any point in time as to the exact dispositions of planetary forces toward an individual. In really elaborate horoscopes, the major times of baleful and beneficial planetary emanations are also scratched into the palm leaf. This sada is kept, usually in a bamboo case, wrapped in a cloth in the home of the individual who paid for it. It is most frequently kept on or near the nat post. The actual content of the horoscope is an affair between the specialist and the client; the document should not be seen or known by others.

In times of trouble, for any event, for giving a large ahlu, for business, for travel, for marriage, for illness, and for gambling, an individual may consult his horoscope to see if planetary forces are well- or ill-disposed toward the event. In Nondwin, the villager usually takes the horoscope information to the East Kyaung pongyi, who has

---

[12] See Scott, 1882, for full details of Burmese practices.

the books and charts, and he tells the proper times for holding shinbyu, or hsungywe, or whatever. Two people about to marry check out the horoscope information to see if they are "star-crossed" lovers, and if they should abandon the union on that account. (I know of no cases where this happened.) In any prolonged illness, the horoscope is consulted, and, if there is a planetary force involved in the illness, certain rites are undertaken. The chief ritual is giving food to, or for, the planetary deity or spirit to placate it or to cause it to be beneficial. This is akin, of course, to the sacrificial idiom in Buddhism proper, to nat feed, and to monk feed, and it says the same thing: A supplicant of inferior spiritual power asks the powerful to protect him, to turn evil from him. In Nondwin there are no planetary deity images, but they can be found in the large pagoda between Nondwin and Sagaing, or in many pagodas in Sagaing and Mandalay. So making the food, and sometimes money, offering to planetary deities is rather close at hand.

Astrological dispositions are the key to an individual's place in the universe. His birth, the moment he is born, is not chance, or accident, but is the outcome of a whole causal chain of previous events as summed up in his kan. His previous kan and kutho determine the moment, plane, and place of birth. The planetary array at that kan-designed moment of material embodiment is the sketch of a person's existence, the clue to how his kan fits into the whole universe, the marker which points to an unfolding future. It is not, as in the corrupted modern superstition found in most newspapers, that the planets and stars rule your fortune. It is that the stars and planets, to use the Nondwin analogy, reflect, like a mirror, the destiny to accumulate kutho and avoid akutho which a person has built up through past opportunities. Astrology thus fits into the primordial notions of village Buddhism as the universe's reaction to the moment of embodiment of kan. The horoscope tells what is laid out for the person because of his birth, a birth earned by previous lives. But even though the horoscope gives the chief trammels along which his life must, and will, run, it is not a bleak destiny, without possibility of shift or change in course. The planetary rites are designed as means to counter baleful influences or black periods in life. The horoscope may be likened to the sailing chart of a seagoing vessel, in giving the course and marking the dangers, but not specifying in full detail, nor predicting, a safe or disastrous voyage. This is the way Nondwin people use and think of planetary dispositions. The astrological element is woven into almost all major decisions, and the planetary forces are the framework for secular decisions. (Even the new state of the Union of Burma was declared independent at a moment deemed propitious by astrologers.) At the death of an individual his horoscope is floated down the creek, to disappear. It is no longer of use.

There are other uses made of the planetary predictive system. One use is to find out if the year itself is a good one or a bad one, in general. Another is to find out if a given activity is specially favored this year or not, or if a given season is right for one thing or another. Part of this kind of information is given in "almanacs" that can be purchased in Sagaing and in Mandalay; part of it is contained in the printing of every Burmese calendar, and part comes from the trouble the experts and near experts take in diagnosing a particular year and in getting their predictions published in the Burmese language press. The form the ordinary villager knows about planetary lore is fairly complex, involving a rigmarole of numbers and planets. The numerical magic (like Pythagorean lore) is woven into the astrological knowledge. To find the general astrological quality of the year, take the number of the year (1960 is 1322 Burmese Era), divide it by seven, and you get 188.8; keep dividing by eights until you get a remainder of 6. Count the number of divisions you make and put them in order in the following ticktacktoe-like square; if the remainder falls in the bottom, middle, it is a particularly bad year. The logic of this ticktacktoe stems from equating it to the human body like this:

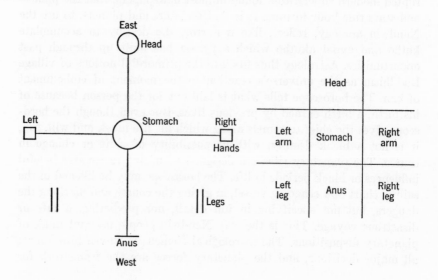

After the remainder (6) is placed in the proper slot, and the character of the year is read from that, there is a poem of the days and number recited (Sunday is 1, on through to Saturday, 7), and the other numbers, corresponding to the days, are placed in their proper slots. For the year 1322, the scheme looks like this:

	3	
5	1	4
2	6	7

This is to be read that the bottom three are bad days (on these days particular troubles are likely to happen to the world), the middle-numbered days fair, and the head position (also east, and hence mingala in the Buddhist idiom, as west is the anus, death, and non-mingala) is by far the best. All this verges on esoteric knowledge for people in Nondwin. What they do know is the general configuration of astrological knowledge, and they deeply believe in this. The actual casting of horoscopes, of year prediction, of event divination, giving numbers to personalities, and other occult mysteries, they leave to experts, whom they pay a fee, if they need any of this knowledge.

There is a little rhyme and jingle of numbers and days (for each letter also has its corresponding number and vice versa) that some farmers use in Nondwin when they get the almanac information that frequently prints the ticktacktoe-like figure I have drawn. On bad years, astrologically indicated, farmers do not plan to expand production, and, if they are cultivating marginal lands, they may decide not to do so that year. On good years they may expand, and they will certainly work the marginal land. All this is not as capricious as it sounds. For a bad year also means, or has ascribed to it, irregular or lesser rains, and higher and more violent winds; this information is also carried in the almanac. The farmers of Nondwin rely on this almanac weather information, for it is the only long-range forecast they get, and it has a good history of being close to the mark according to the verbal reports. There are also some minor number and planet calculations for specific crops. If the day number falls in a mingala spot, it is given its day name (like Thursday equals the letters *pa pha, ba bha, ma* and also 5), and hence, since Thursday falls in a fairly good location in the year grid, all things beginning with its letter will prosper this year (beans, maize, and paddy), and, by the same token, sesamum is not scheduled for a good year.

Now, the astrological year, the rains, and the winds are what they are, and there is nothing a person or Nondwin as a whole can do about them, except take into account what the year is and act prudently in light of that knowledge. There is a vague sort of belief that rains, winds, insects, and other natural factors affecting farming are tied in some way to people's moral behavior in Nondwin and elsewhere. If the rains are poor, the winds destructive, the insects ravenous, it is because, in general, the accumulated kutho of living people that year has fallen below what could have been achieved, and, if these natural factors are favorable, it is because living people have taken advantage of most of the kutho chances they have had. But this is not anything that anyone can act on and does not enter into behavior, except in making sense of the disposition of forces.

From what I observed, the astrological predictions do not have any sensible effect on production, either in the amount or the crops cultivated. These are governed by the straightforward facts of capital, knowledge, labor, ecology, and market prices. Even the small amount of entrepreneurial activity in Nondwin, the onions, was not related to horoscopes, planets, lucky or unlucky signs. It was governed by U Sein Ko's shrewd decision to go into onion growing at this particular time. This is not to say that he did not consult these things, but only to say that they did not govern the situation. He may, as would other Nondwin farmers, attribute part of the outcome to these forces, but he is aware that human effort, knowledge, and kan are the predominant forces shaping events.

The general feeling of prosperity, or lack of it, in Nondwin is dependent upon the crop yield and the market prices for that yield. The year can be whatever the almanac says, but if it is a good crop year, it is a good year, and the reverse. The proverbs one hears about this are to the point:

> In the rainy season the grass grows over the tree stump;
> In the dry season the grass withers, and the trunk is bare.

> The royal symbol of wood once crowned a palace, but it fell
> and became firewood.

Minor Practices. Astrological belief enters into some minor practices beyond those already noted. Each day is governed by a particular planet and has, of course, its corresponding letters of the Burmese alphabet and numbers. The name of an individual is derived from the syllables of his day of birth. That is, children born on Monday have the options of ka, kha, ga, gha, and nga, so that their names would be, for example, Khin, Kyaw, Ngwe, or Khaing, and so on through the week. Each day has its parts of the syllabary, and the first sound of the person's name is taken from these. In Nondwin, only the first name is surely taken from the planetary association. The second name may also be astrologically given, but it is more usual to select the second name for euphonious ends, or to mark some physical feature of the child, or note some habit or character trait, or double the first name, especially for girls, to denote affection and tenderness. For example, a Tuesday girl might, after her planetary initials, be called *Sein* (diamond), and this name might be duplicated for the sound and the feeling of tenderness it gives to *Sein Sein*. Or a Thursday girl might be named *Ma* (Miss) after her planet and *Kala* added to mark her dark skin. Of course nobody literally translates names in Nondwin, unless they are asked. A man named "glorious victory," "beautiful, tall," or "tender tender," or other such vainglorious sounding names hardly thinks of those traits any more than in our society a Smith thinks of forging iron, or a Newhouse of real estate, or Turner thinks of a lathe. Except for a nickname, playfully bestowed, names mean no more than they do in the United States. Occasionally, but very rarely, a person will think his name brings bad luck. Then he will just change it. In Nondwin, the parents themselves bestow names at a simple naming ceremony, at which they may take some suggestions from grandparents. The first name, however, is nearly always a marker of the day and, hence, planet under which a person was born. People born on the same day, bearing the same first sound in their name, do not feel for each other any special affinity, for it is the exact moment of birth, rather than the large category of day, which links fates (combined, of course, with kan, which in the nature of the case must be individual).

The world-circling dragon, the fire breathing *Naga*, is related to planetary knowledge. The Naga is thought to wind around the world, and to be continually shifting the position of his head as he sinuously makes his everlasting girdling of the world. The position of the dragon's head is important to know when a person is about to take a long journey. The rule is simple: Do not travel into the mouth of the dragon. If you travel into the dragon's mouth, you court disaster. In March, April, and May the Naga's head turns toward the West. You cannot travel into his mouth, nor can you bring things across the back of the dragon; so transporting, say, animals to your compound from far away across the back of the dragon will harm the animals. June, July, and August the dragon faces North; late August, September, and October the dragon turns East; and November, December, and January the dragon is southward. The position of the Naga is only important for journeys to, or for bringing goods from, beyond the outer circle of Nondwin's network of social relations; within the circle the Naga's head does not enter into travel decisions.

Alchemy

An important magical system in Upper Burma is alchemy. Alchemy, unlike astrology, or nats, or tattoos, tends to be restricted in two senses. First, it requires considerable cash outlay for the equipment; second, time is required to engage in the cooking of the metals. So alchemy is confined to the rich and the successful, and usually to men over the middle age mark. Alchemists form a sort of secret society; they exchange trade information, and each practicing alchemist has his own particular, private book of recipes which he guards carefully. In Nondwin, only one man is a practicing alchemist, and he is U Sein Ko, the richest man in the village. I find it striking, but not in contradiction, that the most entrepreneurial, rational farmer is also an addict of alchemical experiments. U Sein Ko has a small shed behind his house that holds all of his alchemical supplies. They consist of a small hearth, a bellows to blow the fire to the proper heat, a collection of clay crucibles in which the actual cooking is done, and containers with the metals and other ingredients to be cooked. U Sein Ko had been actively involved in alchemy for about a year, and he explained his involvement as a search for the "abilities." These abilities of the successful *eggiya hsaya* (fire master) are virtually the same as the remarkable powers of the Buddha, except they include some extra ones: turning base metals into gold and silver, eternally youthful bodies, and treasure-locating skills. U Sein Ko knows of no one in recent times who has successfully conducted alchemical experiments, but he tells the tales of "long ago" fire masters who did succeed. Full success is not needed, and there are lesser powers along the route to total achievements. The basic practice of alchemy, as U Sein Ko and his cronies in other villages, whom he visits and who visit him for the exchange of alchemical knowledge, carry it out, is the high heat cooking of mercury in a clay crucible. The notion is to produce a datlon of great power, that is, the ability to absorb baser minerals and turn them to gold. When that datlon is made, it is the ball itself that has the power. In order to transfer the power to a person, the ball must be swallowed by the alchemist, and then he must retire into a place in the forest and be watched over for seven days while the ball works its magic on his body.

The usual routine I observed at U Sein Ko's house and at that of his closest alchemical comrade in Nyaungbinhla was more or less this one. Mercury is cooked in a clay crucible for about three days, a few hours each day. To the mercury are added various plants and leaf substances, chiefly mangosteen, jack fruit, and lime leaf. In the cooking, these vegetable stuffs cover the mercury with a scum, and each time the ball of mercury is cooled, it is scraped clean. It gets harder and harder under the heat. Then begins the high-heat cookery, with the foot bellows turning the crucible a glowing red. First, the mercury is mixed with a bit of silver, and under the pressure of fire the silver spreads out to cover the surface, so that the whole looks like a ball of silver. If the silver spreads evenly without blemish over the mercury, this stage is considered successful. The ball is cooled, and then some gold is added to the silvered mercury. The high heat is applied again, and if the gold spreads evenly over the surface of the ball, this stage is completed.

The next test is to add some more mercury and to have it turn to silver under high heat. This third stage requires more plant and mineral ingredients. It has not yet been done. If the third stage were completed, then the last stage would be the addition of mercury to the silver ball which would then become gold, and the ball would have the power to make all the gold the fire master wanted. He could then purify his ball into pure magic gold and swallow it. Gold rays would emanate from his skin, and he would be ready for the retreat and burial in the forest, while his body was turned to everlasting, or near everlasting, stuff.

The prospect of success, in the total achievement, is not pressing or very real for U Sein Ko and his colleagues. The joys of puttering, of experimenting, of exchanging information, of filling idle hours, of getting limited powers are enough to keep the alchemical urge going. U Sein Ko says all Burmans would, if they could afford the time and money, take a crack at alchemy. Villagers, whom I queried on this subject, could always come up with some alchemical story about a particular datlon which an accomplished alchemist could make perform. The favorite power attributed to alchemists is the ability to recall mercury. In full view of an audience, an alchemist swallowed a mercury ball, and then it appeared in the palm of his hand. Another story is that the dropping of a datlon into a glass of cold water immediately makes the water boil. Or a datlon may be thrown for a distance and then reappear in the hand of the alchemist. Some alchemists also have datlon that are curative for leprosy, eyesores, and other ills.

Villagers have some scepticism about these stories. They think some of the feats, like mercury recall, are mere sleight of hand, and that other trickery is involved in alchemical demonstrations. But they do not doubt that alchemy itself can eventuate in the sorts of magical powers ascribed to it, nor do they disbelieve the possibility of eternal life, or "at will" gold production. U Sein Ko will not and does not claim powers as an alchemist, and the results of his experiments are not made public or even discussed with his family. He talks alchemy only with the initiated alchemical colleagues. They keep books and records and are scrupulously honest about what they have done, for they do not want to deceive themselves or waste time on already performed experiments. This pseudoscience is a matter of belief and trust, and is more a diversion of ardent amateurs in seeking the powerful magic than it is an activity of obsessed men striving for the key to the universe, the cult of Magus.

CURING SYSTEMS

Traditional Medicine

Burmese traditional medicine and curing forms a part of the category of predictive and divinatory systems because: first, it derives from the same historical sources as astrology, alchemy, and charms; second, it follows the same logic as these systems; and, finally, it aims at the restoration of magical balances in the patient, and is not the direct attack on an entity called a disease or an agency like a germ, nor are symptoms clearly related to particular illnesses. My understanding of the rationale of Burmese medicine was at first blocked by an unconscious form of ethnocentrism. I began collecting information about sickness, doctors, and cures in the way I had begun in Mexico and Guatemala in previous fieldwork, by observing the sick being treated, by watching medicines prepared, by interviewing patients and specialists, and by pulling together these data into some ordered whole that would reflect the way these people thought about and acted on illness and curing. This procedure led me into all sorts of confusions, blocks in communications, and finally to puzzlement on my part and on the villagers' part as to what we were talking about. My attempts to get the name of a disease, its symptoms, cause, and treatment, and any comments the *hseihsaya* (medicine master) had to make resulted in lists: I got *gaung kaik* for headache, *baik kaik* for stomachache, *wunthwade* for loose bowels, and hosts of others. But these did not make sense; many of the diseases were nearly the same thing by symptom, treatment, cause, and prognosis. It took a radical shift in the axes of my apprehension before the trouble became clear. There were no disease classes or entities; there was not a direct relation between cause and effect, and treatment was of the whole state of the patient, not of a particular illness. The fact that I did make this leap in category and did shift to the indigenous bases of thought about sickness makes me confident that cross-cultural communication is a real thing, and that even though anthropologists may often see through a glass darkly, they do have the skills and techniques for translating alien systems of thought and behavior into the comprehensible, the familiar, and, sometimes, even into the scientifically useful.

The understanding of the observed facts of Burmese traditional handling of illness and disease depends on the prior appreciation of their theory of human illness and the nature of the human body.

The details of medicine are hseihsaya knowledge, but the general outlines are common village knowledge. The account I give here comes from three hseihsayas interviewed singly, two of them in direct confrontation, and this information was checked out with what the people in Nondwin knew about the total system. My basis for talking to the hsayas was a several-month observation of treatment and illness, and my muddling about in trying to get straight what I saw, and to attribute to what I saw sets of meanings that would echo the minds of villagers.

The human body, according to Burmese medical theory, is composed of *pahtawi* (the earth element which makes mainly flesh) and *abo* (the water element). Abo and pahtawi are complementaries and mix together to make the flesh. (This was demonstrated to me by the mixing of sand and water into a gruelly consistency.) Together these elements make a *meithaka*. The body contains *teizaw* (from the element fire) and this makes for inflammable body gases. The complementary to teizaw is *wayaw* (from the element air) or oxygen. These two complementaries mix or blend together to make another meithaka pair.

Finally, there is *agatha* (an atmospheric element, like that in clouds or in the heavens, an "ether" that envelops the world). These elements, or combinations of the basic ingredients of all matter, are arranged on different sides of the human body. Women are patterned differently from men.

Men		Women	
Left	*Right*	*Left*	*Right*
teizaw	pahtawi	pahtawi	teizaw
wayaw	abo	abo	wayaw
	agatha		agatha

Illness comes from throwing the locus and the amount of the elementals out of proper combination. The immediate agency for throwing these elementals into insalubrious patterns or quantities is "nature." The villagers say, "Nature is our king, and if we violate its laws by getting too hot or too cold, eat improper foods, get too tired, or sleep too little then the balance is upset and nature makes us sick until we restore the proper balance." It is the proper balance of the elementals that is "health" and disturbances of the balance that are "ill health," and medicine is a series of techniques to restore harmony and balance.

The healthy human being has all these elementals in balance; in "line" is the exact metaphor used by hseihsayas, demonstrated by placing five Shan tea bowls in a row and giving each of the bowls the name of one of the elements.

O   O   O   O   O
pahtawi   abo   teizaw   wayaw   agatha

Disturbances of this state are patterned. Too much cold causes this pattern to be manifest:

Too much heat results in this:

These classes of cold- and heat-caused diseases included what I had early taken to be discrete diseases, and the classes by themselves have Pali and Burmese names. Other classes of disturbances look like this (a form of cold-induced):

or this (another form of heat-derived):

Treatment involves giving the patient offsetting medicines, foods, and regimens until the balance is restored. Some examples are: (1) *Kelkala*, a stiffness in the joints, a subcategory of the second form of too much cold. (Immediate and most likely agent is cold bath in overheated state, or too "cold" foods when person is "hot.") Treatment involves giving sugars and bitters. (2) *Weitaphita*, constipation, scant or red-tinged urine, night fever. A cold-caused illness, or illness caused by a change of season so quick that the body could not adjust. Treat with bitter foods.

It is not my intention to write a Burmese manual of the healing arts or a compendium of the pharmaceuticals in ordinary use, but only to give the major axes of reasoning about sickness and disease, and the chief modalities in handling. There are specifics for specific sorts of disarrays of the elements, and some things are better or worse in their efficacy for restoration. Since treatment depends so greatly upon proper intake of the proper balance-restoring foods, most of the foods eaten in the daily diet of Nondwin, and elsewhere throughout Upper Burma, fall into one of the following four classes of tastes or attributes or virtues: *Pu* and *sat* and *hka* are different types of hot; *cho* and *chin* and *a* are different kinds of cold; *sein* is bland tasting; *ngan* and *hpan* are neutral and offset too much hot and/or cold. A balanced diet consists of a harmonious, even blending of these qualities of given foodstuffs. Just to indicate that the "signature" of a food is not necessarily deducible from its physical taste, form, or texture, this list of the common foodstuffs and their consensual categories is given:

rice	not classified	kawethi	cho
bean	sein	reitha	cho
egg	sein	pelonmwethi	cho, a
milk	sein	mango	cho, a
fish	not classified	mangosteen	cho, a
betel	hpan	tamarind	chin
tea leaf	hpan	supoyewhe	sein
salt	ngan	bread	sein
sugar	cho	cake	sein, cho
chili	sat	chakikathi	hka
cooking oil	sein	arrowroot	sein
mutton	not classified	painu	sein
chicken	not classified	potato	sein
bananas	sein	small bean	sein
cabbage	hka, sein	climbing bean	cho, sein
carrot	cho	zadawbeh	cho, sein
cucumber	cho	pepper	sat, pu
onion	pu	duck	sein
kayanthi	pu	deer	sein
tomato	chin	pig	a, sein
vinegar	chin	bird	a, sein
ginger	pu	prawn	cho, sein
saffron	hka	coffee	cho, sein
mahsala	sat	liquor	pu, sat
lime	chin	sesamum	pu, sein

The basic split is between the hot and the cold categories. The different sorts of hot, for example, are chiefly if the heat is communicated to the person by eating, drinking, or sniffing. The sein and ngan and hpan categories are the stabilizers or buffers between the hot and cold categories, and they are particularly effective in neutralizing or preventing ills from an overindulgence of one or another kind of hot or cold food. Burmese try to keep a good balance, and, as can be seen, the listing of the qualities of foods neither hampers almost any conceivable sort of appetite, nor places heavy restrictions on cuisine.

The actual operation of the hsaya-patient dyad is fairly uniform from case to case or consultation to consultation. A hseihsaya takes "all things into account" before treating a patient. This includes such information as the direction from which the patient asking aid comes or from which the doctor is summoned, the time and day, the interview questions of first onset, how the sickness was noticed, what was done before (all Burmese will use home remedies before calling the hseihsaya, and by the time he gets to the case considerable home dosing has occurred), and whether the patient has checked out other possible sources of the malignancy. Great or reputed traditional doctors usually interview one of the family of the sick person before they even come to the village or house where the patient is. If the case sounds hopeless to them, or if it is a variety of illness they do not feel specially skilled in, they will not attend. The hsaya examines and interviews the sick person, takes the pulse, and then prescribes a diet and medicines. Usually a patient is kept in bed, in a closed and airless room, where little light is allowed to enter. Someone else in the family is needed to take care of the patient. Burmese traditional doctors do not charge fees in Nondwin, but they get payment in the form of money "gifts." Five kyats plus a good curry meal is the least one gives a hseihsaya, and 15 to 20 kyats, with the meal, is the very most one gives. But the single fee is not paid at the first visit unless that is all the doctor is to make. He gets paid by the case. He undertakes to cure a given sickness and says, after examination, that this will need a certain number of visits or treatments. The family agrees, so that actual use of hseihsayas runs closer to 20 to 100 kyats per illness.

Hsayas I have seen in action usually carry with them bags of medicines. The medicines are patent types bought in Sagaing and Mandalay and mixed into special combinations by the doctor. Herbs are sometimes part of the medicine kit, and the samples used by doctors are just about what the ordinary villager uses before the doctor comes on the scene. Some hseihsayas use astrology in both the diagnosis and cure if they believe that planetary influences are involved. The most elaborate astrological usage I saw included palm reading, birth date and hour, and computation of the present relations of the gyo to the patient with a complicated 27 planet table, which is a tripling of the usual nine planet system. This case also required that for every year of the patient's life one cup of water and one cup of rice be buried outside of the village fence in order to appease the planets and "drag" the evil from his body.

Hsayas have reputations based on their "curing scores," but these curing scores, although much more public than doctors' hits and misses in the contemporary United States, are not without ambiguity. The patient's kan is, of course, the ultimate factor involved, and the doctor has no control over this. Several systems of medicine are in operation at once, so that the clear role of the hsaya is difficult to factor out. On the whole, the Nondwin peasant does not have a reverential or awesome attitude toward hseihsayas and is at least as technically oriented to medical practitioners as the most careful of Westerners. He shops around for his hseihsaya; he changes doctors if he does not improve, and he refuses a course of treatment if it does not make sense to him. Most of the doctors are not high status people, and most of them are hseihsayas part time, having some other chief occupational role.

Most traditional doctors are hseihsayas because they have a self-developed interest in medicine, and their curiosity and their talent for curing has led them to consult established doctors and to learn from them. Some hseihsayas have spent as long as seven years in apprentice relationships with distinguished town or city doctors. The extent of their practice depends on the reputation they build in the successful treatment of patients. Some doctors develop particular specialties and treat only certain classes of illnesses. Common specializations are in leprosy, in eyes, and in asthma, and there is even a doctor who cures insanity as his specialty. The specialists have special "equipment," in the form of healing charms, which is relevant to their domain. One eye specialist, for example, had a tortoise-shaped piece of brown stone, about ¼ inch long and slightly narrower across. This was a natural tortoise shape, and its efficacy came from that virtue. He received the tortoise piece from a pongyi, who got it originally by breaking up a large mass of rock to find the buried amulet. This stone is placed under the eyelid of a patient and drawn across the eye several times. This treatment is supposed to remove cataracts from the eye. This doctor also had a curing datlon that was the *kobadatlon*, the "nine metals in combination ball." The combination of iron, gold, mercury, lead, silver, diamond, zinc, wolfram, and copper is made into a ball in the alchemical clay crucible by high heat cookery. Sometimes the ashes from human hair or a pinch of melted salt are needed to get the metal into a solid ball. To treat leprosy with this magic ball, a rough patch of the leper's skin is coated with lemon juice, and the ball is rubbed back and forth until some of the skin flakes off. These flakes of skin are drunk in a lemon juice mixture. Either the patient vomits, and thus draws leprosy out, or else he passes it out through the bowels. The treatment is just as good for snakebite, except that coconut water is used in lieu of lemon juice. This particular doctor bragged to me that he has 27 patients in Mandalay, six in Sagaing and 50 in Shwebo. When I asked him if he ever cured anybody of cataracts, leprosy, snakebite, or insanity, he replied, "Of course," and offered to take me to see some of his recovered patients.

The use of the hsaya is only part of the process of recovering health. The massage is an omnipresent technique, both for the maintenance of health and as a cure for minor illnesses, tiredness, or vague body pains. Massaging (*chaungde:* to crick joints) is done vigorously with the hands and the feet of the massager on the full dorsal and ventral sides of a patient. There are no professional masseurs in Nondwin, but some men and women do it as a part-time occupation. The more usual practice is to have a member of the family massage the member in need. Some massages may run up to an hour and are exceedingly thorough. The theory of massage is "decongestion," relief of blood, muscles, and nerves. Sometimes massage is supplemented by magical practices. For a "bad back," massage must be accompanied by two planks, cut from the *yeikyanya* tree, laid parallel to the hips of the patient. A special chant is recited and the planks move together of their own accord. When the planks touch, they should be broken, and pieces of the planks rubbed in the massage on the afflicted back, hip, or arm will result in a cure. The older people are especially given to daily massages, and one of the services of children is to massage their elders.

In home doctoring, these are the most common remedies in use: *

Headache	Boil betel leaf, add salt; drink the liquid. The ensuing sweat cures by restoring hot-cold balance. Grind *thabye* leaf (*Eugenia*) and inhale; or inhale crushed betel leaf; or inhale fumes from crushed saffron roasted over a charcoal fire.
Fever	Grind a mint leaf; to be drunk with water.
Stomachache	Apply a mint leaf paste over the abdomen; drink lemon juice and salt.
Constipation	Drink mint leaf and water; or drink warm salt water on arising; or drink lemon juice in the morning.
Colds	Dry a mint leaf on a brass spoon over a flame, add salt and water and drink; or boil together betel leaf, ginger, jaggery, and drink the solution.
Cuts	Grind tamarind leaf and betel leaf together; place on betel leaf and apply; or squeeze the juice of a mint leaf into the cut, cover with leaf; or smear earth oil over the cut, cover with oil-soaked bandage.
Eye sores	Soak a cloth in tamarind leaf juice, apply; or use cactus tree sap, or bay leaf on cloth.

---

* In giving the Burmese trees, herbs, and plants, I have placed question marks where I was unsure of the botanical name, or where the vernacular had no corresponding English or Linnaean name in Davis's, *The Forests of Burma* (1960).

Itch	Cover with betel leaf, cut a melon (*pethanzi*), mix with crude oil, boil, and smear on itch.
Head itch	Cook bat dung, sparrow dung, chicken dung, or pigeon dung with crude oil and smear on shaven head.
Nerves and veins	Grind dry saffron root and use in hot water compresses.
Swelling	Mix some acacia leaf with rice and eat.
Boils	Plaster with tobacco leaf; or use bark of *padaingzi*.
Vomiting	Drink hot water; mix salt, betel leaf, *thaminza* (*randia dumentorum*), grind, add water, drink.
Diarrhea	Bark of *thale* (*boscia variabilis*) (?), bark of bay tree; grind with water, drink; or take lime juice in a cup of boiling water.
Muscle ache	Bark of *pyoseit* tree (*xylia dolorbrifomis*) (?), mix with water, apply by massage; or mix ginger, betel leaf, and jaggery, boil and drink liquid.
Cough	Wad and suck betel, mint leaf, salt; or drink betel leaf ground with salt.
Toothache	Boil and gargle bark of *malaka* (guava) tree mixed with herb that grows at its base; stuff hole in tooth with clove leaf, or stuff with ashes of clove; decay caused by worm, use *myibok kayan* powder with wax on a hot iron and breathe the fumes. This drives out the worm.
Burns	Smear with lime and cooking oil, apply tea leaves, smear with *kyeikmaywe* to avoid scars.
Menstrual pain	Boil and drink *chenanywe* (?) and three cups of water.
Abortion	Boil *alokyu* (?) with water, mix with whiskey and drink, pound the midriff, squeeze the abdomen, and tie tight girdle; in three days miscarriage.
Earache	Scorch *tazaunnminla* (a variety of *Eurphorbia antiquorum*) (?) over flame, squeeze hot oil into ear.
Bonebreak	Use a kind of bamboo root, pounded, boiled, and steamed as a plaster, and tie up with bamboo splint.

These home remedies are for trivial, nonserious cases of the above ills, for doctors will be summoned if the response is not quick, virtually immediate.

One other sort of medicine is spreading into the countryside and fits well with the older notions of charms, amulets, magic balls, and stones. This is a metal wrist band (*hseit letpat*) imported from Japan and sold in town and city stores, because they are much more popular there than in the countryside. The linked band worn around the wrist is supposed to have a radium content, and it is this "atomic" radiation that is beneficial. It prevents heart attacks, from which the Burmese suffer relatively little anyway, and dizziness; it makes breathing easier and repels those ills that are airborne. The most expensive bands run about 45 kyats, so they have a restricted appeal. That this vogue spread about three years ago is interesting, because the Chinese acupuncture medicine long found in the towns of Upper Burma is still largely confined to Chinese clients, even after centuries of contact with Burmans.

The HA

In addition to the home remedies, the hseihsaya medicine, the charms, tattoos, and patent medicines, there is a form of truly modern medicine in Nondwin. The modern medicine is embodied in the visits of a health assistant and maternity nurse on regular rounds. The HA (health assistant, everything invariably gets into initials in Burma) is stationed in nearby Nyaungbinwin clinic. He comes on his motorcycle to Nondwin and makes rounds. During my stay he was treating heart trouble, vitamin deficiency, anemia, tuberculosis, beri-beri, as well as earaches, stomach troubles, and the usual run of minor complaints. These illnesses were his diagnosis, not mine. The health assistant has the means of injecting penicillin and other antibiotics, which are well received by the people of Nondwin. He has other sorts of modern medicines: aspirins, vitamins, lotions, sulfas, boil lancers, tooth pliers, and other minor surgical tools. He treats villagers at cost for shots and injections or medicines, but he also carries on a sort of private practice, where he will procure medicines not in his government issue kit and charge for his services and the medicines.

From what I have said about medicine, it may seem that the villagers of Nondwin are morbidly concerned with the state of their health, in a continual frenzy of doctoring, treating, dosing, and massaging. This impression, if it is given, is wrong; but it is true that when a villager is ill he goes at the cure hammer and tong and tries everything that he knows, that his neighbors recommend, or any of the experts and quasi-experts suggest. He carries on a vigorous multipronged attack on his illness and is very impatient for results. If, in a day or so, one cure has not worked, he begins something else, and the curing is often, given the bruising massages, the dark rooms, the drinks, more drastic than the illness. But most people recover, and then at the next bout of illness they begin the many-sided, energetic attack on all fronts, using in easy combination the mixture of home, traditional, and modern medicine, and a few forms of magic to boot. When itinerant medicine vendors from Sagaing or Mandalay come with their powders to be ingested, inhaled, or just lapped, men, women, and children, sick and well, cluster around and try the samples.

The only difficulty in the Burmese medical field that I could even get some information about was in the field of preventive medicine. There is a vaccinator who comes around from time to time, but few people turn up for smallpox vaccine. There is no such thing as opposition to vaccination, as was reported in the early part of the twentieth century in Upper Burma, and many people are in fact scarred with the huge marks the vaccination leaves on arm or thigh. It is just that the aftereffects of the vaccine are unpleasant enough to the villager, so that he will not take it as an abstract defense against a disease. But if a year has many smallpox cases, or there is currently an epidemic, the villager and his children submit willingly to what they consider unpleasant.

The Burmese activity in curing stems, in part, from the complete absence of a "stiff upper lip" tradition in response to pain and discomfort. If it is in one's power to alleviate, to cure, one should go at it with a will, and there is no value in stoicism, in the ability to bear pain, to repress suffering. Just the reverse, soft moaning or loud outcry is expected of sick people, and it rallies around their relatives, friends, and attentive sympathizers, all of whom help by offering remedies, condolence, or mere presence outside the sick room to help speed recovery. I think this story of a girl who cut her foot badly in the dead of night illustrates what I have said. This girl cut her foot while trying to ride a bicycle in the dark. The pedal of the bicycle did not have a rubber guard, and the metal entered more than an inch into the sole of her foot, leaving a nasty, ragged hole. Her screams led to a local emergency. The son of U Sein Ko was summoned, and he got his truck out to drive her to the clinic at Nyaungbinwin. Many of the youngsters of the village got aboard the truck to accompany her, as did all the members of her household. U Sein Ko got his shotgun, and he and I sat in the front seat with his son as we sped through the dark to the clinic. The HA was not at the clinic, so the whimpering girl and the truckload of her supporters pushed on to Tatu. Here, at a rudimentary dispensary, the junior HA was flushed out of his bed, and, by candle, flashlight, and oil lantern, proceeded to clean the wound and to stitch it up. During the girl's ordeal, her younger sister held her in her arms; her age-mates around her made encouraging sounds; her aunt held her legs, and her father kept saying, "Pibi, pibi," it is finished.

The girl kept screaming, "Mother, help me, I am going to die, ame, ame, ame." Nobody tried to quiet her, and nobody expected that she could be stitched without all the people holding and comforting her. When it was over, nobody made remarks about the "brave girl, well borne" but went on to tell her to sleep; she would soon be well. Fortitude, capacity to suffer pain, and keeping up a front in illness are qualities that the villagers of Nondwin do not value and do not understand. City doctors, who sometimes get country patients, often characterize them (in contrast, I suppose, to Chinese or Hindus or Europeans) as whimpering, thin-skinned, and self-pitying, since these English and Indian trained physicians share the ethic that the best patient is that sort who does least to get on the doctor's nerves and has a composure that does not frighten waiting clients.

SUMMARY

The ways that Buddhist ritual, nat ceremonies, spirit placation, and personal crises form a whole in the life of the village of Nondwin can be graphically appreciated through the diagram of the Ritual Cycle. The annual round, projected against the calendar months and the agricultural cycle on the outer rims, uses three axes to differentiate among ritual activity: (1) communal versus individual or familial ritual, (2) remote and ultimate benefits versus immediate crisis handling, and (3) laity versus specialist as ritual custodian or performer. The full rationale for the selection of these axes is spelled out elsewhere (Nash, M., 1964). What is intended in the presentation here is to stress the remarkable fact of the interplay of Buddhist and non-Buddhist ceremonies and the weaving together of communal and non-communal ritual. This presentation serves not only as a summary of the meshing of belief systems and activity in Nondwin; it is also a commentary on some widely held generalizations in social anthropology. Ever since Durkheim (1915) noted the analytical importance of the distinction between religion and magic, between a church of believers and a collection of clients, his interpretation has been near standard in anthropological treatments of religion. In one sense, the material from Upper Burma supports Durkheim, but in a more fundamental sense it calls attention to the fact that it is the *interplay* of the opposition between religion and magic, rather than their counterpoise, that accounts for the nature of belief and activity. Furthermore, it is not, as Durkheim also held, the sharing of belief that makes

RITUAL CYCLE IN NONDWIN

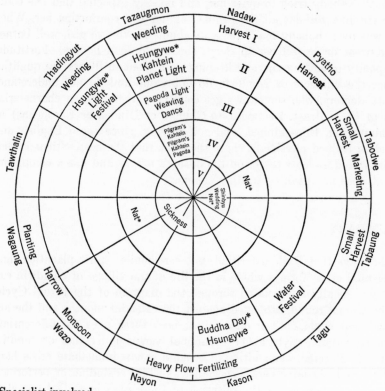

*Specialist involved

RING   I: AGRICULTURAL CYCLE
RING II: COMMUNAL FESTIVAL IN UPPER BURMA
RING III: COMMUNAL RITE IN NONDWIN
RING IV: INDIVIDUAL RITE, CALENDRICAL
RING V: INDIVIDUAL RITE, CRISIS

the religious community in Nondwin, but the other way around; the sharing of social relations is putative evidence for common beliefs. The concrete organization for all communal ritual includes everyone in the village through the mechanism of drawing at least one member from each household. The point need not be labored, the equation is: obligatory = communal. The equation can be expanded to these terms: communal = Buddhist, Buddhist = member of society, member of society = social relation, and social relation = interaction. Hence a villager reasons: those with whom I interact are those with whom I have continual relations, and they are members of my society; as members of my society they are Buddhists, and as Buddhists they must participate in the same rituals I do, so we have common ritual obligations, and we may be reunited in reincarnation. The opposite set of equivalences could be spelled out for nat practice.

The temporal spacing of ritual calls for little comment. Heavy harvest time has no communal rituals, since agriculture demands all available hands. But the coincidence of heavy labor demand and the absence of communal ritual is not perfect, for smaller harvests are interrupted for some festivals. Rituals are heaviest in October and November due to Buddhist canon. This is the end of the Wa, and the contained pressures stemming from the prohibitions of the sacred season are expended. The release comes when people are lowest in their assets, in their stock of money and of food, so that the costliest rituals, shinbyus, come after the major harvests. This is not because time is released but because income goes up. These costly rituals tend to cluster in the two months after harvest, then peter out.

The last two chapters have given a fairly comprehensive view of the belief and ritual system of Nondwin. The current categories for the apprehension and definition of reality, the attribution of meaning to experience, the moral path to salvation, and the local hierarchy of ends leading to the *summum bonum* of Neikban, indicate a belief system much more in harmony with a peasant agricultural society undergoing slow but crescive change. The villager has not envisioned or fully experienced the modern world and has not absorbed it into his world view, or modified the world view to include some of the essentials of modernity. (Ontological uncertainty, predominance of economic ends, high rewards for innovation, artificiality of social order, and tested knowledge as the arbiter of practice are only a few of the themes of modernity as it has characterized the Western world in increasing degree since the 1500's.)

Buddhism is a variable factor in the approach to modernity, and I have stressed, schematically, its Janus-like, protean, and ambiguous nature in dealing with the meaning of economic effort, in contrast to attempts to give it a "score" on the modernization potential table some analysts use when they look at the new nations and their regnant ideologies. Nat practice, spirits, ghosts, and the whole ilk of village demonology I estimated as being extremely liable as modern systems of science and technology make rapid headway in Burma. But one must always temper prediction to unforeseeable events. I am reminded that among the last official acts of former premier U Nu was the dedication of two national nat shrines. This was widely supported by the peasantry as fitting and natural, and what opposition did arise among some urban intellectuals was chiefly on the grounds that it was anti-Buddhist, not antireasonable. Only the Army looked on this activity (as I judged from several officer friends I knew well in the Upper Burma Command at Maymyo) as sheer nonsense. So, it is not only the internal logic of a system of belief, or its adequacy in coping with reality, or the subjective psychological rewards believers experience that are determinative of the vitality of a belief system. But it is also its role as political ideology, its capacity to enlist individuals beneath its banner for political and economic ends, and the ideologies it competes with that are equally crucial in the continued social existence of a framework for the capture of the phenomenal world.

6

Yadaw, an Irrigated Rice Growing Community

Yadaw offers a useful comparison to Nondwin. That is why I chose to divide my field work time somewhat unevenly between them. After I had worked in Nondwin, I made a survey of another village, searching for a social setting that would highlight the facts of peasant life in Upper Burma. I wanted to do two things: first, approximate the range of social and cultural variability in the region from the 40-inch rain line to the hills north of Katha; second, find out how much necessary fit there was in the ways virtually the same social and cultural factors could be combined. In Upper Burma, one does not move from distinct local culture to distinct local culture, nor is the community the locus of cultural organization. There is a fairly common culture throughout the region, but it changes, like the shifts in a kaleidoscope, as one moves from village to village, or village to town. The slight rearrangements in cultural organization are based on ecology, demography, economy, historical factors, and on the networks of communication among communities and the two or three large centers of the region. By selecting Yadaw, a wet rice, irrigated economy, as the anchor of contrast to Nondwin, I think the basic essentials of rural Upper Burma will be thrown into relief. The "ingredients" and the kinds of viable "mixes" they can make are captured through this kind of comparison. Upper Burma, as a region of broad cultural similarity, permits the microscopic approach here suggested; the small variations in culture and society provide not the descriptive completeness of the region but the comprehensiveness that comes from having an inventory of the major institutions and a guide or recipe for the modes of their combination.

I have moderate confidence in this way of solving, or handling, the vexing, perennial, anthropological problem of the *pars pro toto*, at least for Upper Burma. (Geertz, 1963, gives another line of attack for In-

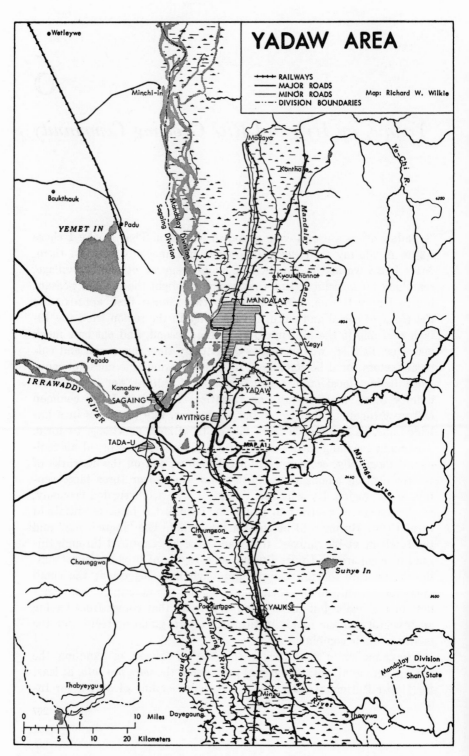

YADAW AREA

+++ RAILWAYS
— MAJOR ROADS
— MINOR ROADS
-·- DIVISION BOUNDARIES

Map: Richard W. Wilkie

Wetleywe

Minchi-in

Mataya

Kontha

Baukthauk

YEMET IN

Padu

Sagaing Division

Mandalay Division

Mandalay Canal

Ye Chi R.

Kyaukthannat

MANDALAY

Yegyi

Pegado

IRRAWADDY RIVER

Kanadaw

SAGAING

YADAW

MYITNGE

TADA-U

MAP A1

Myitnge River

Chaungzon

Chaunggwa

Sunye In

Padunggo

Pan Naing River

Samon R.

KYAUKSE

Thabyeygu

Minzu

Zawgyi River

Mandalay Division

Shan State

Dayegaung

Thanywa

0   5   10 Miles

0   5   10   20 Kilometers

208

donesia.) My confidence comes from the 36 villages I surveyed, my travels from Mandalay to the Chinese border, and from the information Dr. June Nash provided on the three villages on which she did detailed field work.

Yadaw is situated just off the main road which runs south from Mandalay to Rangoon. Seven miles down this road is the village gate. Yadaw is in close connection with Amarapura, in which township's jurisdiction it lies, with Mandalay, and with villages in about a 15-mile diameter (see Map of Yadaw Area). Kyaukse marks about the outer limit of the social circle of usual interaction to the south, and Ondaw junction is the limit to the north. Yadaw means: *Ya* (dry crop —like tomatoes) *Daw* (royal place). And the *bazat yazawin* (the oral history of Burma) recounted by villagers has vague stories that the fifth king of the Alaunghpaya dynasty set aside the land around Yadaw for the growing of cucumbers, tomatoes, and eggplants for the royal household, and from then to Thibaw's time, that was what the people did for a living; they supplied the palace with garden crops. Yadaw is on the edge of the irrigation system centered in Kyaukse. This centuries-old system of canals, ditches, locks, and reservoirs has been traditionally the core of the "granary" of the Burmese kingdoms. Until about fifty years ago, Yadaw was a smallish community living on the dribble from this system. At that time the British extended the canal system so that it fully included Yadaw. The community then shifted to irrigated, wet rice growing, and the garden crops disappeared. The shift was accompanied by two social facts which have continued to form the life of Yadaw. First, there was a migration from surrounding communities, and, second, most of the rice land was owned by large holders in Mandalay (among them resident Englishmen), so that most of the farmers were share-tenant farmers. Some of the migrants came as whole family units, at the behest of the English landlord. About 35 years ago the people from Thabotpin came when new paddy fields were opened by further extension of the canal system, and 30 years ago the Yelonkyaw people came for the same reasons. The Tagundine people migrated because some of their village was taken from them to be paddy land. There is still some clustering of families and households by village of origin, and the lack of community coherence derives in part from the diverse origins of the residents and the relatively short period they have been working out rules of coterritoriality.

A look at the Map of Yadaw Village indicates a tendency for houses to be grouped in bunches, and these quasi-neighborhoods reflect, in large measure, the common time and place of migration. The village

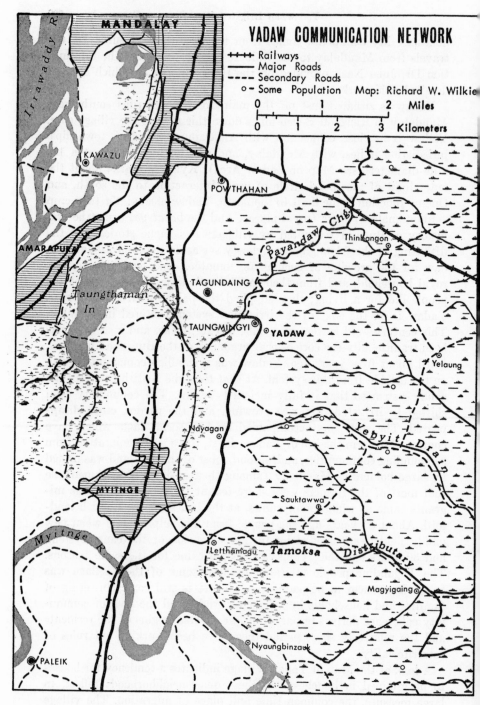

YADAW COMMUNICATION NETWORK

++++ Railways
—— Major Roads
---- Secondary Roads
o- Some Population   Map: Richard W. Wilkie

0   1   2 Miles
0   1   2   3 Kilometers

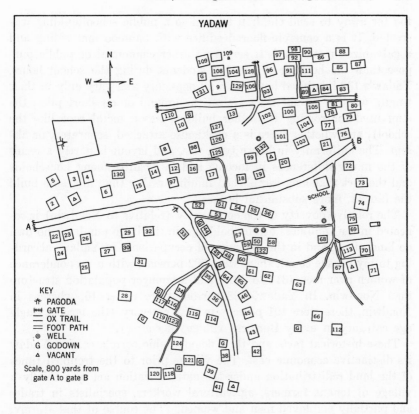

itself shows the casual, historical growth of a community, rather than the orderly planning of a settlement. A main street, really an oxcart trail, runs between the two large gates in the village fence, and another major ox trail runs between two lesser gates to the north of the chief *ywa lan*. The two major axes of settlement reflect part of the history. The smaller road is a vestige of royal times, and the larger road is the result of the rice boom which came in the wake of enlarging the irrigation system. That most of the wells are in the newer part of town is understandable, for older communities in this region always centered about a single or a few wells, and the Englishman who wanted tenants to come and farm his newly opened paddy lands provided the additional attraction of new wells.

The village has a truly public building in the school. The school is not part of the pongyi kyaung, and it sits in the newer part of the village. The two kyaungs, to the east and north of the village, were too far away to send children to, and so a public schoolbuilding was erected. It is a concrete-floored edifice with bamboo mat siding and a galvanized metal roof. It serves no other communal or public purpose than the housing of the 110 students during the school hours. Yadaw's 132 inhabited houses are all one-story and vary only in their length, whether or not they are on the ground or on short piles, the stuff used for roofing (no other building has a metal roof like the school), and whether there is a cookhouse attached, separated, or absent. The uniformity in house type, size, and layout is partly a result of the minor differences in income and in wealth among households and the fact that long-established families rather than migrants build the fancier, more substantial houses.

The relative poverty of the community (relative to Nondwin) is reflected in the smallness of landholdings, in the large number who own no land at all, and in the diversity of occupations. In Yadaw, according to my census count, there were 592 persons, with a preponderance of women over men (311 to 281), and a younger population structure than Nondwin. In Yadaw, 268 persons were under 16, whereas in Nondwin, there were 191 persons in that category (the largest single age category in every Burmese village, of course).

These historical facts and their demographic correlates give Yadaw its distinctive economic cast. The village prior to the troubled times of the land redistribution under the nationalization act was chiefly a village of tenant farmers, agricultural workers, specialists in trades and partially employed men and women. (The course of that stormy, violent, and corrupt attempt to apply the law in Yadaw will be treated under the rubric of politics, for it was, and still is, a matter of political power, not administrative machinery, to apply a land reform code.) Before land reform, only 10 families held land in Yadaw, and these were the size of holdings:

TABLE XVI   Landholding in Yadaw

Family	Acres
One	42
Two	30
Two	16
One	15
One	10
Two	6
One	20

This state of landholdings, in Yadaw's tract land of 1,344 acres, made only 190 acres owner and resident operated and 1,154 acres tenant operated. Tenants are migrants and are not necessarily tied to the piece of land they work. Some tenants had long-standing relations with the landlords; others drifted around to the best bargain they could find, or the landlord got some depressed family to pay a higher rent than his current tenants and so turned them out. There are no tales of great landlord abuse or "rack renting." (In Lower Burma the latter took the form of renting a piece of land to the highest bidder, that is, the family who could pay the largest percentage of the yield, or, what is the same thing, live on the lowest level of subsistence.) There are only tales that the population of residents and the number of cultivators (either owner or tenant) shifted from year to year. More than half of the households in Yadaw have at least one of their senior members from some other community, and this, so far as memory goes, has always been the case. The numbers of people engaged in agriculture as cultivators (not laborers, coolies, women transplanters, or groups who thresh and winnow at the peak periods in the rice cycle) vary from 49 to 74 families over the years. Usually, the headman's tax records show that about 50 families (40 per cent of Yadaw) were, at any one time, engaged as either tenant or owner cultivators during the last decade. Laborers and specialists make up the rest of the labor force, and there are many idle young men and women who would work if they could find something. This state of affairs has not changed, despite the agricultural reforms. When the Japanese came to Mandalay, they drove away the British residents, and the larger land-owners fled. The families of Yadaw who were tenants or owners just stayed on their land. The tenants did what they did before, except that the rentals were no longer remitted. There was not a great expansion in opportunity, just a fortunate shift for those farmers who, at the moment of the collapse of European power, could lay claim to the land they worked. This extralegal, relatively chaotic state of land titles laid part of the basis for the ensuing troubles in land nationalization in Yadaw.

Against this background of a relatively poor, migrant-filled, rice growing community, formerly in the grip of large landholders, I shall describe the contemporary economic organization and its potentialities for innovation, expansion, and modernization.

TECHNOLOGY AND ECONOMY

Technology

The technology of agriculture in a wet rice community is very similar to that of the agricultural complex anywhere in Upper Burma. It is the basic wood, bamboo, and iron complex inherited from neolithic days and supplemented by animal and human power. What I have earlier called colonial and modern technology is peripheral to the work of the village, but some strange, to me, and interesting adaptations from modern technology have indeed penetrated into the economic life of Yadaw. The farmer needs a pair of oxen, costing 300 to 600 kyats depending on age, size, and supply and demand, a cart, costing an average of 275 kyats for the two-wheeled, metal-rimmed variety with the wooden base covered with straw mats, with no fancy carving or silver inlays in the yoke, a metal share plow, 20 to 30 kyats, a dah, from 3 to 5 kyats, with expensive ones costing up to 20 kyats, a scythe, the blade costing 3 to 5 kyats, a spade, 15 kyats on the average, and a bamboo, metal-tipped fork costing 2 kyats, a harrow worth 6 to 10 kyats, and a length of rope worth about 1.50 kyats. Only the cultivator will own all the farming equipment; only he needs the cart and the oxen, the plow, harrow, and spade. Agricultural laborers will as part of their employ own dahs, rope, forks, scythes, and spades. A professional carter, of whom there are several in Yadaw, will own everything but the plow and the harrow. This simple tool kit rests on a complicated, finely adjusted body of technological knowledge about rice: the varieties to plant, the preparation of nursery beds, the transplantation to fields, the harvesting, the threshing, the winnowing, and the preservation of rice straw for sale or use as animal fodder. The same tool kit is useful for the small amounts of sesamum, peanuts, beans, and chickpeas that are eked out of the rice economy of Yadaw. Some machines, either from Mandalay or from more enterprising villages than Yadaw, are used for some stages of rice cultivation by some of the cultivators and, hence, are included in the technological inventory of Yadaw. A few cultivators rent a rice-winnowing machine from a nearby village. The machine air cleans rice at the cost of 5 kyats per basket, which is what hand-labor winnowing costs, but the resultant rice is much cleaner. A fodder-chopping machine sometimes comes from Mandalay and rents for 1.50 kyats to chop up 100 bundles of straw into cattle-sized edibles. Both these machines are powered by

gasoline motors and driven by simple fan belts. The hooking of gasoline motors to indigenous machines seems to be one of the points of
rapid growth in productivity, but this machine has not, as it did not
in Nondwin, become part of the household machinery in Yadaw. The
poverty of Yadaw helps account for this, as does the redundance of
labor. The machines are more efficient, but they free chiefly time and
energy, not the much scarcer good of capital, and there is little to do
with released time and energy in the economic sphere in Yadaw. There
is, then, no compelling reason for most people to shift over to gasoline motors and some good reasons against it; sheer inertia is one.
Farmers will not, at the Yadaw level of development, reach out for
something that requires new knowledge, some capital, and maintenance
unless that item promises visible, short-range, and large amounts of
gain. Furthermore, machine use will disemploy the children of a household who already have plenty of free time, and it might cause them
to drift into the cities and towns and thus work a real hardship with
the heavy labor demands at planting, transplanting, harvest, and cleaning. The technological opportunity in the context of Yadaw is not of
strong appeal, and hardly anyone will be individually worse off if he
ignores the greater potential of the gas motor machines.

Machine agriculture enters only marginally into the economy and
technology of Yadaw. The ARDC has a tractor rental program for
those in the Mandalay region who will plant a second crop that the
agricultural people think feasible. The tractors and drivers are hired
to prepare land for peanuts and sesamum on ground that has been
already paddy harvested. These crops, as well as cotton and beans,
will fit into the temporal spaces left by the paddy growing cycle.

In 1960 the ARDC worked in Yadaw:

TABLE XVII   ARDC Land Worked in 1960

Households	Acres Each	Acres
Three	5	15
One	10	10
Two	3	6
One	4	4
One	8	8
Two	6	12
Total 10		55

In 1961 the ARDC has signed up:

TABLE XVIII   ARDC Land Worked in 1961

Households	Acres Each	Acres
Two	3	6
Three	4	12
Two	10	20
Two	6	12
One	8	8
Total 10		58

So the tractor program is used for 55 to 58 acres, among about 10 households each year. Eight of the ten are repeaters; two new households replaced the two who have dropped the program. Since there are, in any given year, about 50 households that can be called cultivator households, this figure is 20 per cent of all who could on the grounds of property alone be eligible for the program. Given the size of the holdings (below three acres it would not even pay to begin with a tractor, and some smaller holders do in fact plant these second crops with the traditional ox and cart and plow), this response to the tractor program is exceedingly favorable. In the context of small holdings, uncertain ownership, and small return for second cropping, plus the ecological unsuitability of some of the land at Yadaw's disposal, the cultivator's acceptance of the tractor program indicates a rather high sensitivity to new economic opportunity. The blocks to rapid and continuous technological change are not to be found in a "conservative peasant mentality," or in a primitive "attachment to the time honored," in a peasantry already developed to the level of monetary market relations as the prime guide in the level and kind of farm activity. The blockages, and, of course, they do exist as reflected in the slow, virtually static nature of the technology and the economic organization that has characterized the countryside of Upper Burma for half a century, are about the same as those found in most poor, peasant economies: capital shortage, mixture of subsistence with market orientation, great population pressure on available land, interlocking of activities among the economic and noneconomic spheres, lack of knowledge to expand or make more efficient the cultivation of new or old crops, absence of economic organizations beyond the household, uneconomic holdings, and the dependence and claim of household members on the right to work and on the right to share, irrespective of abstract contributions or return calculations. At least Burma is spared some of the more complicating factors above the peasant level, like class structures that block or discourage peasant mobility or a political process dedicated to the preservation of a docile, manipulatable countryside.

There is a whole technology tied to the making of condensed milk in Yadaw. The favorable location of Yadaw, in relation to the herds of cattle in the region that move about for pasture and in relation to the tea shops in Mandalay and Amarapura that are the buyers of the condensed milk, accounts for the location of this industry in Yadaw. The major capital item in condensed milk making is an imported enameled bathtub; this is the only use villagers have for bathtubs.[13] The bathtubs are placed over brick ovens; these tubs are filled with milk, and sugar is added. Then this mixture is slowly cooked until enough water is driven off and a form of condensed milk, suitable for use with tea, is produced. There are three milk makers in Yadaw. Only one is a local enterprise; the others are financed by small capitalists from Mandalay and Amarapura. A cream separator, run by a crank, may be part of the condensed milk industry also. There are two of these in Yadaw, only one in working condition. The other, a Swedish make, lacks a small part. The milk industry here depends on the migration of pasturing herds from Tatu to near Yadaw, from February to July. When the herds return to the Tatu side of the river, the industry ceases. Only the richest household has enough cows to sell milk to the condensed milk makers. They must depend on the transhumance of herds for the rest of the supply.

The condensed milk industry is fairly profitable. A viss of condensed milk made from skim milk sells for an average of 2.50 kyats; a viss made from cream sells for 4.25 kyats; and a viss made from whole milk sells for 4 kyats. Inputs are: 10 viss of milk yields 1 viss of cream; 10 viss of whole milk plus 2½ viss of sugar yields 5 viss of condensed milk; 10 viss of skim milk plus 2½ viss of sugar yields 4 viss of condensed milk. Whole milk sells for an average of 65 pyas a viss. The bathtub cookery can handle up to 200 viss a day. They get

---

[13] They would not bathe in them, for that would not only be hot and uncomfortable, but unhygienic as well. Soaking in your own dirty body water is considered a minor form of European insanity. Yadaw people, like all other villagers in Upper Burma, bathe by throwing jugs or buckets of water over themselves at the edge of a well. This not only cleans and refreshes; it also washes the longyi worn while the bath is taken.

218 The Golden Road to Modernity

this much in February and March; in April it drops to 180 a day, and the new grass in June and July pushes the supply up to 250 viss per day. Considering that a herd of 100 cows yields about 30 viss a day, there must be a considerable, continual migration of cattle just to supply the small industry of Yadaw. Sugar costs 2 kyats per viss and firewood 6 kyats per bundle. Three bundles will do for the busiest day, and two are usually enough. But most of the work on the milk is done for a wage, running from 8 to 10 kyats for each day of operation.

The difficulties of running one's own business are clear from a description of the one Yadaw man who does run his own milk factory of one bathtub and one cream separator. He must make advances to the milk suppliers, for that is the only way he can be sure of a steady supply of raw milk. But even this does not fully insure him a steady supply, and irregularity in the short season can be costly. Furthermore, he says, with bitterness, that almost all the milk sold by Burmans is watered, and he has no recourse for this. He compares the low, grasping ethics of Burmese milk sellers to the high business principles of the Ghurkas of Maymyo who complete their contracts and do not water the milk they sell. (Nonetheless the government milk factory recently built at Maymyo has never produced a drop of milk and is a monument to planning stupidity.) Also, he must employ labor: a runner from Kyigon who takes orders and makes deliveries to the tea shops, and a boy to operate the cream separator, when it is working. The runner's mother came to the owner one day and asked for a 10 kyat advance on the boy's wages. She needed money to buy clothing for a shinbyu she wanted to attend. He gave her the money, but it turned out she had not spoken to her son about it, and the boy was resentful and dragged his feet until he was again earning money. The final trouble is the credit the owner must extend to the tea shops who buy his milk. Getting them to pay up requires frequent trips, much time, and much wheedling. The running of a small business, where business institutions (like contract, trust, credit, labor relations, product specifications, all of which are taken for granted in a developed economy) are little developed, is a nerve-wracking, marginal activity.

The rest of the nonfarm technology of Yadaw is tied to the remainder of the roster of specialized trades and occupations. One residue of the Japanese occupation of Burma is the ubiquitous loudspeaker amplifier units run by storage batteries. These noise blasters are used at all ceremonies and celebrations. They play Burmese records, the jangle of which is fed from the hand turntable through loudspeakers placed at judicious intervals in the village. The rule seems to be the louder, the gayer, the earlier on and the later off, the more the client gets his money's worth. One man in Yadaw was in the festive noise-making business. This young man has a sixth standard education (one of four or five in the village) which he got at Mytinge, where the Burma rail shops are, and where middle schools are available for the qualified. When his mother sold her land and cattle in 1959, he got the 2,700 kyats he needed for the equipment. His fees were 45 kyats a performance, usually a two-day stint of playing, with an added day or two of travel to and from the celebration. Four months a year, the festive months, he was nearly fully occupied, averaging ten performances a month, with a take of 450 kyats a month, and cost of about 300 kyats for help and transportation. The 1,500 kyats yearly take was much above most farm income, and this business was a profitable way to make a living. But even he suffered an unexpected blow. One of his helpers took all the equipment, pawned it in Mandalay, and fled with the pawn money. He does not have the money to redeem his amplifier, battery, and records and is out of business. (Insurance is another business device lacking for the small indigenous entrepreneur.)

A traditional specialty occupation present in Yadaw is the wheelwright. The carts used in transport and in agriculture have large wheels with 12 to 14 spokes, and between each pair of spokes is a section of metal rim (*tagu*). It is the trade of the wheelwright to fit metal rims to cart wheels. For this he keeps a bellows and forge going and uses his hammer and anvil to beat into shape the hot, pliable metal along the wooden curve of wheel. From January to May he does his business; for the rest of the year there is little wheel repair. At peak he can repair five to six carts a day, at 10 kyats for the pair of wheels. On this income he must live the rest of the year. This particular wheelwright is not a very prudent man, and he gambles excessively. When there is a death in Yadaw and the wheelwright gambles at the death house, professional gamblers from Mandalay are apprised of the fact and also come to gamble. They do not cheat, but they are much better than he, and he usually loses heavily. But it is not his reckless use of earned money that prevents him from having any apprentice wheelwrights. He told me he would be willing to train any of the young boys who are willing to learn the craft. None have volunteered. In the face of idleness and unemployment among young men, I was curious as to why. But the reasons are not difficult to find. The youth of Yadaw consider the wheelwright trade a dying institution, much like blacksmithing after the advent of the automobile, and also one without hope of making more than farming. Whether their estimate is realistic or not is beside the point; they are not interested in taking up a long, poorly paid, hard apprenticeship.

What the young men do long for is a training job like those offered at the Burma Mechanical and Electrical Workshop, an army unit. No one from this village tract has ever been employed there, yet it is part of the aspirations of the young men. Fifteen of them have applied for a training job, on the strength of a rumor that such a job was in the offing.

Some of the younger men have taken and left employment on the Irrawaddy Water Transport Line that now runs the flotilla of paddle steamers from Rangoon to Bhamo. For Yadaw boys, this is also an apprentice job. They receive 30 kyats a month, plus room and board on the steamers. Most of them want engineroom work, but what they get is lascar toil, and so after a few months of this they return to the village to join the semi-employed and wait for some chimera of opportunity to come through the haze of idle days.

There are three tailoring establishments in Yadaw. The tailors all use footpedal-driven sewing machines in various stages of sewing machine evolution, plus, of course, the needles, thimbles, scissors, rulers, and threads that are part of the trade. The tailor shop which has the largest volume is run by a man who also teaches the arts of sewing, pattern cutting, and clothes making. He does not get any volunteers to learn from Yadaw, for he charges 150 kyats for a course of instruction, but he has gone to other villages and plied his trade while teaching. The two other tailor shops are run by women. One learned her trade from her brother in Amarapura, the other from a man in Tagundine. Learning to run even a simple sewing machine requires an apprentice relationship or a special course, so, for this reason and for its high capital costs in terms of household assets, the sewing machine does not spread rapidly through the village, and most women in a village cannot and do not sew, but use the expert tailors for things as simple as patching, or changing the length of a garment.

Some women supplement their incomes by selling food at festivals around Yadaw, or in Yadaw every day; others keep in their house compounds small "stores." The cake seller in Yadaw only works during April and May. She buys cakes from Mandalay and resells them. On this she may make five or six kyats a day profit. She does not, of course, count her time. The rest of the year she is a *"kuli,"* as the agricultural workers are called locally.

One man makes and sells "*akyaw*" things—fried goodies that villagers eat. He cooks them himself, keeps a little shack at the edge of the road that passes Yadaw, and hawks his fried foods. His return is about five kyats a day, which is just about what farm labor earns. In this work, nothing is technologically different from the ordinary "heat, stir, and serve" cooking of Burma. Food selling is a regular feature of village life, and those who take this up must compete with food sellers from Mandalay and other villages who come at odd times during the day to walk the streets of Yadaw, with their food baskets slung from their shoulders, calling out what they have to sell. They sell the fried foods, sweets, rice noodles with meat, and *monhinga* (a thin rice noodle with fish curry, onion, and garlic in a soupy form). Village people are likely to eat any time of the day, and children like to nibble, so there is a continual small demand for these foods.

The stores in Yadaw are petty businesses, and they are run by women who can stay home all day. The net earnings of a store average about 30 or 40 kyats per month. The stock includes: rice, salt, oil, nga pi, onions, kerosene, cigars, matches, tea, beans, writing paper, jaggery candy, sesamum sweets, soy sauce, and sometimes cigarettes. Most of this is bought from Mandalay merchants or in the zeigyo in Mandalay. The women who run the shops will take a pony cart once or twice a month to replenish supplies from Mandalay. The goods are sold at slightly higher prices than those obtained in the zeigyo. Since most people do their large shopping in Mandalay, these village stores supply no one with the bulk of necessities, but are merely a convenience when a housewife runs out or is too busy to go to market. The essential requirement of running these minute businesses is that of being available all the time. Only a business-minded woman, one who does not visit and run around, can be successful at this shopkeeping. As such it is virtually limited to older women or widows with time and no great desire to engage in the pleasantries of chatting over tea bowls, and it appeals only to the very poor.

Carpentry skills in housebuilding are also found in Yadaw. The village carpenters also have other occupations, for there is neither enough work for anybody to make a full-time living at it, nor is the work so differentiated that all men do not have some housebuilding skills. Housebuilding is done after the harvest when there is money and time. Most of the housebuilding is a cooperative or exchange labor activity, with the carpenter used, if at all, as we would use an architect. When carpenters are employed, they earn five kyats a day. Houses in Yadaw are not so complex, and ten men working in one full day can put up the smaller kind of house. Just to describe a typical house and to get this bit of technology on the record, I give this account.

The building materials are simple:

> *thetke* (thatch squares of elephant grass, palm leaves, or sugar cane leaves)
> *tayan* (woven bamboo sides)
> wood posts
> bamboo rafters
> nails
> oil (to keep off termites)

The usual house is one-third longer than it is wide, and this one was 15 cubits long by 10 cubits wide, with a height at the center pole of 8 cubits. The cost of materials was 67.50 kyats, and the food for the voluntary builders came to 10 kyats, so the house cost, for building, 77.50 kyats. Before the actual house-building was started, an astrologer set the date, and on the day selected the builders put up the nat pole and an offering of Eugenia to Minmahagiri. The house was oriented to the mingala directions. Except for one man who used a string to "true up" the posts, everybody worked at his own pace, and everyone seemed to know what to do. The people who would live in the house kept the tea circulating. A house like this could be put up in two days by three men and two carpenters. It would cost 10 kyats more than exchange labor, but might, according to villagers, be better put together. Exchange labor is here, then, cheaper than hired professionals. The house is complete when the pots are moved in, the bamboo tubes and baskets wired to the walls, and the few possessions, a box of clothes, some bedding, spoons, a kerosene wick lantern, iron bucket, some wicker hangers, and wire hangings are moved in. This one was the house of a newly-married couple. One other note: even the post holes were dug the hard way, without a post hole digger, and saw, hammer, ax, shovel, and dah were all the tools required.

Of work parties I observed in exchange labor, the core was usually kinsmen: brothers and brothers-in-law are the chief participants, but neighbors and cousins join in. There is reciprocity expected and given in housebuilding and in the periodic reroofing. Other buildings, not to be lived in, like cow sheds or storage godowns, do not require the astrological advice on construction date, but at least a lucky, as against an unlucky, day is always chosen.

The only other nonfarm occupations in Yadaw are carters. These men rent out their services and their carts to haul things to and from markets, to bring manure to the fields, to carry harvests off the fields, and to whatever other transport work they can get. Most of them also work as laborers in the time they do not have carting jobs.

Economy

TABLE XIX   Occupational Structure of Yadaw

Occupation	No. of Persons
Laborer (kuli)	93
Cultivator	59
Tenant farmer	4
Hseihsaya *	1
Food seller *	5
Carter	5
Carpenter *	2
Clerk	1
Masseur *	2
Condensed milk maker	2
Amplifier operator	1
Tailor	3
Teacher	4
Storekeeper *	3
Dairy farmer	1
Wheelwright	1
	187

Total labor force = 224
* Part time.

Considering that 592 people were the total population of Yadaw during the period 1960–61, and that only 224 of these were more than 16 years of age, 187 persons in the labor force is a high percentage of available labor. Thirty-seven young people and three dependent older people made up the "unemployed" of Yadaw. Some of the jobs in the occupation table require working outside of Yadaw. The clerk works in Mandalay and is an off-and-on resident with his parents in Yadaw. Only one of the four teachers is assigned to the Yadaw school. Many of the occupations that are starred as part time require incumbents to work as laborers during the peaks of the agricultural cycle. The natgadaw who lives in Yadaw derives so little income from that specialty that I did not list it as part of the occupational roster. Of all the employed, 156 are directly involved in agriculture, 93 as laborers and 63 as cultivators. But this table does not list all of the people who work in rice growing. For at high, labor-demand times, the wives and children of cultivating families, who do not ordinarily sell labor, pitch into the family enterprise. I would estimate that the labor force in agriculture at transplanting, harvesting, and threshing reaches about 225 persons, rather than 156 listed as agriculturalists of one sort or another. The large percentage of laborers in the work force is a direct result of the distribution of land.

The table of landholdings in Yadaw that I have compiled is based on a house-to-house survey, the tax receipts of the headman on matured crops, and the listings in the squabbles over nationalizations. These facts are combined with checking out with informed villagers to see if information was withheld or distorted.

TABLE XX   Land Holdings, Yadaw

No. of Acres	No. of Households	Per Cent of Households
0	59	48.0
3	1	0.8
4	1	0.8
5	2	1.6
7	3	2.4
8	13	10.6
9	11	8.9
10	10	8.1
11	3	2.4
12	4	3.3
13	2	1.6
14	1	0.8
15	5	4.1
16	2	1.6
20	4	3.3
25	1	0.8
30	1	0.8
704	123	99.9

If one considers the land and occupational distribution together and knows that a 10-acre rice farm is what a family can operate on its own labor resources, barring the peak periods, a nice fit emerges between the two distributions. The symbiotic relations between the landholders and the landless give rise to whatever permanent population and job distribution there is in Yadaw.

Rice Growing. Most of the effort of Yadaw is centered on growing rice. The typical wet rice cycle in Southeast Asia has been described often, so I may skimp on technical factors in order to stress the economic and human aspects of an agriculture dedicated to growing wet rice. Three important features of wet rice growing strike this observer.

1. Periodicity: the compression of work into a six-month period, with resultant idleness (or "make work") during the rest of the year.

2. Peak labor demands: wet rice, as carried out in Yadaw and because of its periodicity, requires huge amounts of labor at transplanting, harvesting, and threshing. This labor must be hired and paid for before the rice is marketed.

3. Constant debt burden: because the rice farmer always needs money for seed and fertilizer to begin cultivation, because he must eat during the growing of rice, and because he must pay off his labor before he sells the rice, he must always borrow at the beginning of the agricultural cycle. He is always paying off an interest-bearing rice loan, in terms of baskets of paddy. Creditors are as necessary to wet rice cultivation as is water and soil.

The other commonly noted features of rice growing—the virtual certainty of crop maturity, the intensive hand skills, the relatively undifferentiated yield from household to household, the dependence on canal and ditching systems, and the inability of small farmers to increase or decrease production as price varies—I shall leave unremarked.

The rice growing cycle begins after the monsoon breaks, in late May or early June. But before the actual work begins in the fields, the people of Yadaw must clean the silt and mud from the canals that feed the rice fields. The rainfall is not sufficient for wet rice growing, and the coming of the rains only makes it easier to break the ground with the plow and harrow. Canal cleaning and repair takes place in March and April before the rains come. The care of canals falls on the cultivator users, although they may hire a laborer to do their stint at this work. Each one of the several canal ditches is assigned by sections to the farmers whose fields the water irrigates. The closer a field is to a runoff ditch, the more valuable it is, for the system works by turns. That is, the farmer nearest the cutoff takes his water first, then he undams the ditch, and the next farmer dams it up until his water needs are filled, and so on down the line of fields. There are about 20 farmers each to the three ditches off the canal system. Each group of farmers is under a *myaung gaung,* whom they elect from their group. The myaung gaung may or may not be from Yadaw, for there are farmers from other village tracts that have land along the canal system. The canal chief does the actual apportioning of work according to how much acreage each farmer has, the share of maintenance being roughly proportional to the landholdings. The canal chief gets no pay, but he is physically exempt from cleaning work; his organization and arbitration are in lieu of physical labor. He also collects two kyats from each canal sharer for hiring labor to keep the canals open during the growing season, when the cultivators themselves may not be able to work at this task. It takes 10 men working one day to clean a 300-foot ditch, and a 300-foot ditch will feed 250 acres with water. Given the 704 acres Yadaw has in rice, it takes about 280 man days to clear the canals. Some hired labor is needed during the season, so that more accurately 300 man days are needed to keep the canals and ditches open. It is not a heavy labor drain on the 63 cultivators, taking about five working days a year from each of them. There are often squabbles about riparian rights, which the canal chief settles. They rarely percolate beyond the level of the common users of the canals to the headman level. In the two groups headed by Yadaw people, there were more troubles in water distribution than in the group headed by a myaung gaung from Kyigon. Disunity or lack of community solidarity is reflected even in canal maintenance. Yadaw, of course, is but one of the hundreds of villages fed by the canal system, and that elaborate system of reservoirs, control gates, and concrete lined causeways depends on a social organization much more complex than the village level. The engineering department in Mandalay is technically responsible for the upkeep of the canal irrigation system, and this department is tied directly to the national government. Irrigated rice growing in this region apparently has always been linked with an administrative and political center, with the peasantry being the dependents on this centralized system of water control. But the present government does not use the irrigation system as a political weapon, nor does it ration water or access according to political relations with villagers. The irrigation system is not a part of the process of political jockeying, and I have no evidence that it ever was.

Planting of rice takes place as early as a cultivator can manage after the first rains. There is a month and a half leeway in getting the rice into the ground. In Yadaw, rice is planted anytime from the middle of May until the first week in July, and the harvest falls in December and January. The chief constraint in rice growing is not the initial time of planting, but the time of transplanting from nursery to flooded field. Here there is a 45-day interval between the time of first planting and the transplantation.

Before breaking the earth with the plow, the good farmer (about 80 per cent) in Yadaw will fertilize his fields. This is done before or simultaneous with the canal cleaning tasks. Fertilizer is cow dung, and five cartloads are used per acre. Cow dung sells for two kyats the cartload, and farmers vary between using three and five cartloads per acre, with nobody using less than three. Those farmers who use only three cartloads of fertilizer say it affects their total yield, but they do not keep records, and exact increments resulting from fertilization are beyond my data. The work of plowing is done in the morning in about four-hour work turns. The heat of midday is too much for both man and beast, although late afternoon plowing or harrowing is sometimes done by those who, for one reason or another, have gotten a late start. The average time involved in plowing and harrowing is eight man days per acre, so it would take one man eight mornings to prepare an acre. The plow, pulled by a team of oxen, digs its metal share into the earth. This share makes a trench rather than a furrow, as would a moldboard plow. When the trench, through repeated runs of the plow, is about six inches deep, the field is considered ready. Between turns of the plow, a simple wooden-toothed harrow is dragged over the field to break the large clumps of earth the plow has turned. Extra weight is sometimes given to the harrow by the farmer who stands on it as it is dragged over the fields. Watching the towel-turbaned plowman, with his longyi tucked up around his legs, usually barechested as he urges his oxen on with words and tree switch, one realizes how hard the work of preparing a field is. What keeps it from being grueling labor is the Burmese habit of bringing along a pot of tea and taking a tea and tobacco break in the shade of a tree, so that both animals and men go back to work with new vigor. If this work were done for hire, it would cost 3.50 kyats per day if the man provided labor and plow or 1 kyat a day for the labor alone (plus tea and a cigar or chew of betel, adding .25 pyas to labor costs).

Rice is planted broadcast, with one and one-half to two baskets of seed to the acre. Seed rice averages about 4 kyats a basket but goes up to 5 kyats during the year. The strains planted in Yadaw (the usual sorts in the region, that is, *Ngasein*, *Theikpan*, and *Taungtheikpan*) apparently do not vary in either yield or hardiness. There is a form of inferior rice, *Maleik*, which can be grown later than the other strains. This variety yields a sort of reddish rice, and when it is cooked it must be eaten immediately, or it gets hard and is virtually inedible. It is so despised by Burmans that it does not even appear in the Mandalay zeigyo, for those who grow it do so to eat it themselves and to eke out a poor life. Only ten cultivators have any of this strain in production this year.

In July and August the rice is transplanted. This is an intense labor job. Men pull up the seedlings, and women transplant them, standing ankle or knee deep in flooded fields. The women usually work in gangs, and in rapid motion they stick the rice seedlings in straight rows about five or six inches apart. Bent over, they move across a field in relentless fashion until the whole area is planted with rice. For this work, a woman will get 1.50 kyats a day, plus 25 pyas in food. Eight persons do an acre in a day, and the whole business is done in a given holding in one or two days, thus requiring teams of women. The other gang work, that of pulling up the seedlings, costs 3.75 kyats per acre. It is three men's work for one morning. The work groups, if large, as in transplanting, pulling up, harvesting, milling, and cleaning the rice, are headed by *gaungs*, or work party leaders. Men and women are leaders, and they guarantee to bring a given number of hands to the task. They are usually in the middle age bracket and have reputations in their neighborhoods of fairness and even dispositions. They oversee the work of the young men and women who make up a large part of the labor force at these peaks, and their presence prevents sexual interplay. They receive extra wages for this work, double the amount given the other laborers. The position of gaung depends upon a person's character as that is estimated by neighbors, and what is sought are forms of gon (virtue), like industry, honesty, fairness, and even temper. The lubyo and aphyo gaungs are, of course, naturals for work gaungs, and they have large parties. Some of the larger tasks require several groups under gaungs, but there is no rivalry and no direct supervision. Everyone knows what is expected and what a fair day's work is, and everyone appears to give it when employed. Besides these character traits, a work gaung needs capital. Some outlay for workers is required during the period because farmers do not settle wages until the festival of the lights.

Until October, when the rice flowers, there is very little work for anyone. Some desultory weeding is done, but the months from the end of August to December are times of idleness. People fill the time by patching out bits of work: selling rice straw in Amarapura and Mandalay, cutting firewood in the hills, doing weaving, and preparing gardens. I talked to farmers who had done no work for 15- and 18-day stretches, and they did not feel that they were idle. They were saving "strength" for the big pushes of harvest and threshing, and they all had bit tasks they were planning to do in the interim period.

They seem to feel that rice growing, with its irregular demands of human attention and effort, is a full-time occupation, allowing them barely enough time and energy to see the pwes, attend races, and work at Buddhist ceremonials.

In December and January, about 120 days after the transplanting, the waving fields of rice are ready for harvesting. Teams of men cut the rice with scythes. Six man days are required to harvest an acre. The harvest costs are usually paid in kind, not cash. One-half basket per work day (average value 2 kyats) is the going rate. The rice sheaves are transported back to the village. There threshing floors have been prepared by smoothing the ground and coating it with a mixture of mud and dung plaster to give an extra hard surface. Oxen, tethered to walk in a circle and muzzled so that they cannot stop to eat the rice straw, trample the rice apart from the stalk and chaff. Women and young people fan the rice with bamboo trays, letting the air do the winnowing, and finally the rice straw is tied into bundles. During this period, until the beginning of February, the whole labor force of the village is active, working both mornings and afternoons. If a farmer does not have the space or the animals for threshing, he rents time from one of the households that does have the plastered threshing floor. This year there were nine threshing floors prepared and in use. Around these nine compounds the whole population of the village clusters. These work groups, tea drinking and cigar smoking, are fully occupied, and hardly anyone is seen loitering in the usual way in front of his house, sipping plain tea from the small green bowl.

After this intense period of work, there is little to do. Rice is either sold to millers who come to pick it up, or put into the godown to be sold later. Some few take their rice to a mill and pay for the milling themselves. The only advantage to this is that they receive the bran (edible for cattle) and the broken rice. In late February the village can be easily sorted into those who just make ends meet and those who have more than bare subsistence, and the key is rice in the go-down. If a man has any withholding power after harvest, he can put his rice in the godown and hope for a .25 kyat increase per basket as the supply dwindles after harvest sale. But if he is pressed by repayment of loans, by paying off wages, and by consumption needs, he must sell all his rice immediately. In Yadaw, only eight households regularly have rice in the godown, and they have the 10 permanent rice storage godowns seen on the Map of Yadaw Village. These are the families who have 16 acres or more at their disposal. The others do not have withholding power.

The economics of wet rice can be appreciated from a sample of the returns to Yadaw cultivators. Rice yields vary from 35 to 50 baskets [14] of paddy per acre. (This is above the national average of 31.7 baskets per acre, but this average is deceptive, including yields from exceedingly marginal cultivations.) Selling price varies from 3.75 to 4 kyats per basket of paddy, but most people sell most of their rice at 4 kyats per basket, so I shall use that figure in the following calculations.

TABLE XXI   Return per Acre of Wet Rice

Cost, Ky		Yield Per Acre		
		Upper	Average	Lower
Plowing, Harrowing	25.00	Gross Yield, baskets	50	40	35
Pulling from Nursery	3.75	Selling Price, Ky	4.00	4.00	4.00
Transplanting	25.00	Money Yield, Ky	200.00	160.00	140.00
Harvest	12.00	Plus Straw Sale, Ky	20.00	20.00	20.00
Thresh and Winnow	8.00	Gross Yield, Ky	220.00	180.00	160.00
Straw Bundling	4.00	Cost, Ky	98.75	98.75	98.75
Seed	4.00				
Manure	10.00	Net Yield, Ky	111.25	81.25	61.25
Canal Cleaning	7.00				
Total Cost	98.75				

Based on 10 cultivators ($N = 63$, 16%) and 150 acres ($N = 704$, 21%).

This return for growing wet rice is known fairly closely by the farmer. When I asked cultivators what it cost to bring an acre to harvest, they uniformly said "100 kyats," which is just about what my pya-pinching counts come to. I have left out of this account another cost that all but one of the farmers in Yadaw contract in the growing of rice: interest on loans. As can be seen in Table XXI, the rice grower needs about 100 kyats for each acre, and his cash returns rarely reach that, so at the beginning of each season he must borrow, either from the government or from private moneylenders. Government loans do not begin to meet the needs of Yadaw farmers. The government in its best years has managed to lend between 35 and 40 kyats per acre to cultivators. Government loans get 1 per cent per month interest, and if the loan is paid back in the prescribed 10-month period, there is an interest rebate of one-half.

[14] One basket of paddy weighs 46 pounds.

In Yadaw, as in other villages, the borrowing from the government is done on a cooperative, group basis. A committee is formed, and it borrows as a corporate group for all the cultivators who make application and are approved. The loan must be paid off on this collective basis. In Yadaw, only 35 cultivators had government loans. The remaining 27 cultivators, as well as 15 of the 35 who had government loans, had to borrow money from private moneylenders. The moneylenders in Mandalay, Amarapura, and other places lend kyats and take back baskets of paddy. They value the baskets of paddy at rates running from 2.50 to 3 kyats. If a man borrows 90 kyats, he will pay back 30 baskets, given the most favorable rate, and this will have cost him 30 kyats in interest, the difference between the 120 kyats he could have sold the 30 baskets for in the market and the 90 he receives from the moneylender 10 months in advance. There is, on the average then, an added cost of 30 kyats per acre in interest charges. The continual cycle of need to borrow, pay off with interest, need to borrow, both to live and to produce, results in a debt burden that is never discharged, nor is it expected to be discharged. Debt is built into the system, and, without the provision of credit by a whole host of moneylenders, the rice would never be grown.

Cultivators in Yadaw do not necessarily borrow all of their money from a single lender, but many tend to build up enduring credit relations with the same lender. The moneylenders are often active, and they seek out cultivators who need money for the roundabout rice production cycle. In most transactions the lender runs little risk. He knows the character of the borrower and his land, and the rice is virtually certain to come in. The lender gets his paddy before the cultivator gets his. Default is almost unknown then, and the activity of the lenders keeps interest rates at high, but competitive (given the 10-month period) rates. The government rate then is a form of subsidy to the farmer. But it is little enough to give him, given the fact that the State Agricultural Marketing Board sets the price of rice. Their price is below what the open market would give, and the current estimate is an 8 to 12 per cent tax taken from the cultivator by setting ceilings on the sale price of rice.

Categories of Wealth. To Yadaw farmers there is only a vague feeling that they are not "better off" than they were in the days of colonialism but "just about the same" in their level of living. This is buttressed by the fact that money in the hand is never very much. Even the money borrowed at the beginning of the cycle comes, often, in part rather than in a lump sum. And by October most people are out of cash except for small amounts gotten by selling straw and fire-wood. Experience with budgeting, with management of sums of money, is not part of the life of most of the farmers. The vise of rice borrow-ing allocates for them most of the money they have without daily or monthly decisions on how to spend. The attitude of getting by on what one has in hand also serves to reinforce the feelings of sameness in their level of living. This attitude, of "pulling in the belt" if resources contract, is expressed in many apothegms and in advice to the young. "If you cannot eat much meat, live on rice, salt, oil, and ngapi, and go to the forest to gather leaves for free cooking of soup. If you are on the way to an ahlu, do not wear your jacket; carry it and put it on when you arrive; it lasts longer that way."

This consequence of avoiding *loba* (greed, desire) stressed by Bud-dhist morality is an economy of Yadaw, probably conducive to greater personal coherence than a striving, gathering ethic, which would cause a psychological problem in the face of deprivation. Wherever in the world the "revolution of rising expectations" is supposedly transform-ing the countryside, Burma is not included. I do not mean either that Burmans have no unfilled wants, or that they would not seize a chance to fill many of their desires, needs, and aspirations; on the contrary, I wish to convey the idea that if needs are not met, if hopes not ful-filled, farmers in Yadaw do not fret, agitate, and riot; what they do is to scale down their wants to match their means. This adaptive mechanism and ideology is well geared to fit a technologically stag-nant society and a society in which great powers and warring groups have from time to time trampled people onto the margins of subsist-ence. So, when the Japanese pressed them into labor brigades, took their cattle, and confiscated many valuables, Burmans did not react with bitterness and violence, but weathered this evil, with their phi-losophy of making do, as their forebears had weathered other tyrannies. Poverty is the common not the crushing fate of farmers, and the chances of ever getting beyond the cycle of making ends meet is remote.

If there is some money left over, after the loans are settled, it goes into clothing and jewelry and merit-making activities. It is not to be used for devising a new economic opportunity, for, really, what is there that a small farmer with small means and little but traditional knowl-edge of farming can do to make much difference in his way of life, in his level of living?

The experiences in getting rich are such that accumulation of wealth is considered truly phenomenal rather than ordinary and natural. There are, in Yadaw, neither the categories of big rich nor really rich, but six households are considered by villagers to have solid withholding power. They do not need to sell rice immediately after the harvest. These six may be considered the rich of Yadaw, and the other two households who have *saba* in the godown just fail, by village standards, to get into that category. These rich (their total assets run from about 15,000 to 20,000 kyats, including the value of land, animals, and jewelry) got that way through different sequences of chance; none of them planned it, strove for it, nor is there an orderly, culturally known way to get ahead in economic terms. (There may be in any society, for all I know, this same accidental quality of getting rich, but many societies have culturally standardized careers of accumulation; Burma does not.)

Two of the rich men were among the larger tenant farmers during British occupation, and when the British landlord fled the Japanese, they held on to their land. For more than ten years they paid neither rent nor taxes, and they became, by village notions, rich. One of the other rich is the son of the last peacetime headman, who also was a large tenant. This man, after much squabbling, has just come into the 30 acres his father used to farm. Another happened to build up a cattle herd after the Japanese left, and his wealth is in the milk cows he owns. The last rich is an old widow who inherited title to land from her husband and from two deceased sons. The amassing of even a small hoard of capital is as capricious as the blowing of the wind, and fortune is the by-product of fate, not the consequence of effort and foresight.

In the control of assets, wealth classes hardly exist in the terminology of Yadaw. They describe themselves as "poor farmers," and only when pressed (by the anthropologist) will they make those distinctions in wealth, between families, that do, in fact, exist. The functionality of these wealth categories is minor, except in second cropping by the larger holders of land and in the withholding power of six to eight households. Only six heads of households are lugyi in the village sense. They also have gon, but none of them is conspicuous enough in worldly success to have the category of a man of pon bestowed on him, and none are rich enough to build the client structure that a man of pon would have.

The 123 social entities I have called households [15] break into three categories:

---

[15] The reasoning behind the grouping of 132 numbered dwellings into 123 households is simple and follows the criteria laid out for functional social units in the section on Nondwin's social organization.

Lugyi (big man):   Those who can withhold and have real dis-
                    cretionary income, rather than rich, with its
                    connotations.
Sufficient: Those who have enough to eat meat and fish
                    regularly, dress in fancy longyis for ceremo-
                    nies, and do not need to hire out as laborers.
Poor: Those who just make ends meet, who must
                    sell labor, chop firewood, and have meals
                    from which meat and fish are often absent.

By combining what I knew of landholdings and cattle with village opinion on the rank of given households, I came to these numbers for each of the categories:

Lugyi	6
Sufficient	30
Poor	87

While there were differences as to the exact ranking of some households, there was no difference into which *category* a household fell.

The import of these categories is manifest partly in what I have already said about occupational distributions, and also in ability and willingness to undertake second crops and tractor or machine hire, and in the family budgets of annual consumption.

In a given year, anywhere from 10 to 20 families do some double cropping, on something like 50 to 80 acres under another crop than wet rice. The ranges are such because many small factors may make the difference in more than 10 families doing more than 50 acres, which numbers of acres and families are minimally involved in double cropping. This minimal group includes the six lugyi, the two households almost in that category, and two of the landholders with more than 10 acres, who have land close to the canal and low-lying land that holds the rain.

Of the second crops in Yadaw, most of the acreage is given over to sesamum. In the year for which I have data, 50 acres were devoted to sesamum. In addition to the six lugyi and the two near lugyi households who normally double crop their holdings, there were eight households trying sesamum crops for the first or second time. The acreage involved ranged from 2 to 5 acres per cultivator. For these new risk takers in double cropping, I found no significant social or cultural categories which distinguished them from the run of the population who were not engaged in double cropping. What seemed to have tipped their decisions in the direction of double cropping were the simple facts

of economics and ecology. Since rain is uncertain, the successful growing of sesamum depends on a pair of fortunately timed showers, and,
if there is a first shower at the beginning of the sesamum growing
period, some farmers may be induced to try a few acres under that
crop on the chance that a second shower will come. In addition to the
uncertainty introduced by rainfall, there is the time involved in getting the sesamum planted and harvested before the rice fields must
be prepared. The time constraint is less for those with higher-lying
ground or ground on the far end of the irrigation net. They can start
their fields at the outer margin of time for planting rice. Another
factor entering into the sesamum as second crop is the composition
of the household. If there is available labor in the household or if the
household is well enough off, there is more likelihood that, given proper
land, sesamum will be essayed. Tied to the above elements are two
purely economic variables. The previous rice yield must leave the potential risk taker with enough money to begin the investment in sesamum; hence, the very poor are virtually eliminated, whereas the lugyi
are favored. The price expectation of sesamum is also considered. Price
does vary from 17 kyats to 25 kyats a basket for sesamum, and, at
the lower expectation, the eight or so households that could, on ecological, resource, time, and labor grounds, undertake a second crop of
sesamum may be put off. With a cost structure for sesamum like that
calculated on page 21, the return to an acre runs from a high of 95
kyats to an average of 47 kyats and to a low return of a net loss. In
Yadaw sesamum is a chance crop, and under the given ecological and
economic conditions sesamum growing is not likely to expand far beyond the 50 or so acres devoted to it by the 15 or so households that
from year to year are willing and able to take the risks.

Other second crops in Yadaw are insignificant and hardly ever
reach the total of 50 acres under cultivation. Peanuts are planted in
some marginal land not suited for rice, and also in 10 acres of dou-
ble-cropped land. The 10 acres of peanuts as a second crop are divided among as many households. Gourds are also planted in 10 acres
as a second crop, and the mapeh bean is sometimes planted along the
bund of the canal. Both gram and sorghum are sometimes interspersed
with the growing rice. This planting of gram and sorghum, in November, in a maturing rice field, gives exceedingly small yields, averaging about 10 baskets to the acre, and in any given year about 100
acres are so utilized.

There are also some small truck gardens in Yadaw, which grow
luffer, cucumber, tomato, and some vegetables whose English equiva-

lent I could not get (*kawethi, takhwathi*). But this is for household consumption and is not commercial or market farming. The area of expansion for truck crops is severely limited by competition with the time needed for marketing of rice straw, by high costs of seed, and the careful attention needed to grow them, when compared with the less rigorous and more open demands of rice growing.

What I have intended to portray are the ecological, economic, temporal, and human effort constraints that limit second cropping in a rice growing economy. Poverty and customary work-leisure periods also curtail the expansion toward second cropping. The returns from second crops are fluctuating and uncertain when compared to the never-failing rice. Second crops need capital; they require special care and ecological conditions, and they cut into leisure time. As such they are not very attractive opportunities for the Yadaw farmer, for the local moneylender, or for the landless to undertake.

The response to poverty in the rice village is not, in this case, a display of agricultural diversity, but rather it is an occupational specialization and a business enterprise. The proximity to Mandalay, the special circumstances of herd transhumance, and the shortage of land have combined to give this community an occupational diversity which exceeds that of most wet rice villages in the region.

Still, the solution to the general problem of the level of living lies in the transformation of the agricultural base of the society and not in the piecemeal addition of ad hoc jobs so that the poor may eke out a living. And, therefore, it is instructive to review some of the attempts of the government agencies to generate agricultural change and the villagers' response to these plans and programs. The machine rental programs described earlier in this chapter have been moderately successful, and, given the pattern of landholding, they are about as well-utilized as could be expected. Smaller machines like the winnower are not in sufficient supply to meet local demand. Of other machines, used in other Asian countries with great success, neither the peasant nor the expert advisor apparently seems aware. The small Japanese tractor, the rice planter, or the thresher are not actively considered in the government programs. Why there is this block in diffusion, this informational lacuna, cannot be discovered from study of the level of society where I worked, and I forgo the inviting opportunity to guess.

About two years ago the agricultural department demonstrated in Yadaw that cotton could be grown successfully and profitably. Since that demonstration, not a single farmer has planted cotton as a second crop. The factors lying behind the indifference to cotton are not far below the surface of casual observation and informants' chance remarks, and, had the ARDC done its anthropological homework with the thoroughness it did its technological preparation, the costs and troubles of the demonstration could have been saved. The obvious facts of land distribution, time and labor constraints in rice growing, the shortages of capital and the unwillingness of local moneylenders to get deeply involved in the cotton business (the cotton speculation here is in the commodity, not in the lending of money to grow it), and the severe violation of the customary rhythm of work and leisure, all foredoomed a serious interest in taking on cotton, especially with the added factor of relatively small returns any single farmer could expect.

The scope of new crop introduction is limited in Yadaw, and the ARDC has made no efforts to demonstrate, other than cotton planting, or to encourage more growing of sesamum and peanuts. The provision of chemical fertilizer has also been suggested, but neither the experts nor the farmers are certain about the profitability of its use.

The most extended and systematic efforts of the government to induce economic change in Upper Burma can be seen in capsule form in the social welfare program. The Social Welfare Department is the heir to the now defunct office of Mass Education. The personnel, when I was in Burma, still overlapped, but administrative reorganization was moving those welfare officers who could qualify into the local government structure as Assistant Township Officers, gradually eliminating the whole Mass Education Program. At the village of Nayakan a week-long school for village farmers was held. The notion of the social welfare officers was to give a course of lectures to instruct selected villagers in topics crucial to the social and economic programs of the national government. Thirty-two villages in the Amarapura township were involved, and they sent 45 students to Nayakan. The students were housed in an empty, red brick building on the pongyi kyaung grounds and were fed in the kyaung itself. The logistics of housing and feeding 45 village Burmans are exceedingly simple. The accommodations are of the barest and crudest. No knives, forks, or eating utensils are required, just a single dish for each man and a single teacup. Chairs, tables, beds, or separate rooms are likewise not needed. Each villager brought his own bedroll and placed it on the matted floor, and the brick building quickly turned into a semblance of a dormitory, or perhaps barracks is more accurate. Night light was not needed, and a few candles provided whatever light the men needed to find their own bedrolls. Sanitary facilities were not necessary in the building—the students washed at the well and eliminated at the edges of the village. Food for villagers was standard, and easily mass-cooked, so the rice, curries, ngapi, and soups came out of the extra cooking equipment the pongyi kyaung had on hand. The sponsoring village was asked to donate 14 kyats, the costs of food for each trainee at the school.

Yadaw, like the other 31 villages in the program, was to send at least two trainees to the Nayakan school. Only one young man attended, although the village did collect the 28 kyats needed to keep two trainees for a week. The selection of the trainee is instructive in demonstrating how little things may doom large programs at the very outset. None of the responsible cultivators were willing to spend the week at Nayakan, for they did not want to "waste," in their words, a week listening to lectures on agriculture, Burma's constitution, the maintenance of village libraries, the suppression of crime, irrigation, animal husbandry, the economics of cooperatives, the meaning of social welfare, and the uses of cooperation. All of these topics and the daily program had come into the village together with the request for two or three trainees to attend the school. When, for two days, I visited the school in session, the daily routine—beginning at 5:30 A.M. and concluding with a 10 P.M. closing prayer—was closely followed. The mature men had other things to do and were not disposed to place themselves in the low status of student or to be run through a taxing program of lectures and activities that they viewed as bearing little on their immediate concerns. In fact, the only reason a delegate came from Yadaw at all was because of the headman's self-interest in keeping on good terms with local politicians. The headman wanted to be able to say that Yadaw, under his aegis, backed the government program of development, and he also wanted to exhibit an earnest of his power. If no one turned up for the school, it would indicate great weakness in the headman, for he would demonstrate to the world that he lacked pon and awza, that he could command no one. The trainee selected by the headman was a young man, dependent on the headman for small favors. Maung Sein, the delegate, went to the school, not because he was a farmer (he was, in fact, among the unemployed youth) or because he was interested in the course material or even because he believed it would be an adventure, but simply because he was obligated to the headman, and the headman was obliged to proffer a token of command. In Burma, an inevitable consequence of sending a young man to learn new things about economic life is that this knowledge will not be diffused to the mature generation, who in fact control most of the resources in the economy. In Burmese social structure knowledge flows from elder to younger. It is presumptuous for the junior to instruct the senior members of society and it is contrary to the village notions of wisdom and knowledge as fixed entities, absorption of which increases over time. What Maung Sein learned at the school, the notes so diligently recorded in the copybook provided by the Welfare Department, remained his private experience. Nobody in the village, not even the headman, asked him what he had learned, and he never talked about it to his peers, except to recount some of the names of other trainees and to describe a particularly hard-fought soccer game in which he distinguished himself.

Apart from the personnel in the training program, there are other equally formidable barriers in implementing the government programs of change. Keeping to the peasant level of social organization, the problem of economic change is chiefly one of bringing together in a viable and appealing mixture the following: opportunity the peasant can perceive and grasp, an incentive structure to move the peasant to the opportunity, the knowledge and technique needed for the peasant to act, and finally the supralocal organization to sustain and expand economic opportunity and growth. The successful emergence of this sort of mixture requires a highly integrated and complementary set of relations and understandings between the government planners and technicians, on the one side, and the peasant farmers they hope to change, on the other. And, in the last analysis, it is persuasion, self-interest, and only a moderate use of force and sanctions that the national elite have at their disposal. In Burma, as elsewhere, peasants can be bullied, exploited, coerced, and taxed, but these techniques cannot, apparently, drive them into modern agriculture. The government programs, as exemplified in the Nayakan school, in the visits by technicians to village meetings on social change, in the propaganda and advice that flow from the various government offices to the villages, and in the plans, decrees, and ordinances made in Rangoon, have not effectively put together the viable and appealing mixture of elements that I have suggested are a necessity for a more than superficial change in the economic structure. Support for this contention is easily found in the Nayakan experience, as well as in the sessions I attended, where agricultural experts came to the village.

One of the recurring themes, both at Nayakan school and in the general ARDC program, is the mechanization of agriculture. The tractor is seen as the means to modern farming, and the tractor program as the symbol of socialist development. In Nayakan the lectures on tractors described, with charts and pictures, how these machines are used in other countries. A glowing picture of the abundance generated by tractor farming was created. The ARDC man announced the gladsome news that 390 tractors were on order for Upper Burma, and that "one of these days" driver training programs for the tractors would begin. The announcement was received with enthusiasm. Five villages, according to their representatives, were willing to buy tractors and pay for them on the installment plan, and these villages had already (as early as 1959) applied to the Subdivisional Officer for permits to buy the tractors when they arrive. Half the package needed for economic restructuring of the countryside is visible in this tractor program. The peasants see the gains from tractor use, and they are eager to try machine farming. So opportunity and incentive exist, at least initially, in the peasant half of the equation. But the government still trades in words, not tractors. The tractors have been a long time in coming (they did not appear during my stay); the schools for drivers and mechanics have not been organized, nor has even a paper plan for tractor purchase or tractor cooperatives been worked out. The supralocal side of the equation has failed to provide organization, capital, knowledge, and technique. They have stopped at the first step, the delimiting of new opportunity and the educational persuasion of peasants to see their self-interest in the new opportunity. Of the two sides of relation between government and the peasants, it is difficult to decide which is the more difficult to create when it is lacking. Apparently the administrative bureaucracy and the politicians are unable to organize and execute any program of scale or deep impact, whatever the reasons for this may be. The peasants likewise have difficulty in organizing themselves for some new tasks, especially in providing incentives for activities requiring more than household-domestic scales of organization (apart from religious activities and the facade and display elements that accompany religious ceremonial).

The state of the tube wells of Yadaw shows what happens in a village when the obvious civic good is not the obvious gain of any single family or individual, and where there are no authoritative public bodies, no traditional sense of civitas, or any framework of organization to span the gap between collective and individual divergences in goals.

Wells provide water for drinking, cooking, and washing the body and clothing. In the dry zone, all villages have at least one working well, and that well is usually communal property. Private wells are a rarity for two reasons: They are expensive, and, if an individual is rich enough to dig a well, he is likely to dig it for the pongyi kyaung rather than for the village. A man who donates a well to the kyaung adds significantly to his kutho and has conferred on him the valued title of *yeidwin daga*. So wells in pre-British Burma were built either through donation or by a levy on the households of a village. Now, wells often are provided by the Welfare Department through its tube-well program. Yadaw has both sorts of wells—the deep-dug bucket and pulley variety and the pump-handle tube well. Tube wells frequently break down because the pumping mechanism either rusts out or the springs give way. The pulley wells, over time, silt up and need to be cleaned out and deepened. Since the tube wells are viewed as a government gift to the village, their repair and maintenance are also seen as a government responsibility. When the tube wells need repair, a villager goes to Mandalay to arrange for someone from the Welfare Department to undertake the repair. The only contribution the village is likely to make is that the households near the tube well, those who in fact benefit most from the well, will feed the repairmen when and if they come. The pulley well requires about 1,000 kyats to pay for the periodic cleaning and deepening. This amount of money appears beyond the village capacity to raise. The immediate users of the well cannot raise it, and the whole village will not raise it because the whole village does not benefit from the well. This is a classical laissez-faire standoff. Public needs do not match private wants. In a community like Yadaw, made up of migrant households, without a strong headman, and lacking an institutional structure for codifying and legitimating a notion of the public good, there is no easy way to reduce this anomaly.

The tale of the wells, like the ARDC programs and indeed even the decisions of cultivators, illustrates an important local constraint on the formulation, apprehension, and implementation of economically meaningful new activities. This constraint lies in the area of organization—organization considered as the procedural means of combining human and nonhuman resources for the achievement of short-range and specific ends. The organizational dimensions absent from Yadaw are political and entrepreneurial. Neither a village council nor anything akin to a firm or other special action body are in the structural repertory of this rice farming community. The organizational dimension is crucial here because the resources of the community could easily provide the needed wells. For example, in one day the community raised 2,000 kyats to bet on its entry in the bullock-cart race at Ta-on. But betting on a bullock-cart race serves the self-interest of each bettor and even provides an increment of kutho, since part of the proceeds from the Ta-on race went for the dedication of a hti on their new monastery. For wells and other obvious communal improvements there is no organizational structure or cultural idiom to make self and other interest complementary.

TABLE XXII   Monthly Expenditure Pattern of Lugyi and Average Household

Item	Price, Ky/Amount	Lugyi Amount	Lugyi Total	Average Amount	Average Total
Cooking oil	4.00	3.50 v	Ky 14.00	3.00 v	Ky 12.00
Firewood	6.00	2.50 cart	15.00	2.00 cart	12.00
Salt	1.00 ky/v	.60 tics	.60	.60 tics	.60
Sugar	2.00 ky/v	.50 tics	1.00	—	—
Tea	.08	20.00 tics	1.60	20.00 tics	1.60
Rice	11.00	3.50 bask	38.50	10.00 bask	30.00
Beans	—	—	—	—	—
Eggs, duck	.15	5.00	.75	4.00	.60
Fish	5.00	.25 v	1.20	.25 v	1.20
Dried fish	10.00	.25 v	2.50	.25 v	2.50
Tobacco	3.25 ky/100	50.00 cigars	1.75	50.00 cigars	1.75
Betel	4.00	.40 v	2.00	.30 v	1.20
Chili, dry	5.00	.50 v	1.75	.30 v	1.50
Napi (prawn)	3.50	.50 v	1.00	.50 v	1.75
Napi (gaung)	12.00	.12 v	—	—	—
Mutton	—	—	—	—	—
Beef	2.00	.50 v	1.00	—	1.00
Chicken	—	—	—	—	—
Pork	4.00	.25 v	1.00	.25 v	1.00
Prawns	12.00	.10 v	1.20	—	—
Peanuts	8.00 ky/bask	—	.25	—	—
Bananas	.50 ky/bunch	.50 head	—	.50 head	.20
Cabbage (Dec.-Mar.)	2.00 ky/ea	1.00 v	1.00	.50 v	1.00
Carrots (Dec.-Mar.)	.50	—	.20	—	—
Buthi (Nov.-April)	—	.50	—	—	—
Onions	2.00 ky/v	—	1.00	2.00 gourds	.20
Kayanthi	—	—	—	—	—
Tomato (Jan.-Feb.)	.50	5.00 v	2.50	4.00 v	2.00
Tomato (rest of yr.)	1.50	1.00 v	1.50	1.00 v	1.50
Cucumber	—	—	—	—	—
Ngabyabye	2.50	1.00 v	2.50	.50 v	1.25
Ginger	2.00 ky/v	.10 tic	.20	.08 tic	.15
Saffron	1.50	.30 v	.50	—	—
Kayekaya	—	—	—	—	—
Mango pickles	—	—	—	—	—
Mangosteen	—	—	—	—	—
Maize (Oct.-Dec.)	1.50 ky/100	500.00 ears	1.75	100.00 ears	.30
Tamarind (Mar.-May)	.60	1.00 v	.15	1.00 v	.15

Item				
Bread	2.00	loose cookies	—	—
Cake	—	—	2.00	.50
Kyethingathi	.50	15.00 v	2.00	2.00
Pehmyint (Nov.–Jan.)	.50	.50 v	2.50	1.50
Potato	—	—	—	—
Pehzinzua	—	—	—	—
Zadawvwe	4.00	.25 lb	1.00	.30
Coffee	.60	1.00 pkg	.60	1.00
Candles	.05	30.00 boxes	1.50	.30
Matches	.30	1.00 qt	.50	.30
Kerosene	(various)	.50 ky/mo	1.00	.30
Fruits	1.00	1.00 v	1.00	.20
Jaggery	—	2.00 cakes	.20	1.00
Soap	.10	1.00 pkg	1.00	1.00
Thanakha	1.00	.10 v	1.00	—
Coconut oil	12.00	—	—	1.00
Powder, lipstick	—	—	.80	—
Flowers	(various)	1.00 ky/mo	1.00	4.00
Medicine	(various)	2.00 ky/trip	2.00	—
Travel	(Mandalay)	5.00 ky/mo	5.00	—
Various greens * (neem, monnyin, gourd leaves, chinbaungywet, nyanyanbin, myuywet, kazunywet, younpateithi, dandalunthi, etc.)	—	—	—	—
Sardines	1.50	2.00 tins	3.00	—
Soy sauce	.50	1.00 bot	.50	.50
Lighter fluid	1.00	.50 can	.50	.30
Garlic	5.00 ky/v	.06	.60	—
Soup powder	2.00	.50 bot	1.00	.50
Noodles	(various)	—	.50	—
Mushrooms (Sept.–Oct.)	3.00	1.00 v	.25	1.50
Purchased foods (chiefly mosikyaw, monhinga, kaukhswe)	—	3.00	3.00	—
Gram	—	—	—	—
Eggplant	.60	.12 v	.05	—
Chili powder	—	—	.25	—
Total average monthly expense			131.45	92.55
Annual food expenditure			1,577.40	1,110.60

* To this item the list is the same as the consumption schedule for Nondwin (pp. 40–41). The items following the asterisk are Yadaw usage, and apparently not Nondwin.

The rice economy of Yadaw, despite the appearance of technological stasis and the organizational inabilities of the local peasantry or the national agencies to provide or invent meaningful economic opportunity, provides for members of the community a level of living carrying all the freighted connotations of "primitive plenty." Hunger, starvation, famine, dire bodily want are not part of the experience of most of the people of Yadaw. The basic elements in the diet everybody gets everyday: the 1.2 pounds of rice per adult, per diem, the cooking oil, the mixture of green, leafy vegetables, the touch of napi, the cups of Shan tea, and the smoke of the cigar, or the bite of a wad of betel. As the comparison in Table XXII reveals, there is not a great difference between the food consumption of a lugyi household and the average household. Only a few items are peculiar to the more economically successful, and the chief difference lies in the amounts of standard articles and foods consumed. Since the rich are only modestly and recently so and because wealth does fluctuate from generation to generation, there is, of course, none of the social cleavage between the habitually wealthy and customarily poor. The tone and atmosphere of Yadaw is one of social equality, with wealth or economic success largely irrelevant as an index of social prestige or power.

The almost certain rice crop, the ease of meeting minimal needs, and the long periods without demanding or concentrated work allow the people of Yadaw to have wide latitude in response to sustained drive toward better economy. There is no severe external discipline, no prod of hunger, no lure of great wealth, no realistic chance to make much of oneself or one's family through economic pursuits. The levels of living of Yadaw can be approximated by the figures in Table XXIII.

TABLE XXIII   Comparison of Annual Expenditures by Wealth Classification *

Item	Lugyi, Ky	Average, Ky
Food	1,577.40	1,110.60
Clothing	750.00	250.00
Religious	250.00	50.00
Household	50.00	30.00
Total	2,627.40	1,440.60

* I do not bother to specify the items of clothing, for they are standard and can be seen in detail in the Nondwin lists

What the description of the economy means, to be aphoristic, is that Yadaw people are more than merely alive and fed, that poverty is common but not crushing, and that wealth is not a real and pressing aim of the units in the economy. Technology and organization have moved to fill interstices in the economy, not to reorient it or build into it a dynamism. The market, money, credit, and even an elaborate supralocal canal system have not pushed this economy into a movement toward economic growth, but have rather combined to make a trendless cycle of low-level sufficiency the axis along which it drifts.

---

of Burmese dress. The figures on clothing, religious donation, and household expenses are self-reported, and not gotten, as were the food expenditure amounts, through systematic observation of actual daily consumption. The figures therefore suffer from selective recall, the human tendency toward rounding, and the usual hazards of getting exhaustive cataloguing. My guess or estimate, for what it is worth, is that the range of error in the total expenditures does not exceed 5 to 10 per cent. At least I am confident that I did not systematically bias the figures, and perhaps the errors are somewhat offset. I have moderate confidence in the comparability with Nondwin. The direction of my inevitable errors in reaching annual consumption figures is toward underestimation. I know, for example, that many of the between-meal snacks (villagers are nearly always eating, smoking, or tea drinking) like the pineapples, mangos, custard apples, plantains, plums, papaya, mangosteen, durian, bits of noodle, fish, and sweets are not adequately estimated by the householders or fully observed by me. Also expenses in going to pwes (though these really are not out-of-pocket), pilgrimages, or races are not included. But again, I do not think the distortion is as great as, say, that in the national accounts of even a fully monetized society, where the decisions to value or not value items are often arbitrary.

I did not bother to calculate the level of living of the poorest families in Yadaw, but my impression, from unsystematic and sporadic budget collection, is that no one lives beyond the extreme of 25 per cent less than the average, whatever the actual income may be. There is for the very poor some sharing of food with the richer households, much dining at other households, and great substitution of more rice to keep the belly full.

7

Social and Political Organization

The community of Yadaw is formed by the interaction and arrangement of families and households. The basic unit of social organization is the family. As in other Upper Burma communities, the family tends to be organized into household units. Coresidents who exhibit the proper kin behavior are the family in group existence. In the ideal state each family and household tends to occupy a single compound. Most of the compounds in Yadaw are marked by fencing or by some other visible boundary. In the Map of Yadaw Village are shown the 132 structures which house the 123 familial units of Yadaw. The number 123 is reached by defining the family with the eight criteria enumerated on pages 45–46. To insure comparability with Nondwin, the 123 family units are divided into the same three types: (A) The conjugal family of father, mother, unmarried children (sometimes with secondary relatives as satellite residents); (B) the extended conjugal family, in which a son or daughter has formed a conjugal family and is coresident with the father and mother and jurally subordinate to the father-mother family; and (C) the joint conjugal family, in which relatives such as siblings or cousins or in-laws live in the same compound with coordinate jural status between or among the families.

SOCIAL ORGANIZATION: THE HOUSEHOLD

The presence of three major types of family organization should not cloud the basic underlying social dynamic of Burmese familial life. The aim and ideal of founding a family is to set up a nuclear household in one's own compound. The existence of varieties in actual family structure and composition is, of course, conditioned by the accidents

246

of birth, death, and other demographic fluctuation, the state of economic well-being, and, most importantly, by the rhythms of the domestic cycle in the independent establishment of a compound. In the field census of Yadaw the following compound compositions were encountered.

Type A	95	77%
Type B	23	19%
Type C	5	4%
Total	123	

A peculiar feature of Yadaw, and of the arrangement especially of its families, is the tendency toward neighborhood clustering. Yadaw, as noted earlier, is a community made up of migrants from surrounding Upper Burmese villages. Migrants from the same or neighboring villages have tended to more or less ghettoize themselves within the village cluster. The fact that 55 per cent of all marriages among the conjugal pair in Yadaw in 1960–61 were contracted with members from other villages is an indication of the high rate of exogamy of the community and possibly of the low rate of internal cohesion across "neighborhoods."

Of the Type B families the mother-daughter extended link accounts for 17, or 14 per cent, and the extension to a male link accounts for 6 families, or 5 per cent of the total in Yadaw. This underlines the contention offered earlier that the basic, or anchor, familial link is the mother-daughter bond. Rather than repeat the facts of kinship terminology, of expected duties between categories of kin, and of the meanings of commensuality, economic communality, coresidence, or role substitutability in Yadaw, for they are the same here as they are in Nondwin and in other Upper Burmese villages I have studied, I shall concentrate more on the meanings and vocabulary of interpersonal familial relations. In reporting on Nondwin I have slurred some parts of the meaning of marriage, the raising of children, and the ways in which authority relations in the family are generalized in the larger social structure. In this description and analysis I hope to amend and extend my earlier observations and remarks on the family.

Marriage and the Family

Marriage is the act that initiates in Yadaw the developmental cycle which may lead to the setting up of a separate familial compound.

In Yadaw there are two sorts of marriage, via arrangement and via courtship. Even the arranged marriage takes into account the tastes of both prospective mates. In actual fact the arranged marriage is not very different from the courtship marriage, since both forms of marriage require that the boy's parents make overtures to the girl's parents on behalf of the boy. Really arranged marriages, exerting the will of parents over or against their children's choices of prospective mates, are not known in Yadaw. These formally arranged marriages take place only among the urban rich, where there are real property stakes involved. Eligible mates are only limited by excluding parent-child or sibling-sibling marriages. First cousin marriages are frowned on but not sanctioned against. In the 192 marriages of people of Yadaw there is no instance of first cousin marriage. The preference is to marry nonkin, at least for a first marriage. Part of this preference stems from the belief that there is some infusion of biological vigor when strangers marry. The interplay of the quasi-arranged marriage and the courtship-ripened marriage gives clues both to the meaning of marriage to the conjugal pair and to the relationship of the newly formed conjugal pair to the families of orientation from which they spring.

Courtship is not a formalized procedure. Boys and girls arrange, during their casual contacts in the daytime at the wells, or in the rice fields, to meet at night. When dusk sets in they slip away from home. They do not meet in groups, but by couples. Boys tend to be the initiators in village romances. They begin by seeking the favors of two or three girls. A girl, conversely, may have, at any one time, two or three admirers. For boys, the usual form of expressing early interest and admiration is the writing of love letters. The love letters are fairly standard compositions and do not vary very much from writer to writer. They are studded with the clichés found in the badly printed manuals for writing such letters. When a boy is favored by a particular girl in however slightly visible a manner (e.g., she waits for him at night on the veranda of her house or returns his love letter), other potential admirers stop their attempts to attract her. The second state of courtship is marked by night visiting between a couple. When courtship has reached the state of night visiting, the visits take place without competing admirers. Competition, among boys at least, would disrupt the amicable relations among the peer group, and it is chiefly this agreement among the young males not to compete with each other for females' favors that accounts for the steady one-to-one relationship in a courtship cycle.[16] So far as I could tell, this male initiation, noncompetition, was the ideal as well as the real pattern. How frequently the steady-state courtship comes to fruition in terms of a marriage I cannot say. But I do know of cases where the steady state was ruptured by disaffection either of the male or of the female. Disaffection, of course, springs from the discovery that the couple may be incompatible. What first attracts a boy is beauty in the female. A woman in Yadaw is beautiful if she has a clear skin, good flesh (which means flesh evenly distributed over her body without too much curvature and with no exaggeration of bosom or buttocks), good bones (not too prominent cheekbones, not too thick wrists, nor too thick ankles), good, long hair and plenty of it (everybody has the same color hair, so there is no preference there). Finally, the woman is not to look old. The air of youthfulness, with no wrinkles around the eyes or worn looks in the face, is valued. These same five characteristics define a handsome male, but not so much attention is paid by women to male appearance. To a woman, intelligence, even-mindedness, and gentleness, along with education are the features sought in husbands. The ideals of both beauty and temperament are built around the notions of proportion or balance or symmetry. For example, fair skin and dark skin are equally disliked. The color of skin *shwe wa yaung* (yellow-gold) is the preferred color. At about age 17 the courtship stage gets under way for women, and they spend a tremendous amount of time primping and arranging. Hair, especially, is glistened with coconut oil and brushed to a high lustre. All young girls take the morning and evening thanakhka face powder treatment to keep the skin "tight." False hair is not now used to increase the size of the *sadon*. Girls are trained in the vanity culture. Ear-piercing for earrings, jewelry on the finger and around the neck, and lacquer wrist bands are part of even the smallest toddler's dress. Women are taught early to walk in a "ladylike" yet provocative manner. Men do not complain about the time, effort, and costs that women from 17 to 40 spend in beautifying themselves. In fact they are proud to see sister, wife, daughter well made-up and beautiful.

Courtship is not necessarily a long affair. Of the many marriages between Yadaw residents to people of other villages, the whole courtship period, the entire time of acquaintance, often does not exceed the short peak season of harvest or threshing when visitors from other

---

[16] The female culture was much more remote from my observation than male culture, especially in the intimate areas of courtship, sex, and marital relations.

villages come to work in Yadaw. This indicates that not much knowledge is needed about potential spouses before a villager can gauge the chances for marriage.

However, no courtship goes without a minimum of romantic love. Love, based on physical attraction and compatibility, is something highly valued by the youth of Burmese society. After the young people have come to an agreement between themselves, the boy informs his parents that he wishes to marry the girl. It is said to be rare, and I know of no cases in Yadaw, for a girl to express a preference to her family before a suitor has presented himself. The parents of the boy will usually accede to his request and make a formal visit on the parents of the girl. This first visit called *kyaung hlande* literally translates as "opening the road." If the visit of the kyaung hlande is well received, the couple is considered as engaged or ready to marry. In most cases the initial visit of discussion, if there is no outstanding cause or trouble between the potential in-laws, opens the way for the two or three other discussions preceding the marriage. Sometimes, however, the initial visit is rebuffed. In cases of rebuff, the pride and sensibility of the parents of the boy are outraged. They will not make another visit. If the boy continues to insist on this particular girl and has the capacity to nag and bedevil his parents, they will send one of the village lugyi. The lugyi presents himself as agent of the suitor, but in fact he reminds the girl's parents that they are laying the ground for ill feelings among neighbors. This appeal usually suffices to reopen negotiations between the two families. The actual negotiations are simple. The parents discuss what, if any, gifts they will make to the couple at the time of the wedding. It is usual for both sets of parents to give to the newlyweds. What is given is dependent on the wealth of the donor, but marriage is not an occasion of great display, and the gifts do not stretch the means of any household. The largest presentations known in Yadaw are gifts of cattle (up to 25 head) or land (up to 10 acres). The family of the bridegroom pays all of the expenses of the actual wedding feast.

A wedding costs from 75 to 700 kyats, depending on the use of these optional elements: printed invitations, loudspeaker, festal foods, mandat, and gift cigars. The core and nonoptional elements in a wedding are the gadawbwe to the elders, the flowers, the leaf of good luck, and tea serving to guests. As in all villagewide or supravillage festivities, guests make donations to hosts, and at every wedding someone, usually the school teacher, sits in a corner with a notebook and ballpoint pen, entering the names of donors and the amounts given.

Marriages, of course, tend to cluster in time. The interdiction on marriages during the period of Wa is strictly observed. Weddings and marriages are entirely secular affairs. The Buddhist monk is never present, not even as spectator; none of the devotions in the village liturgy are chanted; no reference is made to the Buddha and his dhamma. If weddings and marriage are, in some sense, antithetical to spirit of monastic Buddhism and, at the level of the most general values, part of the snare of sensuality and sentiment that makes for attachments to the unending round of life-death-life, what is the meaning of marriage, and why the publicity?

The public ceremony of marriage summons coresidents to witness a change in status and to establish rights in inheritance, property, and exclusive sexual association. At least one representative from each household in the community comes, for some period of time, to the place of the wedding ceremony to drink at least a cup of tea. As in all ceremonies marking important status transitions (birth, marriage, shinbyu, death), the full consensual ratification of all the households is publicly given. The actual marriage ceremony is short and fairly standard. The couple, attired in the best clothing they have and with borrowed jewelry if they are poor, sit in one of the auspicious corners of the wedding mandat or house, if no mandat is built. Invited guests drift in between a line of young girls at the doorway. The young girls are dressed in old-fashioned imitations of the royal maidens, complete to the addition of false hair. They have in their hair the appropriate flowers of good fortune, and to the incoming guests they usually hand a leaf of the Eugenia variety, which also signifies happiness and fortune in this world, along with a cigar. The official community is represented by three or four of the village elders, who are seated in a mingala part of the wedding house. The couple perform the triple shikko for their parents, and the parents recite some homilies on the conduct of married life, the loss of freedom, and new responsibilities. Then the couple shikko to the elders, who say about the same things. This concludes the public ceremony. The newlyweds may have made, prior to the ceremony, a private offering to their mizain-pazain nats. Tea and cookies are served by the lubyo and the aphyo groups, and the respective gaungs also clean up the debris after the wedding, collect the cups, saucers, mats, pots, spoons, and knives which come from the lubyo and aphyo repositories. When the couple are about to leave the ceremonial mandat, a line of the young bachelors stops them, in some cases by holding a silver chain across the path of the newlyweds, and demands the payment of gebo. The payment of the marriage money is said by villagers to keep the newlyweds from being stoned and taunted by the bachelor group. It may be, in part, a survival of that custom, for the payment is indeed higher if the groom comes from another village, but mainly it is a contribution to the peer group as compensation for their work as ushers, servers, cooks, and cleaners at the wedding and is a source of the funds that maintain the unmarried as an organized segment of village social structure.

Marriage forms the basis of a new familial unit, but it does not rupture the ties between the families of orientation of the spouses. There is more change in the role of the male than the female, but both spouses continue to interact with and have strong loyalties toward their families of orientation. Some of the classic conflicts of the Burmese family turn on the unclear cultural stipulation of the respective spheres of the families of orientation and of procreation. This conflict is also one of the chief reasons for divorce. Here is a summary of one of the most exacerbated familial conflicts in Yadaw, and, although it is extreme, it reflects the tension built into a marriage situation where the claims of competing families are unclear, where no alliance structure is created between the families, and where the value system and community organization give but weak underpinning to marriage maintenance.

Maung Mo married and brought his wife to live in the same compound as his parents. He made this decision because his father was troubled with a kidney illness, and Maung Mo wanted to be close to help him. His wife, Daw Chit, did not object at first. They lived in the same compound for nearly four years and had two children during that time. His father's condition got worse and worse. Daw Chit said she could no longer live with the sick old man. His "sickness was an ill omen," and it kept too much of Maung Mo's money involved. Maung Mo was shocked by her suggestion and said it was unthinkable to leave his aged, sick father and old mother on their own. Daw Chit said they could move and still do something toward the upkeep of the aged couple. Now, Maung Mo said, look what happens when sons move far away, and he cited his own brothers, who had families in other villages and did little more than token visiting and support of the parents. And then he brought up the fact that Daw Chit spent a lot of her time at her mother's compound, with her sisters, and he could not tell who was keeping whose household. She replied that daughters must keep close to their mothers, who are after all their best friends and advisors. This sort of argument was kept going, growing more and more acerb for about a year. Then Daw Chit gave Maung Mo an ultimatum: either move away or send away the aged couple, or she was through. Maung Mo said go then. She followed typical Yadaw practice, packed her belongings and moved back to her parents' household. Later she went to the headman, and, since both parties agreed, he wrote out an order for separation, without the more usual attempt by the elders to reconcile the couple. Daw Chit, her belongings, and the children moved away to Amarapura. She has since remarried and is a frequent visitor to her mother in Yadaw, and her mother frequently goes to Amarapura. Maung Mo is still unmarried; he spent a lot of money on his father's illness and now has buried the old man. He supports his aged mother in his compound and says he will never marry again, because a wife would object to his devotion to his parents. When he talks about devotion to parents, he mentions the earnings of kutho and the Buddha's injunctions to care for and honor parents.

The obverse of this marital strife is easily found in Yadaw. Husbands complain about the money and time wives spend on their relations. Usually this sort of tension is resolved far short of divorce or separation, especially if young children are involved. But the potentialities for trouble are constantly on hand. Much lesser sources of strain are: laziness in the husband or wife; bad-tempered or violent spouse; and sexual misconduct. These latter irritations rarely lead to the breakup of the marriage or of the family. In Yadaw there are six divorced men (most of the men who have broken families move away) and 17 divorced women (most of the divorced women stay close to their mothers), so that divorce and separation are not infrequent occurrences. Part of the ease of divorce is due to the structural fact that marriage establishes only a conjugal bond with the potential statuses of pater and mater, and that dissolution means only the loss of a single role, not the rupture of a network of kin relationships or the loss of intimate bonds beyond the conjugal one.

Given the nearly equal social position of women and men in Burma, except in the religious sphere, no really important jural status is gained through marriage or lost through divorce. Women are full, functional members of society, whether they marry or not, as are men, and of course the unmarried are built-in parts of the social structure, not anomalies. The great overlap in the sexual division of labor makes it simple, on the side of the ordinary business of keeping fed, groomed, kempt, and housed, for single persons to live alone. Men can sew, cook, baby-tend, wash clothes, and shop for food. Women can work in the field, drive bullock carts, chop wood, and be prominent in market transactions.

With the establishment of the conjugal family, in incomplete fusion, on the one side, and incomplete fission from the parental generation, on the other, there is no clear pattern of authority between husband and wife. In theory and in public the husband is supposedly dominant, but this dominance is so tenuous, so indefinite and ambiguous that its social visibility is virtually nil. Women are not restrained at home in speaking out, nor in public are they shy and backward or deferential to men. The ordinary household will see men and women sharing tasks and giving and taking orders with about the same frequency. Only on very formal occasions or when exalted visitors come does the male ever play a role that could be called "head of household" in terms of the authoritative decision maker. On all other occasions and in the flow of daily life, authority is light and shared. Burmese marriage then takes place between near equals, held together in first instance by physical attraction, temperamental compatibility, and common decision making. Later, the advent of children may strengthen these bonds, but not necessarily, for keeping a conjugal pair together in a village setting is not seen as absolutely necessary to the rearing of children. And as I shall explicate in the section on child rearing, the socialization of the young is diffused beyond the nuclear family in many important respects.

My data on the daily life of a married couple is much richer in the easily observable externals of task performance, less rich in the meanings attached to daily interaction, and thin in the areas of intimacy and sex life. I do believe the progression of data toward attenuation is not necessarily a reflection of the relative place of these spheres in Burmese culture, but rather of the conditions of my field work, and perhaps my personality. A household in Yadaw is run without order giving or task assignment and with a division of labor allowing great interchange among the persons performing given domestic jobs. The day typically starts with the kindling of the fire either in the cookhouse or outside, and this task falls to whoever gets up first. Tea water is set cooking, and the light breakfast is cooked and served. It is usual for women or for younger children to do the serving. Men are served first, and they get the choicest bits of whatever accompanies the rice and ngapi. During the work day, if not at peak seasons or if the woman has no special occupation, the morning is left to the women and children. Housekeeping takes little time—a few pats on the beds, a cursory sweep with the short-handled broom, and a dip of the dish and cup in hot water about completes the daily maintenance routines. Cooking and pot stirring also are not demanding of time or continuous attention, and child watching is not continuous or overtaxing. Children who can walk and speak are left free to move around the compound; older children are free to come and go nearly as they wish within the village; and smaller children are passed from hand to hand or placed to sleep or rest in the swinging cradles every household has outside in a cleared area. The Burmese housewife, for a peasant woman, seems to be singularly unburdened. One does not see, as I did in Middle America, the ubiquitous child strapped to the back, the continual coming and going of head-burdened women, and the long hours of stooping and squatting before grinding stone and cooking pot. The balance of the day also reveals a flexibility in eating time, in task performance, and the great freedom of women and men, less for children, in gearing their activity together. Certainly a great part of the charm, the feeling of ease, and the unhurried tempo of village life stems from the twin facts of temporal flexibility in domestic tasks and a household that virtually runs without the giving or taking of commands. When not at the peaks of agricultural work, there is, for adult Burmese, much scope for easy and informal interaction. Visiting neighbors and kinsmen, the externally present, bubbling teakettle, and inevitably offered betel box and cigar, frame and encourage much idle conversation and much time killing. No adult is locked into a closed household, and no one confines himself to his own compound. There is an easy and free interchange among at least the neighborhood clusters of Yadaw. Only one house was almost completely outside of the visiting pattern of neighbors, and this clearly was a special case. In this house, a man claimed, against the scoffing of his fellow villagers, to be an adept at fortune telling and astrology. (The majority of his neighbors told me that he was not only a fraud, but that he probably was not fully sane.) He tended a woman, not his wife according to even the minimal definition of marriage adumbrated earlier, who had leprosy in an advanced stage. He also had a notion of cure that was idiosyncratic. These three things, together with a personal arrogance, put him beyond the bounds of the normal neighborhood visiting and tea drinking pattern.

Men, when not engaged in work, have added time-wasting activities. Cards (I was told that this practice came about in 1940) and dominos are played by men in the heat of the afternoon. And in Yadaw there are a few men who gather to drink toddy palm juice when it is just turning sour and slightly alcoholic. Games, like cane-ball kicking (*chinlon*), are for young adults, rarely for heads of households.

In the evening, when work is done, and last meal is taken, the family will most likely stay in its own compound, with only the very closest of neighbors or next of kin likely to visit or be visited. Conversation is usually light and desultory, and the day ends as it began, with the individuals making their obeisances to the Buddha altar and retiring to sleep. Only the smallest children and infants are put to bed; the other children eventually drop off to sleep near a dying fire or held by some adult or in the bed they typically share with older siblings or father or mother.

What happens in the marital bed of a Burmese household is but sketchily revealed by my field notes. There is much joking in a sexual vein among unmarried males, and about half the humor in any pwe turns on the double, better, multiple, entendre of words and phrases. But among married adults, sex and things sexual are not topics of conversation except in epithet or epigram. In four months in Yadaw, I never heard a discussion of sexual things among adults in their own compounds, unless it was gossip about troubles of neighbors or intrigues among those of courting age. In normal married life (my informants ranged from 17 to 45 years of age), at least for the first five years, there is intercourse three or four times a week. As men age this is reduced until they are about 50 years old, when they rarely have intercourse. Most women in Yadaw are virginal when they marry, or else they have had experience with the man they eventually marry, whereas many men have had previous experience with prostitutes in Mandalay. Neither sex has had any instruction or advice from the senior generation, and what sex lore they have is picked up through observation or peer group talk and speculation. As a rule the husband initiates the sex act, but wives may refuse advances. Neither partner is fully undressed, and most villagers go through life without ever seeing a fully disrobed wife. The preferred, if not the only, intercourse position is husband superior, face to face, and none of the men I talked to had ever varied or experimented with other postures. Sexual interplay, despite the vanity culture and the deliberate female allures, is not, I venture to guess, one of the cultivated arts in or outside of the village family. And although there is adultery and even crimes of passion, I would not place sexuality as a major concern of any but the adolescent. At least the manifest causes of domestic trouble never implicate sexual incompatibility as a prime cause, and whether or not a conjugal pair may phrase real sexual difficulties in the more publicly acceptable idiom of family conflict, is beyond my ability to say. Deviations like homosexuality, sodomy, or transvestism seem to be known to villagers chiefly through stories and not through village examples.

Women and men do not, when married, try in any way to restrict the possibility of having children. Coitus interruptus or reservatus is apparently unknown and unpracticed. There is a vague knowledge that women may be more or less fertile at different times during the month, but this is not a guide to frequency or timing of intercourse. Married couples will not practice the several methods of abortion that villagers know, nor is there any contraceptive device in use. The only brake on intercourse, apart from mood, energy, and desire, is a menstrual taboo, which begins with the onset of the menses and ends on the day after their cessation. When pressed, women will say that three (live) children is a good-size family, but they do not begin to complain about the burdens of childrearing until they have six children, and then one may hear from the woman herself and from her neighbors expressions of commiseration about how much work and trouble childrearing is. But, given the fearsome child waste in Burma (infant mortality is the second highest in the world), the problems of restricting family size loom less large than the hazards of bringing infants into childhood.

A pregnant woman must avoid or minimize the intake of certain foods, especially those things classified as hot or spicy or cold. Among the common food taboos for pregnant women are: chili peppers, ginger, tomatoes, leaves from vines, gourds, neem leaves, many green vegetables, with tea and coffee only to be drunk lukewarm.

When a pregnant woman approaches full term, she is put into a room by herself. The delivery room is not in a mingala part of the house or compound. Babies in Yadaw are still usually delivered by midwives, but health service nurses increasingly deliver them. But whoever performs the obstetrical duties, the procedure is not much varied. The baby is delivered, in a normal birth, from a squatting position. Only women are in the delivery room. The woman's mother and sisters are sure to be present in the room, while her husband and father along with neighbors are certain to be seated at a fire just outside the delivery room. A razor blade (rarely, a sharpened bamboo knife) is used to sever the umbilical cord. This, along with the afterbirth, is buried in the south part of the compound.

After the exact moment of the child's birth is ascertained, the baby is relatively ignored. For the first three days of its life it receives honey and water, for the mother is not yet considered "clean" enough to begin feeding. Both mother and child are confined for seven days, and no visitors come into the delivery room, except the father who is allowed to look in from time to time. He and his neighbors are kept somewhat occupied in the heating of continually needed pots of boiling water. The hot water is part of the steam bathing the new mother is subjected to for the seven-day period. After delivery, the new mother is in a particularly dangerous state. Part of the delicacy of her condition stems from the imbalance of her essential body elements which Burmese medical authorities see as consequential in giving birth, and some of the risk comes from vaguely formulated notions about the "uncleanliness," in both a physical and moral sense, of the act of procreation. The seven-day confinement, the seven days of bathing, the seven days of sitting on hot rocks or bricks, the daily smearing of the body with turmeric, the daily taking of turmeric powder in water to encourage sweating, the giving of purgatives on the third day, the special diet of salt fish (for anemia prevention), and the avoidance of cooling foods (meat, eggs, milk, fresh fruit, and vegetables) are all responses to the mixture of ideas about imbalance and impurity involved in giving birth. The impurity notion is most clearly expressed in the giving of purgatives. The new mother may not breast feed her infant until her blood and milk have been cleansed through purges. Usually these occur after the third day. Confinement for the seven-day period after delivery avoids letting sunlight fall on either mother or child, and the room in which they are confined is dark and gloomy, lit only by the flickers of the kerosene lamp and fire. The fear is not of the sun, but of catching cold, for fresh air is considered dangerous to anyone in a weakened condition. On the day the baby first comes out of the confinement room, its head is shaved. The birth hair is considered unclean and is either burned or buried. The first cradle ceremony (*pahketin*) may be held that day or later in the week.

The pahketin ceremony is merely the placing of the baby into a swinging basket of bamboo for the first time. For this event, neighbors and kinsmen are invited, and tea, cigars, and betel are served. At the pahketin ceremony, the father places the child in the cradle and sets it in motion. Then there is a general discussion of what the child looks like, what it might have inherited, the time and moment of birth, and the possibly appropriate names. Children are believed to inherit three major things from parents: character, disposition, and strength. Character is the generalized capacity for morality; disposition is the characteristic of temperament; and strength is the physical ability to weather the wear and tear of life. These inheritances, which are somehow transmitted through the blood or bone, are deep lying and virtually inextirpable. But they combine with two other general forces to shape the actual person and personality: kan, over which there is no control, at least in the perspective of the new embodiment, and environment, the early training period. The pahketin ceremony underlines an important feature of the relation of child training to the responsible adults. First, so much is already given in heredity and in kan that adults have but limited scope for doing either good or harm to the unfolding child, and, second, most of what happens to the child is considered to be an unfolding of what he is. There is little view of the neonate as plastic; rather, the prevailing definition is that babies are helpless miniature adults, who with time and care will mature into whatever their capabilities and experiences permit. In such a conception, parents can hardly ever feel guilt about upbringing, or berate themselves for failure, omission, or commission of nurturing or warping acts. The relative independence of children's fate from parents' guidance makes babyhood and early childhood a time of easeful interaction, where the physical needs are catered to by many ministering adults, and where emotional and ego needs are treated as budding versions of adult needs.

A child will be breast fed for about two or three years, if not displaced earlier by a new arrival. For the first two years of life all food comes directly from the hand or body of a woman, usually the mother, but nursing women who are kin or neighbors will pick up crying infants and feed them. In addition to mother's milk, the child is given food that has been prechewed by the mother. First, rice pap is passed from mouth to mouth; later, other prechewed foods are used.

Young children and infants are frequently put in the care of neighbors, kinsmen, or older children. It is not uncommon for a month-old baby to be left, for an hour or so, with an 11-year-old child, or for a woman to go visiting with a small baby and pass the child from hand to hand, with all adults in the compound taking turns coddling and handling the child. With young children, there appears to be a single cardinal rule by which adults abide: Children should not cry. Nobody abides a wailing child. As soon as it starts to whimper, it is rocked in the cradle, fed, fondled, crooned over, floor walked, changed, or whatever is necessary to stop the crying. Villagers are much less attentive to the troubles that small children can cause themselves. When children can crawl they are allowed to move around almost freely in the compound and are only shooed away from the fire. At the crawling and toddling ages children do not impinge much on adults, and adults play with them if the whim is there or tend to them if they cry, but mostly there is a sort of loose inattention, and the crying, wailing, clarion call is the only means the child can use to mobilize and concentrate adult attention on himself.

When a new baby arrives, the older sibling is suddenly displaced. Concern and attention are fixed on the new arrival. It is true that many Yadaw mothers anticipate the troubles of a new child and tell their older children to be kind to the new baby, to take care of it, and to try to avoid the feelings of rivalry, if the children are closely spaced. The coming of a younger sibling, inevitably, moves the older one away from the concern of adults. His cries are not immediately heeded, his needs and wants come second to the baby's, and some responsibility for the tending of the infant devolves on the older child. Almost uniformly, Yadaw women deny recall of sibling rivalry or displacement troubles. They have no tales to tell of jealousy between children, no incidents to recount of deliberate pain or injury inflicted by older on younger siblings. But one can see, if there are children still young and only a year or so apart, outward signs of trouble. On interviewing a woman with a five-year-old boy and a three-year-old girl, who professed, as did all other women, that the shock of displacement left no trace, I noted that while she spoke she held the girl in her lap; her son kept trying to clutch at her longyi or at her bare arm, and she kept pushing him aside, saying that he was too old to be cuddled by his mother. But later she told me that the only way the boy went to sleep without a ruckus was to share her bed with her and the daughter, whose legitimate sleeping place it was. Similar attempts to keep up the warm, physical contact, the instant need for fulfillment, and the role of dependent child by older siblings can be frequently observed in Yadaw.

In conformity with the concept of children as unfolding, the modes of weaning and toilet training are not standardized as to time or method. Weaning is sometimes forced, by the arrival of a new child, before the second year of life, but, without this, at least two years of breast feeding is common. To the Western eye, it is arresting to see children large enough to walk approach their mothers, unbutton the eingyi, drop the bodice, and begin to feed themselves. The gradual substitution of pap and adult food, from the first year on, cuts down on frequency of breast feeding, but mothers are permissive because there is a belief that a linkage exists between breast feeding and the ability to conceive.

Toilet training practices are in great variety in Yadaw. Some mothers get their children trained within a year to 18 months, and others have told me that they could not depend on children's control of elimination until the child was more than seven years old. Withal, there is a core of custom involved. After the children reach five months of age, women regularly take them outside, just before putting them to bed, and hold them until they urinate. And at night, just before retiring, the mother and her young children will go to the edge of the compound or the village and form a group of squatting bowel eliminators. The youngest children are brought along for this because they learn by example and for the pleasure of being included in this group. One other constant in toilet training is that children, more than a year old, are pushed out of bed when they bedwet, for they are usually sleeping with an adult, and the adult has been made uncomfortable.

All in all, neither toilet training nor weaning is a sudden, shocking, or severe discipline. Children move from the state of complete demand and complete attention, to complete demand and diminished attention, from crisis demand and crisis attention, and finally to minimal demand and virtual inattention to adults. And most of them move without marked events to phase them and without strong recall of this developmental cycle. What this does to the psyche or personality of individuals I do not know, for I am concerned only with the manifest, public expressions of behavior and personality, not the deep-lying and persistent syndromes that underlie these observable and socially understood behaviors. I am, of course, then giving a vocabulary of child-rearing with lexical meaning derived from indigenous attribution, not an anatomy of drive and motive with meaning derived from a more or less sophisticated psychological theory.

Children grow up in this permissive, indulgent, and relatively unprogrammed environment. They are, however, sometimes rudely struck, verbally assaulted, and sometimes publicly humiliated by their parents. Children are spanked for shooting slingshots at birds, they are struck for stealing and for lying, and they are beaten if they seriously get in the way of adult activity. But if you ask a child to fetch a cigar, and he does not, he is not censured or beaten. The child has a "mood" and like adult moods, children's moods are usually respected. If there is an actual confrontation between an adult and his child over an order or about a duty unfulfilled, then real emotion and trouble may ensue. These confrontations are rare, since authority by father and mother is rarely shown in clear "thou shalts" and "thou shalt nots." The child usually knows enough from the normal child's skill and sensitivity for decoding and anticipating adult whims and demands to avoid confrontation, and parents are so relatively undemanding of performance that head-on collision between the unequal wills of children and adults is rare.

Children are drilled in the outward forms of respect and obedience toward parents and elders, and this is what is required, whatever the inward state might be. They learn to shikko to parents before retiring, never use parents' names in direct address, to eat after parents have selected their portions, never interrupt speech of parents, and to respond to direct orders and commands. These observances together with an absence of flagrant lying, stealing, or causing trouble in the neighborhood are what parents expect from their children, and what cause neighbors to say the children are well brought up. A well brought up child in these terms is seen as a credit to the parents, and, oddly, an unruly or ill-tempered child is regarded as a burden on the parents, rather than something they have created. Only the positive aspects of child behavior are thus thought to be influenced by parental guidance.

Besides the sporadic use of physical force and insult to guide child behavior, the main agencies are tale-telling and religious instruction. The stories of ogres, demons, cannibals, even kidnapping Indians, and soul-stealing nats are invoked to threaten children when their behavior is out of line. I have seen children in wide-eyed fright and wonder listen to a parent tell them that a witch or a balu would come after them if they persisted in a given form of disapproved conduct. The parents' tales are all the more convincing, not because parents really *think* a balu is on the way, but because they themselves do believe in the presence and animosity of these creatures, and they do hold that there is a link, however tenuous, between personal conduct and the ability of nats, balus, sonmas, and other malevolent spirits and forces to harm a person. Children are frequently guided in their behavior by invoking *naung bawa*, the next life. If a child kills a fly or steps on ants or willfully shoots his slingshot at birds, he is cautioned that in the next life he will be born in one of the hells. The child is warned that if he lies his breath will turn and stay foul, that his teeth will loosen and fall out, or that the lining of his mouth will be covered by sores. The warnings based on Buddhist cosmology are told children as casually as an American might tell his child not to lean out of high windows, or stay away from strange dogs. Many of the things children see also reinforce this notion of evil consequences inexorably following evil deeds. The paintings on the Arakan pagoda, where Yadaw people may go to shop, show graphically the tortures of the various depths of hell; the jataka tales, told by parents, read in school, acted in pwes, also stress the terrors and tortures of the hell that follows misdeeds.

The core of Buddhist morality is taught to children from about ages five to ten. Before that, they hear, see, and sometimes imitate parents in the devotions, but instruction is not given in any formal sense. Teaching Buddhist codes of conduct is viewed not so much as bringing a child into the fold, but more in the light of making of him a human being, for to the villager the essential condition of full humanity is to be a Burmese Buddhist, to be at least aware of the conditions of salvation and of the minimal methods of assuring rebirth in human form, and with kutho-kan kaunde to be reborn in the territorial, kan-kutho group. Parents, chiefly the father, are responsible for teaching children the Awgatha, the Triple Jewel, the five precepts, about kutho and kan. The cosmological notions, the eightfold path, and anything about the suttas are left to pongyis or the school. The precepts are taught in two phases. The first three: not to kill, not to lie, not to steal, and these mean in the village context, never to knowingly take any form of life, never to knowingly utter falsehoods, and never to take anything that is not freely given, are taught the young children, and they learn to repeat these when they begin to make daily devotions to the Buddha altar or to put out the food for the ants and birds. The second phase is the addition of the last two precepts: not to engage in sexual misconduct and not to cloud the mind with intoxicants. The first means in village understanding never to violate the sexual customs of the community. And, of course, in this construction of the meaning of the Buddhist injunction, this means that having contact with prostitutes and premarital experience with a girl one intends to marry are not violations of the precept. Adultery, incest, and most forms of rape break the precept. Intoxication means almost total abstinence from fermented toddy palm juice or country spirits, the distilled white liquor. Other intoxicants like opium, marijuana, wines, and European liquors are normally beyond the experience and purview of villagers. Children of about 13 years of age are expected to understand and abide by the full five precepts.

Some fathers, about 10 per cent in Yadaw, read excerpts from the *Kyanza* (the book of sacred writings) to their growing children, but, in the main, communication of Buddhism as part of the making of human beings is an oral transmission coupled with example and admonishment and slight physical coercion. Children are trained to be attentive to what they can see of adults acting out the Buddhist code of humanity as they live as familial units in a village community. Some Yadaw people can and do, at least for an anthropologist, reel off lists of familial duties. These are stereotyped codes of groups of five duties among the dyads that make up the family. (But this is formal, bloodless categorization, and everything in the realm of morality and Buddhism is numbered, categorized, and grouped. The logic of classification often eludes both the classifier and the audience, but loose ends apparently are anathema to Buddhist scholastics.) The duties are not, so far as I could see, really used as standards against which to judge anyone's familial conduct, and, in times of troubles, the lists of obligations and rights are not invoked. The elders are much more pragmatic in settling domestic disputes, and the aim is not to move a couple or a family closer to the observance of ethical or religious standards, but rather to talk away the immediate trouble and to restore harmony, however that can be done.

I list the family duties, as I got them, from a 10 per cent sample of the heads of households of Yadaw. Less than half of the sample could give more than a couple of duties in each category, and the list I here present comes not only from the amalgam I made from the verbal reports in my survey, but also from the villagers' expedient of consulting books. The list is offered not because it is a chief guide to familial conduct, or even because it is a major resort in dispute settlement, but rather because it is an example of the mode of impinging a great tradition on the daily life of village families. The point, theoretically, is that, although the flow of life, the nature of reciprocal rights and duties in the Yadaw family, is governed by the skein of local understandings and the personal exigencies of particular families, there is a belief that on some level there exists an ordered ethical code, and that whatever one does, in this world of ungovernable events and pressures, there does exist a world of categorical truth and wisdom, and that this is embodied in canonical literature. And further, the lists underwrite yet another facet of working social systems: The rules are ambiguous enough so that application to the affairs of villagers is problematic. Viability and continuity of standards depend on the inability to be directly confronted and confounded by the actual events of ordinary men pursuing their ordinary lives.

The duties in groups of five are:

Father to Son:
1. keep him from evil doing,
2. instruct him in virtues,
3. provide an education,
4. give a patrimony when he is of age,
5. find him a suitable wife.

Son to Father:
1. help him in his work,
2. take care of him in old age,
3. live a life that entitles you to an inheritance,
4. after his death share your kutho with him,
5. bring no evil reputation to the family.

Husband to Wife:
1. support wife,
2. give her major part of earnings,
3. love and cherish,
4. look after relatives on wife's side,
5. do not think of other women.

Wife to Husband:
1. love, respect, obey,
2. spend money wisely,
3. invest earnings wisely,
4. look after relatives on husband's side,
5. love husband only.

Duties between siblings are not specified as such, but the code to govern relations between friends, with appropriate modifications for age and sex, is said to hold for sibling obligations:

1. give food, clothing, money in case of need,
2. treat as equals,
3. look after their interests,
4. never speak harshly,
5. be trusting of them, never be treacherous.

As children are trained in the morality of village life, they are also prepared for work, chiefly in the family context. At about six or seven years of age, they begin to aid with truly economic and productive task participation. At this time, they also begin to take on the domestic chores of helping with child watching, laundry, cooking, errand running, and cleaning and sweeping house and compound. Young children (between 5 and 15) really are learning as much as they are contributing to economic activity. After 15, they may be considered full members of the work force, and some of them are even in the agricultural labor force, hiring out at the peaks of harvesting, threshing, and transplanting. In this learning of work, boys get much less instruction, in a formal sense, than girls, and they learn much less sedentary, drudge work than do women. In the early years boys accompany fathers to the fields, bring in cattle, or run the foot-powered fodder chopper, while girls are kept closer to the compound in learning to sew, not more than simple overhand stitching to patch clothing, or to mend tears (for patterning and cutting the local tailors are used, to weave, to spin), to peel vegetables and fruits, and to cook. In a case of choice as to which child will tend a younger sibling, the girl is preferred. The teaching and the learning of domestic and economic tasks is, what I suppose it is in all peasant societies, not a formal procedure, but part of ordinary existence, with unsteady and unvig-

orous feedback from the parents. What is moderately unusual in Yadaw is the virtual absence of scaling down adult tasks to fit the child.
The small yet functional loom, the child-sized water pot, cooking pot,
or miniature plow, or whatever is remarkable by its absence. Children
begin on real adult tasks with true adult equipment. Part of the reason for this is the continual parental indifference to or suppression of
childhood curiosity. They cut short queries with traditional answers:
"You will learn in school"; "ask an older child"; "do not bother me";
"you will learn by and by"; and other simple yet effective means of
blunting youthful curiosity. This fits well with the notions of an unfolding nature in children and of age-destined fulfillment. If a child
asks many questions, it is because he has not come to the point where
experience and his own intelligence would give him the answers; thus
a reply is wasted, since he is not truly ready to absorb that information.

Near the age of 11 or 12, children have learned to live on the pe-
riphery of adult society, to stay out of the way in the compound, not
to bedevil adults with inquiry, and to guide their behavior so that it
does not cause domestic or neighbor scandals. The peer-group life becomes much more intense about this time. When I asked the schoolteacher, almost casually, about this (for I thought attendance at his
school might underlie the formation of peer groups and play groups),
he gave me the common Yadaw version of the basis of peer-group
formation. Villagers hold that turning to age mates and extra-com-
pound play groups, rather than the brother-sister or proximate neighbor groups, is a function of the onset of puberty. Puberty makes the
children more active and less able to spend peaceful time sitting or
being with adults. When I brought up the fact that at about age 11
or 12 most children are detached in great measure from the compound-
neighbor complex, the schoolteacher said that this was just the point.
Puberty now comes between 11 and 12 years of age, while in his grandfather's generation it came between 13 and 15 years of age, and so
children get involved in play groups earlier than they did a generation
or two ago.[17]

---

[17] As an aside, I asked what caused the change to earlier puberty onset. He had a
theory I later found to be standard and part of the everyday vocabulary of village
Buddhism. The life span of individuals is getting shorter, and, hence, the age of
puberty is being pushed forward. When I asked him how he knew that life in
general is getting shorter, he said that there are two grounds for this belief: one,
the general notion of cycles of waxing and waning spans of human life between the
comings of new Buddhas, and, two, the closing phrase in horoscopes used to be

Children, as they become somewhat detached from the immediate compound, have quite a bit of free time, and in this time they turn to playing a variety of simple games. *Gonzi hpite* is a clay ball game, resembling in some ways the game of marbles. Mud and clay balls about one-half inch in diameter are lined up, and other balls are pitched at them to try to knock them out of line. It is chiefly a game for 7- to 10-year-old boys. *Zehkonteike* is a girl or young boy's game. This is played by throwing tamarind seeds into small holes in the ground. In the holes, the seeds are flicked against each other, and the winner takes the seeds that he knocks out.

Games for the pubescent child start to get tied to community and public performance. Instrument band groups and dance troupes are the most common forms of play. Groups as large as 15 youngsters will practice with the wooden flutes, brass cymbals, hand drums, bamboo clappers, and brass bells, while young girls dance in imitation of the zat pwes. The *lubyet* (clown) and band interaction will also be mimicked and the elephant dance practiced. All of this is apparently without adult instruction, or any instruction, but in direct imitation of the many pwes children and young adults of this age have seen.

There are also sociability groups among the young men. The core of these groups is the neighborhood-kin clusters. The young men will sit, say, in the tailor's large compound or in a large compound in one of the informal neighborhood clusters, and swap tales of cart races, of soccer matches, of events that have come to them via radio (like the sputnik) or through the newspaper (like the dynamiting of the Dagon Express Train by insurgents).

Burmese Interpersonal Behavior

The finished product of Yadaw socialization is easily described in ideal terms. The valued man and woman is fashioned in the familial con-

---

"may the holder live 120 years," and now nobody lives that long. On these two grounds human life is certainly in the waning phase of the cycles, and longevity is correspondingly curtailed. Also, the weather is continually getting hotter; heat shortens life, and great heat makes food less nourishing. Pagan, the great ruin of Anawratha's reign, is cited as an example of a place that flourished once, but wickedness, heat, and the inexorable rotation among times of increase and times of decrease have turned it into a hot, empty desert, holding the crumbling glories of the past. Now the trees are being cut down all over Burma, and the water is getting scarcer; the end will come, followed by a new and vigorous, green and happy rebirth.

text, but demonstrates his character, virtues, manners, and humanity within the larger context of neighbor and village-wide interaction. By about age 15 the complex of adult behaviors is supposed to be manifest in a person, and from this time on there is a deepening and an enriching of what has been built and given, not a development of new traits or character structures. One of the most crucial aspects of the nature of Burmese interpersonal behavior is summed up in the concept of *a nade*.

A nade is one of those portmanteau, indigenous ideas that is best explicated by inspection of instances. An informant will be talking with me. We have talked, say, for an hour or so; he begins to get restless, manifested chiefly through foot scuffling and eye shifting. Finally, he says *a nabade khimbya*,[18] I must go work; sometime when there is more time we shall talk again. A person of venerable age and reputation drops in unexpectedly on a villager, and if the villager does not have good cigars, cake, or cream to offer with the tea, he starts out by saying a nabade. An older person scolds or corrects a younger one, but the older person is in error. The younger knows this, but he does not speak back or correct the older, and, if one asks why, the answer is a nabade. A man is invited to an ahlu or shinbyu and is unable to make the proper monetary contribution, a nade will keep him from going. Someone wants to borrow something from a neighbor, but before he can do it he must overcome a nade. If you interrupt anyone at work or need to ask a favor, part of the habitually used phrase contains the word a nabade. If one loses an argument, a possible reaction is a nade; in trying to begin courtship, a boy may be stopped by a nade; teachers correcting pupils make the students have a nade; and superiors and more powerful persons can usually stir up a nade in inferiors and the less powerful persons. The constraints of a nade are often inoperative between intimates, among equals, and husbands-wives, sibling-sibling.

The first apparent meaning of a nade is a kind of feeling. A nade happens inside an individual, and rough English equivalents to the content of the feeling might be shame, yielding, melting, disturbance, and inferiority. A nade always comes up in social situations. One does not feel a nade when an action or idea involves no others. A nade is consequent on interaction between status unequals and is absent from the most intimate, full, personal interaction and largely inopera-

---

[18] The use of *ba* in a nabade or in any verb is the polite form. It is optional among peers, but obligatory to persons of respect.

tive among peers and age mates. In a brief definition, then, a nade is complex feeling arising from status nonsymmetry in which the junior or weaker is constrained from direct confrontation of the superior or more powerful by the operation of sentiments like shame, delicacy, and surrender. In the childrearing I have described can easily be found the basis for the deep fixing in villagers of the basis for the emotion of a nade. In social interaction, in daily life, a nade manifests itself in a kind of indirection in most human encounters, a sticking to the surface of persons and situations, and a deliberate effort to take things at their face value, to believe that things are really what they seem. The operation of a nade prevents, or obviates, except for intimate equals, a sharply defined emotional situation, a blazing argument, a direct contradiction, a clash of persons, and the clean and definite statement of what one feels and thinks. This is not to say that villagers do not, in fact, argue, fight, hate, gossip, and kill, but rather that these are explosive events, coming in a wake of overcoming or repressing a nade. A nade is a built-in block to interpersonal spontaneity between villagers of even slightly disparate status. And the sense of delicacy, the unwillingness to cause any inconvenience to another, and the reluctance to speak out, to clear the air are all, in part, tied to instillation of a nade in villagers as a normal process of growing up.

A nade, however, is only one of the ideas that enters prominently in the definition of the ideal person. The Yadaw classification of persons distills down to a dichotomy. Roughly translated, the poles of the classification are a broad, gentle, and wise-minded individual (*thabawdatyide*) and his opposite, a narrow, impatient and foolish person (*thabawdathide*). The features of the broad and the narrow person are most frequently given as:

Broad	Narrow
patient	impatient
meek	aggressive
helpful	selfish
pious	impious
a nade	little a nade
self-reliant	dependent

This is the major way personalities are sorted out, although some minor kinds of persons are also recognized, like the *keba* or beggar, who continually seeks aid and favors, as one who borrows rice and does not repay. The proud man (*kyithawbu*) is one who puts on a serious mien and is snobbish and does not speak to everybody, or else speaks impolitely or not sweetly. Preferred to the proud man is the *chyo pyoncho*, the sweet, smiling fellow, and children are told to grow up in that vein. Mad persons (there were none in Yadaw) are simply called *yude* and are completely irresponsible for their actions; *yode* is simple-minded (people in this category did live in Yadaw), but having limited capacity to live and be responsible. A person with the proper character is called sometimes *lein hmade lu*, a clever person. A clever person is known because he avoids fights and arguments, never uses harsh words, and states things so that hearers get the point easily.

If a man has led a good life, not quarreled with neighbors, and exhibited lein hmade, he may be one of the informal group of *lugyi lugaun* (literally, *lu* means man; gyi means big; lu means man; gaun, from *kaun*, means good, or an adult, for people over 40 may be called *lulyi*, "who is moral"). The lugyi lugauns chiefly give advice, moralize, and express the agreed-on folk wisdom. Lugyi lugauns are rarely directly solicited for their counsel, except by relatives. Rather, they function in the informal conversational groups, in the small parties gathered idly around teacups. In the course of a conversation about the usual topics of crops, animals, pwes, and ahlus, the lugyi lugaun will interrupt to say he heard about a murder because of drunkenness or some trouble over gambling, and he will labor the obvious moral while people listen with approval. The reputation of being known as a good man is enviable, but they do not form a real group, and the number of them in the village falls between 30 to 35, depending upon which sample of informants one uses. The lugyi do not set style; they do not necessarily move anyone to emulation, and they have no power, only the recognized right to use moral suasion in situations of family trouble. However, even these "elders" cannot directly intervene if one of the parties in a familial dispute does not invite them, and the elders are careful to keep their stories abstract, away from real villagers and current village problems. One of the reasons these men are elders is that they do not overstep the vague but delicate line that separates individual responsibilities in Yadaw.

In the ideal, each person is responsible for himself, and even in the family this is operative for adults. The largest span of a villager's sense of involvement, in any affective manner, is the family. There is a large zone of indifference to the behavior of others. In public, at any rate, the indifference to what others do or do not do is scrupulously maintained. Gossip with kin and near neighbors is vitriolic enough, but it is done in a conspiratorial manner, making certain that the object of ridicule or calumny does not ever learn about it. The common saying for avoiding taking a stand on a person or public issue is *Ba jaun amon hkanyamale?* Why should I make myself an object of hatred by speaking up? Village life is a sort of ordered anarchy, and people will not complain or say anything about a neighbor's pestering dogs, children, or behavior if they can in any way tolerate the trouble. Even children are taught early: *Ba jaun thu seik so hkanyamale?* Why make somebody angry (displeased with you)? Keep quiet; do not make enemies. Hurt no one's feelings. Consequently hard truth, frankness, and candor are not public behavior and certainly not manifest among fellow villagers. The contrast between the delicacy and smoothness of interpersonal behavior and the *atin pyawde* (behind-the-back talk) is stark, but the two modes of judging and valuing coresidents never confront each other in the same social situation.

Other concepts about the good, the ideal, the valuable man are captured in the ideas of gon, pon, and awza. I have already given a rather extensive gloss on these concepts in the section on Nondwin political ideals. Here I shall only add some of the subtleties I picked up in Yadaw, after I had already been sensitized by my experience in Nondwin. Awza as formal authority comes from having a powerful office and filling that office like a leader. A leader is a man who has a definite series of attributes. The leader is Nayaka, and he has *Nayaka gon chaukpa*, the six features of a leader (industry, alertness, mercy, patience, judgment, and perspective). A leader is born, not made, and these qualities are manifested in every growing degree in the action and speech of a born leader. In Yadaw, now, there is no Nayaka, and the last real leader died in the time of British rule. No one, then, has awza. Commands from the headman are as likely to be ignored as obeyed. The headman himself is aware of this, so he gives as few commands as he dares. (The upper reaches of administration are forever passing on directives that he must at least announce, but I shall save that story for the following section on political organization.)

I view gon as the moral content of social relations. Gon also has overtones of social presence, even in the sense of "face" to the Chinese. If a person has money and honesty, he has a type of gon. If a student stands first in a class, his teacher and fellow students will have gon. If parents have a bright son, neighbors will say of them gon yude. The major forms of village gon are (1) *thila* gon, morality and good character, (2) *thamadhi* gon, an incorruptible person, beyond bribe or self-interest, and (3) *pyinya* gon, wisdom or learning. Gon, unlike the qualities of leadership, is earned during a person's lifetime and by his efforts. People with markedly different levels of gon have trouble in informal social interaction, for the gon is sort of a nimbus which may blind by its sparkle the lesser person. In my interviewing, my pyinya gon was something of a handicap. As a professor from a faraway university come to study the people of Burma, I had, necessarily, much pyinya gon. This abundance of learning sometimes made villagers reluctant to answer questions, for they thought I would take them to be *mai'te* (foolish) if they did not give learned sounding replies. Only when I made it clear that "right" answers were not possible, but "true" answers were, did the shadow of my unwanted pyinya gon disappear.

Pon is charisma (in the secular realm) and glory (in the sacred realm). Pon describes any power, moral or not, and pon is a mystic quality tied to kan, to kutho, to drive, to energy, to ambition, and to the horoscope. Nobody in Yadaw has pon, and the best example they can give is of an insurgent leader who once held this village in a tribute status. *Pongyi de lu* is a powerful man without any particular office or institutional locus, whereas *pongyi de min* is a man of power who is at the same time an official. Sometimes in casual conversation pon and awza may be collapsed into a single idea, when both are present; for example, U Nu was sometimes called a man of awza or a man of pon. (Now he is reduced to whatever forms of gon he used to be credited with.) A man of pon need not try to dominate, for his power radiates, and people come to him to give allegiance and to offer up services and trust. A man without pon who tries to get authority and power in the village is called a *lu yokma*, a man who wants to dominate, literally a rude man. And one of the perceived political troubles in Yadaw is that many lu yokma compete for power, and none of them has true pon, so factional strife and squabbling is the fate of the village.

The disunity in Yadaw is also thought to be aggravated by two characteristics of the normal villager: (1) *ko ha ko neide*, the drive to live by and for oneself alone, and (2) *hpathi haptha neide*, to be uninterested in others. It seems odd to me that these are said to cause trouble, since in a real sense they are among the honored, desired, and fostered attitudes in the ideal villager. But when cast in the political realm, there is some local appreciation of the negative consequences. If the village is peaceful, unriven by factions, led by a man of pon, then these traits help keep the peace and are fully desired and have no negative consequences. The idea of *myo gyit sei*, love of one's people (possibly patriotism), is something only needed to create the social conditions when it will no longer be necessary, and one can return to the ordered isolation, the regulated individualism, the atomism of village life.

The following six features serve as a summary of the way the family, kin relations, neighborhood bonds, peer groups, and other primary agencies of socialization together conduce to instill the meaning of authority, the set toward the exercise of authority, and the role of individuals in situations of personal conflict.

1. Clear-cut conflict is to be avoided. Authority is not to be directly challenged, unless one is ready for a battle, the outcome of which will be total victory or total defeat.
2. The public content of personal relations is directed toward blandness, toward the avoidance of unpleasant decision and action.
3. When there is trouble, an outstanding grievance, or a sudden attack, catching the antagonist unawares is the way to proceed. Reprisal from a position of great strength and little risk is also acceptable.
4. To get or use power requires coalition formation, and allies are sought against figures of power, for numbers outweigh authority.
5. To get a decision implemented or a request fulfilled when an individual is reluctant to comply, force must be used. Any challenge to authority requires coercion.
6. If something is contested, if a decision is difficult or unpleasant, the best course of action is to contract out. Do not do anything for others that would cause trouble or conflict to you.

These six "rules" of the interpersonal game are abstractions of mine from the welter of daily life, and they are what I take to be the chief, guiding principles used when individuals have any choice in the matter of interpersonal relations. These rules coexist with the stipulations of kin behavior, of age and seniority, and of sex and propinquity, which are the more formal features of the social structure described and illustrated earlier. Together, the conventional understandings and the decision rules account for likely interpersonal behavior, if the full context of what is facing the person is explicated. The rules are neither culture, nor structure, but in the realm of organization. What faces a person in terms of actions, he will take as a given set of events, a given part of culture and social relations impinged upon him. In short, the rules are a decision matrix as that is shaped by a given tradition.

POLITICAL ORGANIZATION

To move directly from the context of interpersonal relations to the realm of politics, even at the village level, is a flight for which there is no ready theoretical vehicle. The sentiments and definitions relevant to authority are, I believe, truly shaped in the agencies of socialization described, but there is not enough information to say very much about how the political realm is likely to be structured or what it looks like in operation. Each subsystem of a social system has its own inner dynamics and its own outer environmental demands, and these factors, as much as the sort of psychological or sentimental energy of the individuals involved, are responsible for the shape and motion of the political organization. I take the words and time to make these somewhat arid and less obvious observations for I do not wish to be misunderstood as to either my line of reasoning or my theoretical stance. The meanings and attitudes engendered in socialization enter into every sphere of social action, but they operate on substantially different task structures, and for substantially different ends, and hence cannot be played out with the same behavioral responses from subsystem to subsystem. They get their fullest play in the institutional segments where they are formed and their least expression in institutional contexts with suprapersonal and more clearly defined ends, chiefly economy and polity. Religion stands somewhere between the family and the polity in allowing full consequential play to meanings and sentiments formed in the agencies of early socialization.

Village Government

The formal political structure of Yadaw is like that of any other village in the dry zone. The chief officer is the thugyi, an elected headman, who, along with an elected committee of four members, forms the local executive branch. Below the headman and the committee are the 10-house heads, each in charge of roughly a 10-house neighborhood cluster. Finally, there are the two ywa gaung, who serve as messengers or runners between the village and the next echelons of local government. Yadaw is linked directly into the township structure of Amarapura, so that the Assistant Township Officer of that municipality and the Township Officer have administrative and some local magistrate functions in connection with the village. From the township level there is a connecting link to the subdivisional officer, and then on up to the divisional officer, the Deputy Commissioner of Mandalay, the Commissioner of Mandalay, and finally to the Prime Minister. All of this, the paper organizational structure in Burma, is typical enough, and sometimes it is even functional in that directives from the office of the Prime Minister filter down the chain of command to the headman, or a complaint from the headman works its way up to the Commissioner of Mandalay. But there are complicating factors that make the administrative structure operate in ways responsive to the play of power politics, rather than the technical imperatives of bureaucratic administration. The ubiquitous facts of political parties, bribery and favor buying, land distribution, village factionalism, insurgents and civil unrest, the attachment to men and cliques, not law and procedures, the gulf between local issues and national concerns, in the history and environment of Yadaw, all combine to make the administrative apparatus operate in the way it does, rather than in the manner it was designed to function.

At the root of Burmese politics, at least at the village-township level and, in the peasants' view, at the national levels, is the continual search for a leader. It is not that Burmans have a "fuehrer" complex, but rather that there is built into the vocabulary of politics the deep-seated notion that only a man of pon, of real power, of charisma, makes a real political difference. There is the sense of attachment to a victorious leader, a man who can get things done, who can build a clientele who will share with him and enjoy with him the fruits of power. The idea of aligning with a powerful, successful leader is old and continuous in Burma's past and much more operative in the shaping of political events, at any level of social organization, than is the recent and alien ideology of government by law and rule by majority. What this principle of a coalition around a man of pon means to local politics is fairly patent. It gives the peasantry an apathetic-galvanic complex in the political arena. The apathetic-galvanic complex is a shorthand for the typical modes of peasant political participation. Yadaw peasants knew before independence, and have had confirmed in their experience since independence, that power is, by and large, self-seeking, and that to be weak in the face of power is to suffer at least material loss and very likely loss of personal freedom or even life. So, the peasants' relation to politics follows this sort of cycle:

Be wary, that is, do not align yourself with anyone who is not clearly a man of pon, rising in power, and able to get something for you. It is always risky to join a coalition around a man of pon, for it identifies you as an adherent, and the fortunes of politics shift; so be sure that your gains will outweigh the inevitable reprisals and losses. Apathy is always safe; you neither gain nor lose anything, but join a coalition when the advantage is clear, for few men amount to anything without belonging to or forming a circle around a man of pon. The timing of the decision of allegiance is delicate, for too early may mean that the wrong side is chosen whereas too late means that participation brings little reward.

Wrong choices drive a man back into apathy; unclear situations of choice promote political apathy; and shifts in the tides of pon make for a resurgence of apathy. On the other side is the galvanic response:

The ill feeling, the frustrations, and hopes for gain, left over from the last battle for power, can be crystallized around an emerging man of pon. When a person joins a clique, he joins in the full awareness that its power is fleeting and that no organizational structure will perdure beyond the ephemeral, nearly mystic power of the man of pon. Thus the high tide of power of the coalition demands swift and far-reaching action; the peasantry must be galvanized into taking the most they can from the current situation. This *carpe diem* imperative means that the power group acts almost to denude and to destroy its opposition. In the village this is a factional struggle, and some men get so committed that there is, for them, no turning back, for they are branded as adherents of a given program. Most people can retract into apathy when the power of the coalition recedes. The really politically committed often have to take to the jungle and join insurgent groups, for they cannot live any more in the village.

This apathetic-galvanic syndrome has three immediate consequences for the political life of villagers in Yadaw: (1) A continual struggle by power-seeking men to enlist villagers in their clique; (2) the politicization of many domestic and trivial issues; and (3) the continual supply of insurgents who harass the villagers. This general interpretation of the political process in Yadaw is reached through informant comment and questioning and also by the activity of seeking the common threads in the discrete political events of elections, land distribution, relations between levels of authority, the modes of official-client interaction, and finally the channels, agents, and types of supralocal impingement on Yadaw.

In Yadaw there are real political parties with real connections to the national parties, whose local branches they are. And the elections for headman turn on party membership, vote canvassing, and direct intervention by political agents from the cities and the capital. But to understand the meaning and role of parties in Yadaw, one must explore some of the local issues around which the national parties have formed. The village has had local troubles since 1953 and has had more or less marked factions since that time, which was the beginning of land nationalization and distribution in Yadaw. But it has only had political parties since the AFPFL split into clean and stable factions. This in part indicates one of the ways local and national politics and power struggles are inextricably intertwined. The national split into political factions gave to pre-existing local factions an idiom and a format for the fixing of antipathies between local factions.

The office of thugyi always had the particular mixture of local leader and cultural broker between villager and political urbanite. At different times the emphasis of the mix was different. First, the headman was an agent of the king and did little except work out royal directives. Later, he became more or less an agent of the British raj and did a bit more in codifying demands of villagers. Now he is a broker between the political parties and local demands; in this position his value to the party depends on whether he can deliver the vote, whereas his value to the peasant turns on whether he can get a grievance attended to or a favor granted. The measure of his authority and power moves between these two pulls. This broker role of the headman defines in large measure the scope of his awza (authority), whereas his pon (power) is dependent upon the kind of coalition he can build internally and the connections he has to higher levels of authority and power.

Yadaw, in the time of the British, just prior to the Japanese invasion had a headman, who had both awza (from his connection with and support by the British) and pon (from his own character and evident skill in the conduct of his and village affairs). U Htun was his name, and for 30 years he was headman of Yadaw. Then there was a headman under the Japanese, who fled to the Shan hills when the British reconquered Burma. After that there was another headman under the British, but, when Aung San and the united AFPFL won independence from England, he was removed from office, and elections were held. Since these elections a satisfactory headman, one who really has pon, as U Htun was said to have in the days before the troubles, has not been elected in Yadaw. Now, the authority of a headman is little exercised on his own initiative. U Htun was reputed to have driven out local illegal distillers, to have forbidden playing cards, and to have curtailed the number of pwes the village sponsored or donated money to, but, since this man of pon, no headman has exercised authority or power on a project he himself initiated. Chiefly and currently the headman either asks higher powers and authorities to act on some village request or refrains from acting. Cleaning the village, building roads, and tax collecting are all done at the instigation of higher authorities. Most of his time, if there is not great pressure from insurgent bands, is spent in trying petty violations (mainly fights and quarrels among villagers, for which five- and ten-kyat fines are the rule), reconciling domestic troubles, or granting divorces. He also transmits or posts notices from the higher levels of government, but he does not try to implement or to enforce these requests or decrees. For example, the headman read a proclamation ordering the movement of rice-straw stacks a given distance from inhabited dwellings. All of the straw was in fact rather closer to houses than the decree required and closer than safety warranted, for the dry straw was continually in danger of being ignited by some carelessly tossed cigar end or a spark flying from a cooking fire. A Burmese village of bamboo and thatch can easily, with the rice stacks in every compound, be turned into a raging holocaust. The reading of the proclamation was completely ignored. Not a single household went to the trouble and work of moving its straw to the required distance. When the Township Officer visited Yadaw, he said nothing about the distance between the straw and dwelling being an open and flagrant violation of the edict he had recently transmitted to the people of Yadaw. He knew, as did the people of Yadaw, that the headman did not have pon, and so, unless force (which he was not prepared to use, it being near election time) were invoked, the rice straw would stay just where each individual cultivator thought it most convenient.

Even the headman's ability to collect taxes is a measure of his pon. The villager pays a fixed tax on his matured crop, the tax varying as to the kind of crop he has grown. The tax is to be paid to the headman, for the headman's chief legal income is 10 per cent of the collected tax. A villager who is in open and direct opposition to the headman will not pay his taxes to that thugyi, but will rather bypass him and pay his taxes directly to the Township Officer, thereby not only scorning the headman, but depriving him of real income. In Yadaw, seven men, political enemies of the incumbent thugyi, refused, after repeated requests, to pay their land taxes to the headman, and paid them to the Township Officer, thus depriving the headman of 50 kyats of income and publicly announcing that they were the core of factional opposition.

If the headman's capacity, in the absence of pon, for doing good or initiating projects on the local scene is limited, his ability to cause trouble is a bit more extensive. Since the government loan program operates through an elected loan committee of which the headman is ex officio a member, the headman can show favoritism in getting loans or demand commissions for processing applications. A headman is the signer for and recipient of government-given seeds, and, if he is venal enough, he may sell the seeds rather than give them at government near-free prices. He can refuse to settle small disputes and magnify them so they must be passed up to the township level, at which time he can take bribes from one side or another as a witness on their behalf. And he can exploit his connections with higher political levels to cause trouble or imprisonment for villagers. All of these activities the headman in Yadaw has engaged in and according to village gossip still engages in. What constrains a headman is the counterpower of factional opposition and the live possibility that some aggrieved person will take a shot at him or ambush him with a dah.

In Yadaw, the two competing political parties (at the time of my visit) are the AFPFL of Kyaw Nyein and the Pataza of U Nu.[19] The headman is affiliated with the AFPFL and has on paper the largest number of adherents, about 100, whereas there are about 50 members of U Nu's Clean faction of the party. There exists a tension between the local and the national level, for, while the AFPFL dominates the village, the Pataza under the recently re-elected U Nu controls the nation. There are also a few adherents of the National United Front party, which the villagers regard as the "above ground" communist party in contrast to Thakin Soe, the leader of the outlawed, or underground, communists.[20]

The presence of competing political parties in Burma and the appeals of these parties to local villagers to vote in local and national elections has taught the villager, in some small measure, to bring demands to political agencies. But at every level politics is strongly tied, as expectation would lead an observer to predict, to persons rather

---

[19] The dates are 1960–61, when the U Nu wing became the Pyidaungzu. The Ne Win revolutionary coup subsequently eliminated all political parties. A discussion of what the course of consensual politics will be in Burma is beyond the scope of this book.

[20] Thakin Soe is known in Yadaw for his three Wa policy: *Wabin* (bamboo), *Wamyit* (bamboo shoot), *Wetwun* (bear). This slogan means that he and his forces will live in the jungle (bamboo), eat of the forest (bamboo shoots), and become as wild as the bear if necessary, but they will fight on until they are the government. The "white flag" communists are identified with the three Wa policy of non-negotiation, while the "red flag" communists under Thakin Than Tun are willing to negotiate with U Nu, but only as one sovereign power to another. Roving bands of white and red flag communists as well as a few free-lance bands of dacoits, some with political tinges and some without, are part of the political environment of Yadaw.

than to organizations or even issues. It is virtually impossible to get villagers to formulate any ideological or policy differences between the Clean and Stable factions of the AFPFL. All differences, even to party adherents, turned on the character of the leading figures of the particular party. Part of this failure to discern differences, of course, is a real reflection of the national scene, for clear, definite issues do not separate the parties, and even in Rangoon the issue is largely a contest of persons for power, not a program for adherents.

To the villager the ideas of socialism, independence, land nationalization, democracy, and prosperity are welcome enough and are espoused by both parties, indeed, even by the outlaw communists and above ground radicals. All the parties subscribe to neutralism, to be really "neutral neutrals" vis à vis the great power blocs in the cold war between the Soviets and the United States. As vague, or idiosyncratically Burmese, as some of these slogans may be, they are the currency of political bargaining, and nobody can hope to seriously enter the politics without first making the proper obeisances to an independent, socialist, neutral, and prosperous Burma.

Within this common cadre of symbolism, inherited from the opposition to colonial status under a capitalist power and sharpened in the gaining of independence, are some special, peculiarly Burmese, political ideas. These ideas are put forth, and in part embodied, by U Nu, the most successful of national politicians among the peasantry. U Nu has become an adherent of the doctrine of a state religion for Burma and the curtailing of the slaughter of beef animals. He also announces that he lives, as closely as possible, the pious life. The doctrine of Buddhism as a state religion, with the official recognition of the sangha as worthy of government support, the reinstitution of government prizes and subsidies for pongyis, has nearly full support in Yadaw. Only five political people of the AFPFL are opposed to it, and even then their opposition is on personal grounds. These people maintain that if U Nu wants to be a pongyi, well and good; let him resign, get his family's permission, and go into a kyaung. But they believe that raising Buddhism as a political issue blinds people to the real evils of corruption and inefficiency in the U Nu regime.

U Nu uses, like a consummate politician, all parts of the religious spectrum in the belief system of the peasantry. He dedicated a series of nat shrines, both in Rangoon and near Maymyo, to the national guardian nats. This was seen by Yadaw peasants as fitting and proper, but some urban intellectuals wrote and said bitter things about the superstition and ignorance of U Nu.[21] U Nu also appeals to the peasantry by his careful attention to astrological portents. U Nu announced he would take a 45-day retreat on Mount Popa, the traditional home of the house nat and a sacred place. The Prime Minister said he would be inaccessible for the full 45 days, during which time he would be engaged in meditation and Buddhist devotions. In the village, this was well received, despite the fact that the insurgent problems were growing, the economy was slipping, and virtually all of the problems of government were pressing. The villager of Yadaw saw the retreat as a good thing because of U Nu's horoscope. They said that U Nu was born on a Saturday, and his particular planet, at this special time, was moving backward from the ninth house of the zodiac to the eighth house, and that this was a very unclear and inauspicious time. The movement of the planet took just 45 days, and any major decision during that period would, in all probability, have been either wrong, incomplete, or perilous, so U Nu was doing himself and the nation a favor by removing himself from the affairs of government during a period when he could not, due to planetary influences, make wise and useful policy decisions.

Outside Effects on Village Government. Another part of the political environment of Yadaw is the now nearly mythological winning of Burma's independence. The figures of Aung San and his assassinated cabinet loom large in the village view of what politics is. The only pictures of politicians in the homes of Yadaw people are of Aung San, the hero of independence, and the President of the Union of Burma. These two men are now above politics. Aung San is thought of as something akin to a nat, a larger than life, powerful figure, who wrested independence from the British. The President is considered a symbol of the unity of the diverse nationalities that make up the Union of Burma. The President is a Karen, but also a Buddhist, and since Karen Christians are among the most dissident members of the Karen National Defense Organization (KNDO) seeking an independent Karen nation, the President is thought of as a strong counterforce making for national unity. Appeal to Aung San, the "thirty heroes"

---

[21] One army officer in the Maymyo command, who has since retired his commission to take up evangelical, Buddhist missionary work among the animists and pagans of North Burma, was particularly vitriolic. He went with a camera to see U Nu dedicate a nat shrine near a lake in the Maymyo region. The lake was dry, and he snapped a picture. A month later he took another picture showing that the lake was still dry. These two photographs, along with a biting letter, he had published in a Mandalay Burmese paper and in one of the English papers in Rangoon.

of the resistance, and the Thakins of the independence movement is a necessary part of the rhetoric of even local politics, as is support of national solidarity. The revolution, the symbols of the young men, especially Aung San, are all invoked to make claim to legitimacy, to the right to hold office, to govern, to be a repository of the national will. The rhetoric of politics and its symbols are then an uneasy mixture (blend would be to overstate their integration) of three sorts of things:

1. The traditional view of a Buddhist, nat Burma, with a culture distinct, peasant based, and long victorious over enemies.
2. A heritage of the independence period under Aung San, which is needed to invoke continuity and bestow some aura of legitimacy over whatever government is in power. (Even the military take-overs use the slogan.) The frontispiece of *Is Trust Vindicated*, a report of the first military government, called the caretaker government, shows a picture of Aung San and a picture of Ne Win, with the single caption *"Bogyoke nauk Bogyoke,"* "After the general, the general."
3. The revolutionary ideas of the postcolonial world: socialism, economic progress, neutrality, Asian-African cooperation, and mutual interests.

All of these ideas come to villagers through newspapers, radios, political organizers, and the cultural brokers who move between the village and the town and city bringing back information, slogans, and ideas. The traditional elements in the political vocabulary are merely what an ordinary peasant thinks about Burmese history, his view of the centrality of Buddhism, the presence of nats, the ineluctability of planetary influences, the pride in the specialness of Burmese culture (as he views it against the despised Kala, the overbearing European, or the tribal peoples of Burma), and a vague history in which Burmese armies conquered the Thai, the Mon, the Arakanese, and other neighboring peoples.

The heritage of the independence struggle is kept alive both by the omnipresence of pictures, stories, and legends of Aung San and the Thakins, and the newspapers who use this theme frequently. Also the twin forces of the need for legitimacy of any government and the chronic complaints of the intellectuals, journalists, the schoolteachers, and the politicians about the colonial period and the inequities of British rule keep alive the feelings and symbols that much of Burma's difficulties, its failures to move swiftly and painlessly into that happy prosperous state most expected after the granting of independence, is due chiefly to what colonialism left behind. The revolutionary ideas of the postcolonial world are also promulgated by the official organs of dissemination, the press, and politicians and literati. These themes are the content of all political parties; they are part of every campaign; they are the stations from which all political discourse departs and the terminals at which it arrives. But they are not the stuff of actual political maneuvering or power seeking, of power use and policy making. They do, however, provide the framework in which the peasant and leaders think and talk about political life, and as such they are necessary environmental or background facts needed to understand the more immediate, causal, and determinate forces in the political life of Yadaw, and perhaps Burma as a whole.

Outside information, propaganda, and political news come into Yadaw in a steady stream. One man, a moderately wealthy individual, regularly gets the *Kyemon* (Mirror) from Rangoon, and he shares it with three neighboring households. One man gets the AFPFL paper (*Mandaing*), and he estimates that 25 other adults in the village regularly see this paper. One man gets the *Bahozi*, a politically neutral paper published in Mandalay, and he shares it with two other households. Two households get the *Rangoon Daily*, and four other households see it from time to time. One household regularly gets the *Bama Khit* (Burma Times) and shares it with five other households. *Bama Khit* is aligned with U Nu. One of the subscribers to *Bahozi* keeps his newspapers on the open table in his compound, and visitors drop by and read it. The newspapers are chiefly concerned with internal politics, scandal, and commentary on their political opponents. Just to check my subjective estimates of the contents of the newspapers regularly coming into and read in Yadaw, I conducted a "current events" quiz on a random basis.

> Who is the new United States President? One man in 10 knew.
> What just happened between Burma and China? Ten of 10 knew that a treaty of some sort had been signed about the border dispute.
> What Chinese official recently came to Mandalay? It took 15 households before Chou En Lai was named.

The chiefs of state in Russia, England, and France are unknown. The United Nations is known, but its headquarters' location is not. These supralocal information gaps contrast strongly with the knowledge of local and national candidates and slogans. The indigenous papers stay close to peasant knowledge and work on peasant interest, and they are not vehicles of education or broad news coverage as much as they are projections of the political ambitions of an editor or paid agents of a party.

The national radio is also a source of government-directed information and news. The party in power has a keen advantage in the way the radio network can be, and is, used, but even opposition speakers are given a reasonable share of time for political broadcasts. Radios are extremely rare in Burmese villages. In Yadaw, as in most villages, the radio would have to be a battery-powered set, for electricity is not available. The radio is mainly directed to town and city people, but many village Burmans do hear important speeches. Since I had a battery-operated transistor radio with me, and there was one other such in Yadaw, this village was doubly supplied with radio news and speeches, as well as the most popular part of the broadcast day, the playing of Burmese records. When U Nu gave his annual government report to the parliament, my radio and the other set were tuned in. My guess is that about 50 to 75 people heard the actual speech at the time it was delivered. When the leader of the parliamentary opposition spoke over the national network the next day, the incumbent headman, one of his adherents, rented the loudspeaker and blared the speech throughout the entire village. Most of the speech was about a recent capture of Koumintang (KMT) nationalist troops in the northeast of Burma by elements of the Burmese army. And it was strange to hear the United States castigated for supplying these troops and supporting them. During the address I moved from neighborhood to neighborhood in Yadaw, and most of the conversation was about the usual topics— buying and selling bullocks, the agricultural yields, and canal water. The United States is just too remote, both in concept and space, to yet be taken too seriously by villagers, for, with the capture of KMT equipment, they considered that the incident was *pibi*, over. In fact, knowledge of the international, modern environment by the peasantry is sketchy: Russia, somewhere, is known; the United States is known in this same vague way; but China is very real and pressing as the big country to the North; Japan is identifiable, so is Israel; England is only known as being far across the seas. The significant world for the peasants is the neighboring Theravada countries: Thailand, Ceylon, Cambodia, and Laos, with China, Japan, and India being definite places that could and do affect the life of peasants. All other nations, of those known, are thought of as just touching or coming into contact with Burma, from time to time and with no serious or permanent effects.

This setting of Yadaw village in the widest set of political relations and political information impinging on villagers is needed to understand its two main currents, land nationalization and electioneering, as the modes of politicizing factionalism. The distribution of nationalized land in Yadaw is a tangled and violent story, and no outsider can expect to get a full, historical, dispassionate account of it. What the tale does tell, apart from the historical fidelity or distortion contained in it, is the sound and the fury and lines of internal stress and cohesion in Yadaw. My account comes from all of the persons who have served over the years on the land nationalization committee of the village, from more than half of the farmers who have received government land, and from the heads of the two political factions. In 1953, the first land was to be distributed to the cultivators of Yadaw. It is recalled that Yadaw was, prior to the invasion of the Japanese and prior to Burmese independence, a village of in-migrants largely devoted to tenant or share farming. The rental hovered around 20 baskets of paddy per acre and provided a comfortable primitivism of consumption for tenants. At first Yadaw followed the legal procedures laid down in the Land Distribution Act. They elected a six-man committee, by the usual open-voice vote procedure, to take charge of the distribution of the land within Yadaw tract. (The tract was larger than the village and included farmers who were not in the political jurisdiction of Yadaw, but this did not affect the history of land distribution.) The six men were all lugyi lugaun, and they proceeded to compile a list of Yadaw men who had actually worked land in the tract as tenants. In accordance with the law only actual farmers could receive plots of land. According to the committee's work, 80 cultivators were eligible to receive 10 acres each. (The 10-acre size of government-grant land was in accord with the belief, and near fact, that a family with a team of oxen or bullocks could farm this much without hiring labor and also maintain themselves in the moderate category of peasant sufficiency.) But the distribution was neither orderly nor equitable. The trouble was basically caused by the different qualities of the land, in terms of soil and nearness to canal runoff, and the fact that some farmers were asked to move from good land they had been farming, as tenants, for years, to poorer land, or other cultivators were shifted about from one plot to another for no apparent reason. The farmers who would lose by movement refused to move; those who would gain insisted on compliance with law and committee mandate. From the distribution in 1954 until 1957, fights, quarrels, and bickerings increased. Some farmers stood firm, others threatened for the right to occupy "their" land. The claims and counterclaims reached a tragic crescendo in 1957. Two murders capped the attempts to implement the law of land distribution in Yadaw. The murders came when the occupants of land given to other farmers refused to relocate. The murders were performed at night, from ambush, and nobody was convicted for the crime, although many men spent many months in jail while the murders were under investigation. The political agents from Amarapura and Mandalay offered, through the aegis of an ambitious villager with political hopes to be at least the next headman, to help the suspects. The U Nu faction, then in power, offered to help those who had legal title to the land. So immediately the factions on the national level tied into the factions on the local level. The split in claims to farm began to be reinforced by identification with town and national political parties who were seeking adherents. In October 1958, the Army took over the government and suspended the program of land distribution. The farmers of Yadaw reverted to the land they had customarily farmed, prior to the program of grant land. When U Nu resumed the reins of government, he legalized the tenancy of farmers on the land they were farming, thus freezing the Yadaw squatter pattern, which emerged after the British landlord had fled the Japanese, and making some of the older "legal" tenants, under the government's own code of nationalization for land, unable to get land. This was a twist, for the AFPFL faction in the village then became the advocates of the people who had originally gotten land from U Nu, but who were now denied it, whereas the Pataza became the supporters of people who originally rebelled against their land law. In short, village factions were formed, and they switched from party to party, and the parties tried to woo them on any grounds they could. The net effect of the land distribution is economically nil; it leaves the same skew, the same resources, and the same distribution of farmers and agricultural laborers. But, politically, land reform has provided a basis for active intervention by national party agents in the village, and this may conduce to an erosion of parochialism and attenuation of traditional control by a man of pon.

It is unclear from the reports I gathered whether the land committee was corrupt, inept, confused, or all three. Certainly some of the people in Mandalay in the higher echelons concerned with land redistribution were not above trying to enlist the committee in schemes for mutual enrichment, to the detriment of orderly and honest land reapportionment. There were cases of paper owners with false tax tickets, and this land was rented to someone who would pay both the committee and the survey people who connived with them. But the committee never had the nerve to actually collect rents from the tenants. The main charge against the committee was favoritism. They listened to pleas of friends, neighbors, and kinsmen for the more favored plots, and when they heeded them this caused great enmity and dissatisfaction.

There was, in any case, great inefficiency on the local level and much going between Yadaw and Mandalay, even with delegations and letters to Rangoon. The net upshot was the dissolution of the committee, a return to *status quo ante* the land act, the formation of factions tied into national parties, the discrediting of the office of headman, the jailing of 42 men, a loss of yield because of the unsettled rights, and the burning grudges that come in the wake of murder and attempted murder.

This is part of the background of the local election I will now describe. The election campaign shows how the forms of democracy may be enacted when the basis for consensual politics have been absent or eroded and underlines how the political process, under adverse conditions like those in Yadaw, may exacerbate rather than heal a breach in civil order.

Elections, whether local or national, are by secret ballot, and all of the village elections I saw in Yadaw and in other villages in Mandalay and Sagaing districts were conducted with the strictest compliance to electoral procedures and with propriety. On the day of voting, small bamboo and thatch huts were erected at the outskirts of the village. In the voting hut were two ballot boxes, one painted red and the other yellow, the colors of the AFPFL and the Pataza, respectively. A voter enters the first hut which houses the registration table and is identified by fellow villagers as he answers to his name. After he is checked off the voting rolls, he chooses either a yellow or a red disc, and he drops this token in the proper box in the voting hut. He is alone when he votes and nobody knows, for sure, just what vote he cast. Around the registration and voting huts are police officers, but they are casual, and their rifles are not loaded nor at the ready position. A festal air surrounds the balloting. Tea, cookies, cigars, and sometimes country spirits are served the waiting voters. Most voters stay around during the entire time of balloting, and the whole scene is reminiscent of a picnic.

The voting turnout was 98 per cent of the eligible men and women of Yadaw. Why does nearly everybody vote? People vote partly because there is some sense of duty, of being a Burman in the very act of casting a ballot, because the novelty of choosing leaders has not yet worn off, partly because voting is assimilated to the notions of village-wide participation in all communal events, partly because candidates urge them to vote, and last and least because there is some real issue at stake which the outcome of the election may influence.

The results of vote canvassing before the election are not obvious. The votes of people already committed to one faction or another are not in doubt, and these people formed part of the volunteer force soliciting votes. Also, party officials from Amarapura and Mandalay visited and asked for votes, and sometimes army officers or township officers with political loyalties to a particular party came asking for support of a candidate. The uncommitted voter (someone not in a faction, in a village like Yadaw, or not in the glow of a man of pon, in a village like Nondwin) usually hedges, so that he will not become aligned with one side or another. In a 10 per cent sample of all eligible voters in Yadaw's election of headman, a pattern emerged among the uncommitted. The man of the house would vote red, and his wife would vote yellow, thereby showing their neutrality and leaving the result of the election to those who have more desperate or compelling needs or wishes to see a particular outcome. For the uncommitted voter, the outcome of an election can have little positive good and may entail negative results in that a headman or a government may turn out harsh and evil. About half of the people I interviewed, when asked about politics, had the standard reply of *na malebu*,[22] "I know nothing about it, and, if I had my way, we would do without local elections; if we could get a decent headman, we should keep him and not put everybody to the trouble of choosing him, election after election."

The AFPFL candidate won the election by a small plurality of the votes, but he left in the wake of his victory a large and determined opposition of U Nu supporters, who have ties to the regional and national hierarchy, and a large number of people who are disgusted and withdrawn from the political life of the village. The factions yet face each other, nearly balanced; most of the village is indifferent to the contending elements; and neither authority nor power exists on the local level. In this state of affairs, the victors try to press for per-

---

[22] This may not be a genuine opinion.

sonal advantage in the land dispute case; the losers try to discredit and obstruct the victors, and people allied with neither faction try to get one of the factional chiefs to press a particular claim or grievance in exchange for a promise of allegiance. Members of parliament are approached by the local politicos, and they give empty promises on things like canal cleaning, land regularization, or reduced costs for fertilizer. Delegates go to Rangoon to plead special cases of villagers, and the whole political process is seen as a means of advancing self-interest by gaining power, with the government viewed as an agency that may be swayed by pleas, promises, or participation. All of this turns on being allied with powerful men and powerful coalitions.

Enough has now been described to characterize, in a few summary sentences, the political life of Yadaw in recently independent Burma. Peasants have the form without the real substance of political power, and their votes do not make policy, even though they elect officials. The gap between the power struggles on the national scene and the similar, more petty struggles on the local level prevents the formation of that context where the exercise of political rights may conduce to the building of political institutions, which may carry the burden of a civil tradition or representative institutions. The roots from which Burmese notions of authority spring, the attitudes and sentiments toward power and government, the search for legitimate symbols and structures of power, and the charismatic, episodic components of leadership, plus the ultimate reliance on either coercion or contracting out of conflict give the Burmese political structure its particular dynamic. The cultural, social, and psychological bases of Burmese village political life and its interaction with the national elite make it patent that a political table of organization, a formal constitution, and even a series of popular and mass organizations do not determine the content and activity of a polity. A regime of civil liberties and democratic institutions, combined with the urgent tasks of cultural modernization and economic development, may take many forms, but it must grow out of the experience of the plurality of the people with real and substantive political power. My impression, not one that can be closely documented from this study or from whatever reading I have done on Burma and other newly independent nations of Southeast Asia, is that there is a strong tension between the powerless peasantry with the hollow forms of democracy and the powerful national leaders who lack the historical, ideological, and institutional commitment to fostering the dispersion of power among the citizenry. The tension is strained to the point of near anarchy or near dictatorship by the desires of the elite to modernize in an orderly disciplined manner and the aims of the peasantry to move toward self-aggrandizement in whatever ways or to maintain customary levels of living, if meaningful economic opportunity is beyond their grasp.

The political dilemma of Burma, seen from the peasants' eyes, is not that it lacks one or another of the almost innumerable so-called prerequisites to democracy, but rather that the political process works on a polity that has not had the time, the occasion, or the power to make consensual politics the vehicle of national integration; yet there is a real urgency in getting registered and acted on the multitudinous and conflicting demands of a people who face each problem with the phrase, "the government should," and an elite who, in part, expect the formal apparatus to provide enough exterior constraint so that they themselves do not need to learn and experiment with the give and take between ruler and ruled.

8

Buddhist Belief and Ritual
and Predictive and Divinatory Systems

The Buddhism of Yadaw is so similar in its major tenets, its ritual, and its place in daily life to that in Nondwin and other Upper Burma communities that to describe it in the detail devoted to Nondwin Buddhism would be unnecessarily repetitive. An alternative course is to emphasize the small differences in accent and in style of handling the same basic body of belief and knowledge and to probe into more of the individual reactions to some of the apparently difficult ideas in the body of village Buddhist belief. The same meanings and activities are attached to the ideas of kan and kutho, to the three worlds, to the precepts, to the four noble truths, to the acts of giving, to pongyis, to the view of a world in which each individual is his own bundle of moral accountability, and finally to the pacing of a single life so that as age increases and death nears one becomes more and more involved in the diligent search for small movements along the nearly endless path toward Nibbana.

VILLAGE BUDDHIST BELIEF

The people of Yadaw are close to the city of Mandalay and hence have more opportunity to see, hear, and judge monks who are not primarily of the village kyaung. This proximity to exalted pongyis and "rogues in the yellow robe" has caused villagers to add a category of pongyi that is not, or very little, current in more remote villages. The pongyis, in general, are graded from the young monk to the eminent abbot, although the same forms of deference must be afforded any wearer of the saffron robe. But in Yadaw the khit pongyi is a real category. Khit pongyi literally means "modern pongyi" and is used in a derogatory sense. A khit pongyi is a man who has taken on the robe and monastic residence and discipline but who is not seriously concerned with his own salvation. He uses the sangha as a means to further some secular end. Some of the khit pongyis are involved in learning trades in Mandalay; some are thought to be interested in building political careers; others are believed to be plain indolent. The villagers are reluctant to talk about khit pongyis, to say anything that is derogatory to the sangha, or to censure behavior. If a villager meets a man he knows or suspects of being a khit pongyi, his immediate behavior is the same as it is toward any wearer of the robe—he will shikko, lower his head, and use the proper status language between monk and layman. This sort of behavior plus the unwillingness to censure monks underlines some important facets of the village conception of the sangha and of the relation of the laity to the monkhood.

A pongyi is a voluntary member of the assembly of the blessed. Any man can enter the monastic life and leave it when it no longer suits him, and most villagers have spent time in the monastery at least as koyin. So the role of pongyi is not so divorced from village experience that it is esoteric. The monk, too, is not the bearer of mystic lore; he is not the vehicle between a layman and divine mysteries, nor is he the shepherd of a flock, responsible for their morality, their link and hope for salvation. To a villager a pongyi is a Buddhist who has reached a level of understanding of the meaning of life that impels him to try to center his energies on salvation. The salvation the pongyi seeks is his own, for each person must be responsible for his own rebirth, his own depth of penetration into the Tipitaka, his own extinction of self and false attachments. In this view, then, it is useless for a villager to censure a monk, to remind him of his duties. The one who suffers from being a khit pongyi is not the community, not the laity, or even the sangha, but the "scoundrel" himself. He is building up his stores of akutho, and, in this world of inexorable moral accounting, the khit pongyi will pay, eventually, for the deceit he lives in. The villager, however, when he has knowledge, does treat monks in some accord with his estimate of their devotion to the rules of order and their abilities to expound doctrine. This differential treatment of monks according to piety and wisdom takes more subtle forms than disrespect or calumny. The villager has the option of choosing to whom he will give the major offerings involved in inviting monks to hsungywe, kahtein, shinbyu, or any other ahlu. The villager does not control the giving in the daily round of pongyi begging. Any pongyi who turns up before noon with begging bowl will receive some cooked food from every household in Yadaw, and the donors will deem it an increment of kutho, irrespective of the estimate of the piety or wisdom of the particular pongyi. It is in the optional spheres of giving, where kutho is reckoned up in part by the worthiness of the monk to whom the sacrifice is made, that the villager exercises his disdain of the khit pongyi. They are never invited to ahlus; they would never be asked to be resident monk in their own kyaung, or to teach the young; and they are largely thus isolated from the points of ordinary contact with laity. Their deception is sealed off from contaminating anyone else, and their falseness becomes a private matter, an affair of impairing their own moral state, not that of others.

This particular view and treatment of khit pongyis, as well as the deeply embedded Buddhist notion that every individual works out his own spiritual state and moral achievement, has obvious sociological corollaries. The decline in the caliber of the sangha need not lead to a revulsion or rejection by the laity, nor need it lead to a reformation within the sangha itself. So long as many, or most, laymen and pongyis take seriously enough the notions of kan and kutho and rebirth as the outcome of these, there is enough self-regulation in the sangha and in the community of believers to keep both the order and the community tolerably within the confines of the religious life.

Even though I could find villagers who were suspicious of particular khit pongyis or of the activities of some of the "political" or "government" monks, I found *no one* who depreciated the sangha as a whole or who showed any scepticism about Buddhist belief. The fact that there is, at the village level, no expression of doubt, of disbelief, or even of incredulity about the wondrous tales of the Buddha, or about the words and teachings attributed to Gotama, requires some explanation.

Part of the explanation lies in those features of village Buddhism explicated in the chapter on Nondwin. The knowledge villagers have of canonical Buddhism is slight, and they have come by that modicum in the way they have come by their language or their kinship relations. With this basic type of enculturation, Buddhism is not a distinct category of thought and behavior to be examined, inspected, and judged any more than is the syntax of Burmese or the wearing of longyis and sandals. Furthermore, the knowledge, even the slight amount of religious and sacred lore, is differentially distributed among villagers. There is a common core, but beyond that, what each man knows, he knows. There is the belief that persons have different capacities to penetrate into the teachings of the Buddha, and thus the differential knowledge is but an expression of varying abilities to understand or apprehend the doctrine. Difference in knowledge is not evidence of conflicting views as to the nature of religious truth, nor can differences form the basis for argument or direct confrontation between believers who hold slightly differing interpretations. In fact, one of the chief ways that time is passed is in conversations about aneiksa, dokhka, anatta. Villagers will exchange anecdotes, meanings, interpretations hour after hour, and in all the conversations I was exposed to, I never heard what would be called a religious argument or an expression of scepticism or disbelief.

If a villager is genuinely puzzled about anything in Buddhism, he will ask either his village pongyi or another learned monk. And the character of the explanation is inevitable. He will receive as reply some metaphor, some analogy, some transformation of the question into a rhetoric he can comprehend. The metaphors of Buddhist explanation are common currency, and apparently the peasants of Yadaw never tire of hearing the same ones—the mustard seed tale and death, the wheel and spokes analogy for no-self, and others.

Another contributing fact to the genuineness of conviction is that village Buddhism permits wide latitudes of behavior, and except for the minimal code of the five precepts, behavioral proscription and prescription are slight. This means that a persisting core of deviant religious behavior has no social or doctrinal basis, and hence there are few people who feel tightly constrained by their belief system. Since the self is the center of Buddhism, a person does not harm others in whatever he does. (Almost never, but there are the territorial and kinship aspects of kutho, so that in actually giving rituals an individual must behave in a more defined manner than in ordinary activity.) And the ultimate recipient of the consequences of abiding by the code of Buddhism or violating it is the person who either abides or violates; other people in the community rarely have any cause to admonish another about his behavior. The social outcome of this is that villagers neither "preach" to each other nor have occasion to hold someone's behavior up to a moral code. Even the monks spend most of the time in their sermons talking about giving, about keeping up the sangha, about impermanence, suffering, and the futility of self, and not about the belief system as something reasoned out or open to reasonable interpretation.

The final basis upon which the sense of Buddhist conviction seems to rest is the structure of the sangha. It is a very loose hierarchy, and what arrangement there is depends upon the age, wisdom, and monastic attachment of a given monk. But there is no authority who can give *ex cathedra* interpretations of Buddhism, nor is there any *ipse dixit* component to a living monk. If these qualities are coupled with the absence of direct temporal power of monks over laity, especially in terms of the nature and content of a lay belief or conviction, then the structure of the sangha and its concern chiefly with itself and not with the spiritual state of lay believers are strong features making for the absence of scepticism, the generality of conviction about the truth value of Buddhism. And, as described earlier, Buddhist conviction requires little interior constraint, little emotional attachment, and little in the way of internal dedication to piety.

What the villagers of Yadaw hold deep-seated convictions about is what I have earlier called the minimal core of bokda batha: the five precepts as the regulatory code of behavior, the ideas of kan and kutho, the boundaries of secular experience set by the trilogy of aneiksa, dokhka, anatta, the discipline of the self by continual acts of giving, the notions of the three loka of existence and the character of existence in these worlds, coupled with the chain of rebirth until the final state of Nibbana, and finally the bits of lore and wisdom in the Jataka tales, in the Thok, and in the many tales and legends still transmitted from generation to generation. This body of belief, while common to Upper Burma, takes on, in different villages and indeed in different minds, variations in emphasis and nuances in deciding relative importance of the parts. But what it does lead to in Yadaw is a body of practice, of individual and social behavior, which is both an expression and a reaffirmation of the core of common conviction.

INTERPLAY BETWEEN BELIEF AND PRACTICE

I now mean to highlight some of the subtle interplay between belief and practice. My own position should be stated so that the logic of organization of the following data may be understood. I hold, as axiomatic, that in daily life the body of religious norms is inherently ambiguous. By that I do not mean the norms cannot be stated by experts (some pongyis) to form a more or less coherent and systematic corpus of ideas, definitions, beliefs, and so forth (although there are, even at this level, edges of thought which are not clear, and scholastic exegesis is, of course, one of the favorite indoor sports of higher level theologians even among Buddhists). But a rather more simple thing, the behavioral counterpart or the action elements which conform or deviate from a given religious norm, cannot be clearly, finally, precisely stipulated. The inherent ambiguity of a set of cultural norms is a testament to their vitality and to their applicability to ordinary life. For a fully understood coherent body of rules, a frozen cultural pattern, is a feature of a dead society, one in which the multifarious behavioral repertory consonant with the norms is forever lost or so clouded by time that rite and belief do in fact appear one and the same. Anthropologists who have chiefly worked in societies without a literate religious tradition are pushed by the nature of their observations into making the possibly erroneous identification between belief and practice. The tricky field problem here is to make an analytic separation between the two. Since a single set of observations underlies both creed and act, an almost inevitable conclusion that they are one and the same thing projected upon the different coordinates of "culture" and of "society" is reached. Although beyond my immediate purposes here, it is interesting to note how this method and data-induced identification have led to the theoretical formulation that religious belief is refracted along the lines of social structure, an epigram that assumes what is wanted to be learned and leaves little room or incentive for new investigation or conceptualization.

The ambiguity of religious norms leads to two sets of social facts: the process whereby the relevant segment of the normative structure is brought to bear on any particular action, and the groupings and organizations that habitually select and express a part of the normative system. These two kinds of activities are the guidelines for the exploration of Buddhism in Yadaw. My intention is to play off the consensual elements in village Buddhism against the variety of behaviors they give rise to and to indicate the areas of free play, the degrees of freedom a villager or a village community has in the implementation of a core of basic conviction. I do not have the skills to follow up the next level of inquiry which would be the contrapuntal interplay between the village system of norms and behaviors with the inscribed norms in the Pali Canon. This would indeed give a picture of Buddhism in Theravada lands which reaches from the hut to the heavens.

The five precepts are, without exception, taken daily by every adult in Yadaw and by most of the children over 12. Younger children take two or three of them, usually leaving out the precepts dealing with sexual misconduct and life taking, since they are thought to be capable of neither. The taking of precepts is an act of making a promise or a vow to oneself. Usually, as the first thing on arising or the last thing before retiring, a person stands before the Buddha altar and recites aloud the five precepts. An altar or image of the Buddha is not necessary, nor is it required that the precepts be uttered. The taking of precepts is an act of individual commitment to the moral code, and the presence of an image of the Buddha and the saying of them aloud provide a setting so that they may be better impressed on the vow taker. If one does not take the precepts at least once a day, one is not really a Buddhist, but just what behavior is consistent with the vows is not so definite. The injunction "do not take life" means to kill deliberately no living thing, yet a man may be a fisherman (although of low social status, forming in part a quasi-endogamous caste in Upper Burma) and still be a Buddhist, or he may be a soldier or even a hunter and still be viewed as a really sincere follower of the path of the middle way. What is universally frowned upon, and in fact not done, is to order any animal killed, to deliberately take a life when it is avoidable. To be either a butcher, or to order a live animal slaughtered, or to kill an insect when it is not annoying is to violate, in a manner insuring rebirth in one of the hells, the first of the precepts. On the other hand, the injunction is tempered with the preservation of one's own life. A villager will not hesitate to kill a threatening poisonous snake, nor to kill a rampaging rabid dog, nor to burn a leech off his leg. At the same time, the villager will brush away, rather than slap at, mosquitos or flies that annoy him, and he will shoo away animal and insect pests rather than crush or stamp them out. Any killing or life taking is immoral, and, when pressed by interviewers, the village Buddhist will affirm that in the ideal it is better to die than to take a life, and he may even describe something akin to martyrdom should a person choose to die rather than take a life. But, on the behavioral level and fully consonant with the first precept, a man may protect himself against the imminent threat of death by killing without accruing akutho, even though in the abstract he foregoes the possibility of getting, at one fell swoop, great increments of merit. In the crisis situation, the theoretically unimportant self is preferred to the religiously significant attachment to nonattachment.

The precept enjoining the telling of truth is also an elastic notion. Not to lie means chiefly not to present falsehoods when under oath or when formally confronted by a request for a specific piece of information. When swearing on the *kyaunza*, the sacred book, a villager wishes on himself all sorts of plagues, diseases, miserable rebirths, horrors, and calamities should his next utterances be lies. In this situation, he will give a straightforward, truthful reply. But in daily interaction, evasion in social relations, manipulation of information, and different degrees of truthfulness are all apparent and are all at the level of awareness of the ordinary resident of Yadaw. Even simple things such as accepting an invitation, when the person knows he will not and cannot attend, are explained by saying it is better to accept and not hurt another's feelings than to speak out and leave bitterness. The villager is a past master at giving vague and indefinite replies to officials, to those who do not need to know, and none of this is considered breaking the precept. Like the precept on killing, the precept on lying is not a rigid rule to cover all possible occasions; rather it is a guideline to conduce in the person a tendency to have a respect for all living things, not to become inured to life taking, to move to a universal tenderness, whereas the injunction not to lie constrains the villager to speak the truth when lying may harm another or may cause trouble and to use speech to promote social harmony. In this context, the "white lie," the evasive reply, and the vague response are functionally equivalent to the truth, for they conduce to a use of speech leading toward universal brotherhood and trust. The first two precepts are the attitudinal basis of myitta—a kindness or tenderness toward all living things.

The next two precepts, not to steal or commit adultery, are interpreted by villagers in a simple and clear manner: do not take anything that is not freely given, and do not violate the local code of sexual morality. Breaking these precepts clearly leads to akutho, and continual breaking means rebirth in the animal form. The draft animals are especially pointed out as expiation for a life of thievery. I do not mean to imply, nor is the reader to infer, that these norms are not violated. My discussion is not about conformity or deviancy to the precepts, but only about their social and behavioral meaning in Yadaw. I do not know the extent of violation of sexual morality in Yadaw, although my impression is that adultery was extremely rare, for there were no such troubles during the time I lived there; likewise there was only one case of suspected theft during the period. This record must be balanced against the roving bands of Buddhist dacoits near Yadaw, with some Yadaw youths in them, and the village joke that rich people have started their careers with a successful stint as a dacoit. The trips by villagers to Mandalay for the services of prostitutes are not considered a violation of the precept, for that is the custom of village boys and hence not in opposition to the teaching. The precept requiring that a Buddhist not cloud his mind with intoxicants implies chiefly that country spirits be abjured, for the toddy palm juice, either sweet or fermented, is hardly considered to have any effect on the mind, and there are not other mind-distorting stimulants available to villagers. (Opium, marijuana, or other narcotics are not in village purview or use, and tobaccos, betel nut and leaf are considered clearers of the mind.) The absence of liquor in the village is remarkable. At no gathering is alcohol ever served. Neither at funerals, nor shinbyus, nor weddings is anyone ever drunk, and leisure interaction goes smoothly without any hard liquor, from the informal conversational dyad to the whole village ceremony. Tea replaces liquor in Burmese social interaction, and it is drunk or chewed mixed with spices and apparently serves as well as alcohol to provide the usual rhythm of large social gatherings. Yadaw did not even have its deviant drunk, as did Nondwin.

The five precepts are then a daily, individual ritual undertaken by every responsible person in Yadaw. In addition, there are opportunities to take the precepts more often than daily. About three times a week there is a Buddhist devotional session in the village *damayoun* (building of the law). Here, under the leadership of an elderly man known as the "Neikban pointer," villagers gather to recite in unison the chief liturgy of Buddhist devotional. Always included are the five precepts. This repetition of the precepts is considered another act of self-discipline, another way of steeping the self in proper attitudes. At these evening meetings are found chiefly the older elements of the Yadaw population, for it is they who, as in Nondwin, are most concerned with religious self-cultivation. There is an interesting difference in attendance compared to Nondwin. In Nondwin, which is judged to be more religious than Yadaw, based on the higher percentage of men who had spent the traditional three Wa in the monastery, the nightly devotional sessions were attended by the young. The elders of Nondwin frequently said their precepts more than once daily but did not need or have a meeting hall to do so.

On duty day (ubonei) villagers have the opportunity to take an additional three or five precepts. Ubonei falls on the phases of the moon and hence may occur four or five times in our calendrical month. The taking of additional precepts adds an increment of merit to the ordinary daily quintet of vows. But it is rare. It is even rarer to see people go to the kyaung on ubonei to take the additional precepts. The full observance calls for extra vows taken at a monastery with the day spent in concentration or in meditation. I have never observed on any ubonei more than seven elderly people, at the kyaungs of Yadaw, involved in the full observance. And from a 20 per cent sample of the households of Yadaw, it appears that the modal observance of extra vows on ubonei occurs from 6–8 times per year. The villagers say they are too busy to take the time to make the extra vows and certainly too pressed to spend much time at the kyaungs. In addition not taking solid food after noon (one of the extra vows) interferes with the ability to work and is hence barred to most working farmers. Apparently the kutho yield from the extra vows is not worth the trouble it causes in the routines of daily life, so the elderly, who are removed from whatever time constraints bind the villager and are most concerned with impending death and rebirth, are those who have both time and motivation to earn the marginal increments of kutho attendant upon the extra vow taking.

Of equal status with the precepts as a ritual of self-conditioning for better rebirth and eventual nirvana is the continual repetition of the trinity of Buddhist theology: aneiksa, dokhka, anatta. Every adult has a string of either 32 or 108 beads, and, at least once per day and frequently much more often, these beads are told to the chant of impermanence, suffering, and no-self. This ritual, also an individual ceremony which can be carried out anywhere and without the prop of the beads, is another form of self-training in the psychological stance of the village Buddhist. I met no villagers who were puzzled by the ideas of change, suffering, and no-self. At least at the manifest level aneiksa means the simple things of biological change: birth, aging, death, decay. At the social level recent history is invoked: The kings have gone; the captains have departed; U Nu comes and goes as Prime Minister; the Japanese have come and gone; and the insurgents wax and wane. At the cultural level there are the tales of the faded grandeur of royal Burma, the ruins of Pagan, the "giants in those days" tales, and the cosmological ideas of the waxing and waning of cycles of human existence and even of the worlds. Dokhka as suffering is similarly understood at a direct and manifest level: to feel pain, to be unhappy, to lose a loved one, to be frustrated, to be poor, to lose a wager, to miss a pwe, to be hungry, tired, and thirsty. All of these are dokhka, dokhka, dokhka (the wail, in interviews, usually comes in the form of a descending three-syllable sigh).

The idea of no-self is for the villager more complex and ambiguous, even at the manifest level of transmission from monk to layman, from adult to child, from informant to anthropologist. If informants are pressed beyond the analogies they have learned in monastic school or overheard in conversation, there is difficulty in saying what absence of an entity like "self" means. The commonest analogies are derived from the "Questions of King Milanda" and have to do with taking an entity apart and seeing that there is nothing more to that entity than its parts. In human terms, this usually means to the villager that the particular arrangement of arms, legs, head, body, muscles, blood, bones, hair, glands, and mucus (these things are enumerated for the human anatomy) is impermanent, and, when death overtakes this arrangement, there is nothing left. There is no entity self, just an arrangement of anatomical bits, all impermanent. This notion is difficult for a villager to hold if one asks him what then is it that goes from existence to existence? What is it that is continuous, that reaps the rewards and punishments of kan and kutho? The most common, first line, answer to this query is the light bulb-electricity analogy. The electric current that goes from bulb to bulb is invisible, continuous, and makes one bulb alive, leaves it dead, and then makes another bulb alive. Since most villagers have only the faintest notions of electricity, I was puzzled into tracking down the source of this analogy, and found that it stems from the popular writings of a Mandalay monk. (If he still is alive, I did not get to see him.) Pushed beyond the level of analogical or metaphorical explanation of what no-self means or what is in fact continuous from existence to existence, villagers come up with a series of different answers, indicating, I think, the real difficulty of holding such a basic notion unless one is a skilled philosopher used to entertaining the sort of idea that patently defies the senses and common experience.

The responses in Yadaw, while various, can be sorted out into two main classes: the believers in the uncanonical notion of soul and the believers in a sort of self or consciousness. Both of these meanings shade into each other and may be held at one and the same time by the same person. What is of importance is that no-self idea is worked over by villagers into a set of meanings congruent with the evidence of their senses and with their common, everyday rationality. Villagers are not, apparently, able to entertain a mystery. In theory, the analogies are explanations meant to obviate the notion of articles of mysterious faith. The Buddhist analog to a sacred, finally inexplicable article of faith is the reliance on intuitive knowledge. Either one knows with the whole being, and not with the intellect, what aneiksa means, or one does not know anything at all about it. Villagers do not use such language, but they effectively communicate such ideas by their insistence that the analogy and the metaphor are sufficient for understanding and that the idea of no-self is self-evident once the poetry of the dhamma has been recited. Yet the intuitive understanding is shaded by the non-Buddhist ideas of soul and of continuing consciousness. The notion of nonself is one of the paradoxes of thought that the villager really does not bear.

The concept *winyin* covers both the notions of a "soul" and a consciousness. It is the winyin that goes from life to life, and the winyin bears in some manner the nucleus of kan which determines the plane of the next existence and the material embodiment of the winyin. The presence of quotes around the word soul indicates that I am somewhat at a loss for a proper translation of winyin. Winyin is not easily described by villagers. Light, airy, a luminosity, like a flame, invisible, bright spark, and breath were some of the terms used in the attempts to communicate to me what the winyin is. In ordinary conversation the contexts in which winyin appears do not add much to a clearer stipulation of its meaning. But, however fragile my understanding is of the implications of winyin, it is clear that the villager does have a notion of some sort of substance or material entity, which moves from existence to existence, and the sheer metaphysical purity of the notion of rebirth is given a concrete vehicle, an agency, and is thus made intelligible for villagers. This consciousness as it moves from life to life does not usually have the ability to recall its former states or former embodiments. But sometimes there are cases of *lu winza*, a person who can recall former existences. This story is told by Maung Sein of Yadaw:

His family (that is, his mother and father) were living in Mandalay. The family lived near "A" road and "A" road is near the three sections of the city where the Manipuris or Ponnas (the astrologers and horoscope makers from Manipur, India) live. His own sister was three or four years old when she asked her mother to take her to see the "mother" of her last existence. She was taken to the Ponna quarters. There she went straight to a woman's house and called her mother. To the Ponna "mother" she described her former life, and how she had left it through being murdered. Her present parents had never heard of the events she described. The girl told of her "older sister" who was wildly loved by a Manipuri whose affection was unrequited. This rejected suitor stormed into the compound and with his dah killed the older sister and the younger. This story was confirmed by the Ponna mother. The Ponna mother brought out for display items of her daughter's apparel, and the lu winza identified them.

The reborn girl could understand Manipuri but not speak it, and she was fond of eating from brass (as Manipuris do and Burmans do not).

Whatever the existential basis of such a story (Manipuri beggars came regularly to Burmese parts of Mandalay, and the actual murder must have caused great local gossip), it is vouched for and believed in by villagers.

Similar fragments of lu winza, such as the girl killed by the Japanese bullet and reborn still bearing the scar in the same place, or the man killed by dacoits, now reborn a woman, are part of the oral tradition of Yadaw. These tales are peasant attempts to elucidate or reactions to the abstract doctrines of no-self and rebirth. They are one means by which philosophical commitments are refracted in mundane life.

The major activities of village Buddhists are centered in the acts and organization involved in ahlu. Ahlu is the term covering giving of alms. To give food to a monk, to hold kahtein, to sponsor a shinbyu, in fact the entire spectrum of sacrificial giving and all the attendant social arrangements consequent on the presentations are denoted by ahlu. Ahlu may be conceived of as the series of activities conducing to changes in the state of individual kan and hence activity designed to insure favorable states of rebirth. Ahlu does not release the person from the cycles which entail aneiksa, dokhka, anatta, but it supposedly refines the personality or character to the point where a serious attempt toward nirvana can be essayed.

Nirvana, the total sacrifice of self, can only be reached in one manner—meditation. It is through meditation, villagers and monks agree, that *wipatthana* (insight) is reached. Only meditation-giving insight is capable of producing the intuitive understanding necessary to cessation of rebirth. With this being the case—*kamahtan* as the means, wipatthana as the vehicle, and Nibbana as the goal—it is somewhat surprising how little meditation is done by either villagers or village monks.

Two things, apparently, account for the virtual absence of sustained meditational practices in Yadaw. First, Nibbana is exceedingly remote, a goal to be reached after countless existences, and, furthermore, the condition of next, immediate existence begins to get pressing and more and more real as villagers age. Second, there is some confusion and doubt as to whether or not kamahtan is really, as against normatively, the *only* way to ever reach the state of complete detachment from desire. There are beliefs that if one is alive in human form to hear the teachings of the next Buddha, this is enough for nirvana, and there are some who believe that sufficient ahlu will make meditation (in some future life) much more efficacious than it could possibly be in this particular span of existence.

Buddhism is part of a round of activity, and, in peasant life, it may be the unqualified source of good; but it necessarily competes with the petty claims of daily life—work, friends, family, status, power, comfort, play, and gossip. Meditation is a form of complete turning inward. An individual pays attention only to his interior process of thought; he keeps before himself the notions of impermanence, suffering, no-self, and in the act of meditation these are the only realities. In effect, then, meditation withdraws a man from society as well as from self, or more tersely, if successful, it leaves no-self to relate to others. Consequently, whatever few sessions of meditation either monks or laity perform are always solitary, away from the sight and sound of fellow beings and their claims for recognition for relating a self to them.

Ahlu, on the other hand, is eminently social in the village context and felicitously a developer of the moral state of the giver. The rituals of ahlu are virtually the same for Yadaw as they are for Nondwin. Except for the daily feeding to monks and the occasional giving to nuns and passing beggars, ahlu is an organized, public, display ritual. The acme of the ahlu cycle for any particular family is the shinbyu. And the shinbyu exhibits all of the features connected with ahlu.

1. It is community wide, at least. (The widest net of intervillage festal organization is involved in the larger shinbyus and pagoda dedications.)
2. It requires the cooperation of the aphyo and lubyo groups, for serving, cleaning, and cooking.
3. It mobilizes at least the neighborhood group to aid in food preparation.
4. Representatives of the sangha must be on hand and be fed.
5. Everybody who attends (at or least the heads of households) makes a monetary contribution.
6. The ostensible focus of ahlu is the building of kutho to strengthen kan, but the major part of the activity is secular display, an invocation of the facade culture of the peasant.

I have elsewhere contrasted the ritual and ceremonial cycles of Yadaw and Nondwin, but here I want to call attention to two major differences which stand as near summaries of the slight, yet important, contrasts in religious life in these two communities. In Yadaw, three sorts of shinbyus are recognized; in Nondwin, only one is recognized. The dimension of recognition is not on ritual grounds, for a shinbyu is a shinbyu, be it the full spectacle of the legend of the Buddha or the simple presentation of a shin at the monastery. The difference lies in the classification of how much money is returned to the sponsors by voluntary contribution of the invited guests. The practice of keeping account books with the name of the contributor and the amount given is said to have originated about 30 years ago, but it is universal now in Upper Burma. The record books are supposed to insure reciprocity in giving, to make certain that exactly the same amount is returned when the recipient becomes a contributor. To give less is to place oneself in an inferior position; to give more is to make claims to superiority; so reciprocity, the general social norm of Burmese village interaction, is supposedly maintained by the keeping of written account books. My guess, based on scattered informant reports and on the general history of the region, is that monetary contribution is relatively recent, and that the number of spectacular shinbyus, with wider and wider networks of invited guests, underlies the now ubiquitous account keeping. But in the giving of shinbyu in Yadaw, three outcomes are recognized in the way the contributions total up: (1) the money-losing shinbyu, in which the sponsors' costs are more than contributions, (2) the break-even shinbyu, in which the sponsors' costs are roughly the same as contributions, and (3) the money-making, in which the sponsors' costs are significantly less than the contributions. In Nondwin, only the money-losing shinbyu, that is the net-drain variety, was recognized, and no one expected to break even or especially to profit from the holding of a religious ceremony in the sacrificial idiom.

How a religious ceremony, designed to be costly, can be converted into a money-making enterprise is clear from the Yadaw example. The people of Yadaw have access to the wealthier persons in Mandalay, and, for some of the wider festivals, they include Mandalay and Amarapura town residents in the list of invited persons. The rich or well-to-do even if one only has casual interaction or acquaintance with them are invited by some people in Yadaw. The lesser integration of the community, the recency of migration, and the history of tenancy makes this feasible in Yadaw but not in Nondwin. To make money from a shinbyu, one need only invite enough rich persons to attend. Most of the people invited (printed invitations are sent) will come. They come on two grounds: Like most Burmans they enjoy the crowd and the display, and it gives them some minor increment of kutho. People give at shinbyus in some measure contingent on their reputation for affluence, for generosity, and for being a lugyi. Well-to-do townsmen may give a peasant family 25, 50, or even 100 kyats as their contribution to a shinbyu. It is unlikely that all of the wealthy who, in fact, come will have occasion to invite the villager to similar ahlus. At any rate, whatever the long-term outcome, the immediate consequence is that some people make money on the shinbyu and that some people consciously contrive to make money on sponsoring a shinbyu. It is only the latter, the conscious intent to profit, that is scorned in Yadaw, for the former, inadvertent money making, is seen as the play of chance.

This fact of the money-making shinbyu, coupled with the other great (in village terms) difference between the villages, that is the great gap in the percentage of men who spend the traditional three Wa after shinbyu in the kyaung (less than 20 per cent in Yadaw, more than 85 per cent in Nondwin), poses the problem in depth of religious conviction between the two communities. I do not believe that on the level of knowledge, belief, or personal conviction (although my evidence for personal conviction about Buddhism is behavioral in the sense of observances, of ritual, of the absence of sceptics, not psychological in the sense of getting information about the structure of sentiments underlying the prevailing Buddhist behavior) there is a significant difference between the communities. In fact, this chapter's emphasis on the similarity between Yadaw and Nondwin comes from the monotonous regularity in my field notes detailing the same orientations, tales, and rituals. What does seem to make the differences between Yadaw and Nondwin in these two areas is probably not, then, differences in piety, but differences in: (1) economy (labor and relative poverty demands of rice growing, against the mixed crops), (2) integration (the factional community against the solidary one), and (3) urban proximity (Mandalay is in the village network for Yadaw; Sagaing is relatively remote for Nondwin). These non- or extra-religious differences between the communities, rather than differences in knowledge or belief, account for the observed variations in the ritual cycle and in the implementation of the common belief system.

The general point about the relation between practice and belief can now be succinctly made. There is a common belief system at the village level in Upper Burma. The Buddhism of Yadaw and of Nondwin are virtually interchangeable at the level of precept, of doctrine, and of meaning. But there are these observable facts. Within the villages, individuals and families vary in the rituals they perform; between the villages, there are differences in some of the major rituals and many of the minor ones, as well. These differences may be accounted for by eschewing the formula that belief and practice are the same things, differentially expressed on the coordinates society and culture, and replacing it with a more adequate conceptualization. This formulation holds, at least for peasant communities whose religion is embodied in scripture as well as in the nerves and brains of living members of the society, that a belief system in the same society gives rise to a variety of behavioral expression, and the same belief system in different local societies likewise is ritually implemented in a variety of modes.

Although village Buddhism is essentially a salvation and rebirth religion, parts of it are adapted to the handling of immediate, pressing crisis problems. The efficacy of the crisis-adapted part of village Buddhism rests, in part, on the pervasive conviction that Buddhism is the proper, complete, and pragmatic description and analysis of human experience in the face of a random, meaningless, and essentially uninteresting world. Yadaw has more recourse to crises ritual than Nondwin, although I cannot reconstruct the precise magnitudes. The relative poverty of Yadaw, its lesser social integration, its greater political involvement, and its failure to produce a man of pon all conduce to a greater incidence of personal and social crisis, and hence a greater frequency of crises activity.

The chief ways Buddhist belief and practice are involved in crises handling are oaths, ordeals, and immediate kan. The Buddhist oath, or act of truth, is a device to test whether or not an individual's kan is equal to the crisis facing him. The oath is taken by villagers chiefly in the form of "stone lifting." If a person is faced with a major decision or is about to undertake some large enterprise, he is likely to use this form of testing the adequacy of his kan. The ritual itself is simple. In most kyaungs and near some pagodas are found smooth rocks placed on stone slabs. The rocks weigh, usually, about 15–20 pounds. The person wishing to test his kan by the stone lifting method stands in front of the rock. He lifts it and holds it a few moments, letting the weight of it register on his mind and muscles. He then replaces the rock on the slab. Next he recites part of the good and bad deeds he has performed in the past, and then he asks if his kan is able to help him achieve the particular purpose or goal. The statement is usually put in the form of asking, "If my kan is equal to the task, may the rock be heavier next time I lift it." After the recitation, the petitioner lifts the rock again, holds it a few moments, and judges whether the rock is indeed heavier. In this usual routine of oath taking, there is a literalness in seeing if the "weight" of past deeds has a tip in the moral direction, for the stone is made heavier by the greater "weight" of kutho over akutho or the stronger influence or predominance of the kutho components of kan over the akutho ones.

A much less practiced form of oath taking is similar to the stone lifting. This oath also tests the disposition of kan toward a crisis situation, usually one in which a person of ill-health has not responded to the various medical and quasi-medical courses of treatment. The oath is taken in front of the household Buddha altar, and the oath taker asks that if he has truly performed his religious duties may the particular crisis be resolved in his favor. When a smallpox epidemic hit Yadaw about seven years ago, for example, the altar oath taking was fairly common. Maung Sein's story is representative. During the epidemic, his daughter was covered with a rash. He went before his household altar and recited this simple oath, "I have taken care of this girl. If I have done my duty to my daughter, may she recover." She improved and did recover. Obviously, such a crisis recourse is available only to a fairly pious Buddhist, and some small part of Buddhist observation and devotion is linked to the eventual use of parts of the ultimate concern system for immediate problem resolution.

The ordeal is seldom practiced now, and, during my stay, I encountered no instances of a person putting himself through an ordeal to test the inclinations of his destiny, and I could elicit no historically verifiable instances of ordeals. Yet the notion of ordeal is present in village culture and considered to be an available means of crisis behavior. The idea of the ordeal is kept in the cultural repository of behavior by ordeal tales. The two most frequently told ordeal stories are the following:

During Pagan times there was a pair of large shears used in judging cases that human wisdom could not solve. Once a man entrusted his money to another. Some time passed, and he came to claim his money. The man to whom he had entrusted it said he had already returned it. The lender of the money went to court, and there was a hearing. But it was one man's word against another, and, without writing or witnesses, no judgment could be made. So the ordeal shears were recommended by the court. The large shears were brought into court, and the complainant put his arm in between the two blades and said, "If this man has returned my money to me, may you chop off my arm." The shears did not act. Then the accused stepped up, and he gave the staff he was carrying to the complainant. In the staff was stuffed the borrowed money. He then said, "If I have not returned the borrowed money, chop off my arm." The shears did not act. The people in the court saw that the shears were impotent to act, and the giant shears lost their reputation, and the judges decided it could try no more cases. Out of shame, the shears jumped into the Irrawaddy and drowned.

Once the Buddha was the son of two blind parents. They lived in seclusion outside the gates of a village. The Buddha as their son brought them water every day from the nearby river. The boy was aided in bringing water by a small deer (*thamin*). One day a hunter passed and shot an arrow at the deer, but the arrow was misdirected and killed the boy instead. His blind parents waited and waited, in vain, for their son's return. But when good and holy people are in trouble, the Thagya Min (king of the deva nats) often comes down to help them. Thagya Min came to the blind parents and asked them what their trouble was. They told him. He then asked them three questions: "Do you want your sight returned?" "Do you want your son returned?" "Do you want a pot of gold?" The blind father took an oath, saying his son was loyal, obedient, and good. "And if this is true," he said, "may I see my son carrying a pot of gold." Since he was holy and his oath true, the wish was fulfilled.

These stories illustrate, by contrast, the points of Buddhist-derived belief in crises situations. The first story is a secular, non-Buddhist tale and tells of the fallibility of human and extrahuman judgment, as well as the shrewdness of some men. The second tale indicates the mode of using Buddhism in crises. It is the devout, the pious, the good Buddhist, and hence the man of strong kan who can survive ordeals and turn oaths to advantage, whereas the impious cannot avail themselves of these tests, for they will suffer. So Buddhism, while not directly able to deal with crisis (except for the pongyi chants to drive sickness from a village or the use of certain thok to intimidate ghosts and witches), can be crisis adapted.

The final mode of using some Buddhist ideas for crises is that of "instant kan." Kan, although clearly the accumulated moral balance over a countless series of existences, lends itself peculiarly to crises. First, kan does not operate as a steady influence in a single direction. For a villager, it is a fluctuating force, and activities in the present may influence the tides of kan. Second, kan inevitably has an astrological dimension. The moment, as well as the condition, of an individual's birth is governed by kan, and hence the planetary disposition toward him are clues to the operation of his fate or destiny. Yadaw villagers do not think that planets have a separate, determining force that by itself affects human life and action, but rather the planets derive their power from the link of kan, and the heavens are to be read as signposts for individual fates.

In an illness that does not respond to ordinary treatment, one usual reaction is to attempt to get immediate kan, either as increment or as changing the predominance of kutho in relation to akutho. The means employed in Yadaw for producing kan are few. Most common is the "feeding" of planetary spirits, also, of course, called nats or devas.

Most pagodas have stone-carved images of the planetary nats on their grounds, and a villager will make food offerings to these devas in a form analogous to feeding monks for the Buddha. But the vocabulary of offering is different—the nats may be called shin, lord, but not shin hpaya, reserved for Buddha pagodas, some exalted monks, nor is the offering itself called *hsun*, the food of the sangha and the Buddha, nor is the act of giving to nats under the *ahlu peide*, almsgiving for merit idiom. However, the nats are given the deferential shikko, and the language of supersubordination in status is employed.

Another form of instant kan is the placing of food offerings outside the village gate. One small bowl of rice, or of hin, for each year of the petitioner's life is the usual offering. This food is eaten by the pariah dogs abounding in the countryside around Mandalay. Akin to this mode of effecting kan is the release of animals. In the Mandalay bazaar there are sellers of birds for this purpose. A petitioner buys one caged bird for each year of his life and sets it "free" thus accumulating kan. The birds, of course, are homing pigeons and eventually return to the seller. Sometimes this is also done with fish, who are released from tank captivity.

The final way to influence kan is by candle offerings, especially at the time of the two festivals of the lights. Since this form of swaying kan is calendrically tied, it is not so widely employed for ill health as it is for economic risk or as a hedge against trouble on a projected sojourn or similar activity in the force of uncertainty.

Beyond these specific uses of Buddhist notions and devices for immediate solution to problems there is a general conviction that monks and parts of the Pali canon are efficacious in times of peril and trouble. This is expressed in the chanting of thok to cleanse a house or even the village from sickness or an epidemic, in the making of in by monks and of other amulets and charms to ward off evil, and in the pongyi tattooing against evils and snakes.

These Buddhist-derived "magical practices" coexist with the village repertory of alchemy (although in Yadaw no one was rich enough to actually engage in these experiments), astrological divination, nat propitiation, and Burmese medicine. These systems, supplemental to Buddhism as salvation strategy, bridge the gaps in dealing with daily uncertainty, personal crises, and the need for the immediate application of power in one's self-interest or the moment by moment warding off of evil.

I have in this section stressed three things about the Buddhism of Yadaw: (1) the variety of individual interpretation of the common core of belief and ritual; (2) the multiplex relations between ritual and belief; (3) the attention to rebirth rather than salvation. These themes, seen as the more personal, individual, and subjective aspects of village belief, taken together with the more impersonal, patterned, and objective aspects stressed in the section on Nondwin, give a fairly comprehensive grasp of the form, meaning, and operation of village Buddhism and of the possibilities for its adaptation to changing social circumstances.

9

Conclusions

In a sense this final chapter should properly be titled "reflections," or "theoretical considerations," rather than "conclusions." My way of work in this book places those empirical generalizations and abstractions I have made close to, and often embedded in, the facts and observations which gave rise to them. This is, in my view, a proper procedure for an anthropologist: to scatter his theory and his generalizations among the facts they are to explain. It is proper because much of anthropological theory is so loosely articulated, much of it so barely above the empirical, that the theory needs the intimate presence of information if it is to avoid the appearance of a mere dance of spectral categories. However, it is necessary, partly for esthetic and partly for scientific reasons, to draw together in one place the chief, guiding, analytic notions, the more outstanding generalizations, and the rationale for the procedures used in gathering and selecting data.

First, this study is a comparison between two peasant villages in Upper Burma. These two communities were selected after a survey of some 30-odd communities in the region north of the 40-inch isohyet. Field work time was nearly equally divided between the villages, although three more weeks were spent in Nondwin than in Yadaw. Roughly five months were spent in each village, and I did supplementary field work on the economics of producing begging bowls in a pottery-making village. Not until the last month of field work was I able, without the aid of an interpreter, to conduct a conversation in Burmese on a fairly complicated topic like Buddhism or politics. In doing field work, I lived alone in the house of a village host, in daily, full-time, and intimate association with the people of the village, dressing in the longyi, eating the local food, and following the ordinary rhythm of village life. I state these conditions of my field work so that the human component involved in the reliability of my ethnographic findings may be assessed. Obviously some things are known "beyond the shadow of reasonable doubt." Some things I know and communicate with moderate confidence. And there are some conclusions about which I have grave doubts. In all cases, however, I have tried to give an expression of my convictions about the ethnographic reliability of reported norms or social relations. I stress reliability for two reasons: (1) the ethnography of contemporary Upper Burma is meagre and I should like to see it grow in a cumulative and orderly manner, and (2) it is important to my further analysis that most of the facts I reason about are just that: facts. This is somewhat antiquarian in modern anthropology, where facts are thought to exist only for the theories or models that can be fashioned after them. I agree on the importance of theories and models and of facts that have, or imply, theoretical significance. But I also have a commitment to explain or account for real behavior in real societies, in actual time and space, and hence a concern with real observations or facts. I do not want, at this stage of development in social and cultural anthropology, to give up so easily and quickly what I consider its chief and greatest resource: as an anchor for our theories in the facts of real social systems.

The two villages selected for intensive field investigation approximate the range of ecological and economic variation in Upper Burma. There are other sorts of communities: fishing villages, plantation communities, special outcast (keba) communities, and artisan communities of lacquer workers, potters, weavers, and stone cutters. By approximating this variation I simply mean that most communities—and most of the people in Upper Burma—are somewhat like Yadaw and Nondwin. These communities are, and have been, the major human adaptations in this region. The culture of the area is fairly uniform. As one moves from community to community, the movement is not from distinct culture to distinct culture but rather an exposure to some small, detailed shifts in cultural inventory and cultural arrangement. Upper Burma has a regional culture, and its small variations from local society to local society are explicable (although I shall not here undertake that explanation) in terms of ecologic, economic, and historic differences among the villages. The point is that Nondwin as a mixed, dry crop farming village is virtually interchangeable with other mixed, dry crop farming communities, and Yadaw is like hundreds of other irrigated, rice communities in most aspects. The significant, even if minor, differences lie between these two sorts of local societies.

The guiding problem in the analysis and description of Yadaw and Nondwin was a result of two major concerns: (1) an interest in the theory of social and cultural change especially in the processes of economic and political change, and (2) the desire to place the peasantry of Burma in the context of a complex national society in a manner aimed at facilitating the understanding of both the peasants and their interaction with segments of the larger social system.

As in all field work, my guiding concerns and major interests were tempered by the actuality of the society under study and the historical flow of events while the field work was being done. The concentration on Buddhism is a reflection of the simple fact that Buddhism is pervasive in the life of the people studied, for I had no explicit, beforehand commitment to go deeply into that subject as I did have in regard to economics and local social organization.

Burma is the locale of study for obvious and somewhat compelling theoretical and empirical reasons. Burma is a new nation. Independent since 1948, it has had time to complete the first stages of decolonization and to put its political and economic affairs in the hands of its people. Here, as elsewhere, one could observe the effects of sovereignty as one spread out into the countryside among a population that had little or no experience with the public forms of consensual and civil politics. The subtle factors that make democracy a working institution in the lives of persons might be revealed in this sort of context, as well as in the modes of peasant mobilization for broad political and economic ends. Burma was first attractive, then, because of the newness of its nationhood and because it had, and has, a commitment to the building of a modern, welfare, and democratic state capable of generating continual economic growth and adapting to a changing world. The chances of Burma building or making of itself what its plans and aspirations called for were not hampered by that virtually omnipresent barrier or impediment in Asia: a dense, heavy population eking by on meagre land and other natural resources. In terms of population and natural resources, Burma had the option of living at a level of primitive self-sufficiency or trying to build a modern economy. It was not locked into an obvious set of vicious circles keeping the economy at a low-level equilibrium. And with the urban, educated and nationalistic elite determined to transform Burma into a socialist welfare state, the conditions for observing and charting the social process of attempted transformation seemed ideal. A peasantry led by a nationalistic, elite segment, in a setting of relative abundance, in a society without great class barriers and with cultural traditions stretching back more than

1,000 years, forms a complex of social features as close to a laboratory for the study of economic and social modernization as the social anthropologist is likely to find.

The attempt to shed light on large problems, such as modernization, economic development, nation building, and the general process of social and cultural change, requires that these large questions be broken down to empirically relevant phrasing and scale. Part of this is an art depending on the skill and ingenuity of a particular investigator, and part of this reduction is related to the methods a field anthropologist has at his disposal. For example, the question of the economic development of the peasantry of Burma resolves itself, from the point of view of the field anthropologist, into the researchable problems of: What is the range and variety of producing farm households in a peasant community? How much do they differ in efficiency and productivity? Are these differences related to some set of social and cultural facts? Which farmers take and seek new economic opportunities, and which do not? Is this resistance or receptivity to change tied to some set of social and cultural characteristics? These queries, and scores like them, raised throughout the body of this book, require a particular kind of data and a special sort of methodology if answers are even to be approximated.

The basic method of anthropology, and the one I have used, with modifications to be spelled out subsequently, is that of observation and informant interview to discover a set of social regularities. When the regularities are gotten, over time, by observing and questioning the behavior and words of people, then the second step, of course, not so neatly separated as these sentences maintain, is to attribute meaning to these regularities. These twin activities add up to a sort of documentary methodology. From social activity and from socially relevant speech clusters, regularities in behavior are documented over a period of time, and then these regularities are given an interpretation or meaning. The whole business of careful note taking, of mapping, of census taking, of pacing off the size of field plots, of tape recording conversations and prayers, of snapping pictures, and of making measurements and sketches is a means of controlling and implementing the process of documenting the social and cultural regularities and attributing meaning to them. In the chapters of this study, the process is fairly well laid out, and a careful reader can see to what extent and by what documents a particular assertion about a social regularity is warranted.

Meaning, however, in the anthropological sense exists on at least two levels: the meaning in the minds of people in the society under study; the meaning in terms of some set of concepts or theories in the mind of the anthropologist. I use the notion of level, for the cognitive awareness of the people in the society must be gotten before the scientific or anthropological meaning can be adduced or attributed. In studying medical practices at the village curing and healing services, for example, I had a difficult and interesting time making sense of the regularities I observed. When, finally, I approximated the principles in the minds of the healers and the patients, I could attribute meaning to the curing activities. When I understood that, by the same cognitive principles as the people of Nondwin, I still had the problem of assimilating it, if possible, into a body of propositions and concepts in anthropology—that is, to give it a scientific meaning or a theoretical relevance.

Anthropological theory is a mixed bag, but it appears to me to be at least torn between two sorts of theoretical commitments, or two kinds of explanations, or two modes of assimilating discovered, cognitive structures to scientific idioms. A good part of the conceptual apparatus of social and cultural anthropology has been developed to explain or account for the presence or absence of kinds of cultural features or social relations. The most developed examples of this sort of theory are, for example, in the area of family and kinship studies. A widely held generalization is that "unilineal corporate kin groups are found in the middle range of technological and economic complexity." In this sentence we find a set of technical terms, unilineal, corporate, and so forth, which takes the family practices of the Hopi or the Tallensi or the Crow or the Omaha and assimilates them to the category in the minds of anthropologists and then links the presence of this category to variables like technology and economy. Another kind of theory which explains the presence or absence of social facts in a given society is exemplified by the numerous studies of "diffusion" and "acculturation." Why are the Burmese Buddhists? The religion was diffused to them from its homeland in India, was adapted by the powerful dynasty of Pagan, and has since been the dominant belief system of the Burmans. These brief examples of structural-functional theory and of cultural-historical theory elucidate the point I want to make. (Both of them must make commitments to psychological theory, for it is human beings that act, not social structures or cultural patterns.) *Most anthropological theory has been concerned with explaining the conjunction or succession of social facts in time and space.* And, of course, this is the major goal of a scientifically oriented social and cultural anthropology: to say why a particular set of customs or social relations are where they are at a given point in time and space. But there is another sort of anthropological theory, less developed but, I believe, no less crucial, and the two sorts of theories blend into each other and in the best of all worlds would be perfectly integrated. The second theory attempts to explain or account for performance of people in a given society and culture. Some examples of this are found in the chapter on the economy of Nondwin; for instance, the poorer among the farmers are the most likely to seek a given kind of innovation, or the solutions the poor find useful do not cumulate into changes in the economic or social structure of Nondwin. Similarly, the section on the conditions for the emergence of the entrepreneur in Nondwin is an example of accounting for the performance of given individuals or given groups in a particular social and cultural context.

These two sorts of accounting for facts are unevenly developed. The presence or absence kind of theory or theories is historically the most elaborated and continues to be, in its various guises from evolutionary modes to radical diffusion models, in the center of anthropological thought. The performance sort of theory is much less developed, and its congeners must be sought in other social sciences. The development of game theory in economics and other forms of decision theory in the social sciences, as well as some of the input-output models in political science and the notions of social behavior as exchange in sociology, are much more akin to the kind of theory I have in mind when I speak of a performance-oriented body of explanatory concepts. To make a performance theory relevant to anthropological data and concerns is more than an act of borrowing or analogizing. It requires the introduction of some new ideas and some extension and reworking of older ones.

The division I find convenient in ordering concepts is, first, between macro- and microstructural analyses and, second, between individuals behaving according to the rules or norms of their society and those who see rules as permitting the exercise or development of certain strategies of behavior. These two axes intersect, and in their intersection lies the embryo of a performance-oriented body of concepts and principles. Macrostructural description and analysis is the usual anthropological report on a whole society. It stresses the social system, the interconnections between roles and the modes of social behavior in the various institutional loci of a given society. In its developed form it eventuates in a description of a social structure and a cultural pattern and gives the range of permissible operation of these structures and patterns. All anthropology is first a macrostructural activity. Until a given society, whether a local community, a tribe, a confederation, or a nation, is described in a structural and functional manner, its anthropologically relevant aspects are virtually unknown. Macrostructural description gives the grid, or frame, for social action in a particular society and provides the types and instances for cross-cultural comparison. The propositions about the coexistence of social features in time and space, the operation of various kinds of societies, the types of societies and cultures in the world, and finally the various modes of social and cultural integration are the theoretical products of macrostructural emphases.

Where macrostructural analyses seem weakest are in the areas of social and cultural change and in accounting for the way particular individuals in a given society will behave in the long or short run. These weaknesses are obviously built into the theory itself, and hence the theory needs supplementing. Microstructural analysis is one way of extending or reorienting the social system notions. Microstructural analysis proceeds from the viewpoint of given individuals or role sets in the framework of a social system. It tries to say what ends persons pursue, what means are available to them, and what are the consequences of the successful or unsuccessful pursuit of given ends. Thus microstructural analysis does not take social action to be purely repetitive, nor does it assume that all individuals follow at all times the norms of their society. Rather, it attempts to see the strategies open to individuals located in particular role sets, commanding specific human and nonhuman resources, and moving toward goals that are partially social and partially individual.

Microstructural analysis uses as its two major terms *choice* and *strategy*, whereas macroanalysis uses *structure* and *function* as its two major concepts. It is in the combination of macro- and microanalyses and in the elevation of the notions of choice and strategy to a par with those of structure and function that I believe further rapid progress will be achieved in the understanding of social and cultural change and of the role of individuals in implementing change.

This theoretical and methodological commitment is stark as it is laid down here, but, when placed against the analyses of the communities of Yadaw and of Nondwin, I think its utility is patent. It does force a reorientation of thought and has a direct influence on method, and it does show where stabilities and liabilities are in a given social order and who, under what circumstances, is likely or unlikely to make or resist a given change or opportunity. It is not, of course, a full solution to the problems of understanding change, but it does open a broad avenue of research and hypothesis on the sources of stability and instability in social systems.

From this theoretical and methodological *apologia pro vita mea*, I move to a brief recapitulation of what I consider the chief yields of this study. The yield is of three sorts: (1) ethnography, (2) propositions about social and cultural change, and (3) concepts about a kind of society and that society's place in a more complex whole. The ethnographic comparisons between a mixed dry crop farming community and an irrigated wet rice community purport to cover the bulk of the peasantry in Upper Burma. Combined with minor variants in the region, they approximate the major ecological, social and cultural arrangements in the area. By labeling and abstracting we can get a shorthand description for the communities of Upper Burma.

The basic settlement unit is a named village. The village may have some dependent hamlets or subvillages. Enclosing a nucleated village settlement is a palisade. The social units are defined by the fenced settlement composed of persons with responsibilities to keep the fence intact. The village is organized in its political dimension under an elected headman and a council of four. Another marker of the social unit, then, are those who vote for the same headman and may pay taxes through him. There are wealth spreads in the community and an ideal four category division with land underlying the wealth divisions. Ten acres of freehold land underlie the customary standard of living which is called moderate. Technology contains the ox-drawn plow, with a steel or iron share, and implements of wood, bamboo, iron, or steel. There is no piece of technology which requires more than two persons to operate: harrowing with the wooden-toothed harrow, the rice pounder, the crosscut saw, the bathtub for cooking milk, the bellows for forging iron, and the earth oven for pottery. Irrigation from canal networks is common and the Persian wheel is used for truck crops.

Single family households are the ideal and statistical norms. Households have great latitude in behavior permissible to them. Women have high status, and the division of labor barely follows the sex axis, except for some religious activities. Senior-junior and age-respect relations based on a kinship idiom are the widest principles of social organization. Power, esteem, authority in the community center around concrete individuals, not offices or statutes. Pon, gon, and awza express these qualities in ideal form.

Beyond the family, the only perdurable groups are based on reli-

320 The Golden Road to Modernity

gious and ceremonial activities; otherwise relationships tend to be contractual, dyadic, and fleeting. Buddhism is the believed in, universal system for understanding life beyond the immediate and empirical. Theravada practice, without much recourse to scripture or emphasis on interior states, is characteristic. The shinbyu is universal, and all men spend some time as koyin. Merit building and giving are the chief elements in village Buddhism. There is a system of animistic belief (nat worship) which is integrated with Buddhism and gives a villager a belief system reaching from hut to heaven and beyond. Any scepticism in belief is directed at nat devotions. Also part of the world view are various predictive and divinatory systems like astrology, alchemy, and omen reading. Witchcraft exists as a minor explanatory device for illness but rarely functions as a means of social control. The villager has a short-time horizon for planning but an eternal one for completion of plans. Life is characterized by attempts to minimize interpersonal conflict, to prevent confrontation, and to allow individuals to pursue their own ways without neighbor or community pressure.

This bald statement of the chief features of Upper Burmese villages can only be understood against the ethnography in this book. How it works as a system and what it means in action are spelled out in the preceding chapters. The utility of this catalogue is to remind a reader what the major axes of life in a village are. On these common themes are many variations among villages: Wealth groups are sometimes three or four; rice communities are poorer and in more debt; migration and endogamy vary; length of time as koyin varies; factionalism is often present, and other contrasts. The full range of variation, bound, it seems on the evidence, to be minor, rests on more ethnography. But this listing will serve as a building block in producing a reliable factual base for the ethnography of Burma.

At the level of immediate observation, villages are not self-contained, isolated social entities. They are connected by trade, by marriage, by migration, by intervisiting, by common attendance at ritual, by sharing kyaungs, by inviting monks, and by other ties. These palpable links I have documented and mapped in the relevant part of this study. What remains is to transcend this empiricism and make the mental leap of placing villages and the peasantry in general in relation to the complex political and economic system of which they are but a part. To place the villages and the peasants in perspective, I have had recourse to the notion of a multiple society with plural cultures. A multiple society may be defined as

. . . a segmented social order welding a territory and its population together by a single set of political and economic bonds. There is a class or segment which commands resources of national scope, carries in it the idea of nation, maintains relations with other nations, and is in some sort of touch with scientific, economic, and political developments of the international community. It is this group, spread out through the national territory, in whom political control is vested and among whom political power is contested. The other segments of the multiple society are organized for regional or local purposes. They do not command political or economic power of national scope. They are, in contrast to the national élite, of small scale in social organization. Plural cultures are sometimes found in the multiple society. Not only is the political, economic, and ideological scope of the segments different, but their cultures may be also (e.g., in Burma the Kachins, the Karens, the Chins, the Shans, the Palaung, the Padung, and the Wa are like this).

The multiple society is different from our own in that the social and cultural variations are not class variations on a basically common culture in a single social structure, but rather the society exhibits poor articulation between segments, disparities in the principles of social structure from segment to segment, and allows only the national, élite elements to be organized for purposeful political action. . . . the multiple society generates tensions in the political and economic spheres which lead to continual conflict until some segment of the multiple society finds and develops a program which can enlist the energies and sympathies of large numbers of people in the national territory, and in the implementing of that program develop the bonds and sentiments to reduce or eliminate the multiplicity of the social organization. (M. Nash, 1964, pp. 420–21)

The concept of a multiple society with plural cultures helps to organize the empirical material about Burma, and it likewise points to the chief modes of interaction between the national elements and the rural peasantry, and finally it provides a guide to the sources of conflict, of change, and of status in a society like contemporary Burma.

If we return to one of the proffered yields of this research, propositions on social and cultural change in the process of modernization, the multiple society idea helps us to see the process in a perspective larger than the local scene. The propositions on change are of two kinds. The first has to do with the persons in the local communities of Nondwin and Yadaw; the second treats the interaction of the peasantry and the elite. The first set of propositions works on the following ideas: An individual is placed in his role; his command over resources and his control over persons is charted, then the ends toward which he strives are listed, and finally his activity in the face of new opportunity is observed. The generalizations on how an entrepreneur, for example, is developed, or what kind of second crop is likely to be undertaken, or why a gasoline motor does not spread throughout the society, or whether or not a community is likely to be riven by factions are all derived from this sort of analysis. The perspective developed here has some novel features when contrasted to the more usual anthropological analysis of change and innovation. It is first *diagnostic* in that it seeks to approximate how a given typical person will perceive, perform, and produce in a situation where there is some latitude or option in his behavior. Second, it conceives of people living social life as something of a discovery process, not enacting a play from a fully known script. This sense of uncertainty, of ambiguity, of chance, and of hope certainly seems more faithful to the way people do in fact live than does the image of adjusting behavior to prescribed rules or norms. Third, the perspective avoids reification and propositions about compatibility between cultural traits or social relations, and it places both social structure and cultural pattern as outcomes of individual activities, as precipitates of historical action.

My conviction is that this mode of analysis yields more than other forms of understanding change based solely on the features of the social system or the value hierarchy, but time and further study, not the expenditure of words, will be the final arbiter.

On the level of the interaction of the peasantry and the national, urban segment, propositions emerge about breaks in communication, divergencies in goals, and the limits of persuasion and of coercion. The chief idea is rather simple: The national elite makes plans and programs without consulting the peasantry. In a multiple society, the national segment is agent and agency, and the other segments are the raw material to be molded. In this sort of social structure, programs are easily made, but implementing them is another problem. Those who devise programs may be as far removed from the social context in which they must be carried out as a man from Mars. They may suffer from poor administrative arrangements, political inabilities to make the needed decisions, and the reluctance, resistance, or indifference of a peasantry for whom the plans and programs promise little but further deprivation or constraints.

The point is that empirical information on the social meaning of a plan or program is woefully inadequate and that the key to development or modernization lies not so much in the elaboration of theory or the proliferation of models as it does in understanding the needs of a people and in the artful devising of suitable means of implementing those needs.

To move from fact and theory to my predilections is perhaps permissible in the final paragraphs of this book. Economic development or social and cultural modernization is on the agenda of history for nations like Burma. Either they will make the transformation or they will disappear as social and political entities. The social science of the West, as well as its technology and science, are important ingredients in making the transition as humanly costless as possible. The chief things that social science has now to offer are, in my opinion, these:

1. A diagnosis of the particular variety of poverty afflicting a given society.
2. A sense of the social and cultural concomitants of different paths to modernity.
3. The insistence that social and cultural modernity is based on the activities and assets of the people involved and is not the mere mechanical transfer of money and knowledge from the richer nations.
4. The hope that society and culture are still evolving systems, and that the trail of discovery from new nations will reveal social and cultural arrangements not prefigured in our theories.

This book is offered as a contribution to the understanding of the different species of traditionality and of poverty, as an example of what sort of human and social data are needed for planning, and as an example of how even the most arcane of social science concerns eventually feed into the main task of all science: to make the world amenable to the dreams of men.

Bibliography

Bellah, Robert Neely, 1963. Reflections on the Protestant Ethic Analogy in Asia. *Journal of Social Issues,* 19:52–60.

Boeke, J. H., 1953. *Economics and Economic Policy of Dual Societies.* New York, International Secretariat, Institute of Pacific Relations.

Brohm, John, 1963. Buddhism and Animism in a Burmese Village. *Journal of Asian Studies,* 22:155–67.

Census Report, 1960. District Commissioner of Sagaing, Burma. Unpublished.

Conze, Edward, 1959. *Buddhist Scriptures.* Baltimore, Penguin.

Davis, John H., 1960. *The Forests of Burma.* Gainesville, Florida, University of Florida.

Durkheim, E., 1915. *The Elementary Forms of the Religious Life.* London, Macmillan.

Furnivall, John Sydenham, 1957. *An Introduction to the Political Economy of Burma.* Rangoon, Peoples Literature Committee and House.

Furnivall, John Sydenham, 1958. *The Governance of Modern Burma.* New York, International Secretariat, Institute of Pacific Relations.

Ginsburg, Norton S., ed., 1958. Burma. In *The Pattern of Asia.* Englewood Cliffs, New Jersey, Prentice-Hall.

Geertz, Clifford, 1963. *Peddlers and Princes: Social Development and Economic Change in Two Indonesian Towns.* Chicago, University of Chicago Press.

Leach, Edmund R., 1954. *Political Systems of Highland Burma.* London, London School of Economics and Political Science.

Leach, Edmund R., 1958. Magical Hair. *Journal of the Royal Anthropological Institute,* 88:147–64.

Leach, Edmund R., 1961. *Rethinking Anthropology.* London, Athlone Press, University of London.

Htin Aung, 1962. *Folk Elements in Burmese Buddhism.* London, Oxford University Press.

Mendelson, E. M., 1960. Religion and Authority in Modern Burma. *World Today,* 16:110–18.

Mendelson, E. M., 1961. The King of the Weaving Mountain. *Royal Central Asian Journal,* 48:229–37.

Nash, June, 1964. Living with Nats: An Analysis of Animism in Burman Village Social Relations. Unpublished.

325

326   The Golden Road to Modernity

Nash, Manning, 1961. Education in a New Nation: The Village School in Upper Burma. *International Journal of Comparative Sociology,* 2:135–43.

— Nash, Manning, 1963. Burmese Buddhism in Everyday Life. *American Anthropologist,* 65:285–95.

— Nash, Manning, 1964. Southeast Asian Society: Dual or Multiple. *Journal of Asian Studies,* 23:417–23.

Ne Win, 1960. *Is Trust Vindicated?* Rangoon, Director of Information, Government of the Union of Burma.

Nu, U, 1954. *Burma Under the Japanese.* New York, Macmillan.

— Pfanner, David E., and J. Ingersoll, 1962. Theravada Buddhism and Village Economic Behavior: A Burmese and Thai Comparison. *Journal of Asian Studies,* 21:341–61.

Revolutionary Council, 1962. *The Burmese Way to Socialism.* Rangoon.

Sawyer, A. M., and Daw Nyun, 1927. *A Classified List of the Plants of Burma.* Rangoon, Government Printing Office.

Scott, Sir J. G. (Shway Yoe), 1882. *The Burman: His Life and Notions.* London, Macmillan.

Singer, Milton, 1961. Review of the Religion of India: The Sociology of Hinduism and Buddhism by Max Weber. In *American Anthropologist,* 63:143–51.

Temple, Sir Richard Carnac, 1906. *The Thirty-Seven Nats: A Phase of Spirit-Worship Prevailing in Burma.* London, W. Griggs.

Tinker, Hugh, 1961. *The Union of Burma: A Study of the First Years of Independence.* London, Oxford University Press, third edition.

Village Manual, no date. The Excise Department, Superintendent, Government Printing and Stationery Office, Rangoon.

Index

Abhidhamma, 107–108, 148
Adultery, attitudes toward, 298
AFPFL (Anti-Fascist People's Freedom
  League), 7, 86, 277, 279–280, 286–
  288
  see also Pataza
Agricultural loans, 97–99
Agriculture, Nondwin, 15–28
  Yadaw, 214–217, 234–240
  see also Nayakan school for farmers
Ahlu, 303
  social aspects of, 304
Akutho, 106, 108–109, 113, 292
Alchemy, 190–192
Alms giving, 302–304
A nade, as personality component, 268–
  269
Anatta, 109, 112–113
Anawrahta, 167, 267n
Aneiksa, 112–113
Anthropological theory, 316
Anti-Fascist People's Freedom League,
  see AFPFL
Apathetic-galvanic complex, 275–276
Apocalypse, 112
ARDC, 214–216, 237, 239–241
Arimittiya, 107
Asia Foundation, 100
Astrology, and Buddhism, 185–186
  and kan, 185
  and naming of children, 189
  and planetary beliefs, 183–190
Aung San, 6, 277, 281–282
Authority, and behavior patterns, 273
  concept, 271

Authority, of headman, 277–279
Awgatha, 114, 263
Awza, 76–79, 271–272, 277
  see also Authority

Bachelors' group, 150–151, 153
Bean crop, 21–22
Beauty, standards of, 249
Begging communities, hereditary, 139
Beliefs, Indian sources of, 183
Bellah, R. N., 156–157, 325
Boeke, J. H., 16–17, 325
Bogyoke Ne Win, 7
British, colonial administration, 5–6, 75
  colonists, 213
  occupation, Yadaw, 233
  railroads in Burma, 4
Brohm, J., 166, 325
Buddha, inventory of abilities of, 148–
  149
Buddhism, 5–6, 14, 102–104, 266n, 267n
  and approach to modernity, 205–206
  and astrology, 185
  collective symbols of, 114
  and community participation, 150–
  151
  cosmology of, 107–114
  and crisis situations, 307–310
  defined, 104–105
  and economic life, 157–163
  and existence, hierarchies of, 108–111
  as individuating force, 149–150
  and the middle way, 112–113
  and spirits, 175
  as state religion, 280–281

Buddhism, as universal system, 320
Buddhist Association, 118, 121–122, 132
Buddhist beliefs, differences in, between
    Yadaw and Nondwin, 291
    and differences in knowledge, 293–294
    and metaphors, 294
    and practice, 295–312
    and scepticism, 293
    and structure of sangha, 294–295
    in village, 291–295
Buddhist giving, acts and status in, 117–
    124
    and gifts to monastic order, 132–138
    hierarchy for, 116
    and hospitality, 139
    and induction into monastic life, 124–
    131
    and kutho, 115–116
    as sacrifice, 115–116
Buddhist morality, and economy of
    Yadaw, 232
Burma, history of modern, 3–7
Burma Mechanical and Electrical
    Workshop, 220
Burma Workers' Party, 86
Burmese national society, organization
    of, 3

Ceremonies, Buddhist and non-
    Buddhist, 203–205
Character traits, Yadaw, 270
Charisma, see Pon
Charms, cabalistic, 177–180
Childbirth, ceremonies, 54–55, 258–259
    taboos, 54, 257
Child rearing, Nondwin, 55–57
Child rearing, Yadaw, attitudes toward
    children, 258–259, 261–262
    and family duties, 264–265
    and maturation, 266–267
    and occupational training, 264–266
    and peer groups, 266–267
    and religion, 262–264
    sibling feelings, 260
    toilet training and weaning, 260–261
Child spacing, 256–257
China, 4–5
Chinese merchants, 4
Chinese Nationalists, 7

Civil War, 6–7
Commissioner of Mandalay, 275
Communications media, 282
Community description, 319–320
Community organization, and Buddhist
    events, 150
Compound composition, Nondwin, 43–
    44
Consciousness, 302
Consumption schedule, Nondwin com-
    pared with Yadaw, 242–243
Conze, E., 325
Cotton crop, 19–20, 236
Courtship and romantic love, 248–250
Cradle ceremony, 258–259
Cultural brokers, 282
Cultural change, theory of, 314
Cultural norms, ambiguity of, 296
Cultural organization, Upper Burma,
    207
Curing systems, 166–206
    see also Nats

Davis, J. H., 199n, 325
Death, natural, 152
    violent, 151–152
Department of Rural Welfare, 99
Deputy Commissioner of Mandalay,
    275
Devotional chant, 114
Devotion leader, Neikban Pointer, 119–
    120
Dhamma, 302
Disunity, political consequences of, 272
Divinatory systems, 166–206
    see also Nats
Division of labor between sexes, 253–
    254
Divorce, 252–253
Dokhka, 112–113
Double cropping, Yadaw, 234–236
Durkheim, E., 203–204, 325
Duty day, and additional precepts, 299–
    300

Economic communality, 45, 48–50
Economy, of Nondwin, 17–44
    of Yadaw, 223–245
    see also Technology

Education, 94–97
  and Buddhism, 95
  and national goals, 96–97
  Office of Mass, 99
  support for at local level, 95
Eight precepts, 113–114
Eight virtues, 113
  see also Five precepts
Election, local, described, 287–288
Electioneering, 285
Entrepreneur, 321–322
Existence, levels of, 105–107
  states of, 111–112
  see also Kan
Exogamy, 247
Expenditure, monthly, pattern in Lugyi
  and average household, 242–243
Expenditures, annual, comparison of,
  by wealth classification, 244

Family, and authority, 56–58
  as basic social unit, 44
  and commensuality, 45–48
  and coresidence, 45
  and economic communality, 45, 48–50
  expenditures, annual, 244
  and extended formation through male
    link, 49–50
  and household altar, 46
  and kinship system, 46, 59–73
  life in, 246–247
  and men-women relations, 52–54
  and mother-daughter bond, 51–54
  organization of, by types, 246
  and pon concept, 52–53
  and recognition, 46
  and role substitutability, 45, 54–57
  social criteria of, 45–46
  and unitary command, 45
  units, Nondwin compared with
    Yadaw, 246
Five precepts, 113–114, 120, 263, 294–
    295
  and individual commitment, 297
  taking of, 296–299
Funeral ceremonies, 151–156
Furnivall, J. S., 2, 4, 7, 66, 325

Gaungs, 228
Geertz, C., 207–209, 325
Ginsburg, N. S., 12n, 325
Goals, collective vs. individual, 240
Gon, 76–79, 228, 271–272
Gossip, Yadaw, 270–271
Gotama, 107, 112, 125
Government, administrative structure
  of, 275
Government loans, for rice growing, in
  Nondwin, 230–231
Government-peasant relationships,
  problems in, 239–240

Haircutting, precautions in, 182
Headman, 277–279
  and elders, 81–84
  see also Thugyi
Hinayana Buddhism, 104
Horoscopes, 184–186
Housebuilding, in Yadaw, 221–222
Household, see Social organization
Household budgets in Nondwin, 33–41
Housewife, role of, 255–262, passim
Htin Aung, 166–167, 325

Ideal person, definition of, 269–270
Impermanence, 300–301
Income distribution, by households, 234
Independence, effect on government,
  281
Independence movement, 6–7, 282
India, 4–5
Induction, into monastic life, 124–131
Infant mortality, 257
Ingersoll, J., 156, 326
Interpersonal behavior, 267–274
  key role of a nade in, 268–269
  and personality types, 269
  see also A nade
Interpersonal relations, 272
Intoxicants, attitudes toward, 299
Intuitive knowledge, 301–302
Irrawaddy, 6

Japanese, invasion, effects of, 6
  in Mandalay, 213
  occupation, 75

Japanese, in Yadaw, 233
Jataka, 114, 148, 295

Kahtein, ceremony, 132–137
    defined, 132
    and giving, 134
    and weaving ceremony, 135–136
Kan, 77, 105–113, 185, 263, 291, 295, 301,
    passim
    emergency, 136
    and feeding of monks, 137–138
    as force in personality development,
    258
    and having children, 171
    and illness, 197
    immediate, 307, 309–310
    and pagoda building, 117–118, 123–
    124
    see also Kutho
Karen Christians, 281
Karen National Defense Organization,
    7, 281–282
Khit pongyi, 291–292
Killing, attitude toward, 297
Kinship, 46, 59–73
    chief features of, 62
    and collateral interest, 66
    and coresidence, 66
    dyadic relations in, 63, 263
    and interaction, 68
    and kin address, 70–73
    and linearity, 66
    and property stewardship, 69
    and seniority, 65
    and sex, 65
    as social organization, 64
    and territorial proximity, 67
Koyin, 320
Kutho, 105–107, 110, 113, 115–116, 185,
    241, 263, 291, 295, 301, 308–309
    accumulation of, 108–109
    emergency, 136
    and feeding of monks, 137–138
    and pagoda building, 123–124
    and support of parents, 253
    see also Kan
Kyanza (book of sacred writings), 263
Kyaukse, 4
Kyaungs, see Monasteries

Kyaw Nyein, 7
    and AFPFL, 279

Land distribution, as index to wealth,
    28–33
Land Distribution Act, 285
Land nationalization, 285–287
Leach, E. R., 164, 325
Leadership, 271, 275
Living levels, 244–245
Lucky and unlucky days, 183–184
Lugyi, 234, 244
    role of in courtship, 250

Macrostructural analyses, 317–318
Magic, black and white, 177–182
    and religion, interplay between, 203–
    204
Mahayana Buddhism, 104
Maize, 21–23
Marriage, 247–267
    attitude toward, 251–252
    costs of, 250
    courtship and, 248–250
    and daily life of couple, 254–255
    husband's role in, 253–254
    and other family ties, 252
    rituals, 251
Marriage studies, Yadaw, compared to
    Nondwin, 247
Mass education program, 99, 237
Maung Maung, 2
Medical services, government provision
    of, 94
Medicine, and illness, 192–202, 316
    see also Curing systems
Meditation, 303–304
Mekgin Shitpa, see Five precepts
Mendelson, E. M., 144, 149, 325
Metaphors, Buddhist, 294
Method, 315
Microanalysis, and social change, 3
Microstructural analyses, 317–318
"Middle way," defined, 112–113
Milk, making of condensed, Yadaw,
    217–218
Mingala Thok, 114
Mixed crop community, setting of, 9–15

Monasteries, autonomy of, 144–145
    descriptions of, 140–142
    gaing, organization of, 144
    and grades of brotherhood, 142–143
    sangha, organization of, 143–144
Monastic life, induction into, 124–131
Monastic order, gifts to, 131–132
Moneylenders, Chettiar, 4
Monks, aim of, 144–145
    attitudes of villagers toward, 292–293
    daily life of, 147–148
    feeding of, 137–138
    and kan and kutho, 137–138
    rules for, 148
    sanctions of, 145–146
Multiple society, concept of, 321–322

Naga, world-circling dragon, 189–190
Nahtwin, ear boring ceremony, 126
Nash, June, 167, 209, 324
Nash, M., 94, 105, 166, 203, 326
Nat, ceremonies, 172–174
    shrines, 280–281
    worship, 112, 320
National government, agricultural
        loans, 97–99
    and rural welfare program, 99–101
    and village, ties between, 93–101
National political parties, attitudes to-
        ward, 86
National radio, effects on village poli-
        tics, 284
National United Front, 7, 86
Natkadaw, see Natwife
Nats, activity of, 167
    belief in, related to levels of social
        relations, 168
    categories of, 167
    and child rearing, 262
    definition of, 75
    as evil powers, 168, 262
    and having children, 171
    hereditary, 170–171
    household, 168–170
    role of in weddings, 251
    royal, 167
    tree, 171–172
    village, 169–170
Natwife, 167, 170, 173–174

Naung bawa, 262
Nayakan school for farmers, minimal
        impact on villages, 239
    recruitment for, 238
Neikban, 107, 116
Neutralism, and political parties, 280
Ne Win, 96, 326
Newspapers, contents of, 283
Nibbana, 107, 295, 303
Nirvana, 303
No-self, 300–301
NUF, see National United Front
Nyun, 17n

Oaths, 307–308
Occupational specialization, 218–222
    in family, 253–254
    as response to poverty, 236
Occupational structure, Nondwin, 157–
        160
    Yadaw, 223–224
Ondaw, shinbyu at, 126–131
Onion crop, 22–26
Ordeals, 307–308

Pagan, 267n
Pagoda, basic form of, 122–123
    building of, 117–124
    festival, 118–123
Pahketin, 258–259
Pali Canon, 105, 114, 296, 310
Party organization, local, 87–92
    national, 87–103
Pataza, 7, 279, 287
Peanut crop, 23, 26–28
Peasant political participation, 275–276
Peasants, and national society, 314
People's Volunteer Organization, 7
Performance, theory, 317
Personal power, concepts of, 76–79
Pfanner, D. E., 156, 326
Planetary predictive system, and aus-
        picious dates, 186–188
Plural cultures, 321
Political dilemmas, peasants', 290
Political life, characterized, 289–290
Political organization, of Nondwin, 44–
        103
    of Yadaw, 274–290

Political parties, competing, 280
  issues in, 280
  in Nondwin, 7
  in Yadaw, 276–277
Politics, vocabulary of, traditional, 282
  rhetoric of, 282
  symbols of, 282
Pon, 52–53, 76–79, 85–91, 233, 271, 275–
    276, 277
  see also Power
Pongyi, defined, 140
Poverty, attitudes toward, 232
  occupational specialization and, 236
  "primitive," 244
Power, 76–79, 277
Prayer groups, 150–151
Predictive systems, 166–206
  and Buddhism, 291–312
  and divinatory systems, 182–190
  see also Nats
President, as Karen, 281–282
Pulse crop, 21–22
Pye, L., 2
Pyidaungzu (Union), 7

Questions of King Milanda, 301

Recreation, adults, 255
  children and young people, 267
Religion and magic, interplay between,
    203–204
Religious behavior, deviant, 294
Religious life, organization of, 140–165
Religious norms, ambiguity of, 296
Research, problems, 315
  procedures, 312–313
  yields, 319
Responsibility for self, 270
Revolutionary ideas, postcolonial, 282–
    283
Rice growing, economics of, 229–231
  harvesting, 229
  organization of, 225–226
  and planting, 226–228
  technological knowledge about, 214–
    215
  transplanting, 228
  and water control, 226
  in Yadaw, 224–231

Riots, 1930's, 6
Ritual cycle, 203–205
Ritual systems, and Buddhism, 296–307
  differences between Yadaw and Non-
    dwin, 304–307
  similarities between, 306
Rural welfare program, 99–101

Sangha, power of, 145–147
Sawyer, A. M., 17, 326
Scepticism, 293, 320
Scott, Sir J. G., 8, 184n, 326
Sesamum crop, 21, 235
Sex life, 256–257
Shan states, 7
Shinbyu, 304, 320
  divination preceding ceremony, 127–
    128
  induction ceremonial, 124–131
  as sacrifice, 131
Singer, M. B., 156–157, 326
Sino-Burman border, 7
Social and political organization, gap
  between, 101–103
Social change, in newly developing na-
  tion, 2
  theory of, 314
Social organization, of Nondwin, 44–103
  of Yadaw, 246–274
Social relations, moral content of, 271–
  272
Social Welfare Department Programs,
  239–241
  see also Nayakan school for farmers;
  Tube-well program
Societal norms, 317
"Soul," 302
Spinsters' group, 150–151, 153
Spirits, 175–176
  malevolent, and child rearing, 262
  see also Nats
State Agricultural Marketing Board, 94
State religion, doctrine of, 280–281
Stealing, attitudes toward, 298
Study locale, reasons for choosing, 1–2,
  207, 314–315
Suez Canal, 3–4
Suffering, 300–301
Suttas, 263

Tattoos, 180–182
Taxes, 93
Technology, 15–17, 214–222
Temple, Sir R. C., 167, 326
Thakin Soe, 279n
Thakins, 282
Theravada Buddhism, 167
    practice, 320
"Thirty Heroes," 281–282
Thok, 295
Three Wa policy, 279n
Thugyi, 277
Tinker, H., 2, 6–7, 326
Tipitaka, 148, 292
Township, 274
    officer, 278
Tractor, problems in adoption of, 239–
    240
Trades and occupations, 218–222
Treasure guards, 177
Trinity, repetition of, 300–301
Triple Jewel, 114, 120, 263
Truck gardening, limited use of, 235
Truth telling, attitude toward, 297–298
Tube-well program, 240–241

U An Gyi, 121–122
U Htun, 277
Union Party, 7, 86
U Nu, 2, 6–7, 101, 205–206, 272, 280–281,
    284, 286, 326
    and Pataza, 279
U Sein Ko, 81–82, 100, 118, 126–127, 175–
    176, 179–180, 188, 190–192, 202–203
    and pon, 77–79, 85–91

Village, and national government, ties
    between, 93–101
    and public welfare services, 93–101
    taxes, 93
Village administration, council of four
    elders, 80–84
    headman in, 75–76
    levels of pon in, 85–91
    manual of, 75–76
    and national political parties, 86–103
    and personal power, concepts of, 76–
    77
    political and administrative unity, 74
    and political constitution of Burma,
    73–74
    and ten house heads, 80
Village government (Yadaw), 274–290
    outside effects on, 281–282
    structures, 274–275
Villages, variations in, 320
Villagers, attitudes of, toward monks,
    292–293
    and information about other nations,
    284–285
Virtue (gon), 228
Virtues, 149
Voter, committed, 288
    uncommitted, 288

Wa, rainy season, 124
    States, 7
Wealth, categories of, 231–234
Weber, M., 156–157
Winyin, 302
Witchcraft, 177–182
World War II, 6